Approaches to Teaching
the Works of Fernando Pessoa

Approaches to Teaching the Works of Fernando Pessoa

Edited by

Paulo de Medeiros

and

Jerónimo Pizarro

The Modern Language Association of America
New York   2025

© 2025 by The Modern Language Association of America
85 Broad Street, New York, New York 10004
www.mla.org

To order MLA publications, visit www.mla.org/books. For wholesale and international orders,
see www.mla.org/bookstore-orders. The EU-based Responsible Person for MLA products is the
Mare Nostrum Group, which can be reached at gpsr@mare-nostrum.co.uk or the Mare Nostrum
Group BV, Mauritskade 21D, 1091 GC Amsterdam, Netherlands. For a copy of the MLA's risk
assessment document, write to scholcomm@mla.org.

The MLA office is located on the island known as Mannahatta (Manhattan) in Lenapehoking,
the homeland of the Lenape people. The MLA pays respect to the original stewards of this land
and to the diverse and vibrant Native communities that continue to thrive in New York City.

Approaches to Teaching World Literature 179
ISSN 1059-1133

Library of Congress Cataloging-in-Publication Data

Names: Medeiros, Paulo de, 1958– editor | Pizarro, Jerónimo editor
Title: Approaches to teaching the works of Fernando Pessoa / edited by Paulo de
    Medeiros and Jerónimo Pizarro.
Description: New York : The Modern Language Association of America, 2025. |
    Series: Approaches to teaching world literature, 1059-1133 ; 179 | Includes
    bibliographical references.
Identifiers: LCCN 2024055078 (print) | LCCN 2024055079 (ebook) | ISBN 9781603296809
    hardcover | ISBN 9781603296816 paperback | ISBN 9781603296823 EPUB
Subjects: LCSH: Pessoa, Fernando, 1888–1935—Study and teaching | Pessoa,
    Fernando, 1888–1935—Criticism and interpretation
Classification: LCC PQ9261.P417 Z5753 2025 (print) | LCC PQ9261.P417 (ebook) |
    DDC 869.1/41—dc23/eng/20250409
LC record available at https://lccn.loc.gov/2024055078
LC ebook record available at https://lccn.loc.gov/2024055079

Für K
　　—PM

For Li
　　—JP

CONTENTS

Acknowledgments   ix

Introduction: Teaching Pessoa's Infinite Plurality   1
  Paulo de Medeiros and Jerónimo Pizarro

PART ONE: MATERIALS

  Editions and Translations   13
  Further Reading for Students   18
  The Instructor's Library   20

PART TWO: APPROACHES

Historical and Cultural Context

  Orpheu, Modernism, and Europe   29
    Steffen Dix

  Gender in Pessoa   47
    António Ladeira

  Pessoa and Popular Culture   71
    Ellen W. Sapega

The Book of Disquiet

  The Book of Disquiet and World Literature: Notes from the Seminar Room   81
    Paulo de Medeiros

  The Problem of Genre in *The Book of Disquiet*   93
    Bernat Padró Nieto

Other Works

  Mensagem: The Ideas behind a Poetic Vision   111
    Onésimo T. Almeida

  The "Great Book," Caeiro, and Pessoa's Theory of Poetry   125
    Irene Ramalho-Santos

  The Political Poetry of Álvaro de Campos: At the Margin of the Margin   139
    Sofia de Sousa Silva

Curriculum

Bringing Pessoa into the Philosophy Curriculum   155
    Jonardon Ganeri

Reframing Writerly Identity with the Works of Pessoa and Other
    Modernist Poets   162
    Meghan P. Nolan

Editing

From Meta-Editing to Virtual Editing: The *LdoD* Archive as
    a Computer-Assisted Editorial Space   178
    Manuel Portela

Editing Pessoa's "Radical Scatters"   193
    John Pedro Schwartz and Jerónimo Pizarro

Notes on Contributors   211
Works Cited   215

ACKNOWLEDGMENTS

We thank the international Pessoa community, as well as our many dear colleagues, for their continuous support and interest. We also express our gratitude to our respective institutions and to various publishing houses and national libraries, including the Biblioteca Nacional de Portugal, for supporting our research. Closer to home, Paulo wishes to acknowledge his direct colleagues in the Department of English and Comparative Literary Studies, especially the Warwick Research Collective, which has been a key source of intellectual stimulation since he joined Warwick. Jerónimo extends his appreciation to the many scholars, editors, friends and publishers with whom he has worked to bring new editions and critical perspectives on Pessoa's work to light.

Introduction: Teaching Pessoa's Infinite Plurality

Paulo de Medeiros and Jerónimo Pizarro

Teaching Fernando Pessoa requires addressing a complex array of challenges. It is as if Pessoa, Portugal's greatest twentieth-century poet, indisputably one of the key figures of modernism and now widely recognized as one of the most important names in world literature, in his own inimitable manner had succeeded in his goal to become plural like the universe. Teaching Pessoa with fidelity to the texts always involves a plural reading. That is, any reading of Pessoa must understand itself as limited, temporary, always only in the process of becoming, and always leading into yet another reading. A reading that fails to do so also fails to grasp the core of Pessoa's project, which was, paradoxical as it may seem, only a project inasmuch as it continuously attempted to reinterpret itself through a process not just of refinement but of a relentless questioning of the self and the world.

Pessoa explored the plurality of the self in many ways, none more forceful than his creation of heteronyms. Even if he was not the only great writer to use fully formed alter egos to compose different kinds of works—think of Søren Kierkegaard, for example—he went further than any other before or after him. Pessoa started creating other forms of the self very early on, and, although counts vary, one can easily see more than a hundred names that Pessoa invented in order to further explore the world he was busy creating. Of those, a few were given great salience, and Pessoa divided most of his production among them: Álvaro de Campos, arguably the most extreme of all in his opinions and feelings; Ricardo Reis, a trained classicist and Epicurean who excelled in the writing of odes; Alberto Caeiro, the "Keeper of Sheep," whom Pessoa named as the master of them all, including himself; and Bernardo Soares, whom Pessoa preferred to designate as a semi-heteronym, feeling he was the closest to himself. It was to him, in part, that Pessoa gave the authorship of what has come to be recognized as a masterpiece, the unfinished and until 1982 unpublished assemblage of prose fragments known as *The Book of Disquiet*.

Then there are the different Pessoas we need to take into account besides the heteronyms. For one, there is a private Pessoa about whom not much is known. Richard Zenith's recently published biography runs to more than a thousand pages and contains a plethora of facts about Pessoa, his life, and his writing, yet much of Zenith's narrative is, as it had to be, conjecture (*Pessoa: A Biography* and *Pessoa: An Experimental Life*). Within what can be known, however, there are fascinating elements to the plurality Pessoa was. We can look at the photographs that are available to us, taken in childhood, young adulthood, and not long before Pessoa would die, and be surprised by the image that looks back at us in turn. Or consider the author's move from Lisbon to South Africa at the age of seven, when his mother joined his stepfather in Durban, and his eventual return to Lisbon after completing his secondary education. Or contemplate Pessoa as a participant in an extensive love correspondence with Ophelia Queiroz, to whom he was twice engaged. Or note that, even though Pessoa wrote most of his work in Portuguese, he first tried writing poetry in English and maintained the use of both English and French for writing throughout his life. There is Pessoa the modernist as well as Pessoa the monarchist sympathizer, Pessoa the translator—something he did to earn a living but also for other reasons—and Pessoa whose sharp wit and impeccable, if paradoxical, logic went hand in hand with a deep interest in the esoteric. One may at any given time emphasize one or another of these aspects of Pessoa—as indeed we must—yet should remain always aware of the remarkable complexity that made Pessoa as distinct as he was. As all of us, but more intensely than most of us, Pessoa was not who he was so much as he was who he was in the process of becoming.

Any consideration of Pessoa's plurality must also take into account that he wrote in various genres; that his poetry runs a wide gamut of poetic forms; that his prose—chiefly, though not only, through *The Book of Disquiet*—has by now come to be seen as equally important as his poetry; that he also wrote drama, a few short scripts for film, and, on occasion, marketing slogans.[1] Furthermore, even as important a work as *The Book of Disquiet* was pieced together only long after the author's death. Each subsequent edition, not to mention translation, even at the hands of the same editor, reshuffled the fragments, reordered them, dropped some, and added more—sometimes many more. In a concrete rather than simply metaphorical sense, *The Book of Disquiet* itself is always in the process of becoming a book without ever quite achieving that. Some may see that as a failing characteristic of Pessoa the inveterate dreamer, whereas others, such as ourselves, prefer to see in the text's incompleteness a sense of its remarkable openness.

Confronting Modernity

Pessoa was acutely aware of the way in which the advent of modernity threatened to question all assumptions, shake up the most deep-seated convictions, and hurl everything and everyone forward at what must have seemed a devastating pace. In one of the fragments intended for *The Book of Disquiet*, presumably from 1915, his sense of his generation's profound rift with the past is more than clear: "Pertenço a uma geração—ou antes a uma parte de geração—que perdeu todo o respeito pelo passado e toda a crença ou esperança no futuro. Vivemos porisso do presente com a gana e a fome de quem não tem outra casa" ("I belong to a generation—or, rather, to part of a generation—that has lost all respect for the past and all belief or hope in the future. This is why we live in the present with the desperate hunger of someone who has no other home"; *Desasocego* 103; *Disquiet* [New Directions] 90). This sentiment, a mixture of melancholy with a kind of pride, is given an even starker and more developed expression in a subsequent fragment, possibly from 1917, worth citing here at some length:

Pertenço a uma geração que herdou a descrença no facto christão e que creou em si uma descrença em todas as outras fés. Os nossos paes tinham ainda o impulso credor, que transferiam do christianismo para outras formas de illusão. . . .

Tudo isso nós perdemos, de todas essas consolações nascemos orphãos. Cada civilização segue a linha intima de uma religião que a representa: passar para outras religiões é perder essa, e por fim perdel-as a todas.

Nós perdemos essa, e ás outras tambem.

Ficámos, pois, cada um entregue a si-proprio, na desolação de se sentir viver.   (*Desasocego* 142)

I belong to a generation that inherited a disbelief in the Christian faith and that created within itself a disbelief in all other faiths. Our forefathers still felt an impulse to believe, which they transferred from Christianity to other forms of illusion. . . .

We lost all this and were orphaned at birth of all these consolations. Every civilization cleaves to the intimate contours of the religion that represents it: to go after other religions is to lose that first religion and ultimately to lose them all.

We lost both our religion and the others too.

Each of us was left abandoned to ourselves, amidst the desolation of merely knowing we were alive.   (*Disquiet* [New Directions] 122)

The clash between generations, not only between systems of belief but between belief and its complete loss, can be said to derive from, and to reflect, the loss felt by Pessoa as a human being. When Pessoa was only five years old, his father died, a trauma renewed and extended one year later with the death of his younger brother. Moving from Lisbon to Durban, from Europe to Africa, and from Portugal to a British colony was also a process of dislocation that may have further propelled Pessoa into a reliance on himself. In Durban, Pessoa was exposed to the stark contrasts between colonial rule and local traditions, witnessing firsthand the cultural tensions and conflicts of a divided society. These early experiences deeply influenced his worldview and some themes that would emerge in his work.

Upon his return to Lisbon Pessoa witnessed the clashes of his time in a very direct way. Portuguese politics were in constant turmoil, the king and the crown prince were both assassinated on the streets of Lisbon in 1908, and the country became a republic in 1910. The first Portuguese Republic was marked by fundamental instability, averaging three different governments a year in the fifteen years it lasted, and by an intense desire to modernize the country, update its outdated laws, and raise the levels of education. Economically, however, the country was constantly on the brink of collapse when not actually bankrupt. Portugal's active entry into the First World War on the side of the Allies in 1916 further increased the general sense of devastation, which in turn contributed to the brief resurrection of the monarchy in Porto in 1919 and the success of the military coup that made Portugal a dictatorship in 1926.

Perhaps it should come as no surprise to see Pessoa's texts developing constantly as a never-ending process of folds upon folds. His texts can be intensely self-referential yet are always extremely expansive, alluding to a myriad of sources that reflect his own multiplication into the heteronyms. But at the same time, it is important to avoid falling into the trap of imagining Pessoa as a kind of self-centered aesthete, a poetic mandarin alienated from reality. Pessoa felt deeply the world around him as the source of all that he knew and longed to know, everything he could experience and imagine. It has become a kind of commonplace to refer to the Portugal of his time as a backward, underdeveloped country, seemingly still almost unaffected by the Industrial Revolution, and to Lisbon as a sort of cocoon where its bourgeoisie lived a sort of splendid idyll of times long gone by, sustained by cheap manual labor provided by a largely impoverished rural population and fueled by a distorted and illusory sense of superiority derived from the nation's imperial "glories." One should be wary of such facile explanations. For one, the bourgeoisie has always been defined by its international connections. As the editors of a recent study of the rise of the middle classes globally put it, "Many social structures that emerged in the long nineteenth century can be traced back to activities of such cosmopolitan bourgeoisies and in turn can be considered a reason for the emergence of these groups" (Dejung et al. 4).

This is not to say that one can simply view the bourgeoisie in Lisbon as akin to its counterpart in London, Paris, or Berlin, to stay just within a western European reference. Portugal was then a very minor power, as its influence had steadily diminished after the golden age of its global expansion in the fourteenth and fifteenth centuries. Pessoa was keenly aware of this, and his call for a Fifth Empire to rejuvenate Portugal, however misguided one might deem it, was always intended at the cultural, not the political, level. Following on the foundational work of Immanuel Wallerstein on world-systems theory and on its direct application to Portugal by Boaventura de Sousa Santos ("Between Prospero and Caliban"), Portugal's designation as a semiperipheral country can be of some help in understanding Pessoa's positioning toward modernity. Pessoa was living and writing in a country that was far from being at the core of Europe but was, by its geography, history, and imaginary, a constituent part of it. In a sense, Pessoa did not have the same access to the latest developments and trends in art and culture that writers had in London or New York, Paris, or Berlin. Yet he was deeply cosmopolitan and very receptive to all that was happening in those centers. And he certainly managed not only to overcome any disadvantage he might have felt (apart from his reduced financial circumstances) but also to surpass many of his more fortunate contemporaries. Indeed, we may want to see Pessoa's achievements as a prime example of the importance of the periphery in bringing about cultural innovation and of what Fredric Jameson named "a singular modernity" that takes into account specific societal conditions shaping various forms of modernity across time rather than producing different ones at different times and in different places.

Pessoa and the Idea of the Canon

Pessoa has come to embody not only modernism in Portugal but also Portuguese poetry in the twentieth century, such is the impact of his texts in the Portuguese cultural imagination. Indeed, if there are unassailable names in Portuguese literary history, for many that of Pessoa is second only to that of Luís Vaz de Camões, the sixteenth-century author of *The Lusiads*, who is still revered as the national poet. And even if Pessoa's international reception has been spotty and rather late, since relatively few of his texts were made available during his lifetime, he has also come to occupy a firm place in the canon of European and world literature. In other words, Pessoa's cultural capital is as solid as can be and certain to keep increasing as successive generations discover him and let themselves be seduced by the enigma of a body of work in which paradox and failure are not vices or weaknesses but are advanced as proof of the writer's feelings and intellectual restlessness. Teaching Pessoa today, one can therefore bank on both the established reputation of a master writer and on his infinite malleability to guarantee that students will approach their reading prepared to encounter greatness while discovering how contemporary Pessoa is.

Pessoa can be used to represent tradition and the glory that modernism was but also to let students see how tormented he was and how defiant of tradition and especially of conformity. It is useful to keep in mind Walter Benjamin's sixth thesis from his widely known "Über den Begriff der Geschichte" ("Theses on the Philosophy of History"). In it, Benjamin is concerned with historical materialism and the relation to the past, noting that both tradition and those who receive it are constantly in danger of becoming mere tools (*Werkzeuge*) of the ruling class. Consequently, what matters is to resist and "von neuem dem Konformismus abzugewinnen, der im Begriff steht, sie zu überwältigen" ("to wrest tradition away from a conformism that is about to overpower it"; "Über" 695; "Theses" 255). This directive could be applied, without any changes, to Pessoa. His writing is a constantly renewed effort to dispel the moldy fumes and cobwebs of a hollow veneration of tradition for tradition's sake whose entrenched judgment of what constitutes value obstructs its perception of the art that it pretends to venerate.

Of course, it would be false to label Pessoa as a revolutionary, politically or otherwise. Yet in all of his texts there is an implicit or explicit resistance to mediocrity, to the lack of imagination and any subservience to established power. In yet another fragment of *The Book of Disquiet*, Pessoa starts by refusing the dichotomy employed by "revolutionaries" between the aristocracy and bourgeoisie on the one hand and the common people on the other for being too simplistic. He proposes instead another opposition, between those who conform and those who do not. He offers representatives of culture and counterculture that come close to forming an antinomy:

[T]enho por irmãos os creadores da consciencia do mundo—o dramaturgo
atabalhoado William Shakespeare, o mestre-escola John Milton, o vadio
Dante Alighieri, e até, se a citação se permitte, aquelle Jesus Christo que
não foi nada no mundo, tanto que se duvida d'elle pela historia. Os outros
são de outra especie—o conselheiro de estado Johann Wolfgang von Goethe, o senador Victor Hugo, o chefe Lenine, o chefe Mussolini.

Nós na sombra, entre os moços de fretes e os barbeiros, constituimos a
humanidade.   (*Desasocego* 178)

I have as brothers the creators of the consciousness of the world—the
unruly playwright William Shakespeare, the schoolmaster John Milton, the
vagabond Dante Alighieri . . . and even, if I'm allowed to mention him,
Jesus Christ himself, who was so little in this world that some even doubt
his historical existence. The others are a different breed altogether—
Councillor of State Johann Wolfgang von Goethe, Senator Victor Hugo,
heads of state Lenin and Mussolini.

It is we in the shadows, among the errand boys and barbers, who constitute humanity.   (*Disquiet* [New Directions] 160)

One of the key aspects of Pessoa is precisely that rather than reject tradition he
surpassed all his contemporaries in learning it, following it, and mastering it.
Returning to Portugal having spent his adolescence learning the English poetic
tradition, especially the Romantics, and above all Shakespeare, Pessoa proceeded
to make the Portuguese literary tradition his own. And it was by wresting Portuguese literature from conformism, as Benjamin would advocate, that Pessoa
was able to stay true to it while propelling it to a new height. Even when one
may think that Pessoa is sticking close to the precepts of the canon, as in Caeiro's
pastoral motifs or the neoclassical odes of Reis, one should keep in mind that he
draws on the power of tradition as but a necessity in transforming it into a modernity that, like the classics, goes on speaking to successive generations instead of
becoming a stale repository of truisms. And this can be tested every day anew
either by reflecting on the incredible influence Pessoa has had, not just on all
Portuguese writers who succeeded him but all across the world and through all
forms of art, from music to painting, graphic novels to sculpture—or by simply
reading Pessoa.

Pessoa and the Archive

Pessoa, like Wittgenstein, only published one book in his lifetime; this work, published in 1934, a year before his death, was *Mensagem* (*Message*). This means
that he can be considered a largely posthumous author, although he collabo-
rated with several newspapers and magazines between 1912 and 1935, and
even before 1912 if we include some juvenilia. We are aware that there might
be an aporia, a contradiction, when the notions of author and posterity are

brought together. Generally, an author is one who creates or gives existence to something. Thinking about an author as posthumous is to reason about paradoxical objects, since many of the notions associated with the concept of authorship become problematic. But this is one of the challenges of Pessoa. He left an archive more than a set of works; he left a Mallarméan promise of a book but not an "actual" book.

Pessoa was not included in an excellent volume edited by George Bornstein, *Representing Modernist Texts: Editing as Interpretation*, but editing Pessoa crucially bridges the gap between modern textual scholarship and literary criticism, to bring together "lo que la tradición occidental alejó tenazmente: por un lado, la comprensión y el comentario de las obras; por otro lado, el análisis de las condiciones técnicas o sociales de su publicación, circulación y apropiación" ("what the Western tradition tenaciously distanced: on the one hand, the understanding and the commentary of the works; on the other hand, the analysis of the technical or social conditions of their publication, circulation, and appropriation"; Chartier 11; our trans.). Editing Pessoa—like editing W. H. Auden, H.D., William Faulkner, James Joyce, D. H. Lawrence, Marianne Moore, Ezra Pound, William Carlos Williams, Virginia Woolf, W. B. Yeats, and many others— raises issues to which Bornstein calls attention on the back cover of his book, namely, "the construction of a writer's canon and the effect of newly available 'uncanonical' manuscript materials on existing works and orderings; the replacement of the older idea of a fixed, stable text by a more contemporary notion of the text as process; and the interrogation [of] notions of 'author,' 'intention,' and 'stability of the text'" as well as of the processes of "authorship attribution," *constitutio textus* (establishment of a critical text), and construction of a work (like *The Book of Disquiet*) or set of works.

We don't know if one day a still nonexistent Pessoa Foundation will announce publication of the complete works of Pessoa. But it is possible that if they did, the president of that foundation would issue a statement along the lines of Nicholas Cronk's conference keynote address as director of the Voltaire Foundation, presented here in abstract:

> The *Complete Works of Voltaire* published by the Voltaire Foundation were begun in 1968 and will be completed in 203 volumes in 2021. In so far as discoveries of manuscripts and editions will continue to be made, this monumental edition is necessarily incomplete. But it is also incomplete in another more profound sense. Eighteenth-century editions of Voltaire present an often-unstable version of the text; Voltaire cultivates an open and fluid style, making frequent use of self-quotation, and blurring traditional generic boundaries; Voltaire's characteristically slippery authorial posture, making frequent use of anonymity and pseudonymity, adds further instability to the *œuvre*. For all these reasons, Voltaire's works present a particular challenge to the critical editor of a print edition—a challenge that perhaps can only be fully met in a digital critical edition.

It might take at least half a century to publish the two hundred or more volumes of those imaginary complete works; any edition of Pessoa is "necessarily incomplete," not only because new discoveries are possible, but because Pessoa's "characteristically slippery authorial posture . . . adds further instability to the *œuvre*." That future edition might only exist as a digital critical edition—and possibly not as a singular one but as a plural one. If we study the digital transformation of Pessoa's archive, still in process (see Aldabalde and Pittella), we can conclude that it is still necessary to discuss how to democratize reading and how to encourage a network of reappropriations of certain digitized objects.

In a special issue of *Portuguese Studies*, conceived mainly to pay tribute to Pessoa and to reflect upon the destiny of his literary estate, it was noted:

> Like many other modern writers, such as Goethe and Flaubert, Fernando Pessoa was an authentic "keeper of papers." Whoever has opened his *arcas* [trunks] and gone through his *espólio* [literary estate] has been struck by the fact that anything that could be written on was used and kept, from his childhood to his death: napkins, business cards, bits of posters, book covers, envelopes, notebooks and calendar pages, not to mention writing paper (headed or not) from the offices where he worked, and from the cafés where he used to write or meet his friends. . . . Hardly a day went by without Pessoa writing a poem, a prose passage, the beginning of a translation or a short reading note; almost all of these were neatly folded into his pocket and then put in the trunks—most likely as a silent pledge to posterity. Over the years at least two trunks were filled with papers. They were like a labyrinth of overlapping papers, whose investigation began in the late 1930s when Luís de Montalvor and other poets, editors, literary critics and friends associated with the magazine *presença* (without a capital P) initiated the posthumous publication of Pessoa's writings—a task that is far from concluded to this day. In view of the vast quantity of these fragments, and their open-ended character, this editorial adventure remains as stimulating now as it was then. Pessoa's restless need to write, his incessant preoccupation with gathering his autographs, his elaborate but slow plans to edit, and a hesitation to publish, all account for the impressive number of papers that exist: currently they are over 30,000. For, to the 27,000 or so documents kept in Portugal's National Library we must add those still with Pessoa's heirs (about 10%), the few in the Casa Fernando Pessoa [House of Fernando Pessoa], and those in literary collections and with some anonymous and silent individuals (about 2%).   (Pizarro and Dix 6)

All these papers, written between 1900 and 1935, are still slowly coming into the public domain, and we might say, as ten, twenty, or thirty years ago, that Pessoa's editorial future remains almost as open as ever. We are still making our way through the vast labyrinth of Pessoa, a labyrinth of languages, identities, and all sorts of documents.

Reading Pessoa Today

Teaching and learning about Pessoa are always forms of reading Pessoa. Certainly, the ways in which Pessoa resonates with us and those in which we, in turn, react to his words, have been changing, as could not but be. Yet even if nowadays we have many more forms of "reading" Pessoa, such as in painting, film, sculpture, graphic novels, or music, we always go back to his words. Pessoa, like any great poet and artificer, excels at filling our minds with images and rhythms, such that his words are always already appealing to our visual and aural imagination. Still, it would be disingenuous to pretend that the classical, philological teaching of Pessoa has not greatly changed, having been extended and redirected. This reflects in part the fact that we have much more at our disposal today: many more texts of Pessoa have come to light; new editions constantly introduce different, sometimes more precise, readings; improved technological conditions have increased access to film, musical recordings, and digital formats. But perceptions of Pessoa—his place in the history of modernism and his relation to modernity—have also changed. And so have our own sensibilities. Questions that might not have arisen fifty, twenty, even ten years ago have come to the forefront. Shifts in critical perspective, like an increased attention being given to materiality and less of a focus on the more romanticized versions of the poet, always play a part.

The present volume seeks a certain plurality of perspectives, not so much in emulation of Pessoa's own plurality but rather because of the conviction that teaching Pessoa today, as his work is read in an ever-larger number of university courses in the humanities, is indeed plural. Here and in part 1, "Materials," we try to provide a quick, if rough, map of a wonderful universe that can at times appear as somewhat of a labyrinth. The first section in part 2, "Approaches," titled "Historical and Cultural Context," fills in the map in detail. Steffen Dix's essay sets out not only Pessoa's immediate context—the writers in the orbit of the *Orpheu* magazine—but also a European context that is crucial to understanding Pessoa. Gender questions, which were always there, have assumed an ever more pressing, and more open, position in our societies and in our personal lives. António Ladeira's essay provides several readings that can both deepen our understanding of Pessoa's texts and allow for an integration of some of his works in courses beyond the traditional ones in literary studies. Ellen W. Sapega's innovative study of Pessoa and popular culture further expands the volume's inquiry into the area of cultural studies and helps dispel notions of Pessoa and our interest in his work as an elitist activity disassociated from reality.

Many students, instructors, and members of the general public may find that *The Book of Disquiet* is the first, or even the only, text by Pessoa that they get to read. Although its fragmentary nature may be appealing, its complexity can make it seem daunting. The next section attempts to deal with the mix of fascination and puzzlement that *The Book of Disquiet* can evoke. Whereas Paulo de Medeiros draws on his own experience teaching the book in courses on literature and philosophy, reflecting on questions of world literature and form, Bernat Padró Nieto delves into one of the book's most pressing questions—that of genre.

Even if today many may come to know Pessoa through his prose, he remains one of the most important poetic voices of the twentieth century. In the next section, "Other Works," Onésimo T. Almeida discusses *Mensagem*, the sole book Pessoa published while he was alive. Considered controversial by virtue of its supposed nationalist character and acknowledged as one of the most rich and complex works Pessoa ever composed, it can be difficult to approach, even with instructor guidance. Yet it is not unusual for selections from it to feature in undergraduate reading lists. Almeida's essay should prove very useful for all those attempting to read and teach this most fascinating work. Irene Ramalho-Santos tackles another thorny issue in Pessoa's poetics, the role of the heteronym Alberto Caeiro, whom Pessoa designated as the master of all the other heteronyms and of himself, in a manner designed to ease beginning readers into an appreciation of the full import of Pessoa's poetic theorizing. Sofia de Sousa Silva argues that Álvaro de Campos uses his poetry to challenge the dominant values of early-twentieth-century society, rejecting notions of progress, conformity, and social norms. His work serves as a space for transgression against the constraints of civilization.

The last two sections may at first appear more geared toward the interests of instructors, but we hope that they will appeal to students in equal measure. The first "Curriculum" essay, by Jonardon Ganeri, focuses on "bringing Pessoa into the philosophy curriculum," which we think is one of the great tasks of teaching Pessoa today. The second, by Meghan P. Nolan, relates Pessoa to other great modernist poets in a way that can serve as a point of entry for students without any knowledge of Portuguese literature. The last section, "Editing," offers two complementary essays. Manuel Portela goes over his own hypertext edition of *The Book of Disquiet*, a most timely issue, and John Pedro Schwartz and Jerónimo Pizarro take on the question of Pessoa's fragments from an editing perspective, drawing on examples of manuscript study using the archives of Jorge Luis Borges, Emily Dickinson, and Herman Melville. Both essays, drawing from extensive experience in editing, allow a glimpse into the workshop behind the production of the texts that we can read and admire. As such, they may motivate some students to engage themselves in learning more about a crucial, though usually invisible, aspect of any textual work, without which our reading experience would be vastly different and certainly less rich.

NOTE

1. Before the Salazar regime banned Coca-Cola in Portugal, Pessoa composed the slogan "Primeiro estranha-se, depois entranha-se" ("On the first day it tastes odd. On the fifth day it takes hold"; Pittella and Pizarro 74; our trans.).

Part One

MATERIALS

Editions and Translations

The work of Fernando Pessoa has been widely disseminated, even if usually not in a systematic way. Editions of his works have been appearing in isolated volumes or in series since shortly after his death in 1935. During his lifetime, Pessoa published frequently in periodicals but published only one book, *Mensagem* (*Message*). Most of his work has only been published posthumously.

Portuguese Editions

The first systematic Portuguese edition of Pessoa's works was brought out by Ática, starting in 1942, in Lisbon. These volumes, which primarily reflected choices made by Pessoa's friends of texts they believed would contribute to his image, included eleven volumes of Pessoa's poetry, organized according to heteronym or genre, including his English poetry, and nine books (two of them published together in a two-volume edition) of his prose, starting with the *Páginas íntimas e de auto-interpretação* (*Intimate and Self-Interpretative Pages*) in 1966 and concluding with the *Livro do desassossego* (*Book of Disquiet*) in 1982. Besides ephemeral and occasional editions, usually of selected poems, there have also been pirated editions that are generally considered bibliophile rarities.

Many respected publishing houses—Presença, A Regra do Jogo, Manuel Lencastre, Dom Quixote, Livros Horizonte, Europa-América—have produced editions of Pessoa's works. Among the Brazilian editions, of note are those by the Companhia das Letras, which draw from the Portuguese editions by Assírio e Alvim, and the single-volume *Obra poética* (*Poetic Work*) edited by Maria Aliete Galhoz and included in the Biblioteca Luso-Brasileira.

The Edição crítica das obras de Fernando Pessoa (Critical Edition of the Works of Fernando Pessoa) is a monumental project of the Imprensa Nacional–Casa da Moeda, Portugal's national press, that has been underway for several decades now. With initial funding from the Portuguese government, a team of Pessoa experts and other scholars are working to bring out detailed critical editions, complete with a full scholarly apparatus, to establish a proper reading text that can also be shared with the general public. It has been organized in twelve volumes, some of which are further divided into individual books as follows:

1. *Poemas de Fernando Pessoa* [*Poems by Fernando Pessoa*]
   Volume 1: To 1914. Edited by Luís Prista.
   Volume 2: 1915–1920. Edited by João Dionísio, 2005.
   Volume 3: 1921–1930. Edited by Ivo Castro, 2001.
   Volume 4: 1931–1933. Edited by Ivo Castro, 2004.
   Volume 5: 1934–1935. Edited by Luís Prista, 2000.

Mensagem *e poemas publicados em vida* [Message *and Poems Published during His Lifetime*]. Edited by Luiz Fagundes Duarte, 2008.

Quadras [*Quatrains*]. Edited by Luís Prista, 1997.

Rubaiyat. Edited by Maria Aliete Galhoz, 2008.

2. *Poemas de Álvaro de Campos* [*Poems by Álvaro de Campos*]. Edited by Cleonice Berardinelli, 1990.

3. *Poemas de Ricardo Reis* [*Poems by Ricardo Reis*]. Edited by Luiz Fagundes Duarte, 1994.

4. *Poemas de Alberto Caeiro* [*Poems by Alberto Caeiro*]. Edited by Ivo Castro, 2015.

5. *Poemas ingleses* [*English Poems*]

Volume 1: *Antinous, Inscriptions, Epithalamium, 35 Sonnets.* Edited by João Dionísio, 1993.

Volume 2: *Poemas de Alexander Search* [*Poems by Alexander Search*]. Edited by João Dionísio, 1997.

Volume 3: *The Mad Fiddler.* Edited by Marcus Angioni and Fernando Gomes, 1999.

6. *Obras de António Mora* [*Works of António Mora*]. Edited by Luís Filipe Teixeira, 2002.

7. *Escritos sobre génio e loucura* [*Writings on Genius and Madness*]. Edited by Jerónimo Pizarro, 2006.

8. *Obras de Jean Seul de Méluret* [*Works of Jean Seul de Méluret*]. Edited by Rita Patrício and Jerónimo Pizarro, 2006.

9. *A educação do stoico* [*The Education of the Stoic*]. Edited by Jerónimo Pizarro, 2007.

10. *Sensacionismo e outros ismos* [*Sensationism and Other Isms*]. Edited by Jerónimo Pizarro, 2009.

11. *Cadernos* [*Notebooks*]. Edited by Jerónimo Pizarro, 2009.

12. *Livro do desasocego* [*The Book of Disquiet*]. Edited by Jerónimo Pizarro, 2010.

Between 2010 and 2012, Ática attempted a brief revival of its historical edition and brought out six volumes that complement the ones it had published up to 1982, some of which are still available as reprints:

Provérbios portugueses [*Portuguese Proverbs*]. Edited by Jerónimo Pizarro and Patricio Ferrari, 2010.

Argumentos para filmes [*Film Arguments*]. Edited by Patricio Ferrari and Claudia J. Fischer, 2011.

Associações secretas e outros escritos [*Secret Societies and Other Writings*]. Edited by José Barreto, 2011.

Sebastianismo e quinto império [*Sebastianism and the Fifth Empire*]. Edited by Jorge Uribe and Pedro Sepúlveda, 2011.

Prosa de Álvaro de Campos [*Prose by Álvaro de Campos*]. Edited by Jerónimo Pizarro and Antonio Cardiello, 2012.

Ibéria: Introdução a um imperialismo futuro [*Iberia: Introduction to a Future Imperialism*]. Edited by Jerónimo Pizarro and Pablo Javier Pérez López, 2012.

Currently, there are two main editions that present reliable texts for most readers in attractive paperback versions. The oldest one is published by Assírio e Alvim, a tradition-rich publisher of poetry with arguably the most important catalogue of its kind, now an imprint of the large Porto Editora. From 1997 to the present it has brought out thirty-seven separate volumes (and selected sixteen to include in its Colecção Pessoa Breve, with a lower price point):

A hora do diabo [*The Devil's Hour*]. Edited by Teresa Rita Lopes, 1997.

A língua portuguesa [*The Portuguese Language*]. Edited by Luísa Medeiros, 1997.

Livro do desassossego, Bernardo Soares [*The Book of Disquiet, Bernardo Soares*]. Edited by Richard Zenith, 1998.

Correspondência, 1905–1922 [*Correspondence, 1905–1922*]. Edited by Manuela Parreira da Silva, 1998.

Correspondência, 1923–1935 [*Correspondence, 1923–1935*]. Edited by Manuela Parreira da Silva, 1999.

O banqueiro anarquista [*The Anarchist Banker*]. Edited by Manuela Parreira da Silva, 1999.

Ficções do interlúdio [*Fictions of the Interlude*]. Edited by Fernando Cabral Martins, 1999.

Poesia, Alexander Search [*Poetry, Alexander Search*]. Edited by Luísa Freire, 1999.

Eróstrato e a busca da imortalidade [*Erostratus and the Quest for Immortality*]. Edited by Richard Zenith, 2000.

Poesia de Ricardo Reis [*Poetry of Ricardo Reis*]. Edited by Manuela Parreira da Silva, 2000.

Poesia Inglesa I [*English Poetry I*]. Edited by Luísa Freire, 2000.

Poesia Inglesa II [*English Poetry II*]. Edited by Luísa Freire, 2000.

Crítica: Ensaios, artigos e entrevistas [*Criticism: Essays, Articles, and Interviews*]. Edited by Fernando Cabral Martins, 2001.

A educação do estóico, Barão de Teive [*The Education of the Stoic, Baron of Teive*]. Edited by Richard Zenith, 2001.

Poesia de Alberto Caeiro [*Poetry of Alberto Caeiro*]. Edited by Fernando Cabral Martins and Richard Zenith, 2001.

Quadras [*Quatrains*]. Edited by Luísa Freire, 2002.

Mensagem [*Message*]. Edited by Fernando Cabral Martins, 2002.

Poesia de Álvaro de Campos [*Poetry of Álvaro de Campos*]. Edited by Teresa Rita Lopes, 2002.

Aforismos e afins [*Aphorisms and the Like*]. Edited by Richard Zenith, 2003.

Canções do beber: Rubaiyyat na obra de Fernando Pessoa [*Drinking Songs: Rubaiyat in the Work of Fernando Pessoa*]. Edited by Maria Aliete Galhoz, 2003.

Escritos autobiográficos, automáticos e de reflexão pessoal [*Autobiographical, Automatic, and Personal Reflection Writings*]. Edited by Richard Zenith, 2003.

Poesia, 1902–1917 [*Poetry, 1902–1917*]. Edited by Manuela Parreira da Silva, Ana Maria Freitas, and Madalena Jorge Dine, 2006.

Poesia, 1918–1930 [*Poetry, 1918–1930*]. Edited by Manuela Parreira da Silva, Ana Maria Freitas, and Madalena Jorge Dine, 2006.

Poesia, 1931–1935 y sin fecha [*Poetry, 1931–1935 and Undated*]. Edited by Manuela Parreira da Silva, Ana Maria Freitas, and Madalena Jorge Dine, 2006.

Obra essencial de Fernando Pessoa [*Essential Works of Fernando Pessoa*]. Edited by Richard Zenith, 2006–07. 7 vols.

Quaresma, Descifrador [*Quaresma, Decoder*]. Edited by Ana Maria Freitas, 2008.

Forever Someone Else. Edited by Richard Zenith, 2008.

Encontro Magick *seguido de* A boca do inferno [Magick Meeting *followed by* The Mouth of Hell]. Edited by Miguel Roza, 2010.

Teoria da heteronímia [*Theory of Heteronymy*]. Edited by Fernando Cabral Martins and Richard Zenith, 2012.

Cartas de amor de Fernando Pessoa e Ofélia Queiroz [*Love Letters of Fernando Pessoa and Ofélia Queiroz*]. Edited by Manuela Parreira da Silva, 2012.

O mendigo e outros contos [*The Beggar and Other Stories*]. Edited by Ana Maria Freitas, 2012.

Histórias de um raciocinador e o ensaio "História policial" [*Stories of a Reasoner and the Essay "Police Story"*]. Edited by Ana Maria Freitas, 2012.

O regresso dos deuses, e outros escritos de António Mora [*The Return of the Gods, and Other Writings by António Mora*]. Edited by Manuela Parreira da Silva, 2013.

Cartas, visões e outros textos do Sr. Pantaleão [*Letters, Visions, and Other Texts by Mr. Pantaleão*]. Edited by Ana Maria Freitas and Manuela Parreira da Silva, 2014.

A estrada do esquecimento e outros contos [*The Road of Forgetting and Other Stories*]. Edited by Ana Maria Freitas, 2015.

English Poetry. Edited by Richard Zenith, 2016.

A porta e outras ficções [*The Door and Other Fictions*]. Edited by Ana Maria Freitas, 2017.

More recently, Tinta-da-china, one of the most vibrant publishing houses, which also maintains a presence in Brazil, has begun presenting up-to-date texts in attractive and inexpensive editions:

Livro do desassossego [*Book of Disquiet*]. Edited by Jerónimo Pizarro, 2013.

Eu sou uma antologia: 136 autores fictícios [*I Am an Anthology: 136 Fictional Authors*]. Edited by Jerónimo Pizarro and Patricio Ferrari, 2013.

Obra completa de Álvaro de Campos [*Complete Works of Álvaro de Campos*]. Edited by Jerónimo Pizarro and Antonio Cardiello, 2014.

Sobre o fascismo, a ditadura militar e Salazar [*About Fascism, the Military Dictatorship and Salazar*]. Edited by José Barreto, 2015.

Obra completa de Alberto Caeiro [*Complete Works of Alberto Caeiro*]. Edited by Jerónimo Pizarro and Patricio Ferrari, 2016.

Obra completa de Ricardo Reis [*Complete Works of Ricardo Reis*]. Edited by Jerónimo Pizarro and Jorge Uribe, 2016.

Teatro estático [*Static Theater*]. Edited by Filipa de Freitas and Patricio Ferrari, 2017.

Poesia: Antologia mínima [*Poetry: Minimal Anthology*]. Edited by Jerónimo Pizarro, 2018.

Fausto [*Faust*]. Edited by Carlos Pittella, 2018.

O mistério da Boca do inferno: Correspondência e novela policial [*The Mystery of Hell's Mouth: Correspondence and Detective Novel*]. Edited by Steffen Dix, 2019.

Prosa: Antologia mínima [*Prose: Minimal Anthology*]. Edited by
   Jerónimo Pizarro, 2020.
Mensagem [*Message*]. Edited by Jerónimo Pizarro, 2020.
Cartas de amor [*Love Letters*]. Edited by Jerónimo Pizarro, 2023.

English Editions

It is perhaps no surprise that editions of Pessoa's works in English are also widely scattered and various. The number of able translators, some poets in their own right, who have tried to render Pessoa into English is large. Some of the most successful editions have even been reedited to incorporate the changes in our knowledge of Pessoa's works as more and more manuscripts have made their way out of the archives and into print. The best-known translations, such as those by Margaret Jull Costa or Richard Zenith, are readily available. In addition to these, we recommend Edwin Honig's *Selected Poems by Fernando Pessoa*, with an introduction by Octavio Paz; Honig and Susan Brown's *Poems of Fernando Pessoa*; David Butler's *Selected Poems*; and Zenith's *A Little Larger Than the Entire Universe: Selected Poems*. Especially significant translations of Pessoa's prose include *Always Astonished: Selected Prose*, translated by Honig, and *The Selected Prose of Fernando Pessoa*, translated and edited by Zenith. Although there is no planned large-scale edition of Pessoa's works in English at the moment, New Directions has initiated a series of publications, with Jull Costa as translator, which include *The Complete Works of Alberto Caeiro*, edited by Jerónimo Pizarro and Patricio Ferrari and translated by Jull Costa and Ferrari. Finally, a special mention should be made, given its worldwide importance, to *The Book of Disquiet*, of which there are several translations and even several editions by the same translator. In 1991, a banner year, not one but four different translations appeared: *The Book of Disquietude*, translated by Zenith; *The Book of Disquiet: A Selection*, translated by Iain Watson; *The Book of Disquiet*, translated by Alfred Mac Adam; and *The Book of Disquiet*, translated by Jull Costa. Ten years later, Zenith would bring out a revised edition under the title *The Book of Disquiet*. And in 2017 Jull Costa also brought out a significantly revised translation, based on the text of the critical edition edited by Pizarro and published by New Directions in New York and Serpent's Tail in London.

Further Reading for Students

Although instructors will not want to overload students with extra reading, providing the necessary context to enter Pessoa's universe should be seen as a must. There are several introductions to Pessoa that discuss a large number of his works as well as the critical issues surrounding them in a concise, clear manner that can guide students' first attempts at understanding the complexity and richness of Pessoa's texts and encourage further explorations. Jerome Boyd Maunsell in "The Hauntings of Fernando Pessoa" provides the quickest means of entry. Furthermore, instructors can choose from two book-length introductions, excerpting as needed: Darlene J. Sadlier's *An Introduction to Fernando Pessoa: Modernism and the Paradoxes of Authorship* and Pizarro's *Fernando Pessoa: A Critical Introduction*. Students wishing to go a bit further or to delve into specific questions may benefit as well from "Fernando Pessoa's Critical and Editorial Fortune in English," by José Blanco. *A Centenary Pessoa*, edited by Eugénio Lisboa and L. C. Taylor, brings together a variety of critical perspectives that remain of interest and are generally accessible.

For historical context, we recommend David Birmingham's *A Concise History of Portugal*, first published in 1998 and updated for its third edition in 2018. Also fundamental is the chapter by Ellen W. Sapega on Portugal in *The Cambridge Companion to European Modernism*, edited by Pericles Lewis. In order to gain a fuller appreciation for Portuguese modernism in general, and especially the group of artists around Pessoa, the first resource should be the volume of essays edited by Steffen Dix and Pizarro, *Portuguese Modernisms: Multiple Perspectives in Literature and the Visual Arts*. Students wishing to see Pessoa in the context of world literature may find a point of entry in Paulo de Medeiros's "Fernando Pessoa, Singular Modernity, and World Literature."

Instructors who do not wish to assign traditional extra readings might opt for digital presentations on Pessoa, other Portuguese modernists, or places and items related to them. Images can be easily assembled, drawing from photos of Pessoa, Mário de Sá-Carneiro, José de Almada Negreiros, and other members of the *Orpheu* group (see the various photobiographies mentioned in "Background Studies"), or from paintings, for instance by Amadeo de Souza-Cardoso, whose work was included in the famous Armory Show of 1913 in New York. Information about this and indeed on other art forms that avail themselves of Pessoa and his texts can also be found easily in a simple Internet search. Some instructors may also find it useful to use images of facsimiles of some of Pessoa's papers or direct students to the resources available through the site of the Pessoa House Museum (casafernandopessoa.pt). Likewise, images or maps of Lisbon can be profitably used to give students a better sense of the streets Pessoa continuously walked and used as reference points in his writing. A recent episode of a classic BBC Radio 4 program, *In Our Time*, hosted by Melvyn Bragg, presents a range of facets of Pessoa's life and works in a round table with Juliet Perkins, Cláudia Pazos-Alonso, and Medeiros ("Fernando Pessoa"). The Instituto Camões also provides some useful resources ("We, Orpheu").

The Instructor's Library

Biography

Many studies of Pessoa include at least a smattering of biographical detail. Pessoa was not a recluse by any means, and by now much is known about his life, yet he could be discreet, and there are many areas that remain obscure and as such provide fuel for ample speculation. Published in 1950, the first sustained biography of Pessoa, *Vida e obra de Fernando Pessoa: História duma geração* (*Life and Work of Fernando Pessoa: History of a Generation*), by João Gaspar Simões, was in its way a monumental work by an influential literary critic who had known, corresponded with, and helped edit Pessoa. As its title indicates, it fit in with the then current model of lives and works of great men. Today, its psychologizing attempts strike one as dated, but the work has remained in print and has had little competition until recently. In 1988, Ángel Crespo published *La vida plural de Fernando Pessoa* (*The Plural Life of Fernando Pessoa*), and eight years later Robert Bréchon brought out his *Étrange étranger: Une biographie de Fernando Pessoa* (*Strange Stranger: A Biography of Fernando Pessoa*). José Paulo Cavalcanti Filho wrote a large, much-publicized, and somewhat polemical biography that blurred the line between author and subject: *Fernando Pessoa: Uma quase-autobiografia*, published first in 2011 and then in an English translation by Filipe Faria in 2019 (Cavalcanti Filho, *Fernando Pessoa: A Quasi Memoir*). The first biography in English was written by Hubert D. Jennings. Plans for its publication in 1974 were disrupted by the 25 April Revolution, and the work is only now available for the first time as *Fernando Pessoa, the Poet with Many Faces*, an edition that also includes a selection of Pessoa's poems edited by Carlos Pittella. It does not cover the entire life but focuses very much on the time Pessoa spent growing up in South Africa. Another partial biography that focuses on Pessoa and South Africa was written as a doctoral thesis by Alexandrino Severino at the University of São Paulo in 1969 and later published in revised form as *Fernando Pessoa na África do Sul: A formação inglesa de Fernando Pessoa* (*Fernando Pessoa in South Africa: The English Education of Fernando Pessoa*). The most recent biography, by Zenith and variously titled *Pessoa: A Biography* and *Pessoa: An Experimental Life*, is again a voluminous and much celebrated undertaking that dialogues with its predecessor by Gaspar Simões and with the biographies of other influential modernists. It can be seen as a good work of reference for the present.

Background Studies

To the sources of historical and social context listed in the section on further readings for students should be added books rich in personal and other photographs of Pessoa, his family and friends, and places and objects directly related to him. Among those, Maria José de Lancastre's *Fernando Pessoa: Uma Foto-biografia* (*Fernando Pessoa: A Photobiography*) holds the distinction of not only being the first but also one of the most lavish, in large format. After several reprintings, it eventually went out of print, though major academic libraries should have a copy. A second, revised edition was published as a smaller paperback at a more affordable price in 1998. It cut some photographs from the first edition but added others; the text itself was also revised and updated. This edition is also no longer in print, though used copies can be found. Ten years later, another photobiography in large format, *Fernando Pessoa*, was brought out as part of the series *Fotobiografias Século XX* (*Photobiographies of the Twentieth Century*), with extensive texts by Zenith.

Complementing these, Manuela Nogueira's *Fernando Pessoa: Imagens de uma vida* (*Fernando Pessoa: Images of a Life*) offers a personal perspective on Pessoa's life by his niece and includes useful contributions by Galhoz and Zenith as well as images not available elsewhere. Although there is no comparable work in English, the book *Pessoas Lissabon* (*Pessoa's Lisbon*), prepared for the forty-ninth Frankfurt Book Fair, where Portugal was designated the guest of honor, includes many images as well as a series of brief essays on Pessoa and his context, translated into English and German. Common to all these resources is a chronology of Pessoa's life, which is useful in a classroom setting. Finally, a volume and two CDs issued with the exhibition *We, the "Orpheu" Lot / Nós os de "Orpheu,"* curated by Antonio Cardiello and colleagues, is recommended. Where the volume itself is not accessible, the exhibition can be visited virtually at the Instituto Camões site ("We, Orpheu").

Critical Studies

The body of scholarship and criticism on Fernando Pessoa is vast, rapidly expanding, and available in a variety of languages. Critical studies are still most frequently written in Portuguese, but important contributions have been made in English, French, German, and Spanish. Sometimes, an influential study appears in translation. Any attempt at comprehensiveness would be either misguided or futile since Pessoa studies have become an expanding universe including multiple intersections with other disciplines and fields of study. When a semblance of comprehensiveness in Pessoa studies was still somewhat imaginable, José Blanco, one of the most distinguished Pessoa scholars, produced a large bibliography, which he referred to in terms of a sketch (*Fernando Pessoa: Esboço de uma bibliografia* [*Fernando Pessoa: Outline of a Bibliography*]), followed by a later attempt, *Pessoana*, in two volumes. Here our goal is to provide a short and selected guide for instructors who may be pressed for time and want to focus on specific issues related to Pessoa studies.

Articles on Pessoa appear in many scholarly journals and other types of publications. Special issues of academic journals have covered a wide range of questions on Pessoa and can be easily accessed (Sadlier and Martins; Mendes;

Pizarro and Dix, *Pessoa*; Pizarro and Ferrari). It is also useful to note the academic journals dedicated to Pessoa studies. The first journal dedicated to Pessoa studies was *Persona*, published at the Centre for Pessoa Studies then in operation at the Universidade do Porto, in twelve issues, from 1977 to 1985. In the light of its historic importance and relative inaccessibility, a facsimile edition was published in 2019 that also included two essays, one by Arnaldo Saraiva, *Persona's* editor, the other by Pizarro, who was responsible for its reedition (*Persona*). For a long period after the dissolution of the Centre for Pessoa Studies and the demise of *Persona*, there was no comparable publication. This gap was filled in 2012 with the publication of the first issue of *Pessoa Plural: A Journal of Fernando Pessoa Studies*. An open access, peer-reviewed electronic journal, coedited by Pizarro, Almeida, and Medeiros and hosted by Brown University, *Pessoa Plural* has been continuously publishing articles, reviews, and original documents in facsimile. A useful resource for critical opinions of any facet of Pessoa studies regardless of interpretative or theoretical perspective, the journal has published a large number of documents from various archives, making it uniquely valuable for instructors who may want to focus on the material aspects of Pessoa studies. Another open access electronic journal focused on Pessoa studies, *Estranhar Pessoa (To Find Pessoa Strange)*, has been published since 2014 under the editorial direction of Pedro Sepúlveda.

Renowned critics such as George Steiner and Harold Bloom also held the work of Pessoa in very high esteem and wrote about it. Steiner's well-known critical review of *The Book of Disquiet* in Zenith's second translation of 2021, which appeared in *The Guardian* as "A Man of Many Parts" is worth many essays much longer and is ideal for introducing students to some of the thorniest issues in Pessoa's studies. Bloom, for his part, included Pessoa with Franz Kafka, Sigmund Freud, Virginia Woolf, James Joyce, Samuel Beckett, Marcel Proust, and Jorge Luis Borges when naming the canonical figures of modernity (*Western Canon* 421). He also wrote a chapter on Pessoa for his book *Genius: A Mosaic of One Hundred Exemplary Creative Minds* (595–99). Two of the most important interpreters of Pessoa, especially in cultural terms, are the late Eduardo Lourenço and José Gil. Although much of their work is still awaiting translation into English, some of it can be found in recent translation or in French. A selection of Lourenço's essays has been edited and translated by Ronald W. Sousa and published as *Here on Douradores Street: Essays on Fernando Pessoa*. Gil, who at one point was programming director for the Collége International de Philosophie, had there a research program on Fernando Pessoa. From his several works dedicated to Pessoa, especially noteworthy are *Fernando Pessoa ou la métaphysique des sensations (Fernando Pessoa or the Metaphysics of Sensations)* and *O devir-eu de Fernando Pessoa (The Becoming-I of Fernando Pessoa)*. Many other authors have taken a philosophical approach to Pessoa. Ricardina Guerreiro published a large study of *The Book of Disquiet* in relation to Walter Benjamin, focused on the notion of melancholy: *Do luto por existir: A melancolia de Bernardo Soares à luz de Walter Benjamin (Mourning for Existence: The*

Melancholy of Bernardo Soares in the Light of Walter Benjamin). Judith Balso
has published variously on Pessoa and philosophy, and one of her books is available in English as *Pessoa, the Metaphysical Courier* (see also Balso, *Affirmation* 35–46). One of the most thought-provoking essays on Pessoa and philosophy
is chapter 4 of Alain Badiou's *Handbook of Inaesthetics*, "A Philosophical Task:
To Be Contemporaries of Pessoa" (36–45). Badiou's essay "The Age of the Poets"
also makes ample reference to Pessoa. Among the most recent studies of Pessoa
and philosophy are *Nietzsche e Pessoa* (*Nietzsche and Pessoa*), edited by Bartholomew Ryan and colleagues; Jonardon Ganeri's *Virtual Subjects, Fugitive
Selves: Fernando Pessoa and His Philosophy*; and *Fernando Pessoa and Philosophy: Countless Lives Inhabit Us*, edited by Ryan and colleagues. Pessoa, who
earned a living as a commercial translator, also attempted literary translation.
The most systematic attempt to analyze this important element of Pessoa's writing up to now has been published as a collection of essays in a special issue of
the *The Translator, Fernando Pessoa and Translation* (Pizarro and Medeiros).

Many critical studies look at the work of Pessoa from the perspective of genre,
not least because Pessoa so often evaded, redefined, and subverted traditional
genres. The most comprehensive study along these lines is K. David Jackson's
Adverse Genres in Fernando Pessoa. Thomas Cousineau reads *The Book of Disquiet* as a kind of novel in *An Unwritten Novel: Fernando Pessoa's* The Book of
Disquiet. In her major study *Fernando Pessoa and the Lyric: Disquietude, Rumination, Interruption, Inspiration, Constellation*, Irene Ramalho-Santos presents some of the most important theoretical reflections on Pessoa's poetry and
poetics. A crucial study of Pessoa's poetics in comparative perspective is provided
by Ramalho-Santos in *Atlantic Poets: Fernando Pessoa's Turn in Anglo-American
Modernism*. Comparative studies of Pessoa have been growing recently and can
be among the most useful for instructors introducing Pessoa to students who have
some prior knowledge of either Anglo-American modernism or contemporary
theoretical approaches. George Monteiro, one of the most influential scholars
of Pessoa, wrote several studies that remain as important today as when he wrote
them. Instructors may profit especially from *The Presence of Pessoa: English,
American, and Southern African Literary Responses* and *Fernando Pessoa and
Nineteenth-Century Anglo-American Literature*. Monteiro also edited a series
of essays, *The Man Who Never Was*, stemming from an important colloquium
on Pessoa that took place at Brown University, where he was professor in the
Department of English as well as in the Department of Portuguese and Brazilian Studies, which he had helped to found. Mariana Gray de Castro collects a
variety of studies in *Fernando Pessoa's Modernity without Frontiers*. From a
number of influence studies, we note two of the most recent: Patrícia Silva's
Yeats and Pessoa: Parallel Poetic Studies and Castro's *Fernando Pessoa's Shakespeare: The Invention of the Heteronyms*. In *Pessoa's Geometry of the Abyss*
and *O silêncio das sereias* (*The Silence of the Sirens*), Medeiros discusses Pessoa in relation to Kafka and Benjamin. Reflections on Pessoa and world literature from a world-systems theory perspective are carried out by Ramalho-Santos

in *Fernando Pessoa e outros fingidores* (*Fernando Pessoa and Other Feigners*) and by Medeiros in "Transnational Pessoa" and the already mentioned "Fernando Pessoa, Singularity, and World Literature." David Frier edited a volume of essays on the question of intertextuality, *Pessoa in an Intertextual Web: Influence and Innovation*.

Given Pessoa's multiplication of the self into all the various heteronyms, it would seem that psychoanalytical approaches to Pessoa would abound. However, perhaps owing to the fact that such a perspective is less frequent in traditional Portuguese studies than in literary studies generally, that is not the case. Nonetheless, two authors have written strong contributions along Freudian and Lacanian lines. Leyla Perrone-Moisés, a Brazilian scholar, has published several studies, including *Aquém do eu, alem do outro* (*This Side of the Self, Beyond the Other*) and *Pessoa, le sujet éclaté* (*Pessoa, the Shattered Subject*). José Martinho, a practicing psychoanalyst in Lisbon, has contributed a very accessible book entitled *Pessoa e a Psicanálise*. Pizarro's critical edition of Pessoa's *Escritos sobre génio e loucura* not only collects practically all of the many texts Pessoa himself wrote on the subjects of genius and madness but also includes an extended introduction. More recently, Nelson da Silva, Jr., published *Fernando Pessoa e Freud: Diálogos inquietantes* (*Fernando Pessoa and Freud: Unsettling Dialogues*). Although hardly mentioned in the early days of Pessoa studies, scholarship on sexualities and the body in Pessoa have been developing considerably in the last twenty years. A groundbreaking volume of essays on this subject, *Embodying Pessoa: Corporeality, Gender, Sexuality*, was edited by Anna Klobucka and Mark Sabine. Aníbal Frias has written extensively on this topic in his *Fernando Pessoa et le quint-empire de l'amour: Quête du désir et alter-sexualité* (*Fernando Pessoa and the Fifth Empire of Love: Quest for Desire and Alter-Sexuality*), as have both Zenith and Cavalcanti Filho in their respective biographies of Pessoa already mentioned. Most critics concur on seeing Pessoa's texts as exhibiting a degree of misogynism, not altogether uncommon in other modernists. The study that has explored this furthest is José Barreto's *Misoginia e anti-feminismo em Fernando Pessoa* (*Misogyny and Anti-Feminism in Fernando Pessoa*). One other main issue for the interpretation of Pessoa concerns politics and the political, and here too Barreto has blazed a trail. Instructors will certainly profit from his two essays available in English: "António Ferro: Modernism and Politics" and "Salazar and the New State in the Writings of Fernando Pessoa."

Film

Instructors who want to use film in relation to Pessoa, whether as a complement to the texts or as part of an interdisciplinary approach, have several options. First of all, Pessoa himself was interested in film and tried his hand at writing several film scripts. Admittedly, he never fully developed any of them. Nonetheless, it is certainly important to consider those scripts, both in terms of historical context and periodization as well as in terms of what they can tell us about the author's relationship to modernity and new representational technologies. The six film scripts, written in Portuguese, French, and English, have been published together in a volume edited by Ferrari and Claudia J. Fischer (Pessoa, *Argumentos para filmes*). The critical analysis made by both editors is the most important contribution to an understanding of Pessoa in relation to cinema. Beyond this, instructors can avail themselves of several films that base themselves on texts by Pessoa. Arguably the most significant of these to date is João Botelho's *Filme do Desassossego* (*Film of Disquiet*), an intense, at times experimental, film closely based on the *Book of Disquiet*. Medeiros made some reflections on this in his *Geometry of the Abyss* already mentioned (69–73). Another film by Botelho, *Conversa Acabada* (*The Other One*), concerns Pessoa and Sá-Carneiro, one of his close friends and another great modernist poet. José Fonseca e Costa's film *Os Mistérios de Lisboa / What the Tourist Should See* is based on a text Pessoa wrote in English as a sort of tourist guide to Lisbon. Giulio Base's film *Il banchiere anarchico*, which premiered at the Venice Biennale in 2018, took as its inspiration a short narrative by Pessoa, *The Anarchist Banker*. In 2021, two new films based on Pessoa were released. One, directed by Leandro Ferreira, was jointly produced by RTP, the Portuguese State Television, and Marginal Filmes, with the title *Um jantar muito original* (*A Very Original Dinner*). The other, *O ídolo* (*Note for a Thriller*), is a short film directed by Pedro Varela that has the distinction of having been shot entirely with a mobile phone as part of a campaign by Samsung. Although critical, scholarly studies of these more recent films are not yet fully available, instructors can find interviews as well as brief reviews of them with a simple Internet search. New studies were published in *Pessoa and Cinema*, a special issue of *Pessoa Plural*, in 2024 (Pizarro et al.).

Archives

At the moment, there are two main archival sources for Pessoa that are publicly accessible (some materials remain in private collections). The most significant of these is housed in Portugal's National Library in Lisbon, which has acquired Pessoa's estate and has made a selection of materials available digitally ("Espólio Fernando Pessoa"). The Museum Casa Pessoa houses Pessoa's own personal library. The entire collection was digitized by Pizarro, Ferrari, and Cardiello in 2010 and can be accessed electronically ("Biblioteca Particular"). Instructors wanting to acquaint themselves with questions related to Pessoa's collections can read an extensive discussion with full bibliographical details and profusely illustrated in "Livros, objectos, manuscritos e fotografias: doação e venda" (Pizarro and Filipe).

Audiovisual and Electronic Resources

Whereas an Internet search most probably will reveal a wide and growing variety of materials related to Pessoa, whether from scholarly journals, personal blogs, and the popular press or in the form of theatrical interpretations of Pessoa's texts or even impersonations of the poet promenading through the streets of Lisbon, some can be particularly useful to instructors, either as supplements or on their own. *The Book of Disquiet*, with its many variants, competing editions, and successive translations, is an ideal text for a comprehensive digital project such as the *LdoD Archive* (ldod.uc.pt), which offers multiple possibilities for engaging with Pessoa and *The Book of Disquiet*, making available different editions and the materials associated with them and offering possibilities for developing other editions as well. Instructors wishing to quickly have access to Pessoa's texts may avail themselves of the *Arquivo Pessoa* (arquivopessoa .net). And instructors with an interest in translation studies may want to take advantage of the many versions of one of Pessoa's key poems, his "Autopsicografia" ("Autopsychography"), that have been collected electronically at disquiet .com/thirteen.html.

Part Two

APPROACHES

Orpheu, Modernism, and Europe

Steffen Dix

In 2011, Pericles Lewis edited *The Cambridge Companion to European Modernism* and divided European modernism into "core" and "peripheral" modernisms. This structure is implicitly based on the world-systems theory of Immanuel Wallerstein, which represents an attempt to establish a theory capable of explaining the expansion of worldwide capitalism dividing the modern world into a center, a semiperiphery, and a periphery. By standing in this sociological model, Lewis identifies modernism in Portugal as peripheral.[1] It is a historical coincidence, but this division had already been anticipated by Fernando Pessoa in reference to his sensationism: "Cubism, futurism and other lesser isms have become well-known and far-talked because they have originated in the admitted centres of European culture. Sensationism, which is far more interesting, a far more original and a far more attractive movement than those, remains unknown because it was born far from those centres" (Pessoa, *Sensacionismo* 214). However, "far from those centers" does not—at least not always—mean "in the periphery," because economic growth and sociocultural development do not necessarily coincide. In the nineteenth and twentieth centuries, the relationship between economic growth and sociocultural development became overly complex, and it would be more appropriate to point out European modernism's transnational physiognomy than its division between center and periphery.

Nonetheless, when considering the expansion of world capitalism, the division into a center, semiperiphery, and periphery becomes intelligible, and Portugal was described as a semiperipheral society, characterized by "uma descoincidência articulada entre as relações de produção capitalista e as relações de reprodução social" ("a clearly outlined lack of coincidence between the relationships of capitalist production and the relationships of social reproduction"; B. Santos, *Estado* 109).[2] At the end of the nineteenth century, Portugal remained disconnected from the great economic developments, urbanization, and bourgeois modernity that were transforming other European nations. At the

Conferências do Casino (Casino Conferences), held in 1871, Portuguese intellectuals sought to sought to establish a connection of their nation with the rest of Europe in terms of social, economic, political, and cultural transformation. In 1880, in his poem "O sentimento de um ocidental" ("The Feeling of a Westerner"), Cesário Verde describes Lisbon as a melancholy and lackluster city, contrasting greatly with Baudelaire's Paris, whose flaneur lives the intense life of a city in full urbanization and industrialization. In the first decades of the twentieth century, Portugal was still, economically and socially speaking, in Europe's periphery, but there are several reasons why modernism in Portugal cannot be called peripheral.

It would probably be more appropriate to say that there was, in Portugal, a certain asynchronism between modernity, modernization, and modernism. To understand this asynchronism, let us look at a generic description by Fredric Jameson, who understood "modernity as the new historical situation, modernization as the process whereby we get there, and modernism as a reaction to that situation and that process alike, a reaction that can be aesthetic and philosophico-ideological, just as it can be negative and positive" (*Singular Modernity* 99). There is in this perspective a dialectic between industrialization or urbanization and aesthetic or philosophico-ideological reactions to these developments. This dialectic notion is pertinent, but there is a certain incongruence when we try to apply it to Portugal. In the modernist context, Fernando Pessoa's Lisbon is today as representative as Virginia Woolf's London, Alfred Döblin's Berlin, or Robert Musil's Vienna. Yet Lisbon was far from matching the sociocultural and economic infrastructure of London, Berlin, or Vienna. *The Man without Qualities'* first chapter has enormous suggestive strength in its description of a beautiful day in August 1913 in a great city (whose name is not stated, although it clearly is Vienna): "sie bestand aus Unregelmäßigkeit, Wechsel, Vorgleiten, Nichtschritthalten, Zusammenstößen von Dingen und Angelegenheiten, bodenlosen Punkten der Stille dazwischen, aus Bahnen und Ungebahntem, aus einem rhythmischen Schlag und der ewigen Verstimmung und Verschiebung aller Rhythmen gegeneinander, und glich im ganzen einer kochenden Blase . . ." ("it was made up of irregularity, change, forward spurts, failures to keep step, collisions of objects and interests, punctuated by unfathomable silences; made up of pathways and untrodden ways, of one great rhythmic beat as well as the chronic discord and mutual displacement of all its contending rhythms. All in all, it was like a boiling bubble . . ."; Musil, *Mann* 10; *Man* 4). On her walk, Clarissa Dalloway fuses her inner world with the bustling streets of Westminster, "the swing, tramp, and trudge; in the bellow and the uproar; the carriages, motor cars, omnibuses, vans, sandwich men shuffling and swinging; brass bands, barrel organs; in the triumph and the jingle and the strange high singing of some aeroplane overhead was what she loved; life; London; this moment of June" (Woolf 4). In *Berlin Alexanderplatz's* first chapter, Franz Biberkopf gets out of prison in Berlin Tegel, takes tram no. 41, and heads into the city center, going through "Schuhgeschäfte, Hutgeschäfte, Glühlampen, Destillen" ("shoe stores, hat stores, streetlights, bars"), always surrounded by a "Gewimmel, welch Gewimmel" ("crowd, what a crowd"; Döblin 13–14). Unlike these bustling cities, in Lisbon's city center we can still find the somnolent peace of the countryside: "Ha momentos, sobretudo nos meio-dias de estio, em que, nesta Lisboa luminosa, o campo, como um vento, nos invade. E aqui mesmo, na Rua dos Douradores, temos o bom somno" ("Even the city has its moments of country quiet, especially at midday in high summer, when the country invades this luminous city of Lisbon like a wind. And even here, in Rua dos Douradores, we sleep well"; Pessoa, *Desassossego* [Tinta] 494–95; *Disquiet* [New Directions] 442). This excerpt, in which Pessoa goes on to speak of his "villa de provincia" ("provincial town"), was written on 29 August 1933, around eighteen years after the publication of the two issues of the journal *Orpheu*, which was the first (and most important) modernist manifestation—or even manifesto—in Portugal and which created a considerable scandal in the petty bourgeois world of Lisbon. Considering this excerpt, as well as Verde's poetry or the Casino Conferences, as general witnesses, we could easily conclude that modernism in Portugal came in a fairly provincial and sleepy environment. Modernism in Portugal anticipated the country's sociocultural modernization; *Orpheu* emerged in a landscape that was practically in a premodern state. That is to say, it at least did not possess the typical modern and urban fertility that gave birth to works such as *The Man without Qualities*, *Mrs. Dalloway*, or *Berlin Alexanderplatz*. Despite this, in Lisbon, *The Book of Disquiet* was born, which is as much a key work of European modernism as those of Musil, Woolf, or Döblin.

Nevertheless, the argument of asynchronism between modernization and modernism in Portugal does not contradict the notion that sees modernism in a dialectical relationship with modernity and the process of modernization. This dialectical relationship remains valid, and modernism tended to emerge in a temporal succession during or immediately after modernization. But modernism is also a transnational phenomenon with hybridization tendencies, and Western modernity must be faced in the context of early globalization. Some global tendencies inevitably affect any given location, and modernism can—in certain circumstances—anticipate modernization or modernity locally. Notwithstanding his not mentioning a relationship between modernism, modernity, and modernization, Pessoa described this effect and defended explicitly, in a 1912 article on new Portuguese poetry, the hypothesis that an artistic movement can anticipate or precede a sociocultural state ("Nova poesia portuguesa").

The first goal of this essay is therefore a detailed observation of how modernism preceded, in Portugal, modernity in general or sociocultural modernization. This observation has a singular effect because it allows for a historical reconstruction of some transnational itineraries of European modernism, which is then revealed as a plural unity. Considering its transnational character and its national particularities, European modernism is at once a single and multiple phenomenon, understandable only in its particular identity and irregular shape. In this sense, modernism in Portugal was a modernism in the periphery of Europe but not a "peripheral modernism." It might be better to state that modernism in Portugal was a mosaic modernism that mirrored the characteristic cultural diversity of the continent. That is, modernism in Portugal was truly European in the way it represented a large variety of European artistic conceptions and languages. The second goal of this essay is to try to shed light on how Fernando Pessoa's modernism should be understood as a real contribution to the European project. Regardless of Ezra Pound's famous dictum "Make it new," it is possible to observe, in many modernist writers and artists, implicit or explicit attempts to find a hypothesis and build a new European culture. As a modernist writer, Pessoa represents the attempt to establish a new European conscience built on a cosmopolitanism and an individualism that are free of nationalist or cultural resentment. He represents the individual Friedrich Nietzsche called a "good European" ("guter Europäer"; *Jenseits von Gut und Böse* 183), bringing together the diversity of European culture, understanding well the ambivalences and dangers of modernization processes. The second part of this essay therefore faces Pessoa's modernism as a construction project of a modern Europe, sketched right in the center of "the great seminal catastrophe" of the continent (Kennan 3).

Orpheu

Notwithstanding the political disturbances that roiled the Lisbon of Pessoa's time, the author understood his city as provincial and melancholic in contrast to the dynamic European metropoles where modernist works were constantly being produced. Álvaro de Campos is a personification of this contrast. The naval engineer composed his main modernist texts in London or in the industrial town Barrow-on-Furness (home to an important shipyard that during the first decades of the twentieth century was heavily engaged in the construction of warships), where he celebrated local factories, laboratories, music halls, and Luna Parks. His most nostalgic or even nihilistic texts were written in Lisbon, where he felt "o tedio dos dias que passam" ("the boredom of passing days"; Pessoa, *Obra completa de Álvaro de Campos* [2014] 214). Yet the notion of provincialism in Pessoa is ambiguous. On the one hand, there is a pleasant provincialism when he speaks, in *The Book of Disquiet*, about the drowsiness of the midday heat or, with marked affection, about the waiters in the small cafés, or about the little barbershops. On the other hand, there is a provincialism that is revealed in his countrymen in their thoughtless admiration of great European capitals, modernization, or progress. In his text on Portuguese provincialism, Pessoa recalls a conversation, contemporary with *Orpheu*, between himself and his close friend and fellow modernist writer Mário de Sá-Carneiro: "V. é europeu e civilizado, salvo em uma coisa, e nessa V. é vítima da educação portuguesa. V. admira Paris, admira as grandes cidades. Se V. tivesse sido educado no estrangeiro, e sob o influxo de uma grande cultura europeia, como eu, não daria pelas grandes cidades. Estavam todas dentro de si" ("You are European and civilized except in one matter, and in that thing, you are a victim of Portuguese education. You admire Paris, you admire the great cities. If you had been educated abroad, and under the influence of great European culture, as I was, you would not notice the great cities. They would all be within you"; Pessoa, *Crítica* 371–72). This provincialism is revealed as well by "amor ao progresso e ao moderno" ("love of progress and modernity") in combination with an inability to create progress or modernity independently (371). Sá-Carneiro confirms, implicitly and on several occasions, this supposition of Pessoa, as in a letter to José Pacheco, written on 11 August 1915, referring to the stay of the Delaunay couple in northern Portugal: "[os Delaunay] representam, em todo o caso, a arte mais avançada—e, Europa. Deve-lhe em verdade ter sido um consolo os ins-tantes 'Europeus' que com eles terá vivido" ("[the Delaunays] represent, in any case, the most advanced art—and Europe. It must have been a consolation for you, the 'European' moments you lived with them"; Pires 131).

In fact, a close look at the sociocultural context of Portuguese modernism reveals an asynchronism between a semi-industrialized environment and an artistic movement that developed an enormous cultural impact. Modernism in Portugal was not a genuine product of advanced industrialization or vibrant urbanization. It was instead the result of importing various notions or different cultural agendas that were adapted nationally or transformed into an authentic product. Paraphrasing Boaventura Santos, modernism in Portugal is the prod-uct of an articulated lack of coincidence between the relationships of a socially stagnant establishment and those of a reproduction artistically cosmopolitan. This lack of coincidence is implicitly present in the conversation between Sá-Carneiro and Pessoa that happened—as Pessoa points out—during the time of *Orpheu*, and this divergence was made explicit by the violent attacks against the members of generation *Orpheu*. From this the pertinence of these questions fol-lows: "O que é o *Orpheu*?" and "O que quer *Orpheu*?" ("What is *Orpheu*?" and "What does *Orpheu* seek?"; Pessoa, *Sensacionismo* 76, 74).

Orpheu—as the most emblematic representation of Portuguese modernism—does not allow itself to be described in a broad sense without a closer look at a European modernism that was, always and everywhere, a trans- or supranational phenomenon. The Italian Filippo Tommaso Marinetti launched his futurism in Paris, the American Pound had a central role in the consolidation of imagism and vorticism in London, cubism was born from a French-Spanish dialogue and was disseminated by a German gallery owner, and Dadaism was founded in Zurich by artists of German, Romanian, and Israeli origin—to name just a few examples. Bearing visible influences from Paris, London, and Rio de Janeiro, both of *Orpheu*'s issues (and even the unpublished third issue) reveal the same trans- or supranationality. Theoretically, *Orpheu* represents a synthesis or inter-section of the great artistic movements that anticipated or were directly a part of European modernism. In *Orpheu* we can find traces of symbolism, cubism, futurism, imagism, and vorticism, imported directly from abroad to Lisbon and nationally synthesized.

Sá-Carneiro announced on several occasions—sometimes openly, other times more ambiguously—his fascination with futurism and cubism. In some passages from his letters to Pessoa there is clear amazement regarding these artistic movements, as in his letter from 10 March 1913: "confesso-lhe, meu caro Pessoa, que *sem estar doido,* eu acredito no cubismo. . . . O mais celebre, o mais incompreensível destes pintores é o espanhol Picasso, de quem tenho visto imensos trabalhos que é fundador da escola. . . . Resumindo: eu acredito nas intenções dos cubistas; simplesmente os considero artistas que não realizaram aquilo que pretendem" ("I confess to you, my dear Pessoa, *without being crazy,* that I believe in cubism. . . . The most famous, the most incomprehensible of these painters is the Spaniard Picasso, from whom I have seen a large number of works, who is this school's founder. . . . In short: I believe in the cubists' intentions; I simply consider them artists who have not accomplished what they intended" (*Em ouro* 96–97). Sá-Carneiro saw his poem "Bailado" ("Dance") as his "cubist work," and his famous poem "Manucure" refers to "Meus olhos ungidos de Novo, / Sim!— meus olhos futuristas, meus olhos cubistas, meus olhos interseccionistas" ("My eyes anointed with New, / Yes!—my futurist eyes, my cubist eyes, my intersectionist eyes"; *Poesia* 161), proclaiming,

MARINETTI + PICASSO = PARIS < SANTA RITA PIN-
TOR + FERNANDO PESSOA
ALVARO DE CAMPOS
! ! ! !

(167)

The mathematical symbols and the size of the font in the last lines suggest that Sá-Carneiro saw the work of Santa-Rita Pintor, Pessoa, and Campos as superior to the works produced in Paris. On 30 June 1914, one year before the publication of *Orpheu*, he declared, not without pride, Campos's "Ode triunfal" ("Triumphal Ode") to be an "obra-prima do Futurismo" ("masterpiece of Futurism"; *Em ouro* 168). And on 13 August 1915, after both issues had been published, he referred to a visit to the gallery Sagot, "o templo cubista-futurista" ("the cubist-futurist temple"; 223), where he bought the anthology *I poeti futuristi* (*Futurist Poets*), containing "uns Fu fu . . . cri-cri . . . cucurucu . . . Is-holá . . . etc. muito recomendáveis" ("some Fu fu . . . cri-cri . . . cucurucu . . . Is-hello . . . etc. highly recommendable"; 351). Contrary to this enthusiasm, Sá-Carneiro had a curious aversion to the work of Amadeo de Souza-Cardoso, who was, for him "um tipo *blagueur, snob,* vaidoso, intolerável, etc. etc. Parece que não se pode ser cubista sem se ser impertinente e *blagueur* . . ." ("a *blagueur,* snob, vain, intolerable guy, etc., etc. It seems one cannot be cubist without being impertinent and *blagueur* . . ."; 118). Generally, Sá-Carneiro's attitude is hard to describe because it oscillates between fascination and some ambiguous interpretations, that is, between a deep understanding and a certain ignorance. In this way, Sá-Carneiro's reference to Souza-Cardoso is largely incomprehensible, considering that Manhufe's painter was, at the time, the only Portuguese modernist with an international reputation, participating in important international exhibits, such as Salon des Independants (1911, 1912, and 1914), Salon d'Automne (1912–14), the Armory Show (1913), *Erster Deutscher Herbstsalon* from Galerie Der Sturm (1914), and an exhibit from the Allied Artists' Association (1914), and enjoying commercial success. In his derogatory comment, Sá-Carneiro refers to his visit to the Salon d'Automne in the Grand Palais, where three paintings by Souza-Cardoso were exhibited, among them *Avant la corrida* (*Before the Race*), which can be interpreted as a work tendentially cubo-futurist, considering it combines the static fragmentation of cubism with a dynamic shattering of futurism. In fact, this painting could be interpreted as intersectionist, since it joined static with dynamic, yet, curiously, Sá-Carneiro did not recognize this. It is also interesting to know that Sá-Carneiro's comment is a response to a very explicit question—an expression of interest rather than derision—Pessoa had asked him in his previous letter about the "célebre pintor avançado português" ("famous advanced Portuguese painter"; *Sensacionismo* 400).

An even more open and practically unconditional fascination with futurism than in Sá-Carneiro—one contrary to Souza-Cardoso's artistic independence—can be found in Santa-Rita Pintor, José de Almada Negreiros, and Raul Leal. In 1916, Santa-Rita and Almada Negreiros founded the Comité Futurista (Futurist Committee), and in 1917 they organized a futurist section in the Teatro República and published the journal *Portugal Futurista* (*Futurist Portugal*). Santa-Rita was a devoted disciple of Marinetti and attended, in 1912, the lectures the Italian held at Gallery Bernheim Jeune, located on Boulevard de la Madelaine. Almada Negreiros published, in 1917, several futurist texts, such as *Ultimatum Futurista às Gerações Portuguesas do Século XX* (*Futurist Ultimatum to Portuguese Twentieth-Century Generations*) or *Saltimbancos* (*Contrastes Simultâneos*) (*Circus Performers [Simultaneous Contrasts]*) and shows in his visual work a profound influence from Picasso, incorporating his favorite theme, *saltimbanques*, and from the Delaunays' orphism, which he combined with futurism (M. P. Santos 253; P. Silva, "*Orpheu* Generation" 92). Leal was not only a little "*Orpheu* de mais" ("overly *Orpheu*"), as Sá-Carneiro mentioned to Pessoa (*Em ouro* 413); he was possibly also a little *futurista de mais* ("overly futurist"), considering a long, confused letter in which he explained to Marinetti that his religious system corresponded to a futurist church: "Et c'est une Gloire pour le Futurisme que la Religion elle-même sache profiter de ses enneigements. L'Église Paracletienne dont la fondation Dieu M'ordonne d'annoncer, c'est une Église essentiellement Futuriste!" ("And it is a Glory for Futurism that Religion itself knows how to take advantage of its snowfall. The Church of the Paraclete whose foundation God commands Me to announce is an essentially Futurist Church!") It is not known whether this letter, which exists only as a manuscript in Fernando Pessoa's estate (BNP/E3, 113F-6), was ever sent to Marinetti (see M. Silva). One might assume, however, that if Marinetti read this letter, he probably got real vertigo reading this somewhat hallucinatory document. One can also assume that the great fascination with futurism in these three members of *Orpheu* is explained by the desire to end Portugal's provincial past and to build a future society that could resemble European modernity.

Like Souza-Cardoso, Sá-Carneiro, Santa-Rita, or Leal, Pacheco got his inspiration from the artistic productivity of Paris and became responsible for the cover of the first volume of *Orpheu*, which represents an antique landscape. The two candles recall Greek columns, and the graphic illustration of the cover of the first issue of *Orpheu* may be a portrait of Isadora Duncan, who at the time was attempting to develop a new dance with visible references to the art of ancient Greece. In his letter from 30 June 1914 to Pessoa, Sá-Carneiro refers to "umas sanguineas sobre a Duncan que são muito belas" ("sanguine drawings on Duncan that are very beautiful"; *Em ouro* 225) that Pacheco had recently made— probably those which can be found today in the Calouste Gulbenkian Foundation collections. From 1910 to 1914, with brief interruptions, Pacheco lived in Paris, where he was in contact with his countrymen Souza-Cardoso and Sá-Carneiro and with many international artists, including Constantin Brâncuși and Amedeo Modigliani, who is believed to have portrayed Pacheco in a painting known today as *Portrait d'un homme au chapeau (José Pacheco)* (*Portrait of a Man with a Hat [José Pacheco]*).

Ronald de Carvalho, Eduardo Guimaraens, and Luiz de Montalvor brought the editorial experience they had gained from the Brazilian journal *Fon-Fon!* to *Orpheu*. Although not exactly a modernist or avant-garde journal, *Fon-Fon!*— founded in 1907 in Rio de Janeiro—identified itself with the principles of modernity in its onomatopoeic name (representing the sound of a car honking); in the articles on social habits of the Rio de Janeiro metropolis, the arts, cinema, and theater; and in the "proliferação de anúncios de projetos editoriais" ("proliferation of advertisements of editorial projects"; R. Sousa, "Bastidores brasileiros" 165) that also appear in *Orpheu*.

Finally, there are certain elements in Pessoa's work that stem, less directly, from London—most notably from imagism and vorticism. While *influence* may not be the most fitting term—perhaps *inspiration* is more accurate—one can observe a clear proximity to these two strands of European modernism in Pessoa's writings from this period. Pessoa had both issues of the vorticist journal *Blast*, which have a strong resonance in his sensationism, and at least the first issue of *Blast* became a clear graphic inspiration for the second issue of *Orpheu*. A detailed and careful analysis of the parallels between the two journals and the general impact of vorticism on Portuguese modernism can be found in a noteworthy article by Patrícia Silva ("Mediating Transnational Reception"). In Pessoa's private library, there are two imagist works—*Images, 1910–15*, by Richard Aldington, and *Cadences*, by F. S. Flint—and there is some probability that he also received, though after the publication of both issues of *Orpheu*, the 1 May 1915 special issue of the journal *The Egoist*, which was dedicated entirely to imagism. In May 1915, Pessoa wrote a draft of a letter to an unnamed addressee, but someone connected, with some certainty, to the imagist group: "I . . . await with much interest the specimen number of the 'Egoist'" (*Sensacionismo* 385). In this letter, eventually addressed to Richard Aldington, who in 1915–16 edited *The Poets' Translation Series* and who was the assistant editor of this special issue of *The Egoist*, Pessoa clearly distances himself from futurism and presents his own sensationism as an independent movement. Declaring an intention to make sensationism a central element of the modernist movement in England, this letter, along with another written in May 1915, serves as a crucial document for classifying Portuguese modernism within the broader European context. The second letter was addressed to Harold Monro, who from his Poetry Bookshop in London published the most important imagist poetry. Not unlike the first letter, the second represents an attempt to publicize *Orpheu* (or at least some parts of it) in England. Although oscillating between "intersectionism" and "Sensationism," these two letters are a clear attempt to show the artistic independence of Portuguese modernism, declaring that "the Portuguese Sensationist Movement is a thing quite apart from Futurism and having no connection therewith" or explaining that "the term 'intersectionist' applied to the poem is not the distinction of a school or current, like 'futurist' or 'imagist,' but a mere definition of process. . . ." At the same time, however, Pessoa recognizes that "the recent literary movement in Portugal [represents a] complex inclusion and absolute fusion of elements drawn from the four quarters of the intellectual earth." We can read it even more explicitly in another theoretical text: "The Sensationist movement (represented by the Lisbon quarterly *Orpheu*) represents the final synthesis. It gathers into one organic whole (for synthesis is not a sum) the several threads of modern movements, extracting honey from all the flowers that have blossomed in the gardens of European fancy" (Pessoa, *Sensacionismo* 385, 387–88, 159).

The first attempt by Pessoa to internationalize modern Portuguese poetry is from 26 December 1912, the day Pessoa wrote to *Poetry Review* with the intent of promoting "to internationality the extremely important and totally ignored movement represented . . . by contemporary Portuguese poetry" (*Correspondência 1905–1922* 59). Sá-Carneiro congratulated Pessoa on this attempt to make internationally known some of the poets who lived "num canto amargurado e esquecido da Europa" ("in a bitter and forgotten corner of Europe"; Sá-Carneiro, *Em ouro* 59). However, this task seems herculean because Portugal in the early twentieth century simply did not have the social and economic conditions to become an important piece in the cultural game of Europe.

Being aware of this, Pessoa and Sá-Carneiro found an easier solution: reversing their direction, they tried to bring Europe into Portugal. That is, before—or synchronously with—the international promotion of Portuguese modern poets, the Europeanization of the country would be necessary: "O que é preciso ter é . . . uma noção do *meio internacional*, de não ter a alma . . . limitada pela nacionalidade. Cultura não basta. É preciso ter a alma na Europa" ("What is needed is . . . a notion of the *international environment*, of not having one's soul . . . limited by nationality. Culture is not enough. It is necessary to have the soul in Europe"; Pessoa, *Sensacionismo* 177). These lines were written before May 1913, and the reference to "soul limited by nationality" was clearly a criticism of the journal *Renascença Portuguesa*, which intended to give cultural content to the republican revolution and based itself on Teixeira de Pascoaes's theory of saudosism. Sá-Carneiro confirms Pessoa's intuition, stating that he is "inteiramente de acordo" ("in full agreement") and emphasizing the "verdade monumental" ("monumental truth") of the need to have "Europa na alma" ("Europe in the soul"). The affirmation that Sá-Carneiro "gostava de desenvolver aqui ideias" ("would like to develop ideas here") appears to represent the definitive birth of the plan of creating a journal called *Europa* (*Europe*). In the same letter to Pessoa, Sá-Carneiro is enthusiastic about the "ideia sobre a revista" ("idea concerning the journal")—which at the time was provisionally named *Esfinge* (*Sphinx*)—and immediately takes responsibility for the material realization (Sá-Carneiro, *Em ouro* 177, 181). In June 1913, Sá-Carneiro was in Lisbon, where he would remain until the end of May 1914, and it seems there was then a concrete conversation about creating a modernist journal with the title *Europa*. On 5 July 1914, again in Paris, Sá-Carneiro writes, "*Europa! Europa* (revista) é que preciso sobre tudo!" ("*Europe! Europe* (journal) is what I need most of all!"; *Em ouro* 231). Nevertheless, the publishing plans of both Portuguese poets were overtaken in an instant by the geopolitical events happening in Europe. It is a fatal coincidence that Sá-Carneiro wrote a letter to Pessoa on 28 July 1914, almost prophetically begging, "Ai a *Europa!* a *Europa!* como ela seria necessária!" ("Oh *Europe! Europe!* How it would be necessary!"; *Em ouro* 250). This exclamation happened at the precise moment that Austria-Hungary declared war on Serbia—in other words, on the very day "the great seminal catastrophe of the twentieth century" (Kennan 3) began—and it would be another asynchronism to title a modernist journal with the name of a continent that was at the beginning of major and unprecedented self-destruction.

At the end of the summer of 1914, Pessoa and Sá-Carneiro were aware of the impossibility of naming the journal *Europe*. At the same time, the outbreak of war accelerated the journal's publication, given that all the main characters were in Portugal again, all of them with rich European experiences in their luggage, and their physical proximity finally eased practical tasks. A few years later, after 1922, Pessoa recalls a meeting with Sá-Carneiro and Luiz de Montalvor, who had recently arrived from Brazil, in the café Montanha. Montalvor also had the idea of publishing a journal, specifically under the name *Orpheu*. Pessoa and Sá-Carneiro welcomed the idea "com enthusiasmo" ("with enthusiasm"; Pessoa, *Sensacionismo* 87), since they were perfectly familiar with Greek mythology, knowing that Orpheus, as the greatest of all poets and musicians, was able to find his way back from the underworld. Europe was also coming back from the underworld it was in. Thus the journal *Orpheu* gathered several European artistic influences and established the "unica ponte entre Portugal e a Europa, e, mesmo, a unica razão de vulto que Portugal tem para existir como noção independente" ("only bridge between Portugal and Europe, and even the only major reason why Portugal must exist as an independent notion"; Pessoa, *Sensacionismo* 70). This is exactly what *Orpheu* was and sought.

Pessoa's Modernism: A European Project

Pessoa's modernism can and should be seen as a European project. This assumption is justified by answering two characteristic questions frequently asked in the field of modernist studies: What is the "old" one tries to overcome, and, second, what is the "new" one tries to create? Since European modernism mirrors the historical and cultural complexity of the continent (Bru et al. 3) from the first decades of the twentieth century, the answer to these two questions is likewise complex. In his book *Die Welt von Gestern* (*The World of Yesterday*), Stefan Zweig describes prewar Europe as a region in full development, a territory in cultural and economic growth. Vienna, Milan, Paris, Berlin, and London, all great cities, were growing prosperous. New theaters, libraries, museums, and galleries opened across Europe. The quality of middle-class life rose significantly with the addition of bathrooms and telephones to homes and the use of bicycles, buses, and trams to shorten travel times. For Zweig, the Europe of this age was strong, rich, and beautiful. Yet Zweig also recognizes a sort of "elektrisches Knistern im Gebälk" ("electric crackling in the woodwork"; 261–77) happening at the time, and a small spark was enough to ignite the fire. Referring to the years before the First World War, other testimonies speak of a suffocating, stifling atmosphere and the need for an invigorating thunderstorm. In fact, there seems to be a certain diffuse intuition that a disruptive event was coming.

In 1909, Marinetti, in his first famous manifesto on futurism, published in the French newspaper *Le Figaro*, glorified war as necessary hygiene—stressing that only warlike aggression could bring about beauty. A significant number of expressionist poems and paintings depicted apocalyptic imagery, and in most cases, it is not easy to tell whether such imagery signifies jubilant anticipation of great hygiene or anguish at a cataclysm of blood and mud. The happy glorifications from many modernist artists and writers during the first weeks of war make one believe the war was seen as a purifying force, an invigorating thunderstorm, or a great cleaning that would make room for a new beginning. Pound's modernist imperative "Make it new!" seemed to come true. The initial enthusiasm was, despite all this, quickly replaced by pitiful death in muddy trenches and mass destruction. Paul Valéry wrote in 1919, right after the war, of the pain of learning that not only the most unexpected but the most absurd thing can happen and the most certain thing can come suddenly to nothing:

Il n'a pas suffi à notre génération d'apprendre par sa propre expérience comment les plus belles choses et les plus antiques, et les plus formidables et les mieux ordonnées sont périssables par accident; elle a vu, dans l'ordre de la pensée, du sens commun, et du sentiment, se produire des phéno- mènes extraordinaires, des réalisations brusques de paradoxes, des décep- tions brutales de l'évidence.   ("Crise" 988)

It has not been enough for our generation to learn from its own experi- ence how the most beautiful and ancient things, and the most formida- ble and best ordered, are perishable by accident; it has seen, in the order of thought, of common sense, and of feeling, extraordinary phe- nomena, sudden realizations of paradoxes, brutal disappointments of the obvious.

From a contemporary perspective, the First World War was a traumatic experi- ence since it was the moment when technical and industrial modernity—initially celebrated by almost all modernists—made possible a terrible carnage that broke out almost without warning. The times before the First World War resemble a kind of refashioned Janus head, looking at the same time at a prosperous future and a hellish deep.

This contradictory situation is described in Musil's *The Man without Quali- ties*, which starts, as I said above, on a beautiful sunny August day in 1913. A couple is walking and stares at a road accident. A lorry driver has been unable to brake in time to avoid hitting a man who now, after the collision with the vehicle, is seen lying "wie tot" ("as if he were dead") on the pavement. After observing the scene for a few minutes, the couple keeps walking and the man remarks on a statistic from the United States: "dort [werden] jährlich durch Autos 190.000 Personen getötet und 450.000 verletzt" ("one hundred ninety thousand people are killed there every year by cars and four hundred fifty thousand are injured"; Musil, *Mann* 11; *Man* 5). The numbers of casualties do not, of course, reflect the reality on American roads in the year 1913 but rather refer to the many deaths that the coming world war would soon bring with it. Between the next summer in 1914 and November 1918, another seventeen million people would die, a large part in the fields of war and with the support of new technologies. The war thus made some modernist statements obsolete. In other words, it was increas- ingly harder to agree with the conviction that a car's engine, which roars and seems to work like machine-gun fire, was more beautiful than the Niké of Samo- thrace. In his classical interpretation of Igor Stravinsky's *Le sacre du printemps* (*The Rite of Spring*), Modris Eksteins describes the First World War as the "psychological turning point for modernism," where the modernist semantics of creation and destruction changed meaning. Destruction became more intense, and the intention to create appeared more and more abstract (329).

Pessoa's generation experienced this abrupt passage from great movements and developments to a sudden disturbance caused by the extreme violence that spread throughout the entire continent. Many texts before the war saluted "a riqueza inédita de emoções, de idéas, de febres e de delirios que a Hora euro-pêa nos traz" ("the unprecedented wealth of emotions, ideas, fevers, and delir-ium the European Hour brings us"; Pessoa, *Sensacionismo* 188). In "Ode triunfal" or in "Ode marítima" ("Maritime Ode"), the whole semantics of modern life has positive connotations; the adjectives *bela* ("beautiful"), *moderna* ("modern"), *maravilhosa* ("wonderful"), *triunfante* ("triumphant"), *estupenda* ("stupendous"), and *estrénuos* ("strenuous") all appear with an exclamation point. The "European Hours" provoke in Campos a true euphoria: "a Europa! Eia e hurrah por mim-tudo e tudo, máquinas a trabalhar, eia!" ("and Europe! Hey and hooray for all in all and all in me, machines at work, hey!"; Pessoa, *Obra completa de Álvaro de Campos* [2014] 56); *A Little Larger* 160), as we can read in "Ode triunfal," writ-ten on 8 March 1914, on Pessoa's famous "triumphal day." Be that as it may, it is important to note that the original publication of "Ode triunfal," in the first issue of *Orpheu*, ends with the date June 1914 and with the indication that the ode was written in London (Pessoa, *Obra completa de Álvaro de Campos* [2014] 56). That is to say, this enthusiastic celebration of a modern Europe was written only weeks before the outbreak of the First World War, and it is interesting to know how Pessoa was able to sustain his European passion over the following years. One might have expected him to produce some verses comparable with T. S. Eliot's "The Waste Land," expressing disappointment or despair, or meditating on death. Pessoa's curious statement that *Orpheu* was more interesting than the current war seems, under these circumstances, more a signal of despair than an inconvenient provocation: "It may be silly, though it is true, to say there is more unexpectedness and interest in 'Orpheu' than there is in the present War" (*Sensacionismo* 220).

In fact, his affirmation is not all that honest. Pessoa was extremely interested in the First World War and followed current debates closely. Since 1914, one could see in Portugal's intellectual life a growing Germanophobia, which started with an influential article Pascoaes published in December 1914 in the journal *Águia* under the title "Portugal e a Guerra: E a Orientação das Novas Gerações" ("Portugal and War: The Orientation of New Generations"), in which he defended the thesis that in that war there were "duas almas se degladiam: a celto-romana e a germanica" ("two souls clashing: the Celtic-Roman and the Germanic"; qtd. in Barreto, "Fernando Pessoa" 178). On 1 July 1915, the republican official João de Barros published in the newspaper *O mundo* (*The World*) an appeal to Por-tuguese writers and artists defending a similar thesis that there were in that war "civilizações antagonicas que se degladiam, tendo como mentoras supremas de um lado a França, do outro lado a Alemanha" ("antagonistic civilizations clash-ing, with France on one side and Germany on the other as supreme mentors"; Barreto, "Fernando Pessoa" 189). Barros demanded a patriotic position in sup-port of the allies. Pessoa probably already knew the thesis that identified the ambiguous relationship between Germany and France as the main reason for the outbreak of the Great War, or he read that same reason again a little later, since this idea was also present, in a somewhat more scathing way, in the editorial of *Blast* journal: "The Essential German will get to Paris, to the Cafe de la Paix, at all costs; if he has to go there at the head of an army and destroy a million beings in the adventure." In the vorticists' opinion, there was "un amour malheureux" ("an unhappy love") at the basis of this war that the German felt for the French but that the latter did not feel back ("Editorial" 6). In any case, it seems that Barros's article was the starting point from which Pessoa began directing his intellectual attention to the psychological and sociological reasons that were behind this "seminal" and unpredictable "catastrophe" (Kennan 3). In his answer to Barros—which was never published—Pessoa intended to demonstrate that "a alma portuguesa deve estar com a sua irmã, a alma germânica, na guerra presente" ("the Portuguese soul must be with her sister, the Germanic soul, in the present war"; *Ultimatum* 199). This answer is part of a large number of texts that Pessoa, and mostly his literary character António Mora, wrote "a favôr da Allemanha e do seu procedimento na guerra presente" ("in favor of Germany and its conduct in the present war"; *Obras de António Mora* 153). Despite these controversial opinions, Pessoa's interest in Germany and its role in the war was never superficial. Even today in his private library there are many books on the First World War, and particularly on the relation between the war and German culture (for example, *Treitschke and the Great War*, by Joseph McCabe; *The Menace of German Culture: A Reply to Professor Münsterberg*, by John Cowper Powys; *L'Allemagne et la guerre* (*Germany and the War*), by Émile Boutroux; *Civilisés contre allemands* (*Civilized versus German*) by Jean Finot; etc.), and in his estate there are several editorial plans and fragments that manifest his involvement, at least implicit, in the intellectual debate on the war. However, his defense of Germany must not be automatically confused with a true Germanophilia or a feeling of disgust toward the allies. In other words, being supposedly at the same time Germanophile and Allyophile (or, more specifically, Anglophile)—that is, "simultaneamente ambas as coisas" ("simultaneously both things")—Pessoa, in Barreto's fair assessment, "não foi propriamente nenhuma delas, no sentido usual que esses termos tinham" ("was not likely either of them, in the usual sense those terms had"; "Fernando Pessoa" 170).

Although it is not that obvious at first sight, there is in this contradiction a likely answer to the two questions posed above: What was the "old" Pessoa wanted to overcome, and what was the "new" Pessoa wanted to create? Pessoa criticized the "old" on several previous occasions, and mostly in his texts on the new Portuguese poetry. He remarked on the strong nationalism of the Portuguese literary movement *saudosismo* ("saudosism"), whose name derives from the word *saudade*, which can only be roughly described as a kind of bittersweet melancholy, and which is associated, in this context, with a deep nostalgic sense of national belonging. That same nationalism is again present in the context of war, and very explicitly in the essay by the saudosist poet Pascoaes:

A atmosfera europeia é tragica, magnifica, sublime, contraria a esse depri-
mente cosmopolitismo em que as nações se diluiam, e reveladora e crea-
dora do seu caracter, da sua presença viva sobre a terra. . . . Se fôrmos para
a guerra, mostraremos ao mundo que estamos prontos a morrer pela patria,
que sômos Alguem que vive porque quer viver, e Portugal creará então
novas raizes na Historia. Por elas absorverá nova seiva, nova energia. Che-
gou a hora de se não viver de Portugal, mas para Portugal. E viver para
Portugal, que está em perigo como todos os povos latinos, é morrer por ele.
(Barreto, "Fernando Pessoa" 183)

The European atmosphere is tragic, magnificent, sublime, contrary to that
depressing cosmopolitanism in which nations were diluted, and revealing
and creating its character, its living presence on earth. . . . If we go to war,
we will show the world that we are ready to die for our homeland, that we
are Someone who lives because they want to live, and Portugal will then
create new roots in History. Through them new sap, new energy, will be
absorbed. The time has come not to live of Portugal, but for Portugal. And
living for Portugal, which is in danger like all Latin people, is dying for it.

Theoretically, Pascoaes found the reasons for the war not in different imperial-
istic aspirations or economic interests but in a profound conflict between oppos-
ing races and civilizations facing each other with hostility on the same European
ground. The contradiction consists in the fact that Pascoaes justly identifies
nationalism as one of the main reasons for war but explicitly defends a nationalist attitude to position himself in this conflict.

Nationalism is historically a creation of modernity, and Europe's catastrophic
biography from the twentieth century began with the aggressive consolidation
of national interests. From this perspective, one can understand, on the one hand,
the unusual theory of Pessoa's literary character António Mora, who wished for
Germany's victory, and, on the other, Pessoa's concept of "nacionalismo cosmopolita" ("cosmopolitan nationalism"), which is much less paradoxical than one
might think. On the contrary, this concept has a surprising contemporary
relevance.

Despite having defended Germany's proceedings in the war, Mora pointed
out that he never considered Germany as a cultural ideal but saw in it a means
to "unificar a civilização europeia contra o ideal christão" ("unify the European
civilization against the Christian ideal"; Pessoa, *Obras de António Mora* 358).
Mora's argument is based on the possibility of a European unification forced by
the German victory. As a consequence of this forced unification, the desire was
going to rise within Europe to split itself up again into very small forces, thus
reconstituting the city-states of ancient Greece. Mora understands this process
as the "repaganização" ("repaganization") of Europe, which was going to include,
necessarily, the elimination of nationalisms. The rebuilding of the city-states as

the secondary result of a German victory would prepare the fertile soil for the return of the classical culture of the ancient world: "Eu não admiro, em si, a cultura alemã. . . . Mas admiro nella o passo preciso dado para a repaganização do mundo moderno . . . a recondução da cultura europeia para o ideal classico. . . . Só atravez do domínio alemão da Europa eu podia sentir esperança no futuro da Europa" ("I do not admire, in itself, the German culture. . . . But I admire in it the necessary step taken toward the repaganization of the modern world . . . the reconduction of European culture towards the classical ideal. . . . Only through the German rule over Europe could I feel hope in the future of Europe"; Pessoa, *Obras de António Mora* 358).

However, that is Mora's argument, and it is unlikely Pessoa believed in the possibility that Christian roots could be completely eliminated in a culture where they had long been fixed. In contrast to the unusual—and certainly not feasible—thinking of Mora, Pessoa developed the notion of "nacionalismo cosmopolita," which can be understood as a more viable solution for the European question. One of the most striking moments in reading Pessoa's work is in his extreme attention to the sociocultural and political events of his time. It would be too one-dimensional to hold nationalism solely responsible for the outbreak of war, and Pessoa never connected nationalism directly to war. Nonetheless, there are at least two texts in which he distances himself very clearly from a kind of nationalism that aims at an inner isolation and advocates an outer superiority. More specifically, he distinguishes between different types of nationalism. The first one is linked exclusively to a national Catholic and monarchist tradition, unable to adapt itself to the general conditions of European civilization. This "nacionalismo integral" ("integral nationalism"), which was theorized mainly by the French author Charles Maurras, is represented, for Pessoa, by the members of the reactionary and pre-fascist group Integralismo Lusitano (Lusitanian Integralism), who saw themselves, in the middle of the war, as a "resposta eloquente" ("eloquent response") to the "delírio pacifista" ("pacifist delirium")—thinking of the motto "guerra para defender a pátria, guerra para a legitimamente a engrandecer!" ("war to defend the homeland, war to legitimately make it great!"; *Questão Ibérica* 5). The second type of nationalism is also a kind of "nacionalismo integral" ("integral nationalism"), but much more liberal than the reactionary nationalism propagated by the Integralismo Lusitano. Even if this rather liberal form of nationalism feels committed to global humanitarianism, it still insists on the unrestricted primacy of a national soul, attributing to "uma nação determinados attributos psychicos" ("a nation certain psychic attributes"). This more liberal type of integral nationalism is represented by Pascoaes's saudosism, which also defended "a intervenção de Portugal na guerra, como oportunidade de reencontrar a pátria, o 'fim colectivo' de que os portugueses andariam transviados, como forma de educar o povo e as novas gerações, bem como solução digna e eficaz de assegurar a independência nacional" ("Portugal's intervention in the war as an opportunity to rediscover homeland, the 'collective purpose' that Portuguese people had been led astray from, as a way to educate the people and the new generations, as well as worthy and effective solution to ensure national independence"; Barreto, "Fernando Pessoa" 171). Lastly there is Pessoa's own "nacionalismo cosmopolita" ("cosmopolitan nationalism")—or "nacionalismo synthetico" "(synthetic nationalism")—which consists in attributing a nationality to "um modo especial de synthetizar as influencias do jogo civilizacional" ("a special way of synthetising the influences of the civilizational game"). By integrating in itself "todos os elementos cosmopolitas" ("all the cosmopolitan elements"), this nationalism is represented, according to Pessoa, by Shakespeare and Goethe, and, obviously, by *Orpheu's* collaborators (Pessoa, *Sensacionismo* 66–68).

Regarding Europe, Pessoa's "nacionalismo cosmopolita" recognizes and legitimates all national peculiarities, linguistic diversities, or different sociocultural characteristics. Receptivity to the cultural plurality of the continent makes it possible to extract the best pollen of "all the flowers that have blossomed in the gardens of European fancy." Europe's modernity and its artistic movements became, for Pessoa, an endless source of inspiration. Through a permanent interaction with the most important literature and art of his time, Pessoa became the maximum example of a "good European"—a cosmopolitan without fear of losing his nationality. In this sense, Pessoa implicitly foresaw a vision of Europe that was presented and debated ninety years later. In 2004, Ulrich Beck and Edgar Grande, in *Das kosmopolitische Europa* (*Cosmopolitan Europe*), defended an idea of a Europe that is surprisingly close to the great Pessoan imperative: plurality is not a problem, it is the solution. Considering that this plurality was, for Pessoa, a categorical necessity, one can better understand the "old" to be overcome and the "new" to be created. The "old" is a one-dimensional vision that tendentially suppresses all other possible perspectives. The "new" is the synthesis of all possible perspectives. It is a cosmopolitanism that defends heterogeneity in all aspects, be they religious, cultural, social, or political. Pessoa's insistence that a "criatura de nervos modernos, de inteligência sem cortinas, de sensibilidade acordada, tem a obrigação cerebral de mudar de opinião e de certeza várias vezes no mesmo dia" ("creature of modern nerves, of intelligence without curtains, of awakened sensitivity, has the cerebral obligation of changing their mind and certainty several times in the same day") is not relativism but an unconditional opening to the plurality of a modern world, a conditio sine qua non of a cosmopolitan spirit. The next sentence of this text, published on 5 April 1915 with the title "Crónicas da vida que passa" ("Chronicles of a Passing Life"), does not allow for a different interpretation: "Deve ter, não crenças religiosas, opiniões políticas, predilecções literárias, mas sensações religiosas, impressões políticas, impulsos de admiração literária" ("It must have not religious beliefs, political opinions, literary predilections, but religious sensations, political impressions, literary admiration impulses"; Pessoa, *Crónicas* 35).

In terms of his modernism, Pessoa understood his sensationism as a synthesis of all aesthetic currents of his time. In terms of Europe, Pessoa advocated for cosmopolitanism and thus foreshadowed a debate that became current only at the beginning of the twenty-first century. Simply put, as a modernist writer,

Pessoa was also an innovative thinker of Europe who—not by chance—expressed grandiose ideas in extremely accessible sentences: "O meu quintal em Lisboa está ao mesmo tempo em Lisboa, em Portugal e na Europa" ("My backyard in Lisbon is at the same time in Lisbon, in Portugal, and in Europe"; *Ultimatum* 3).

NOTES

1. See Sapega in that volume for a good general perspective on the members of the *Orpheu* and *presença* generations ("Portugal").
2. All translations not otherwise attributed are my own.

Gender in Pessoa

António Ladeira

The readers of Fernando Pessoa generally associate his work with the notion of a problematic gender.[1] For the sake of argument, let us imagine an article or book offering a history of the perception of gender in Pessoa. The first important moment in such a history is the moment when the author himself addresses the subversive eroticism of his English poems "Antinous" (homoeroticism) and "Epithalamium" (heteroeroticism). In a preemptive defense against accusations of immorality, Pessoa justifies what he labels the "obscenity" of the aforementioned poems by telling João Gaspar Simões:

> Há em cada um de nós, por pouco que se especialize instintivamente na obscenidade, um certo elemento desta ordem, cuja quantidade, evidentemente, varia de homem para homem. Como esses elementos . . . são um certo estorvo para alguns processos mentais superiores, decidi, por duas vezes, eliminá-los pelo processo simples de os exprimir intensamente.
>
> (Simões 54)[2]

> Regardless of how little one specializes in obscenity, there is in each of us a certain element of this order, whose quantity, naturally, varies from man to man. Since those elements . . . constitute an impediment to some high mental processes, I have decided, twice, to eliminate them through the simple process of expressing them intensely.[3]

A second key moment can be found in the essay the poet published in *Contemporanea* after editing *Canções* (*Songs*), a collection of homoerotic verse by his friend António Botto (Pessoa, "Antonio Botto"). Pessoa claims that Botto is, of all Portuguese authors, the only true aesthete that he knows: that his artistic predilection for the homoerotic (independently of his personal sexual orientation, never addressed directly) follows the Greek model according to which the male body is the only example of total beauty, as opposed to the female body, whose beauty is only partial since it lacks the physical strength that male bodies (allegedly) possess. It is tempting to interpret Pessoa's defense of Botto as a justification for his own deviation from a normative gender, particularly in relation to the genderic model that was dominant during his time. It is a deviation not only from gender broadly understood but also from the subdivision of gender we now call "masculinity."

Having said this, I believe that the issue of "subversive sexuality" in Pessoa (one component of the wider concept of gender) has not been as thoroughly discussed as it should have been. Despite the identification of a few poems as highly sexualized and some important studies on the subject (discussed below),

Pessoa has been (and still is, to a certain extent) perceived as a quasi-asexual figure, a "man without a body," who lacked a biography or even a "real" life. Pessoa's case, in fact, could be presented as an illustration of a phrase that he coined about his poet friend: "dele [Pessoa] se poderia afirmar o que ele afirmou de Sá-Carneiro: 'O Sá-Carneiro não teve biografia: teve só génio. *O que disse foi o que viveu*'" ("Of [Pessoa] one could say what he said about Sá-Carneiro: 'Sá-Carneiro did not have a biography: he only had genius. *What he said was what he lived*'"; Sena, "O heterónimo" 48). This view helps explain the famous characterization of Pessoa by Jorge de Sena that later became the title of the first international conference on Pessoa in the United States: "the man who never was."[4]

A third moment that contributed to the poet's sexually (or corporeally) aseptic image can be located in studies by Sena. According to Sena, Pessoa is—essentially—a poet devoid of "erotic affection," in whose works one finds

> uma frieza amorosa que perpassa na sua obra poética inteira, mesmo quando [se] fala em termos de amor. A obra poética de Fernando Pessoa, excepto nestes dois poemas em inglês [Epithalamium e Antinous], é como a *noche oscura* do sexo, deserto da privação absoluta, "normal" ou "anormal", da afectividade erótica . . .   ("O heterónimo" 31)

> an amorous coldness that traverses all his poetic oeuvre, even when [one] speaks about love. The poetic works of Fernando Pessoa, except for these two English poems [Epithalamium and Antinous], are like the *noche oscura* of sex, desert of the absolute deprivation, "normal" or "abnormal," of erotic affection . . .

Paulo de Medeiros has said, "Se bem que a crítica nunca tenha ignorado completamente estas questões, pode-se afirmar que durante muito tempo quer a representação do feminino, quer a corporalidade da escrita não foram propriamente temas importantes, a par da mitificação e mistificação do autor como ser spectral e fantasmagórico" ("Although the critics have never completely ignored these questions, one can say that, for a long time, both the representation of the feminine, and the corporeality of writing were not necessarily important themes, along with the mythicization and mystification of the author as a spectral and ghostly being"; *O silêncio* 105).

One book in particular attempted to correct this image of a man without a body (an image that over the years became an ossified trope and a myth, as Medeiros suggested). *Embodying Pessoa*, a volume edited by Anna Klobucka and Mark Sabine, proposed a revisionist image of Pessoa as an author with both a body and a sexuality.[5] This renewed interest in that aspect of Pessoa's work (and biography) is due to the fact that the field of gender studies—as it evolved—forced academics to adopt new perspectives and interrogate old texts in different ways. In other words, Pessoa "changed" (or his image changed) because so did the perspectives of the critics.

My approach to gender in Pessoa differs from others in that I employ, as I believe, a wider concept of gender. Doing so will—I hope—permit a new, more complete and nuanced image of a gendered Pessoa to take shape. Commonly, gender studies scholars tend to focus on the unconventional relationships that Pessoa's subjects have with sexuality. Academics usually pay particular attention to homoeroticism and homosexual desire. While not excluding this important aspect of Pessoa's (literary) gender, my approach here also considers how his poetic subjects and narrators fail to follow (and, for that reason, expose) the social norms of what was viewed as the acceptable masculinity of his time—that is, what some critics characterize as "normative" masculinity. Pessoa's gender is both subverted and subversive: first, in his unconventional sexuality or erotic desire (or lack thereof, as Sena would say); second, in the way he engages in a relatively discreet, tense (yet fruitful and eloquent) dialogue with gender-related social norms and behaviors. Analyzing excerpts found in Pessoa's English poems; in the poetry of Ricardo Reis, Alberto Caeiro, and Álvaro de Campos; and in *The Book of Disquiet* shows how Pessoa's subversive gender displays both a sexual and a social dimension and thus how his work undermines gender in ways that are at once sexual and social.

The editors of *Embodying Pessoa* suggest that Pessoa's heteronymical impulse is inseparable from a quality of gender fluidity on the one hand and the expression of a certain homoeroticism on the other hand (Klobucka and Sabine, "Pessoa's Bodies" 24)—an impulse toward sexual alterity (and alterity in general), toward making oneself other.[6] A few years before *Embodying Pessoa*, one of the first authors to write about Pessoa's sexuality, Richard Zenith, said, "[T]here is still a vast, fascinating area of research that awaits exploration: homosexuality as a motivating factor for the very origin and concept of Pessoa's heteronymy" (Zenith, "Fernando Pessoa's Gay Heteronym?" 36).[7] As she studied the relationship of certain aspects of Pessoa's production with Shakespeare's sonnets, Mariana Gray de Castro suggests (evoking T. S. Eliot) that Pessoa's claims of "impersonality" allowed him to—disguisedly—express more freely his personal feelings (*Fernando Pessoa's Shakespeare* 177). This vocation toward the heteronymical process—as it has been theorized—could stem from a problematic identity (a diminished or hypertrophied identity). A similar identitary fluidity may be found in Pessoa's other alterity, the linguistic one: "o Pessoa ele-mesmo tinha duas pátrias linguísticas, ambas seus amores infelizes: o inglês que não viera a reconhecê-lo como cidadão estético, e o português em que se 'naturalizara'" ("Pessoa himself had two linguistic homelands, both were unhappy love stories: the English language, which did not recognize him as an aesthetic citizen, and the Portuguese language, in which he became a naturalized citizen"; Sena, "O heterónimo" 25). Sena himself argued that it is also "significant that Pessoa chose to publish the two poems in Portugal, where, being in English, they were likely to attract little public attention" (qtd. in M. Castro, *Fernando Pessoa's Shakespeare* 180). This idea is echoed by a passage in which "Robert Bréchon argues that Shakespeare's native language was, for Pessoa, a dramatic mask" (183).[8]

In other words—whether this had constituted Pessoa's deliberate strategy or not—creating and publishing these poems in English, in Portugal (where very few people could read in English at the time, as Sena claimed [Pessoa, *Poemas ingleses* 27–28]) was the safest way of publishing poems of this nature. It is not by chance that one of the most illuminating and moving texts on gender subversion (and exuberant, quasi sadomasochistic mental humiliation) is the now famous "Carta da Corcunda ao Serralheiro" ("Letter of the Hunchback to the Metalworker"; Pessoa, *Eu sou* 627–32), a text that has garnered renewed attention as new work on Pessoa's gender has come to the fore. This character (I feel tempted to call her a "quasi-heteronym") is not only a woman (one of the few cases in Pessoa's prose) but one who has long lived with a severe curvature of the spine and is now dying of tuberculosis. Yet—secretly, in a letter that she never sends—she declares her desperate and unrequited love for an able-bodied, attractive member of the working class: a certain Senhor Antonio, a metalworker, who does not seem to be even aware of her existence:

> Tem-me visto á janella quando o senhor passa para a officina. . . . Deve sempre ter pensado sem importancia na corcunda do primeiro andar da casa amarella, mas eu não penso senão em si. . . . Adeus senhor Antonio, eu não tenho senão dias de vida e escrevo esta carta só para a guardar no peito como se fosse uma carta que o senhor me escrevesse em vez de eu a escrever a si. Eu desejo que o senhor tenha todas as felicidades que possa desejar e que nunca saiba de mim para não rir porque eu sei que não posso esperar mais. Eu amo o senhor com toda a minha alma e toda a minha vida. Ahi tem e estou toda a chorar.   (627)

> You've seen me look at you from my window when you pass by on your way to the metalworks. . . . Doubt you've ever given a second thought to the hunchback girl who lives on the second floor of the yellow building, but I never stop thinking about you. . . . Good-bye, Senhor António. My days are numbered, and I'm only writing this letter to hold it against my chest as if you'd written it to me instead of me to you. I wish you all the happiness I'm able to wish, and I hope you never find out about me so as not to laugh, for I know I can't hope for more. I love you with all my heart and life. There, I said it, and I'm crying.
> (Zenith, "Fernando Pessoa's Gay Heteronym" 43)

Her desperate words eloquently capture the previously mentioned spirit of this Pessoan articulation between heteronymy, subjective openness—or identitary amorphousness—and gender fluidity: "e eu não sou mulher nem homem, porque ninguém acha que eu sou nada" ("and I am neither a woman nor a man, for no one believes that I am anything"; Klobucka and Sabine, *Embodying Pessoa* 19). We should pay particular attention to the interesting association made by this character (who is, obviously, Pessoa in drag) between being *nothing* and possessing an undefined gender: being neither a man nor a woman. In other words, not fitting in either gender, not agreeing to a binary model, signifies that one's humanity is questionable, challenged, or denied. Pessoa is, patently, a masculine-feminine (or nonbinary) outsider, pathetically and perversely in love with a humanity that lives in the grip of a patriarchal system and that does not return that love. In this binary world, Pessoa, as a poet, man, and citizen, clearly does not fit in. The advent of Ricardo Reis is not alien to the interconnectedness of these genderic and identitary processes. The birth of the classicist in the universe of Pessoa (i.e., the birth of Reis as a heteronym) happens as a direct consequence of the creation of the master of all heteronyms: Caeiro. The birth of Caeiro, whom Pessoa called "meu mestre" ("my master"), is a career-defining event for Pessoa, narrated in a famous letter to Adolfo Casais Monteiro in which the Portuguese poet describes how, in a trancelike state, standing up, he once wrote a torrent of poems on the flat top of a wardrobe he used as a desk ("Letter"). Omitted in the aforementioned letter to Casais Monteiro is the fact that—alongside the phenomenon of heteronymy or heteronymism—a new stage of gender reshuffling is inaugurated: "Ricardo Reis deixou de ser mulher para ser homem, ou deixou de ser homem para ser mulher—como se preferir—quando teve esse contacto com Caeiro" ("Ricardo Reis stopped being a woman in order to be a man, or he stopped being a man in order to become a woman—if you prefer—when he had that contact with Caeiro [as master]"; Pessoa, "Notas para a recordação" 460).

In addressing Pessoa's most obviously erotic production—his English poems—I focus on sexuality and not on the social elements of gender since the latter are less visible in settings that are not contemporary but classical. A famous passage concerns a case of necrophilia in "Antinous." In this poem, Hadrian kisses the corpse of his recently deceased lover. The unifying effect of the kiss causes the men to figuratively exchange places and in a sense merge into each other, becoming equal. Hadrian, symbolically, dies, while the object of his affection symbolically comes back to life; or, alternatingly, they both appear dead and alive.

> Then his cold lips run all the body over.
> And so ice-senseless are his lips that, lo!,
> He scarce tastes death from the dead body's cold,
> *But it seems both are dead or living both*
> And love is still the presence and the mover.
>
> *(Poemas ingleses* 96; my italics)

"Ephithalamium," by contrast, presents an extreme fantasy of heterosexual, conjugal love—during a wedding night—in a highly suggestive and at times raw, violent manner.

He feels the battering ram grow large and itch.
The trembling glad bride feels all the way hot
On that still cloistered spot
. . . .
The maiden mount now her first rider bears!
Flesh pinched, flesh bit, flesh sucked, flesh girt around.
Flesh crushed and ground,
These things inflame your thoughts and make ye dim
In what ye say or seem!   (*Poemas ingleses* 140–44)

Although the most obvious examples can be found in Campos (analyzed below), there is no doubt that these verses introduce us to the very important representations of sadism in Pessoa's erotic poetry. These sadistic elements have been classified as manifestations of an English culture of flagellation, also known as the "English vice":

> Em outras palavras, o que fica claro em "Epithalamium" é que a poesia erótica de Pessoa revela uma fantasia sádica específica, e que ela se alimenta dos componentes dessa fantasia infantil que informou a produção discursiva inglesa a que [Pessoa] esteve não só exposto, mas que sofreu diretamente como educando numa escola inglesa.

> In other words, what is clear in "Epithalamium" is that Pessoa's erotic poetry reveals a specific sadistic fantasy, and that it feeds on the components of that childish fantasy which informed the discursive production in England to which [Pessoa] was not only exposed but one that he himself "suffered" as a student in an English school.   (Vieira 74)[9]

I will now address two poems by Ricardo Reis. Excerpts of the first one feature what we, readers, believe to be a conversation between two lovers, although only the poetic subject can be heard:

> Vem sentar-te comigo, Lídia, à beira do rio.
> Sossegadamente fitemos o seu curso e aprendamos
> Que a vida passa, e não estamos de mãos enlaçadas.
>   (Enlacemos as mãos).
>
> Depois pensemos, crianças adultas, que a vida
> Passa e não fica, nada deixa e nunca regressa,
> Vai para um mar muito longe, para o pé do fado,
>   Mais longe que os deuses.
>
> Desenlacemos as mãos, porque não vale a pena cansarmo-nos
> Quer gozemos, quer não gozemos, passamos como o rio.
> Mais vale saber passar silenciosamente.
>   E sem desassossegos grandes.
>   (Pessoa, *Poesia: Antologia mínima* 197)

Come sit beside me, Lydia, on the river's bank.
Let us gaze in peace upon its course and learn
That life passes, and we're not clasping hands
    (Let us clasp hands.)

Then let us think, as adult children, that life
Passes and does not stay, leaves nothing and never returns,
Flows towards a distant sea, nearing the very foot of Fate,
    Still more distant than all the gods above.

Let us unclasp our hands, for it's worthless to tire ourselves.
Whether or not we indulge in life, we pass like the river.
It is worth more to know how to pass silently
    And without great intranquillity.   (*Poetry: Minimal Anthology* 201)

These verses are about the transitoriness of life, a motif found in all of Reis's universe. Here, we encounter the well-known Horatian-Epicurean position of not worrying excessively or expecting too much from life. It is significant that the poetic subject and his lover—Lydia—appear childlike, almost presexual or asexual.[10] The poetic self invites his interlocutor to slowly "pass" (i.e., to transition from life to death as they age) silently and discreetly, like the river. They should not, Reis forewarns, fight or resist the passage of time. In the ethereal, quasi-static atmosphere of the poem, one important effect is obtained by the clasping and the unclasping of hands—one of the few things that, diegetically, actually *happen* in the poem. First, the poetic subject—through a formal verbal tense, the second-person plural—asks his interlocutor to hold hands ("clasp hands"); then, moments later, he asks her to unclasp them. Even the sober (very chaste yet romantic gesture) of clasping hands—as opposed to the more conventional, and sensual, embracing or kissing—is interrupted when the subject suggests that they should unclasp hands in the end. In the fourth stanza, the subject intensifies his progression toward a quieting of the senses, of all passions, and of emotions of all kinds:

Sem amores, nem ódios, nem paixões que levantam levantam a voz
Nem invejas que dão movimento de mais aos olhos
Nem cuidados, porque se os tivesse o rio sempre correria,
    E sempre iria ter ao mar.   (*Poesia: Antologia mínima* 197)

With neither loves nor hates, nor passions that raise their voices,
Nor envies that stir the eyes to fevered glances both this way and that,
Nor cares, for if we had them the river still would flow
    And then rush headlong into the sea.

(*Poetry: Minimal Anthology* 201)

The following stanza provides a culmination to the series. Contrary to appearances, Reis is not denying Lydia his love. He is, instead, proposing a different kind of love that could nevertheless be understood as the negation of conventional love. Reis calls it "peaceful love." The poem reaches its dramatic apotheosis when the subject declares that they are free to express their romantic feelings through conventional means (kisses, caresses, embraces) should they wish to do so. However, liberatingly, their choice appears to be a different one. Self-repression of erotic impulses is—in this poetry—a particularly common occurrence. These acts of abnegation are not viewed as the acceptance of an all-powerful dictatorial, internal (or external, generic) sexual impulse or drive but as the exercise of a personal freedom to oppose these internal and external forces. For these reasons, these poems could also signify the problematization or rejection of heterosexual love, homosexual love, or romantic love in general.

> Amemo-nos tranquilamente, pensando que podíamos
> Se quiséssemos, trocar beijos e abraços e carícias,
> Mas que mais vale estarmos sentados um ao pé do outro
>   Ouvindo correr o rio e vendo-o.   (*Poesia: Antologia mínima* 197)

> Let us love each other peacefully, reflecting that we could,
> If we wanted, exchange kisses and caresses and embraces,
> But that it is worth more to sit at each other's side,
>   Hearing the river and seeing it flow.
>   (*Poetry: Minimal Anthology* 201)

The second and final poem by Reis, known as "Os jogadores de xadrês" ("The Chess Players"), eloquently illustrates the second dimension of gender subversion—the social one. Here we notice an outrageous challenge to the common expectations placed upon men in general and in the unspecified time and society (*some* war in Persia) depicted here:

> Ouvi contar que outrora, quando a Persia
>   Tinha não sei qual Guerra,
> Quando a invasão ardia na Cidade
>   E as mulheres gritavam,
> Dois jogadores de xadrês jogavam
>   O seu jogo contínuo.   (Pessoa, *Obra completa de Ricardo Reis* 106)

> I've heard that once, during I don't know
>   What war of Persia,
> When invaders rampaged through the City
>   And the women screamed,
> Two chess players kept on playing
>   Their endless game.   (*A Little Larger* 97)

The poem begins with a group of men rejecting one of the most recognizable of all codes of masculinity: in case of conflict, able-bodied men are expected to come to the defense of women and children before anyone else. The rules of war (and of chivalry) go hand in hand with the codes of honor (or of "manliness," understood as a synonym of "honorable behavior") such as showing mercy for the defeated, respect for those who surrender, generosity toward the "weak and the defenseless" (as women and children were perceived to be at the time). The obligation of these chess players was therefore to defend their own wounded honor, which, in this case, implies salvaging the damaged honor of their wives and children: "In terms of masculinity, the invocation of personal honor—with its links to family, tribe, and nation—gives eternal justification to an act of immediate violence" (Brady 49). Pierre Bourdieu said, "Manliness, understood as a sexual or social reproductive capacity, but also as the capacity to fight and to exercise violence especially in acts of revenge, is first and foremost a duty" (50–51). Instead of intervening, these men not only ignore their duty to avenge the attacks on the women but, selfishly and cruelly, continue to engage in a recreational activity: a game of chess. The situation becomes not just unacceptable but a scandalous violation of the rules of gender (rules that shape our culture and our lives, whether we realize it or not).

> Ardiam casas, saqueadas eram
>   As arcas e as parêdes,
> Violadas, as mulheres eram postas
>   Contra os muros cahidos,
> Trespassadas de lanças, as creanças
>   Eram sangue nas ruas . . .
> Mas onde estavam, perto da cidade,
>   E longe do seu ruido,
> Os jogadores de xadres jogavam
>   O jogo de xadres.   (Pessoa, *Obra completa de Ricardo Reis* 106)

> Houses were burning, walls were torn down
>   And coffers plundered;
> Women were raped and propped against
>   The crumbling walls;
> Children, pierced by spears, were so much
>   Blood in the streets . . .
> But the two chess players stayed where they were,
>   Close to the city
> And far from its clamor, and kept on playing
>   Their game of chess.   (*A Little Larger* 97)

As one of the players takes a glass of wine, the reader is shown close-up scenes of plundering; of homes burning; of women and children being, respectively, raped and pierced by spears; of blood gushing, running on the streets.

The contrast with the quiet, impassable players has never been starker. Grotesquely, the poetic subject asks that this abhorrent behavior be imitated by men generally ("my brothers"):

> Meus irmãos em amarmos Epicuro
>   E o entendermos mais
> De accordo com nós-proprios que com elle
>   Aprendemos na historia
> De calmos jogadores de xadres
>   Como passar a vida.   (*Obra completa de Ricardo Reis* 108)

> My brothers in loving Epicurus
>   And in understanding him
> More in accord with our view than with his,
>   Let's learn from the story
> Of the impassive chess players how
>   To spend our lives.   (*A Little Larger* 99)

All those genderic responsibilities weigh heavily on the hearts of men, and yet those responsibilities are "nothing"—or should be viewed as nothing—if one assigns them no importance. Men should devote their lives not to heroic masculinity, not to the wars of daily life, but instead, for example, to a board game in which war is merely simulated. Only under these circumstances (after the heavy burden of manhood is lifted) will life be bearable, since it will feel like a dream and not at all like real life, a very Pessoan trope: "O jogo do xadres / Prende a alma toda, mas, perdido, pouco / Pesa, pois não é nada" ("The game of chess / Completely absorbs one's heart but weighs little / When lost, for it's nothing" (*Obra completa de Ricardo Reis* 109; *A Little Larger* 99).

Similarly to Reis's, Caeiro's concept of love is linked to a platonic mode. He elects the thrill and the relative safety of engaging with the memories of someone who is absent over the unpredictability (and the sexual and social consequences) of the physical encounter.

> O amor é uma companhia.
> Já não sei andar só pelos caminhos.
> Porque já não posso andar só.
> . . . .
> *Mesmo a ausencia d'ella é uma coisa que está comigo*
> E eu gosto tanto d'ella que não sei como a desejar.
> Se a não vejo, imagino-a e sou forte como as arvores altas
> Mas se a vejo tremo, não sei o que é feito do que na ausência d'ella.
>   (Pessoa, *Obra completa de Alberto Caeiro* 79; my italics)

Love is a companion.
I no longer know how to walk alone along the paths.
Because I can no longer walk alone.
· ·
Even her absence is a presence.
And I like her so much that I don't know how to desire her.
If I don't see her, I imagine her and I'm as strong as the tallest trees.
But if I see her, I tremble, and I don't know what has become of what
    I feel in her absence.   (*Complete Works* 111; my italics)

As I switch to the social aspects of gender, the following verses introduce the reader to a social type common at the time: the activist of socialist or communist ideological beliefs. He visits a lonely *aldeia*, an (imaginary) place where (imaginary) Caeiro, the shepherd, resides. The man hails from a place of suspicious mores and mentalities—the city—and has just arrived in the countryside, universally associated with innocence and purity. In this Caeirian atmosphere, in which a particular brand of honesty coexists with a wise, sarcastic type of (paradoxical, cynical, sometimes violent) innocence, both the honest, empathetic activist (our visitor) and the dishonest, selfish politician will feel out of place. Caeiro—with the same conviction—rejects both the typical politician, activist, or humanitarian and the conventional poet, along with the rules of poetic convention, which in his time (he seems to be saying) would direct him more toward metaphysics (à la Teixeira de Pascoaes) than toward the pure expression of a natural world (of which Caeiro claims to be an interpreter). As he distances himself from both these masculine types—the diligent activist and the metaphysical poet—Caeiro is also extricating himself from the society of his fellow men— that is, from what Eve Kosofsky Sedgwick calls his "male homosocial bonds" (*Between Men* 131).[11] By—provocatively, perhaps sarcastically—claiming that he does not care about injustice, he is opening himself up to the accusation of being callous and insensitive or barbarous and inhumane (like the chess players in Reis's poem), which conflicts with elements of his own poetry that could be interpreted as humanitarian. Since idealized "masculinity" (still to this day) is also expected to be an expression of gentleness and generosity toward the weak, "masculinity," in this context, is a particular brand of humanitarianism. It has been said that all forms of war (including team sports, which are, simultaneously, games and forms of simulated war), whether "devastating or courteous . . . always [include] the elements of grandeur, generosity and disinterestedness" (Nye 219).

Hontem á tarde um homem das cidades
Fallava á porta da estalagem.
· ·
Fallava da justiça e da lucta para haver justiça

E dos operarios que soffrem,
E do trabalho constante, e dos que teem fome,
E dos ricos, que só não se importam com isso.

E, olhando para mim, viu-me lagrimas nos olhos
E sorriu com agrado, julgando que eu sentia
O odio que elle sentia, e a compaixão
Que elle dizia que sentia.

(Mas eu mal o estava ouvindo.
 Que me importam a mim os homens
E o que soffrem ou sentem que soffrem?
Sejam como eu—não soffrerão.
Todo o mal do mundo vem de nos importarmos
                              uns com os otros . . .)
. . . .

Eu no que estava pensando
. . . .
(E isso me commoveu até ás lagrimas),
Era em como o murmurio longinquo dos chocalhos
. . . .
Não parecia os sinos d'uma capella pequenina
A que fossem á missa as flores e os regatos
E as almas simples como a minha.
            (Pessoa, *Obra completa de Alberto Caeiro* 61–62; my italics)

Yesterday evening a man from the city
Was talking at the door of the inn.
. . . .
He was talking about justice and the fight for justice
And about the suffering workers,
And about their unending labors, and about those
                              who are hungry,
And about the rich, who don't care about any of this.

And, looking at me, he saw tears in my eyes.
And he smiled, pleased to think that I was feeling
The hatred he was feeling, and the compassion
He said he was feeling.

(But I was barely listening.
What do I care about men
And what they suffer or feel they suffer?
Let them be like me and they won't suffer.
All the evils of the world come from us taking an
                              interest in one another . . .)

. . . .

What I was thinking about

. . . .

(And it was this that moved me to tears),
Was how the distant murmuring of sheep bells

. . . .

Sounded nothing like the bells of a tiny chapel
To which the flowers and the streams
And simple souls like mine might go to mass.

(Complete Works 72; my italics)

The last image is the culmination of a series of cynical rejections of common solidarity with the subject's "fellow men." This circumstance consolidates his position as an isolated poet and a man, and in that sense—in Caeiro's provocative style—as a flawed human being, since being a man (in our contemporary Western culture) ideally means being an honorable and empathetic member of the "homosocial community" dedicated to the improvement of the lives of others or, at least, to social pursuits and interactions with other men. Instead (through "tears," which are not typically associated with masculinity) he is displaying the hubris of claiming to be the only true interpreter of nature. The greatest irony happens when Caeiro—as he presents himself in this defiant and isolated manner—also claims to be a "simple soul," just like all other men: "Bemdito seja o mesmo sol de outras terras / Que faz meus irmãos todos homens" ("Blessed be the same sun of other lands / That makes all men my brothers"; *Obra completa de Alberto Caeiro* 65; *Complete Works* 83).

Turning now to Campos's unconventional sexual masculinity, we observe how his subversive, sadomasochistic traits (so named by Pessoa himself) are by far the most exuberant of those found in all personas. In "Triumphal Ode," he says:

Eu poderia morrer triturado por um motor
Com o sentimento de deliciosa entrega duma mulher possuída.
Atirem-me para dentro das fornalhas!
Metam-me debaixo dos comboios!

. . . .

Masóquismo através de maquinismos!
Sadismo de não sei quê moderno e eu e barulho!

(Pessoa, Obra completa de Álvaro de Campos [2014] 52–53)

I could be shredded to death by an engine
And feel a woman's sweet surrender when possessed.
Toss me into the furnaces!
Throw me under passing trains!

. . . .

Masochism through machines!
Some modern sort of *sadism*, and I, and the hubbub!

(A *Little Larger* 157; my italics)

The poem "Ode maritima" ("Maritime Ode") famously includes passages of outrageously raw and violent homoeroticism. Here are some moments evocative of the sensuous working-class figures presented by Whitman:

Eh marinheiros, gageiros! eh tripulantes, pilotos!
Navegadores, mareantes, marujos, aventureiros!
Eh capitães de navios! homens ao leme e em mastros!
. . . .
Homens que dormem co'o Perigo a espreitar plas vigias!
Homens que dormem co'a Morte por travesseiro!
. . . .
Que enchestes o vosso olhar de costas que nunca verei!
Que fôstes a terra em terras onde nunca descerei!
Que comprastes artigos tôscos em colónias à prôa de sertões!
E fizestes tudo isso como se não fôsse nada,
Como se isso fôsse natural,
Como se a vida fôsse isso,
Como nem sequer cumprindo um destino!
. . . .
Homens do mar actual! homens do mar passado!
. . . .
Para a aventura indefinida, para o Mar Absoluto, para realizar
    o Impossível!

(*Obra completa de Álvaro de Campos* [2014] 82–83)

Hey sailors, look-outs! Hey shipmates, pilots!
Navigators, seamen, mariners, adventurers!
Hey ship captains! Hey men at the helm and on the masts!
. . . .
Men who sleep with Danger peeking through the portholes!
Men who sleep with Death for a pillow!
. . . .
Men who've feasted your eyes on the coasts I'll never see!
Who've landed in lands where I'll never set foot!
Who bought primitive goods in colonies at the fore of hinterlands!
And you did all of this as if it were nothing,
As if this were natural,
As if life were simply this,
As if you weren't fulfilling a destiny!
. . . .

Men of today's ocean! Men of yesterday's ocean!

. . . .

Into an uncertain adventure, on the Absolute Sea, to achieve the
    Impossible!   (*A Little Larger* 174–75)]

    The following passages contain denunciations of the abuses of masculinity—a
masculinity that is simultaneously subject and object of its own cruelty. One may
claim that they expose the general violence of gender. Having said this, I do not
believe that this (poetic) condemnation of violence is incompatible with a broad
homoerotic fascination (possibly ironic) with masculine violence. This fascination
turns here to acts perpetrated by navigators and colonizers (themselves victims of
harmful patriarchal codes) who thus achieve a certain mark of hypermasculin-
ity, regardless of how idealized—or fragile—it may be:

[Homens] Que destes o primeiro espasmo europeu às negras atónitas!
Que trouxestes ouro, missanga, madeiras cheirosas, setas,

. . . .

Homens que saqueastes tranqùílas povoações africanas,
Que fizestes fugir com o *ruido de canhões* esas raças,
Que matastes, roubastes, torturastes, ganhastes
Os prémios de Novidade de quem, de cabeça baixa,
Arremete contra o mistério de novos mares! Eh-eh-eh-eh-eh!
A vós todos num, a vós todos em vós todos como um,
A vós todos misturados, entrecruzados,
A vós todos sangrentos, violentos, odiados, temidos, sagrados,
Eu vos saúdo, eu vos saúdo, eu vos saúdo!

. . . .

Quero ir comvôsco, quero ir comvôsco,
Ao mesmo tempo com vós todos
Pra toda a parte pr'onde fostes!
    (*Obra completa de Álvaro de Campos* [2014] 83–84; my italics)

(Men) Who bestowed the first European spasms on startled Negro
    women!
Who brought back gold, beads, fragrant woods, arrows,

. . . .

Men who pillaged peaceful African villages,
Who put the natives to flight with *booming cannons*
Who killed, who robbed, who tortured, who won
reward of New Things for rushing headlong
Into the mystery of new seas! Hey-ey-ey-ey-ey!
I salute all of you in one man, and one man in all of you,
All of you mixed together, all intermingled,
All of you bloody, violent, hated, feared, fabled,

I salute you, I salute you, I salute you!
. . . .

I want to go with you, I want to go with you,
With all of you at the same time
To every place you've been!   (*A Little Larger* 176; my italics)

After identifying with these men (who are the opposite of the mild-mannered Pessoa, effeminate by comparison) he invites them to "use" him as they have treated women they enslaved, in a ritualized, sadomasochistic way. I would like to expand on the idea that the heteronymical process could be a homosexual enactment (already suggested by Richard Zenith and others) by adding to the equation the masochistic component of this sexuality,[12] which strengthens the idea of depersonalization and of the (sexual, social, poetic) game of losing one-self in order to acquire the (totalizing) power of becoming another. The follow-ing comments about Sacher-Masoch's *Venus in Furs* could shed light on these verses by Campos:

> In short, Severin does not merely override Wanda's autonomy, he *becomes* Wanda and various other alternative selves, while never losing . . . auton-omy and individuality. This is the fundamental structure of the masochist subject, and what makes it more than mere role-playing and masquerade. Its simultaneous power and powerlessness are really a manifestation of a deeper structure of the dream of a total subject that is both itself and other . . .   (Mansfield 8)

Campos offers himself in sexual sacrifice to these mariners so that he may acquire the masculine power that they possess and represent (and which he lacks) by merging with them and in them:

> Sim, sim, sim . . . Crucificai-me nas navegações
> E as minhas espáduas gosarão a minha cruz!
> Atai-me às viagens como a postes
> E a sensação dos postes entrará pela minha espinha
> E eu passarei a senti-los num vasto espasmo passivo!
> Fazei o que quizerdes de mim, logo que seja nos mares,
> . . . .
> Que me rasgueis, mateis, firais!
> . . . .
> Quebrem-me os ossos de encontro às amuradas!
> Fustíguem-me atado aos mastros, fustíguem-me!
> . . . .
> Derramem meu sangue sôbre as ágoas arremessadas
> Que atravessam o navio, o tombadilho, de lado a lado,

. . . .
Ser o meu corpo passivo a *mulher-todas-as-mulheres*
Que fôram violadas, mortas, feridas, rasgadas pelos piratas!
Ser no meu ser subjugado a fêmea que tem de ser dêles!
   (Pessoa, *Obra completa de Álvaro de Campos* [2014] 85–89; my italics)

Yes, yes, yes . . . Crucify me on your ocean crossings
And my shoulders will revel in my cross!
Tie me to your voyages as if to stakes,
And the sensation of the stakes will enter through my spine
And I'll feel them in a vast, passive ecstasy!
Do what you like with me, as long as it's at sea,
. . . .
Wound me, rip me open, kill me!
. . . .
Smash my bones against the gunwales!
Tie me to the masts and thrash me, thrash me!
. . . .
Spill my blood over the raging waters
That sweep across the poop deck
In the storms' wild convulsions!
. . . .
To be in my passive body the *woman-all-women*
Ever raped, killed, cut and mauled by pirates!
To be in my submissive self the female who needs to be theirs!
   (*A Little Larger* 177–81; my italics)

Campos's poem titled "Poema em linha recta" ("Poem in a Straight Line") expresses, in an intense manner, the feelings of inadequacy of a man who has obviously fallen outside the norms of masculinity of his time. The poetic subject confesses his failure to reach some key goals of manhood: he is not dignified (honorable) in the eyes of society but "ridiculous," not strong but weak, not courageous but a coward; he is not even respected by men on a lower social stratum (such as "moços de recados," or "errand boys"). The poem reads like a satirical catalogue of nonmasculine, shameful behavior that highlights the unfairness of these so often unacknowledged codes. By (sarcastically) claiming that he is the only dishonorable male in the world—"nunca conheci quem tivesse levado porrada" ("I've never known anyone who took a beating"; Pessoa, *Obra completa de Álvaro de Campos* 280; *A Little Larger* 246)—he is stressing the fact that many men (if not most men) brag publicly about their victories and virtues while being secretive about their faults and failures. As Michael Kimmel and other sociologists and anthropologists have noted, the mark of perfect manhood is, by definition, impossible to reach (see, e.g., M. Almeida 17).

Nunca conheci quem tivesse levado porrada.
Todos os meus conhecidos têm sido campeões em tudo.
E eu, tantas vezes reles, tantas vezes porco, tantas vezes vil,
Eu tantas vezes irrespondivelmente um parasita,
Indesculpavelmente sujo,
Eu, que tantas vezes não tenho tido paciência para tomar banho,
. . . .
Que tenho sido grotesco, mesquinho, submisso e arrogante,
Que tenho sofrido enxovalhos e calado,
Que quando não tenho calado, tenho sido mais ridículo ainda;
Eu, que tenho sido cómico às criadas de hotel,
Eu que tenho sentido o piscar de olhos dos moços fretes,
Eu, que tenho feito vergonhas financeiras, pedido emprestado sem pagar,
Eu, que, quando a hora do soco surgiu, me tenho agachado
Para fora da possibilidade do soco;
. . . .
Toda a gente que eu conheço e que fala comigo
Nunca teve um ato ridículo, nunca sofreu enxovalho,
Nunca foi senão príncipe—todos eles príncipes—na vida . . .
Quem me dera ouvir de alguém a voz humana
Que confessasse não um pecado, mas uma infâmia;
Que contasse, não uma violênica, mas uma cobardia!

(Pessoa, *Poesia: Antologia mínima* 293–94)

I've never known anyone who has taken his lumps.
All my acquaintances have been champions at everything.
And I, so often worthless, so often swinish, so often vile,
I, so often irrefutably parasitic,
Unforgivably filthy,
I, who so often have lacked the patience to bathe,
. . . .
Who have been grotesque, petty, submissive, and arrogant,
Who have suffered insults and kept quiet,
Who, when I haven't been quiet, have been still more ridiculous;
I, who have appeared ludicrous to chambermaids,
I, who have felt the blinking eyes of delivery boys,
I, who have made shambles of my finances,
borrowed money without repaying it,
I, who, when the fists began to fly, have ducked
Out of the way of flying fists,
. . . .
All the people I know and talk to daily
Never did a ridiculous thing, never suffered an insult,
Never were anything but princes—all of them princes—in life . . .

I wish I could hear from somewhere a human voice
That confessed, not a sin—but an infamy!
That told, not of violence—but of cowardice!

(Poetry: Minimal Anthology 297–98)

Sexual and romantic relationships with women and men are a clear impossibility for the narrators of *The Book of Disquiet*. What follows are confessions of
romantic (sexual, social) failures. These observations also point us toward elements of misogyny, not present in the whole of Pessoa, necessarily, but certainly
found in this Pessoa:

O meu horror ás mulheres reaes que teem sexo . . . As da terra, que . . .
teem de supportar o peso agitado de um homem—quem as pode amar,
que não se lhe desfolhe o amôr na antevisão de prazer que serve ao sexo
°enfernizado de negro? Quem pode respeitar a Esposa sem ter de pensar
que ella é a mulher n'outra posição de copula? Quem não se enjoa de ter
mãe por ter sido tão vulvar na sua origem, tão nojentamente expellido para
o mundo? Que nojo de nós não punja a idéa da origem carnal da nossa
alma—d'aquele irrequieto ◊ corporeo d'onde a nossa carne nasce, e, por
bella que seja, se desfeia de origem e se nos desfeia de nata.

(Pessoa, *Desassossego* [Tinta] 44)[13]

My horror of real women, sexual women . . . Those earthly women, who . . .
must bear the agitated weight of a man—who can love them? Who does
not feel love dissolving at the mere thought of sexual pleasure? Who can
respect his Wife and not think of her simply as a woman in another sexual
position? Who does not feel disgusted to have had a mother, to have been
so vulval in his origins, so vilely expelled into the world? Who is not revolted
by the idea of our soul's carnal origin, of the corporeal turbulence out of
which our flesh is born, and which, however beautiful, is soiled by its origins, its birth?   *(Disquiet* [New Directions] 10)

These misogynistic elements of *The Book of Disquiet* (with obvious ties to
other misogynistic moments in Pessoa's work) can bring us back to the idea
(already found in the preface to Botto's *Songs* and in the English poems in general, particularly "Epithalamium") that women are somewhat inferior and their
eroticism is negative or threatening. Medeiros, for example, has commented, "As
ideias elitistas de Pessoa, a defesa de uma 'aristocracia da inteligência', bem como
as suas concepções estéticas modernistas, tudo isso o afastava do mundo feminino, que ele desdenhava como intelectualmente inferior, tradicionalista, mono-
teísta e incapaz de de criatividade ou génio" ("The elitist ideas of Pessoa, his
defense of an 'aristocracy of the intelligence,' as well as his aesthetics and modernist concepts, all of that removed him further from a feminine world, which
he disdained as intellectually inferior, traditionalist, misoneist and incapable of

creativity or genius"; *O silêncio* 110). *The Book of Disquiet*, in a sense, presents a man enthralled in a generic dilemma, one with which Pessoa's attentive reader is already familiar: excluded from the only homosocial network that would allow him to validate his identity as a "proper" man, he ironizes, problematizes, and dramatizes his efforts to fit into this patriarchal model that rejects him and that he (ultimately) rejects. The narrators of *The Book of Disquiet* are located at the opposite end of the spectrum from what would be a dominant, "hegemonic" male: they live in almost complete social isolation, lacking friends or lovers. At the beginning of the *Book* Pessoa elects a narrator—another fictional version of himself—to be his close confidant: "Nunca teve de se defrontar com as exigencias do estado ou da sociedade. Ás proprias exigencias dos seus instintos elle se furtou. Nada o approximou nunca nem de amigos nem de amantes. Fui o unico que, de alguma maneira, estive na intimidade d'elle" ("He never had to deal with the demands of state or society. He even avoided the demand of his own instincts. He had never acquired friends or lovers. I was the only person who, in some way, became close to him" (*Desassossego* [Tinta] 36; *Disquiet* [New Directions] 6). Near the end of the book, a different narrator expands on his discomfort with the masculine (social) role by reflecting on the archetype of the self-made man or the self-made millionaire. In Lisbon, at the time a city of nascent capitalism, this archetype could be the epitome of the hardworking entrepreneur or businessman, exceptional and heroic, envied by other men and admired by women. Toward the end of the excerpt, the narrator replaces this generic model of masculinity (just like Caeiro did) with another male, who—while defying all the conventional codes of manhood or perhaps for that reason—takes on the status of some kind of superman of literature, an Übermensch of the arts (a classical model of sublimation, to use Freud's term). This man, who is obviously Pessoa (everyone is Pessoa in Pessoa's universe, after all), claims for himself an alternative "masculine" hegemonic status: that of the aesthete (possibly like Botto). This aesthete is intoxicated by hubris, although it is likely a nonpatriarchal (or perhaps parapatriarchal) kind of hubris. The ascendancy that he possesses over all other men derives from the fact that he creates his own rules of masculinity or creates his own masculinity (albeit in a fantastic, literary manner). In the following passage, Bernardo Soares dismisses the enviable accomplishments of an American millionaire of the time. This man's great accomplishments, he says, differ only in degree from those of a certain traveling salesman from his neighborhood in Lisbon. The tremendous triumphs of the famous self-made man are, in his opinion, not important at all, or, at most, they are no more important than those of the Lisboan traveling salesman's. The ideal man—Pessoa claims—is the one who rejects these palpable (and, therefore, petty) trappings of success that everyone craves. Instead, Soares strives toward unique, higher, spiritual, individual goals. Only in solitude—he claims—does he achieve the goal of becoming himself. Soares is referring to the goals of becoming another, of completely othering himself—or birthing himself, along with his own gender, a gender of one—as he struggles in the process of becoming an accomplished artist.

Quanto mais alto o homem, de mais coisas tem que se privar. No pincaro não ha logar senão para o homem *só*. Quanto mais perfeito, mais completo; e quanto mais completo, menos *outrem*. Estas considerações vieram ter commigo depois de ler num jornal a noticia da grande vida multipla de um homem celebre. Era um millionario americano, e tinha sido tudo. Tivera quanto ambicionara—dinheiro, amores, affectos, dedicações, viagens, collecções. . . . [O] mesmo, na sua esphera, poderia dizer o caixeiro de praça, mais ou menos meu conhecido, que todos os dias almoça, como hoje está almoçando, na mesa ao fundo do canto. . . . Não ha ninguem no mundo que não conhecesse o nome do millionario americano; mas não ha ninguem na praça de Lisboa que não conheça o nome do homem que está alli almoçando. . . . Variava nelles o comprimento do braço; no resto eram eguaes. Não consegui nunca ter inveja d'esta especie de gente. Achei sempre que a virtude estava em obter o que se não alcança, em viver onde se *não* esta, em ser mais vivo depois de morto que quando se esta vivo, em conseguir, enfim, qualquer cousa de *difícil*, de *absurdo*, em vencer, como obstaculos, a propria realidade do mundo.

(Pessoa, *Desassossego* [Tinta] 371–72; my italics)

The higher a man rises up the scale, the more things he must relinquish. On the mountain peak there is only room for that man *alone*. The more perfect, the more complete; the more complete, the less *other* he is. . . . These thoughts came to me after reading an article in a newspaper about the . . . multifaceted life of a famous man. He was an American millionaire and had been everything. He had everything he could have wanted—money, love affairs, affection, devotion, travel, private art collections. . . . [T]he same could be said, in his own sphere, of the travelling salesman, an acquaintance of mine, who has lunch every day, as he is today, at the table in the corner at the back. . . . Everyone in the world knows the name of the American millionaire, but everyone in this part of Lisbon knows the name of the man currently eating his lunch over there. . . . The length of their arms might be different, but otherwise they are the same. I've never been able to feel envious of such people. Always felt that virtue lay in getting what lay beyond one's reach, in living where you were *not*, in being more live when dead than when alive, in achieving, in short, something *difficult*, something *absurd*, in overleaping—like an obstacle—the obstinate reality of the world.   (*Disquiet* [New Directions] 316–317; my italics)

One could say—as I have suggested—that Pessoa is proposing an alternative to masculinity, perhaps a more fluid, less binary version of it or one less predicated on patriarchal norms. We could call it antimasculinity or negative masculinity. Interestingly, the way he describes this solitary and heroic undertaking reminds me of a classic definition of masculinity, that of heroic self-superation: "Masculinity is an homosocial enactment. We test ourselves, perform heroic feats, take enormous risks, all because we want other men to grant us our manhood" (Kimmel 129). Whether this new, Pessoan generic subject, thus described, is predominantly masculine, feminine, or androgynous I do not know.[14] It seems certain that this persona tends toward the hubris of poetic exceptionalism that appears to be typical of modernist or avant-garde movements; Pessoa is no exception, or, rather, he is (or claims to be) *the* exception in practically every respect. As I have tried to demonstrate, Caeiro is the nonhumanitarian, platonic lover (or nonlover) who is also the only true poet of nature. Campos is the sexual masochist and the only nonprince in existence in the world (the only one not to have taken a beating). Reis—in a world of sensualists—is contented with the Stoic-Horatian secret pleasure of being the only one knowing that he could "embrace" and "kiss" if he really wanted to. Finally, each of the narrators of *The Book of Disquiet* rejects two of the main goals of patriarchally sanctioned masculinity—namely, the pursuit of heterosexual love, which they find vulgar, vulvar, and repulsive (possibly no less so than real, physical homosexual love), and the pursuit of the classically masculine trilogy of wealth, fame, and glory. In his work, Pessoa presents himself—in his radical independence—as different from all other poets, and he does so substantially through the creation of his own gender, a gender that he himself birthed and made permanently other (i.e., not closed, or polarized, or completed) in its many liberating idiosyncrasies.

NOTES

1. Paulo de Medeiros uses the term *paradox* to refer to the concept of gender in Pessoa: "A representação do feminino, assim como tudo o que tem a ver com questões de género, ou sexualidade, sensualidade e eroticismo, constitui um emaranhado de paradoxos no *Livro do Desassossego*, assim como no resto da obra de Fernando Pessoa" ("The representation of the feminine, as well as with everything that relates to gender issues, or sexuality, sensuality and eroticism, constitutes an entanglement of paradoxes in the *Book of Disquiet*, and also in the rest of Fernando Pessoa's work"; *O silêncio* 105).

2. A similar interpretation of this excerpt can be found in Mariana Gray de Castro's study *Fernando Pessoa's Shakespeare*. Castro notes that Pessoa read Shakespeare's sonnets as proof of the latter's real homosexuality or pederasty yet rejected a similar biographical extrapolation on the part of the critics who analyzed his own homoerotic poetry. She also suggests that Shakespeare's sonnets may have initially inspired and shaped Pessoa's own homoerotic production (167) and implies that the possibility of personal criticism eventually inhibited that production and increased his objections to biographical readings of his own poetry. For example, she explains, "Pessoa's encounter with psychoanalysis . . . prompted him to offer Gaspar Simões a pre-emptive Freudian explanation for 'Antinous' and 'Epithalamium' as artistic sublimations of libido, designed to dissuade the biographer from performing his own" (179).

3. Unless otherwise attributed, all translations are mine.

4. *The Man Who Never Was* subsequently became the title of a volume, which contained the proceedings of the conference, edited by the American scholar George Monteiro. See also G. Monteiro ("First International Symposium").

5. On corporeality and sexuality in Pessoa, Medeiros also mentions Allegro and Barreto (*Misoginia*).

6. The editors note, "These shape-shifting, transgendering materializations of the superior man's imaginary body illustrate in a particularly vivid and synthetic way the foundational interrelatedness of thought and sensation, as well as of self-consciousness and becoming other, that are at the core of Pessoa's literary experience" (Klobucka and Sabine, *Embodying Pessoa* 6).

7. The passage continues thus: "Pessoa offers a clue on this subject when he writes, 'The multiplication for the I is a frequent phenomenon in cases of masturbation . . . , because masturbation—which is 'sexual inversion' in the most literal sense, that is, monosexuality—is the only kind of sex that remains for repressed homosexuals, unless they take the (for them) unnatural, heterosexual route" (Zenith, "Fernando Pessoa's Gay Heteronym?" 36). Zenith's important biography of Fernando Pessoa (*Fernando Pessoa: A Biography*) was published as I was writing this essay, and, consequently, I did not have a chance to read it. However, I am told that the author may have revised his initial position on Pessoa's sexuality. Here is a passage, from a review by Carlos Adriano, that may suggest an evolution (or, on the contrary, a confirmation) of Zenith's position on this issue: "Nesta biografia, evitei definir a sexualidade de Pessoa, mas, com base em suas explicações espirituais e, como demonstrado por sua própria 'prática', tal como era, é possível afirmar que o poeta em última análise não era heterossexual, homossexual, pansexual nem assexual; era monossexual, andrógino. Os heterônimos podem ser vistos como fruto de sua autofecundação . . . [é] quase certo que Fernando Pessoa morreu virgem" ("In this biography, I avoided defining Pessoa's sexuality, but, based on his spiritual explanations and, as demonstrated by his own 'practice,' as it was, it is possible to affirm that the poet was not ultimately heterosexual, homosexual, pansexual nor asexual; he was an androgynous monosexual. Heteronyms can be seen as the fruit of his self-fecundation . . . it is almost certain Fernando Pessoa died a virgin"; qtd. in Adriano).

8. M. Castro refers readers to Bréchon, *L'innombrable* 177–85.

9. According to Vieira, Pessoa also possessed in his library the book *The Boyhood of Algernon Charles Swinburne*, by Mrs. Disney Leith (Mary Charlotte Julie), which, famously, displays elements of this culture of flagellation (10).

10. Some scholars believe that Lydia may be male. "In a typed text first published by Teresa Rita Lopes . . . Campos points out that the female lovers whom Ricardo Reis addresses in his odes—Chloe, Lydia, Neaera—were mere abstractions . . . and he goes on to prove that the beloved flower extolled by Reis in an ode published in 1924 is not his ethereal Chloe or Lydia but a young man" (Zenith, "Fernando Pessoa's Gay Heteronym?" 40).

11. Sedgwick claims that all men negotiate their lives according to a network of social and political relationships with other men. She calls this network "male homosociality" (*Between Men* 17). One of the unwritten rules of such homosocial communities is homophobia. Paradoxically, Sedgwick declares that "intense male homosocial desire [is] as at once the most compulsory and the most prohibited of social bonds" (*Epistemology* 187).

12. Vieira comments, "One should not forget that the flagellant imagination is intimately related with other aspects of sexuality, such as homosexuality, sadomasochism and pedophilia, all of them verifiably present in the sexual discourse of 'other Victorians'" (Vieira 13).

13. In the cited edition, an asterisk indicates a "leitura conjecturada" ("conjectured reading"), and a diamond indicates a blank space left by Pessoa. The conjectured text in this case may be translated as "darkened by sickness."

14. Pessoa may not be looking to establish an androgynous empire or "imperialism of poets," as suggested by Irene Ramalho-Santos (*Atlantic Poets* 221), but perhaps an imperialism of a poet—an imperialism of one.

Pessoa and Popular Culture

Ellen W. Sapega

In early 2007, the Portuguese comedy troupe Gato Fedorento aired a brief
television sketch titled "Big Brother Grandes Portugueses" ("Big Brother the
Greatest Portuguese"), a mash-up of two popular reality shows: the internationally syndicated series *Big Brother*, in which viewers who watch a group of strang-
ers occupying a shared domestic space are invited to vote to evict contestants
from the house, and the contest *Os Grandes Portugueses* (*The Greatest Portuguese*), which was based on the BBC series *One Hundred Greatest Britons*.[1] At
the time, the Portuguese national television station, RTP1, was in the midst of
broadcasting the latter show. On 14 January 2007, a list of the ten most voted-
for personalities, selected from a group of one hundred candidates, had been
revealed on the social media platforms surrounding *Os Grandes Portugueses*.
On that list were the names of Portugal's two most celebrated poets: Luís de
Camões and Fernando Pessoa. In the Gato Fedorento satire, Pessoa, Camões,
D. Afonso Henriques (the founding king of the Portuguese nation), and the
eighteenth-century despot the Marquês de Pombal are sharing a house outside
Lisbon in a town called Venda do Pinheiro. The fifth occupant is Marco Borges,
a contestant who had gained fame for his aggressive behavior in Portugal's first
season of *Big Brother* seven years earlier. As the Marquês de Pombal complains
that it is Pessoa's turn to wash the dishes, he receives a series of answers from
the person lounging on a couch that he is not Pessoa but is rather, successively,
Alberto Caeiro, Ricardo Reis, Álvaro de Campos, and Bernardo Soares. This
sequence is then followed by a quick shot of Pessoa and Camões uncomfortably
sleeping in the same single bed; a conversation between Pombal, Pessoa, and D.
Afonso Henriques about their preferred sexual positions; and a short bit where
Pessoa refuses to leave the bathroom. At the sketch's end, the Marcos Borges
character explains to the camera, in an expletive-laced monologue, that while
he is angry with each of the house's residents, the two poets were the most "lin-
grinhas" ("inconsequential").

In this witty and irreverent appropriation of Pessoa, the producers draw upon
visual cues that are regularly associated with the poet. As is to be expected, the
actor portraying Pessoa has a mustache and is dressed in a dark suit with a vest,
a bow tie, and a hat. The sketch also presumes the audience's knowledge not only
of the heteronyms but also of certain elements of Pessoa's personal life or purported psychological profile (an ambivalent sexuality, melancholia, etc.). No direct
references were included, however, to the content of Pessoa's work, to his poetry
or prose.

This was not the first time that a reference to Pessoa appeared in Portuguese
popular culture, nor would it be the last. The sketch does illustrate the extent to
which the figures of Pessoa and his principal heteronyms have entered what

might be considered the Portuguese collective consciousness and have become significant elements in contemporary popular discourses. Over the past three decades, there have been movies made about Pessoa; he has entered novels as a character; his words and images appear in advertisements, popular songs, and comic books, to name just a few genres.

To date, as very little research has been done on the topic of Pessoa and popular culture, there are several ways of approaching this intersection. One course would be to interrogate the poet's own relationship to popular culture of his time. This would entail examining his work to find influences or references to popular culture. It might include studying the *Quadras*, popular quatrains that Pessoa wrote toward the end of his life; the proverbs that he compiled, translated, and sought to publish in 1913; or the film arguments (or scripts) that he toyed with over the years. All these projects were left unpublished at the time of his death. Another approach to Pessoa and popular culture would involve seeking to understand the poet's presence as an element within contemporary popular culture by identifying allusions, adaptations, and appropriations of Pessoa's work or his character. In this essay, I follow the latter line of enquiry, examining several key examples that constitute well-known representations or remediations of Pessoa in Portuguese popular culture that mark different moments in a continuum that dates from the 1980s to the recent past, asking by what means and to what end popular culture seeks to explain, understand, or even exploit his work.

As Robert Shaughnessy has noted, "The 'popular' itself is hardly an uncontested term or frame of reference: seen from some angles, it denotes community, shared values, democratic participation, accessibility and fun; from others, the lowest common denominator, the reductive or the simplified, or the shoddy, the course, and the meretricious" (2). Writing about the transmission and appropriation of Shakespeare, Shaughnessy reminds his readers that questions of class and cultural ownership are bound up with considerations of taste and aesthetic value. Thus, the tensions or contradictions of a given society often come to the fore when the works or the memory of a given author or artist move from high to popular culture. As I examine specific instances in which Pessoa's image and work have been appropriated, reevaluated, or consumed in the decades following the Portuguese Revolution of 1974, I identify certain elements of his persona and his work that have been employed in new contexts.[2] In most cases, the viewer, reader, or consumer of these remediations must possess a minimal knowledge of Pessoa's life and poetics in order to make meaning of the appropriation at hand. When this is the case, they may derive pleasure from the appropriation, or they may reject it as tasteless or reductive. As the Gato Fedorento sketch illustrates, contemporary Portuguese popular culture has eagerly embraced Pessoa. In the material that follows, I hope to provide a better understanding of the various ways that Pessoa has become a sign or an icon that is both powerful and productive in its connotations (Lanier 93).

José Saramago's 1984 novel *O ano da morte de Ricardo Reis* (*The Year of the Death of Ricardo Reis*) is one of the earliest appropriations of the figure of

Pessoa. While Saramago cannot strictly be considered a "popular" writer, it is worth noting that in the 1980s the future Nobel Prize–winning author had yet to enter the canon of Portuguese letters. In fact, as Ronald W. Sousa has speculated (88), the implied readership of this novel, members of the Portuguese intelligentsia that came of age under the Estado Novo, tended to dislike what Saramago was doing with the novel form in this book and in his previous novel, *Memorial do convento* (*Baltasar and Blimunda*). In broad terms, both these "historical" novels rely on an intrusive, third-person narrator that the reader is asked to take as the "implied author" (R. W. Sousa 71). The stories told by this speaker lack the sort of character development that most readers have come to expect from the genre, which frustrates our attempts to identify facilely with the protagonists (95).

In *O ano da morte de Ricardo Reis*, the reader is invited to enter into a complex textual game based on the premise that Pessoa's heteronym Ricardo Reis has returned to Lisbon from his self-imposed exile in Brazil upon learning of the former's death. The reader accompanies Reis over a period of eight and a half months, during which time he circulates through the capital city reacquainting himself with the social realities of a homeland that he had abandoned some sixteen years earlier. For a reader familiar with Pessoa's work, the protagonist's status as a fictional creation is quite evident throughout, and the novel is filled with sly comments and observations about Pessoa and his heteronyms, intertextual references to Reis's and Pessoa's verse, and the ironic situation in which Reis becomes emotionally involved with a housekeeper at his hotel named Lídia. Reis himself, however, is apparently unaware of the fact that he never truly existed, except on paper, even as he maintains regular contact with his already-deceased creator.

From the opening sentence, which reverses a well-known line from *Os Lusíadas* (*The Lusiads*), to the closing words that, like a mirror, reflect and recast this incipit,[3] this novel points to and celebrates the creative possibilities that may be opened through actions, narrative and otherwise, that entail the appropriation of literary texts and their authors. At the same time, the possible dangers that can lurk behind such appropriations are also duly exposed. Throughout, the narrator explores the power of certain literary figures to serve as sites of memory (*lieux de mémoire*) and demonstrates more specifically how the figure of Camões has played multiple symbolic roles in the Portuguese national imagination since the mid-nineteenth century. This is articulated through the figure of Pessoa, which the narrator has commandeered, recast as a ghostly presence, and sent out into the city with his own literary creation, the heteronym Ricardo Reis. Reis, the protagonist, is drawn into an urban labyrinth, a labyrinth that literally has the figure of Camões at the center of its symbolic order (I refer to the statue of Camões that was erected near the top of the Chiado neighborhood in the mid-nineteenth century). The reader, on the other hand, is drawn into a textual labyrinth constructed around both Pessoa's work and his memory (see Sapega, "Saramago's 'Genius'").

There are many aspects of this novel's treatment of Pessoa and his work that
could be explored here, and an extensive bibliography on this topic has emerged
in English and Portuguese in the decades since its publication. For my present
purposes, I would like to focus on one facet in particular, which Ronald W. Sousa
has described as the narrator's actions in respect to the "putting-in-place of the
fascist symbolic order" (104). As Reis disembarks in Lisbon on 29 December 1935
(Saramago, *Ano* 37; *Year* 25), just under a month after the death of Pessoa, almost
all of the novel's action takes place in 1936, a year that witnessed the outbreak
of the Spanish Civil War and the rise of German and Italian fascism. Saramago's narrator also reminds us that the year in question was a key moment in the
consolidation of the Estado Novo's repressive structures. In response to the turmoil across the border, Salazar approved the creation of the Mocidade Portuguesa ("Portuguese Youth") and strengthened the powers of the political police
(PVDE); he also authorized the establishment of the Tarrafal penal colony on
the Cabo Verdean island of Santiago.

Upon his return to Portugal, Reis is obliged to confront the political realities
that he had sought to evade in his life and his work. This coming to terms is
achieved by several means: through the protagonist's reading of propagandistic
books and heavily censored newspapers, his attendance at public events and
performances (a play, a political rally, and a pilgrimage to Fátima), and observation (on his daily walks through Lisbon, Reis is confronted by many scenes of
misery and abject poverty). The combination of these modes of access to information impels the reader to evaluate the various discourses employed by the
Estado Novo to impose on the public its specifically one-sided views of national
experience.[4] While Reis maintains a mostly passive stance in the face of the
events he witnesses, it is clear that he does not accept the regime's propaganda.
When his allotted time is up, he willingly follows Pessoa's ghost and abandons
his place on earth.

Through the appropriation of Pessoa's heteronym, Saramago inserts the poet
and his work into the concrete sociopolitical context of 1930s Portugal. While it
may not have been the implied author-narrator's primary intent, the reader is
reminded that the poet was in fact dead well before many of trappings of the
regime were fully put into place. This, in effect, has the result of "freeing" Pessoa from his associations with the imperial ethos of the Salazar regime and makes
an important contribution to new ways of imagining the poet's life and interpreting his works.[5] In the years that followed, a series of events surrounding the
commemoration of Pessoa's death (fifty years in 1985) and his birth (one hundred years in 1988) would provide multiple opportunities to reassess the poet's
work and his relationship to the city in which he spent his entire adult life.

When Saramago published *O ano da morte de Ricardo Reis*, the well-known
statue of Pessoa in front of Lisbon's Café Brasileira had yet to be commissioned
(fig. 1). In fact, the capital city did not have any monument or other physical tribute to the memory of Pessoa, save for a plaque identifying the building in which
he was born.[6] That would change very quickly in the coming years as new facets

Figure 1. Lagoa Henriques. *Statue of Fernando Pessoa*. 1988, Lisbon. Photograph by Daniel Villafruela, 17 Sept. 2014, *Wikimedia Commons*, commons.wikimedia.org/wiki/File:Lisboa -Rua_Garrett-Estatua_de_Fernado_Pessoa-20140917.jpg.

of Pessoa's work were revealed to the general reading public. In November 1985, multiple activities were organized to recognize the fiftieth anniversary of the poet's death. At that time, Pessoa's remains were transferred from the Prazeres Cemetery to the Cloisters at the Jerónimos Monastery.[7] Three years later, another cycle of commemoration marked the centenary of his birth. On 13 June 1988, Lagoa Henriques's statue of Pessoa was inaugurated in Chiado. This near-life-size representation of the poet is seated at a table that resembles those found inside the historic café. His left leg is crossed over his knee and his empty right hand is raised as though in deep thought or conversation. To his left, an empty chair invites passersby to join him for a moment in his apparent reverie. Since the day of the statue's inauguration, countless foreign tourists and Portuguese nationals have done just that. On the day of the statue's inauguration, the first to join the poet was Mário Soares, the president of the republic, who, upon looking west to the Praça de Camões, remarked that he could "contemplar Pessooa e ver Camões" ("contemplate Pessoa and see Camões"; Vilela and Fernandes 213). If the nearby statue of Camões, which was dedicated in 1867, was seen by many as representing the "the monumental national history promulgated by fascism" (R. W. Sousa 92), this bronze likeness of Pessoa, located just several steps away, has become emblematic of the contradictory ways that his likeness has been pressed into service in support of a wide variety of commercial and commemorative projects during the past three decades.

There were many serious academic events related to the celebration of the centenary of Pessoa's birth in 1988. The general public celebration that took place on 12–13 June bordered on the carnivalesque, however, in acknowledgment of the date on which the festivities took place. Pessoa's birthday, 13 June, coincides with the popular municipal celebrations in memory of St. Anthony, who died in Padua on 13 June 1231 (this is the reason why, following on tradition, Pessoa was given the middle name António). As St. Anthony was born in Lisbon in 1195, the city considers him one of its patron saints and celebrates his day with lively festivities in the streets that begin on the night of 12 June and last until dawn. The series of events organized in 1988 to commemorate the one hundredth anniversary of Pessoa's birth incorporated elements traditionally associated with St. Anthony's Day. Hence, in the Largo de São Carlos, in the shadow of the building where Pessoa was born, images of the saint and potted sweet basil plants were for sale alongside T-shirts bearing the poet's likeness. A stage was erected in the square, on which a disparate series of performances took place. Besides the expected declamations of Pessoa's poetry,[8] a folkloric dance troupe from the Ribatejo region (where Alberto Caeiro was purportedly born) performed, followed by a fashion show and a trained dog act. When questioned about the rationale for these eclectic programing choices, João D'Ávila, the event's organizer, explained that the party was *for* Pessoa; it was not merely a celebration of his life and work ("Isto não é um espectáculo sobre Fernando Pessoa mas para Fernando Pessoa" ["This isn't a show about Fernando Pessoa but for Fernando Pessoa"; J. A. Dionísio 53R]).

Festivities of a similar nature continued in the Largo de São Carlos on 13 June 1988, while several blocks north, in the Largo do Chiado, the now-famous statute of Pessoa was officially inaugurated. If Mário Soares was the first to occupy the empty seat at the table, joining the bronze likeness of the poet in the convivial act of contemplating the world passing by, many others would follow his lead, both on the day of the statue's inauguration and in the years that followed. From the start, however, the statue was not without controversy. Some critics were quick to point out that Pessoa tended to favor other cafés, such as the Café Martinho da Arcada or the Brasileira do Rossio (which closed in 1960), while others lamented the fact that the poet was depicted without his glasses. The well-known writer Sophia de Mello Breyner Andresen explained her dislike of the statue in the following terms: "Vê-se o que se fez com o Pessoa para lhe criarem uma imagem que ele não tinha e não queria ter, ele que não queria ter uma imagem nenhuma. Era um homem embiocado e puseram-no bastante pinoca sentado no Chiado. Se ele lá estivesse, estaria num sítio escuro, com uns amigos que o escondessem" ("Look what they did to Pessoa by creating an image for him that he didn't have and didn't want to have, he who didn't want to have any image. He was a reserved man and they made him into a bit of dandy seated in the Chiado. If he were there, he'd be in a dark corner, with some friends who would help hide him"; Vilela and Fernandes 212).

The most scathing assessment of the statue came from the Associação Portuguesa Internacional dos Críticos de Arte, who were attending parallel celebrations of the Pessoa centenary in Paris. In a communiqué released in the week of 12 June 1988, this group called for the immediate removal of Henriques's "ridiculous" likeness "por razões de decência intelectual e pública" ("for motives of public and intellectual decency"; "7 dias" 4). The art historians may well have been objecting to the realist codes used by the sculptor, which could be considered historically and aesthetically out of place. Besides drawing upon some of the most well-known (and stereotypical) images of Pessoa that circulated after his death, the very gesture of adopting a realist aesthetic might be interpreted as misguided. The sculptor's reliance on mimetic, albeit simplified, codes of representation harked back to the cultural politics of an earlier era that in many respects recalled the work of his teacher and mentor, Salvador Barato Feyo, who had been a favorite of the Estado Novo regime.[9] In 1988, this style did not conform to the postmodern tastes that were shaping Lisbon's urban fabric. Additionally, as Andresen alludes to in her critique of the sculpture, up to that time, Pessoa's "presence" or being was mostly articulated through language itself ("ele que não queria ter uma imagem nenhuma" ["he who didn't want to have any image"; Vilela and Fernandes 212]).

It is important to note that most negative reactions to this statue came from well-known Portuguese intellectuals. In retrospect, their disparaging remarks about Henriques's sculpture may have betrayed a certain anxiety on the part of Portugal's literary and artistic elites, an anxiety born of the fear that they were losing control of the discourses related to the poet's significance. For many years, Pessoa's family and a small circle of friends, colleagues, and a select group of scholars had tightly monitored his work and image. As the popular public events surrounding the centenary of Pessoa's birth attest, his place in the collective imagination was rapidly changing, nonetheless. In fact, as time wore on, a saying began to circulate that declared, "Tanto Pessoa já enjoa!" ("So much Pessoa can make you queasy!"; F. Martinho 23).

During the centenary year of Pessoa's birth, the poet's image was also appropriated and put to the service of commerce in an advertising campaign for Café Delta, one of the country's largest coffee roasters and distributors.[10] In a slightly altered version of a famous painting of Pessoa that his friend and contemporary José de Almada Negreiros completed in 1954 ("Portrait"), this campaign presented an image of the poet seated at a café table, sipping a small cup of coffee (Zenith, *Fotobiografias* 178). In the original painting, the coffee is placed on the table, next to a sugar bowl and a copy of *Orpheu 2*. Pessoa's right hand rests on a sheet of paper, and he holds a cigarette in his left hand. As to be expected, in the advertisement, the well-known logo for Delta coffee can be seen on the cup that Pessoa holds. Beneath it, we find the Delta triangular logo and the slogan "A verdade do café," which might be loosely translated as "The real coffee." Across the bottom of the poster, an ironic declaration states in capital letters, "TODOS OS PESSOAS BEBEM CAFÉ DELTA." In Portuguese the noun *pessoa* is feminine, and the expression "Todas as pessoas" in English would translate as "everyone." By utilizing the definite article in its plural masculine form (*os*), and rendering it in a contrasting black typeface, this declaration invites the viewer to chuckle at its clever wordplay, as it implies that the heteronyms, as well as their creator, enjoy this particular product. The playful declaration that calls attention to the appropriation of Almada's iconic image of the poet would make any viewer who got the joke feel clever and culturally aware.

As with several other examples I have discussed, full appreciation of the Café Delta advertising campaign requires some previous knowledge of Pessoa and his work. In order for viewers of this image to derive pleasure from it, they must be capable of understanding at least some, if not all, of the layered references it presents. While some viewers might not immediately identify the original painting that the advertisement appropriates, most would recognize it as a well-known likeness of the poet. Additionally, they would know Pessoa as the creator of the heteronyms. Although a comparison to Saramago's novel might seem a stretch, it is possible to affirm that in both cases, if readers or viewers do not possess this basic knowledge about the heteronyms, they will be denied access to many of the different codes that are employed in the text. In this sense, and following Roland Barthes's famous distinction between a readerly text and a writerly text, we may conclude that both the Café Delta advertising campaign and Saramago's novel belong in the latter category.

Henriques's sculpture, on the other hand, can be appreciated without the benefit of much, or even any, knowledge about Pessoa, and this may help explain its continued popularity, especially among the foreign tourists that flock to Lisbon's central Chiado district. Since 1998, this statue has been integrated into the Café Brasileira's outdoor seating area just across from a particularly busy entrance to the Lisbon metro. Passersby are drawn to the sculpture, which provides them a delightful photo opportunity. It is safe to assume that this is some visitors' first encounter with Pessoa, who they would have learned from their print or digital guides was Portugal's most famous poet. This in turn may lead to an interest in learning more about his life and his work. Inside the café and in many of the shops that fill Lisbon's Baixa, these tourists can then acquire translations of Pessoa's poetry and *The Book of Disquiet*, as well as postcards, T-shirts, and myriad other objects printed with his likeness. The sculpture therefore points to an important role that the image and works of Pessoa have played since the 1980s. Pessoa is now an internationally celebrated author that has helped awaken a wider interest in Portugal and its literature and culture. As Fernando J. B. Martinho, a well-known critic of Pessoa's work, has remarked, the poet now serves as a loco-motive that generates interest in Portugal and Portuguese culture: "he paved the way to the others; he aroused interest for the country and its literature and culture and that continues to be one of his main roles" (21). Thus, we can con-clude, perhaps, that the seemingly endless circulation of images of Pessoa in popular culture, the appropriations and adaptations of his words and his like-ness, and the playfully ironic allusions to his life and his work, go well beyond a simple commodification of his work. They speak as well to an increasing inter-national interest in Pessoa's literary project and serve as a point of Portuguese national pride.

NOTES

1. Gato Fedorento (meaning "smelly cat") was a Portuguese comedy group com-posed of José Diogo Quintelo, Miguel Góis, Ricardo Araújo Pereira, and Tiago Dores. The group is known for its unique, surreal humor that was inspired, in part, by *Monty Python's Flying Circus*. Their show *Diz que é uma espécie de magazine* (*It's a Sort of Talk Show*) ran on the Portuguese channel RTP1 for two seasons, from 2006 to 2008 ("Gato Fedorento" [*Wikipédia*]). Several recordings of the episode referred to here may be viewed online (see, for example, "Gato Fedorento" [*YouTube*]).

2. I take this date as my point of departure because it marks the beginning of a period of important political, cultural, and economic change for Portugal. More than five decades of state censorship came abruptly to an end, and many historical figures and symbols previously associated with the Estado Novo were scrutinized and reevaluated.

3. The novel's opening line reads, "Aqui o mar acaba e a terra principia" ("Here the sea ends and the earth begins"; Saramago, *Ano* 11; *Year* 1). Its closing sentence is "Aqui onde o mar se acabou e a terra espera" ("Here, where the sea ends and the earth awaits"; *Ano* 415; *Year* 358).

4. As Ronald W. Sousa explains, the reader is "implicitly asked to look to Reis and Pessoa as the interpreters, but while they do draw some conclusions, it is unclear that they are involved in any general interpretation project. Instead, on this score they func-tion principally to pose issues in need of interpretation" (95).

5. Over the years, the Estado Novo's educational apparatus consistently promoted the ostensibly nationalist poem *Mensagem* (*Message*; 1934). Already in January 1935, ten months before Pessoa's death, *Mensagem* was touted in the national press as "a pro-phetic announcement of 'Portugal's tomorrow' already dawning in the 'Portugal of today'" (see Barreto, "Salazar" 182). In the 1950s and '60s, as Pessoa's work became the subject of academic study, conservative exponents of a line of thought that promoted the idea of a "Portuguese philosophy" sought to inscribe Pessoa's name in the list of its prac-titioners (R. W. Sousa 20). By the time of the 1974 revolution, Pessoa's work, like that of Camões, had become symbolic for many readers of a shared, national ethos that located the roots of Portuguese exceptionalism in the Age of Discovery.

6. This plaque was installed and inaugurated on 30 November 1958 (Zenith, *Foto-biografias* 176).

7. The church of this monastery, erected in the sixteenth century, is the resting place of Manuel I and John III. In the late nineteenth century, the remains of Camões and Sebastian I were transferred to tombs housed in the same space.

8. According to the report of this event published in *Expresso*, most of the poems that were declaimed came from *Mensagem* (J. A. Dionísio 55R).

9. Besides creating well-known monuments to such writers as Alexandre Herculano and Almeida Garrett (both located on Lisbon's Avenida da Liberdade), Barata Feyo contributed a sculpture titled *Raça* to the 1939 New York World's Fair and another titled *D. João I* to the 1940 Exposition of the Portuguese World. In 1952, he produced a statue of Bartolomeu Dias that is located in Cape Town, South Africa, and in 1960 his bronze likeness of Prince Henry the Navigator was inaugurated in the Praça de Portugal in Brasília.

10. This advertising campaign appears to have been launched on a series of different platforms (e.g., calendar, poster, billboard). A copy of the poster can be found in the *Fotobiografias de Fernando Pessoa* (Zenith, *Fotobiografias* 178), and I have seen the calendar for sale on the Internet ("Calendario").

The Book of Disquiet and World Literature: Notes from the Seminar Room

Paulo de Medeiros

> Tão superfluo tudo! nós e o mundo e o mysterio de ambos.
>
> (All so superfluous! We, the world, and the mystery of both.)
>
> —Fernando Pessoa, *Livro do desasocego* (my trans.)

Teaching Fernando Pessoa's *The Book of Disquiet* is like embarking on an infinite journey of discovery and, especially, of self-discovery. The first time I had occasion to assign *The Book of Disquiet*, close to twenty years ago, it was in the context of a small and highly specialized seminar for postgraduate students at the University of Utrecht. Even though some could have read the original Portuguese, most were dependent on a translation. In this case, the publication of Richard Zenith's translation in the Penguin Modern Classic Series in 2001 had been the necessary catalyst for my decision. Not only was this edition extremely accessible at bookstores and public libraries, its being marketed as a "modern classic" also guaranteed it as a canonical choice that students, however unfamiliar with the author or with Portuguese literature on the whole, would not immediately reject. It was not without some trepidation that I embarked on that first seminar. Yet, even before the semester was over, I knew that the book, for all its intrinsic strangeness, did not come across as an oddity. Students were perplexed by Pessoa's—or rather Bernardo Soares's—labyrinthine, complex, and paradoxical thought, in a form that, to borrow one of Gerhard Neumann's insights into Franz Kafka, could be described as a "gleitendes Paradox" ("sliding paradox") . Yet they also were being taken over by the intensity of feeling—even when concerning tedium—and the beauty of the text. They were relentless in their questions, and I found myself, time and time again, without satisfactory answers, having to probe further, research and think further, in order to suggest a better answer, however tentative, at a later meeting. The sense of wonder and awe of a first reading was not—indeed, still is not—extinguished. And seeing it multiplied on the faces of students can be addictive, as anyone engaged in teaching can recognize beyond a doubt.

Other settings in which I have been able to discuss *The Book of Disquiet* with students at Warwick, besides at conferences and other such events, include a postgraduate seminar on world literature, in which Pessoa's work was read alongside selections from Kafka, Walter Benjamin, and Marcel Proust; and, more recently, in the undergraduate senior seminar required of students in the joint honors BA in philosophy and literature. Both new settings, even more than the first, are at the base of my current reflections. Both posed new questions, challenges, and opportunities, especially as not one of the students had access to the original text, or even any previous knowledge of who Pessoa was or what *The Book of Disquiet* might be—in itself already a most disquieting prospect.

That basic ignorance concerning *The Book of Disquiet*, rather than being a hindrance, has proved to be a most useful heuristic platform. Obviously, there is no such a thing as a tabula rasa—indeed, all the knowledge that students bring to seminars concerning literature, modernism, modernity, and the canon is of great importance. *The Book of Disquiet* calmly but inexorably challenges all certainties concerning those cornerstones of literary studies, and the clash between the text and a priori notions elicits resistance as well as surprise and, not infrequently, marks the beginning of yet other, multiple, journeys of discovery. In order to understand how Pessoa can have such an effect, it is useful to keep in mind how literary studies, even when set up according to the principles of comparative literature and no longer bound by a strict understanding of national literary history, traditionally acknowledges a certain canon and the place within it to which the various literatures, and individual works, have been assigned. Portuguese literature, when it figures at all, is mostly understood as a "minor" literature—in itself a concept that gets misused all the time. Consequently, Pessoa, even though he is one of the most canonical figures in Portuguese literature, cannot but be seen as semiperipheral at best. Approaching *The Book of Disquiet* in the seminar inevitably leads to a confrontation with such notions and often leads to an exposure of the flawed principles undergirding such hierarchical organizations of literature as always based on certain kinds of privilege. Such an exposure is sure to contribute to a fuller understanding of the significance of art, the individual work of art, and the function of each in society, when not to a downright discarding of the old set of norms and an adoption of a critical understanding of the operations of the literary system as part of the world-system as suggested by Immanuel Wallerstein.

Wallerstein's analysis of the world-system and his tripartite structure of core, periphery, and semiperiphery are crucial to a reading of *The Book of Disquiet* as world-literature (as differentiated from the more conventional field of world literature). In such a reading, there is no point in elevating Pessoa to a pinnacle of world literature, even though of course he rightly belongs there as one of the key writers and thinkers of modernism. Rather, the point is to understand Pessoa as a writer from the semiperiphery who, precisely because of—as opposed to instead of—occupying such a liminal, in-between space, can point the way toward the future. Many contextual elements need to be taken into account when adopting such a view. For one, Portugal at the turn of the nineteenth to the twentieth century was considered a minor European country whose limited say at the table of European and world politics had been driven home by the British ultimatum of 1890 (which basically forced Portugal to revise its imperial ambitions concerning southern Africa by asserting the predominance of Britain's competing colonial claims). This reality can be said to have marked Pessoa's entire generation. Having grown up in South Africa from the age of eight, when his mother took him to Durban to join his stepfather, Pessoa had direct experience of the multiple contradictions of colonialism and of the clashes between England and Portugal and their respective imperial pretensions. Lisbon was already paradigmatically representative of the semiperiphery given its mixture of cultural conservatism and provincialism on the one hand and the overwhelming remnants of its past imperial splendor on the other. Whereas Portugal existed simultaneously on the periphery of Europe and at the center of a reasonably large empire, Durban was even further away from being at the center even of South Africa, but, more importantly in terms of a cultural clash, it was part of the British Empire (Zenith, *Pessoa: An Experimental Life*). Pessoa's upbringing and education, and thus his literary references, were a mix of both influences—and his exposure to and propensity for English literary models led him to further distance himself from the majority of the Portuguese of his generation, who were still largely dependent on French culture.

One of the most obvious ways of incorporating *The Book of Disquiet* in the literary curriculum is, as I once also did, to juxtapose Pessoa with other great writers. My own choice of Kafka, Benjamin, and Proust was perhaps contingent yet not aleatory. Certainly, other great literary figures of the period might be invoked instead. My choice had to do with the fact that, like Kafka's, Pessoa's writing often involves the construction of subtle, though very charged, paradoxes; that, like Benjamin, Pessoa gave much attention to the function of images and to dreams, indeed to dream-images; and that, though not quite in the same way, Pessoa's attention to memory and his ability to create a sense of sensory intensity not unlike Proust's must be seen as clearly distinct and representative. Reading *The Book of Disquiet* alongside *The Trial*, *The Arcades Project*, or *In Search of Lost Time* can have the advantage of immediately signifying to students that Pessoa is one of the canonical masters of modernism while simultaneously also inviting them to discover the profound similarities and significant divergences among them all. Students encountering Pessoa in this context may be less prone to doubt his claim to be in such company. Yet they may also be less clear on how the notion of periphery is fundamental in understanding not just the work of Pessoa but also that of some of the greatest names of modernism.

In this regard both Kafka and Benjamin (Proust less so) provide excellent points of departure for a decentering of the canon of European modernism. Some may even want to think of a kind of anticanon, and there is much to be said on that score, as Pessoa by now could be said to embody the very image of the canon, first on a national level, but increasingly more so on an international, even global scale. George Steiner in his review of the translation of *The Book of Disquiet* for Penguin refers to the day Pessoa credits as being his "triumphal day," when he created the principal heteronyms "in a kind of trance," with a question expressing an intense appreciation verging on awe: "Was 18 March 1914 the most extraordinary date in modern literature?" ("Man"). Yet this reverence had not always been forthcoming and the reception of Pessoa was indeed late, even in Portugal, as many of his texts remained unpublished for a long time. *The Book of Disquiet*, for instance, had to wait until 1982 to see first publication of a truncated version. Critics and scholars knew then they had something both strange and complex on their hands, yet few, if any, might have guessed how much *The Book of Disquiet* would come to contribute to a reevaluation of Pessoa as not only a great poet but as a great writer *tout court*. Perhaps one of the important points that can be made from this is the recognition that Pessoa's work is not belated; rather, it is our appreciation of it in its true significance that has taken its time. Alain Badiou has gone arguably the furthest by declaring that "philosophy is not—at least not yet—under the condition of Pessoa. Its thought is not yet worthy of Pessoa" (*Handbook* 36).

However tempting the notion of an anticanon might be, with *The Book of Disquiet* as an *antibook* at both its core and its periphery, more on which later, I still would rather do away with it. If anything at all, it should never be seen as more than a stage in a dialectical process leading to the annulment of the very notion of canon, with its mechanisms for inclusion and exclusion, predicated as it is on rigid notions of hierarchy, origin and originality, and value designed to reinforce and duplicate reigning forms of privilege. Rejecting the notion of canon should not be confused with rejecting any type of framing within a given cultural tradition, be it national or wider. Understanding Pessoa's, and in particular, *The Book of Disquiet*'s achievement is only possible by keeping in mind precisely how this author and his text amplify and reshape, honor and subvert literary tradition and how, consequently, they earn their place in that same tradition. All the while, though, one cannot lose sight of the fact that Pessoa died before he could arrange and edit the multitude of fragments that have now been variously assembled by successive editors. Although it is pointless to speculate on what Pessoa might have done, one question should still be considered, as Pessoa perhaps never intended to publish *The Book of Disquiet* as a book. It is in that light that I prefer to refer to *The Book of Disquiet* not just as a nonbook (Pessoa, *Disquiet* [Penguin]; Zenith, *Pessoa: An Experimental Life*), nor as an antinovel (Ganeri, *Virtual Subjects*), but rather as an antibook, in which "the use of the absolute fragment as a mode of composing enables the formulation of an anti-systemic way of thinking" (Medeiros, *Pessoa's Geometry* 93).

The form of *The Book of Disquiet* is one of the key elements for discerning how important Pessoa's work is in the context of modernism and beyond. The "book" is an assemblage of a multitude of widely disparate "parts" written across a long span of time, possibly from as far back as 1913 to 1934. As such, the themes, the images, and even the choice of language necessarily reflect different phases of Pessoa's writing, just as the "book" at one point had been assigned to one heteronym, Vicente Guedes, before Pessoa decided to replace him with his semi-heteronym, Bernardo Soares. Elsewhere I have had occasion to reflect on this, noting that "Pessoa settled for one signature only, even if one must still see those of Guedes and Pessoa himself as if under erasure, palimpsest-like." This is something I still subscribe to even though my next assertion, that "the *Book of Disquiet*, in contrast to so much of Pessoa's writing, does not depend on, nor does it contribute to, a multiplication of the Self," needs amplification if not correction. Indeed, I think that by settling on the figure of Soares, Pessoa engaged in a sustained kind of self-reflection that, even though not narcissistic, borders on the entropic. In any case, it is important to also emphasize how Pessoa rejects any return to a view of a unified Self, as "in the extreme fragmentation of the *Book of Disquiet* there is a consummate representation of a shattering of the Self into myriad splinters—the *Book of Disquiet* enacts a mirroring of the Self that is both true and false, inasmuch as Soares both is and is not a double of Pessoa. And it is a doubling that both lacks and exceeds that which it represents, indeed, exceeds it by virtue of its own lack" (Medeiros, *Pessoa's Geometry* 13).

Without entering into an extended discussion of the fragmentary nature of *The Book of Disquiet*, I still think that it should be remarked on as one of the most significant theoretical characteristics of this text. Indeed, in terms of teaching the text it can be seen as an important element to pair with—and help diffuse—the subject of heteronymy, which tends to overshadow most discussions on Pessoa and what makes him unique. This is not to say that the question of the multiplicity of selves Pessoa not only imagined but enacted and performed is not extremely important and should not be addressed as indeed a central one or, to follow Jonardon Ganeri, as an enigma, "the challenge to provide an analysis of the functions of the first person . . . and so of the phenomenology of self-consciousness" (*Virtual Subjects* 19). The way Pessoa uses the fragment form in *The Book of Disquiet* as well as his deployment of heteronyms can, and should, be seen then under the sign of excess. A logical conclusion, then, will be to regard excess as a constitutive feature of Pessoa's relationship to, and framing of, modernity. In that, he is in good company, of course; and yet Pessoa also again demarcates himself by the very intensity that drives his writing into a most relentless form of self-critique that, even though at times appearing to proceed dialectically, never actually finds resolution, synthesis, or peace. Or, as we read in one of the poems from 1930 signed by Pessoa, whose soul was certainly always open to plurality, "Quem tem alma não tem calma" ("Who has a Soul does not have rest"; *Novas poesias* 48).

The Book of Disquiet is one of the best texts with which to teach what is meant by modernism as a period and by modernity as a condition—not only because it shares many of the defining features of modernism as we have come to know them through the works of writers such as Virginia Woolf, Ezra Pound, James Joyce, Thomas Mann, and the already mentioned Kafka, Benjamin, and Proust, as well as a score of others, but because it does so posthumously. Most obviously, what I mean by referring to *The Book of Disquiet* has to do with an accident of late publication as well as a protected dissemination and circulation in translation. Yet to see *The Book of Disquiet* as a posthumous text is also to see it as a text that was ahead of its time in many ways. Indeed, if one wants, one may even use the text to test our understanding of the postmodern as a movement or period that is inextricably linked with—and continues but also challenges our set of expectations drawn from—modernism. The fragment as the privileged form through which Pessoa chose to construct *The Book of Disquiet* is not new, of course. However, whereas often all that survives of a work are scattered fragments, in Pessoa's case, much more is at work and at stake. It is true that no one can know what Pessoa might or might not have done had he lived longer—and we only need remind ourselves of Kafka, his destruction of a number of originals, and his last request to his friend and editor Max Brod to burn all his unpublished and mostly incomplete texts to realize that Pessoa might likewise have destroyed the myriad texts he left unpublished. Instead, Pessoa preserved not only all those fragments that are clearly of a more transient nature, often written on the odd bit or other of paper, but also many fragments that are complete texts in themselves while remaining overall still fragmentary in relation to an imagined whole: *The Book of Disquiet*, which in itself was not, nor perhaps could ever be, a totality, except perhaps in Pessoa's imagination or in our own contemporary, that is, posthumous, reading.

This is how Fredric Jameson reasoned when considering the question "Joyce or Proust?" in his *Modernist Papers*, invoking Samuel Taylor Coleridge and his emphasis on the imagination: "Coleridge's great distinction takes on the metaphysical proportions of a vision of the world's gap, between an absent totality and a meaningless contingency, or between form and content, or spirit and matter . . ." (172). Had Jameson drawn on Pessoa, he might have taken this one step further. As much as I share (what I take to be) Jameson's frustration concerning the indefensibleness of the canon (any canon, but certainly the modernist canon) that goes hand in hand with our apparent need to rely on it—"Canonical questions are as contradictory for modernism as they are unavoidable" (Jameson, *Singular Modernity* 170)—I would like to suggest that Pessoa, and *The Book of Disquiet* most certainly, may offer a way out. And to do so I would invoke not so much Coleridge but Friedrich Schlegel and his conceptualization of the absolute fragment in the often-cited fragment 206 of the *Atheneaum* and its famous comparison of the fragment to a hedgehog, complete in itself ("in sich selbst vollendet . . . wie ein Igel"; *Kritische Friedrich-Schlegel-Ausgabe* 197). In this I am following Irene Ramalho-Santos and Carla Gago, who proposed and developed a link between Pessoa's use of the fragment and Schlegel's (Ramalho-Santos, *Atlantic Poets* and "Tail"; Gago, "Interstícios"). Besides its obvious importance to a proper understanding of the theoretical importance of *The Book of Disquiet*, this perspective also opens up various avenues in terms of teaching. On the one hand, the notion of interstice is useful to students with a background or interest in questions of literary theory and history as well for those hailing from philosophy departments. On the other hand, it becomes vital as a way of problematizing received notions about periodization in general and the troubled relationship between modernism and postmodernism. Indeed, one way of understanding the posthumous quality of *The Book of Disquiet* might be to discern to what extent it is not only a major exponent of modernism (in spite of its late dissemination) but also in many ways a work that adumbrates postmodernism in its radical writing strategies. With its dependence upon, and emphasis on, the impossibility of separating the world of dreams from reality, to imagine the self as anything other than an infinite multiplication and an infinite performance, even in its use of the notion of the simulacrum as inexorably linked to that of the fragment (Medeiros, *Pessoa's Geometry*), *The Book of Disquiet* clearly anticipates key postmodern positions.

In the undergraduate senior seminar for students majoring in philosophy and literature, the students, a colleague from philosophy, and I read a series of paired texts, one of which was always more closely linked to a philosophical tradition and the other to a literary tradition. To go with *The Book of Disquiet* we chose Benjamin's *Illuminations*, with a special emphasis on his essay "The Work of Art in the Age of Its Technical Reproducibility" (217–52). The structure of the seminar naturally steered the discussions along several weeks to a coherent cluster of topics that tried to blend a focus on aesthetics with one on politics and was anchored on a discussion of the vexed question of modernity even more than on that of modernism. In this regard, a text that I had occasion several times to refer to was Fredric Jameson's influential work *A Singular Modernity*. His argument for a view of modernity as singular, fraught with what Trotsky identified as a "combined and unequal development," is crucial, I think, to an ability to see *The Book of Disquiet* as a key text in world literature. In this I follow the position defined by the Warwick Research Collective, which offers two related advantages. First, invoking the concept of a "singular" modernity allows us to view the inclusion of Pessoa—rather than as a gracious acknowledgment by the center of a bit of the exotic periphery or a recognition of the necessary belatedness of some literatures—as a full-fledged part of the system called world literature (Medeiros, "Fernando Pessoa"). Second, it allows us to start grasping, on a conceptual level, rather than just on an emotional level, what it means to view Pessoa as a contemporary.

Before returning to the issue of the contemporary and developing it further, I want to introduce a separate, though related, set of questions. Reading *The Book of Disquiet* now, in the third decade of the twenty-first century, is not the same as reading it either when it was written (a few fragments had been published in

Pessoa's lifetime, though without in any way explicitly constituting parts of the book to come) or even in the eighties, when it was first published. In a sense, our distance from those times may even be what allows us to recognize the importance of *The Book of Disquiet* to a reconceptualization of our image of Pessoa as a poet or of his place in the literary system. We can—and should, of course—avail ourselves of whatever historical information we have in order to properly contextualize our reading. The critical edition prepared by Jerónimo Pizarro (*Desasocego*) reveals the extensive amount of research that went into the manuscripts in the archive, including the employment of various tools to aid in the dating of the individual pieces of paper as well as the methodologies behind genetic criticism, in order to render a text as accurate as possible. The ease of access to digitized documents today makes such accounts all the more informative for students while also revealing how some questions will have to remain without answer.

Our seminar also explored the framing of the text beyond its existence as writing. Artists in all media and from all over the world have either incorporated some aspects of Pessoa and of *The Book of Disquiet* in their work or have sought to create new versions of the book in their own chosen media. During the seminar we focused mostly on photography, taking advantage of my colleague's specialization and my own interest as well as the fact that both Benjamin and Pessoa—though in different registers and drawing unequal critical attention—wrote on photography. Given the present's focus on visuality, and the explosion of the interest in photography with the advent of the digital age and the incorporation of cameras in mobile phones, this is an especially fruitful area to explore with students, drawing upon, for example, the work of Maria José de Lancastre. A focus on photography is also important in exploring further questions of modernity. In reading Pessoa with Benjamin, it is useful to read against the grain—that is, rather than reading Pessoa through a Benjaminian lens, we can read Benjamin with a perspective informed by *The Book of Disquiet*. Take the question of the aura, certainly one of the most celebrated, if polemic, ideas in Benjamin's conceptualization of the work of art in modernity. Pessoa also reflects on the question of the "originality" of the work of art and on our desire to hold photography as a true representation of reality. Yet his, or, rather, Soares's, perspective is devoid of any form of nostalgia for some lost and irretrievable past. In that, Pessoa may be even more modern than either Benjamin or Proust, as nostalgia in *The Book of Disquiet* is never anything more than a performance that gets enacted, a mask that is donned so as to play to the expectations of the world but is always pulled off to let readers see the trappings of the performance brought on by memory and the pretense of remembrance.

Another area that must be mentioned and that offers distinct challenges is cinema. Critical attention to Pessoa and film has been relatively scarce, and opinions on Pessoa's own interest in film are more divided than consensual. To some, Pessoa was concerned most of all with the written word, and his scant involvement with cinema must be seen in the context of his interest in theater (Matos

Frias). Conversely, I see Pessoa's interest in film as yet another expression of his fascination with the visual as well as his resolute problematization of traditional notions of self (Medeiros, *Pessoa's Geometry*). Arguably, the most relevant way of approaching the question of the relations between *The Book of Disquiet* and film resides not so much in an exploration, however important, of direct textual references to film or of Pessoa's own attempts at writing for the cinema (Pessoa, *Argumentos para filmes*) but on an examination of how *The Book of Disquiet* has been taken up in film.

Wim Wenders, for instance, in *Lisbon Story* not only lifts passages from *The Book of Disquiet* and uses them as mysterious (exotic) aphorisms but even offers a kind of Pessoa double, walking through the same streets of the Chiado area of Lisbon that Pessoa also used to walk. Even if that film's relation to Pessoa is somewhat residual, it opens up many possible lines of inquiry into Pessoa given Wenders's preoccupation with seeing, with the ontology of vision, and with the troubled relationship between the past and the present (Medeiros, "Tal como Lisboa"). Ultimately, however, even though it is an important film in Wenders's portfolio and perhaps in the history of film, and in spite of Wenders's sincere and deep involvement with Portugal, Lisbon, and Portuguese artists, it fails to go beyond a co-optation of Pessoa that redoubles the notion of a mythical, quaint, and ghostlike figure from a longed-for but irretrievable past. Much the same could be said about a more recent and also celebrated film, *Night Train to Lisbon*, an adaptation of the novel *Nachtzug nach Lissabon* (Mercier), directed by Bille August and featuring a star-studded cast, including Jeremy Irons and Bruno Ganz. Whereas Wenders's film may appear somewhat puzzling to a general audience, August's film, which tries to preserve the literary feel of the original novel and leans on the writing contained in a mysterious Portuguese book, will much more easily appeal to the public. That mysterious book is modeled to a great extent, I would suggest, on *The Book of Disquiet*, something that might have lent itself to some very interesting experiments in terms of film as a medium. Yet, more so than was already the case with Wenders, this film also ends up appropriating the image of a highly introspective writer as a simple, if effective, means of creating an air of mystery and exoticism where again Portugal plays the role of an idealized periphery to the central European mind.

A completely different option is given us by João Botelho's *Filme do Desassossego*, the title already indicating that is not an adaptation of Pessoa's book but a new, and necessarily different, version of it.

> Imagine the *Book of Disquiet* as film. Not as a reference in a film, or as part of an exploration of Pessoa's life and oeuvre, but the text itself rendered as a film. . . . [Botelho's film] transposes Pessoa's work into another medium and, even though language remains extremely important, with whole, extensive fragments quoted in full, what makes this an important film is its transposition into filmic language of some of the premises of the *Book of Disquiet*.   (Medeiros, *Pessoa's Geometry* 69)

As I have had opportunity to argue, Botelho's film can be seen as an enactment of Jacques Derrida's notion of film as always already spectral. Rather than just drawing on the often-cited mythical allure of Pessoa as "the man who never was," or, as Octavio Paz once put it, as the "taciturn ghost of the Portuguese mid-day" ("taciturno fantasma del mediodía portugués"; my trans.; "El desconocido de sí mismo" [*Revista*]), Botelho manages to produce a specular, haunting version of *Disquiet* that instead of substituting for the text, or simply affecting to reproduce it, transfers it into another medium and as such veritably enacts a further performance of the text and not just of the (freely rudimentary at best) plot. Or, to put it in yet another way, Botelho has managed, as perhaps few readers of Pessoa have done, to follow Badiou's injunction to be Pessoa's contemporary.

Each succeeding age will have to come to terms with Pessoa's contemporaneity, which is also to say, with the way in which, though being very much a man of his time, Pessoa was also untimely in a Nietzschean sense. As a way of bringing these brief notes to a conclusion, I wish to suggest two possible ways for reading *The Book of Disquiet* in the present. One, already indicated by Badiou, refers to the way in which Pessoa, in all of his work, but even more so in *The Book of Disquiet*, radically disrupts the established categories on which we depend in order to make some sense of the world. As Badiou puts it:

> If Pessoa represents a singular challenge for philosophy, if his modernity is still ahead of us, remaining in many respects unexplored, it is because *his thought-poem inaugurates a path that manages to be neither Platonic nor anti-Platonic*. Pessoa poetically defines a site for thinking that is truly subtracted from the unanimous slogan of the overturning of Platonism. To this day, philosophy has yet to comprehend the full extent of this gesture.
> (Badiou, *Handbook* 38)

Giorgio Agamben offers another way with his reflection on the meaning of *contemporary*: "The contemporary is he who firmly holds his gaze on his own time so as to perceive not its light, but rather its darkness" (44). Pessoa was certainly not unique in his ability to see through the obfuscating appearance of radiance promised by modernity, but he was as lucid as possible when he diagnosed his generation as one marked by loss: "Pertenço a uma geração que herdou a descrença no facto christão e que creou em si uma descrença em todas as outras fés ("I belong to a generation that inherited a disbelief in the Christian faith and that created within itself a disbelief in all other faiths" (*Desasocego* 142; *Disquiet* 142).[1] He can be even more precise, noting how, of course, within each generation there are still many, often profound, differences: "Pertenço a uma geração—ou antes a uma parte de geração—que perdeu todo o respeito pelo passado e toda a crença ou esperança no futuro. Vivemos porisso do presente com a gana e a fome de quem não tem outra casa" ("I belong to a generation—or, rather, to part of a generation—that has lost all respect for the past and all belief or hope in the future. This is why we live in the present with the desperate hunger of someone who has no other home"; *Desasocego* 91; *Disquiet* 104).

These are not the words of a nihilist. Pessoa's ability to avoid being blinded by the light of his time and see through to the darkness might have made him melancholic as opposed to nostalgic, but he was never defeatist. For all its insistence on inaction and its excessive forms of introspection, *The Book of Disquiet* is more a manual for resistance than an affidavit of surrender. Pessoa (Soares) cannot be said to work systematically, and *The Book of Disquiet*, in its fragmentariness, openness, and call for an infinite form of writing, is paradigmatically antisystemic (Medeiros, *Pessoa's Geometry* and *O silêncio*; Ornellas). It also would be wrong, though not completely, to see him as a materialist (after all, Soares never ceases to affirm the primacy of the sensations for reaching knowledge, so that, in an important sense, epistemology is always already somatic). Pessoa might not proceed dialectically, yet his thought, at least as expressed through Soares in *The Book of Disquiet*, can be said to approach the dialectic, not as a kind of argumentation but much more in the sense of a negative dialectic. Without any pretensions (or illusions?) of linking Pessoa with Theodor Adorno, there are still striking points of convergence. This, for instance, is how Adorno opens his *Negative Dialektik*:

> Die Formulierung Negative Dialektik verstößt gegen die Überlieferung. Dialektik will bereits bei Platon, daß durchs Denkmittel der Negation ein Positives sich herstelle; die Figur einer Negation der Negation benannte das später prägnant. Das Buch möchte Dialektik von derlei affirmativem Wesen befreien, ohne an Bestimmtheit etwas nachzulassen. Die Entfaltung seines paradoxen Titels ist eine seiner Absichten.   (9)

> Negative Dialectics is a phrase that flouts tradition. As early as Plato, dialectics meant to achieve something positive by means of negation; the thought figure of a "negation of negation" later became the succinct term. This book seeks to free dialectics from such affirmative traits without reducing its determinacy. The unfoldment of the paradoxical title is one of its aims.   (*Negative Dialectics* xix)

For both Adorno and Pessoa, paradox was not a logical dead end but rather a necessary response to the world.

Soares, and with him Pessoa, never abdicated from life, insisting instead on the power of dreams to create and to give rise to an alternative reality, perhaps more real than what normally goes by that name. *The Book of Disquiet* borders on the utopic: "Sem illusões, vivemos apenas do sonho, que é a illusão de quem não pode ter illusões" ("Bereft of illusions, we live on dreams, which are the illusions of those who cannot have illusions"; *Desasocego* 142; *Disquiet* 143). Inaction of course can easily be construed or misconstrued as resignation, abandonment, or capitulation. Pessoa (and Soares) constantly walk this fine line as if intent not so much on surveying it as on exploding the very boundaries the line signals. Another closely related passage from *The Book of Disquiet* reads thus:

> Quanto mais contemplo o spectaculo do mundo, e o fluxo e refluxo da mutação das cousas, mais profundamente me compenetro da ficção ingenita de tudo, do prestigio falso /da pompa/ de todas as realidades. E nesta contemplação, que a todos, que reflectem, uma ou outra vez terá succedido, a marcha multicolor dos costumes e das modas, o caminho complexo dos progressos e das civilizações, a confusão grandiosa dos imperios e das culturas—tudo isso me aparece como um mytho e uma ficção, sonhado entre sombras e desmoronamentos.   (*Desasocego* 143)

> The more I contemplate the spectacle of the world and the ebb and flow of change in things, the more deeply am I convinced of the innately fictitious nature of it all, of the false prestige given to the pomp of reality. And in this contemplation, which any reflective person will have experienced at some time or other, the motley parade of costumes and fashions, the complex path of progress and civilizations, the magnificent tangle of empires and cultures, all seem to me like a myth and a fiction, dreamed up amidst shadows and oblivion.   (*Disquiet* 144)

That, I would argue, is not giving up on life but rather seeing its darkness. And in that seeing lies a whole lesson in resistance.

NOTE

1. The English translation cited in this essay is the most recent one by Margaret Jull Costa in *The Book of Disquiet* (New Directions), with occasional slight alterations when needed to stay closer to the original.

The Problem of Genre in *The Book of Disquiet*

Bernat Padró Nieto

Much has been written about the oddness of *The Book of Disquiet*. Indeed, it is a unique work and difficult to classify. Written over more than twenty years and unpublished for almost half a century after its author's death, it is the editorial result of a selection and combination of fragments that Fernando Pessoa kept in various stages of production. A few were published in the press during his lifetime, whereas others are not much more than mere notes or drafts. The National Library of Portugal has catalogued some 1,445 facsimiles as parts or possible parts of the project of *Desassossego* and, of these, 390 contain explicit references to the *Livro* (Giménez 276). There is no indisputable evidence of the order they should take, and specialists are divided over the matter of their inclusion in the whole. There are as many versions of *Disquiet* as there are editors, no two versions with the same number of fragments, and neither is there any agreement regarding the heteronymic authorship. Hence, "hoje temos menos um livro do que diversas incarnações editoriais" ("Today we have not so much a book as different editorial incarnations"; Pizarro, "Ansiedade" 290), and its history is the history of its editors and its editions (Sáez Delgado 10).[1] Its writing, moreover, seems to defy all known genre forms. In his review of the first edition in English, George Steiner wondered, "What is this *Livro do Desassossego*? Neither 'commonplace book,' nor 'sketchbook,' nor 'florilegium' will do. Imagine a fusion of Coleridge's notebooks and marginalia, of Valery's philosophic diary and of Robert Musil's voluminous journal. Yet even such a hybrid does not correspond to the singularity of Pessoa's chronicle" ("Man").

We might fall into the temptation of seeing in *Disquiet* confirmation of Benedetto Croce's thesis postulating that great works are either devoid of genre or constitute a genre in themselves. Throughout history, artists have tended to disobey the laws of genre:

> While making a verbal pretence of agreeing, or yielding a feigned obedience, artists have, however, really always disregarded these *laws of the kinds*. Every true work of art has violated some established kind and upset the ideas of the critics, who have thus been obligated to broaden the kinds until finally even the broadened kind has proved too narrow, owing to the appearance of new works of art, naturally followed by new scandals, new upsettings and—new broadenings. (37)

So should we forget, then, about the genre dimension of *Disquiet*? Is there such a thing as works without genre? Quite the opposite. Even in such an extreme case, we would always be left with the option of proposing a class of works of no genre, not to mention the distinction between literary and nonliterary works, which also requires a classificatory criterion. *Disquiet*'s particularity does not prevent one from seeing in it a certain "family air," as Wittgenstein might say (32), vis-à-vis other texts. It is often compared with works like Giacomo Leopardi's *Zibaldone*, Henri-Frédéric Amiel's *Journal Intime*, or Friedrich Schlegel's *Philosophical Fragments*. Others point out its resemblance to an autobiography without a life trajectory, or to a diary without a calendar, or to a novel without vicissitudes. Its fragments have been compared with essays and prose poems. Why, then, this obsession with highlighting these possible resemblances in *Disquiet*? The answer is clear-cut: the genre dimension of a work is one of the aspects of its intelligibility. The elusive nature of Pessoa's masterpiece, which both claims and rejects classification, is what makes it a privileged object for theoretical reflection on literary genres.

Dialectics of the Genre Law and Its Transgression

David Jackson has suggested that all of Pessoa's writing shows what he calls "adverse genres," a literary game flying in the face of formal conventions (15). Transgression against traditional genres is a core phenomenon in the poetics of modernism. The self-referentiality one finds in many works is due to resistance to adopting external, preexisting criteria, as is the case of genres. Accordingly, "[these] works are increasingly unclassifiable, and begin to resist the commercial categories of the genres in the effort to distinguish themselves from commodity forms at the same time that they invent various mythic and ideological claims for some unique formal status which has no social cognition or acknowledgement" (Jameson, *Singular Modernity* 159). Nonetheless, as Maurice Blanchot admitted, the law of genre is paradoxically manifested when it is transgressed:

> [Literature] might be developed, not by engendering monsters, shapeless works, without law and without rigor, but uniquely by provoking exceptions to itself: which form a law and at the same time suppress it. . . . We must rather think that, each time, in these exceptional works in which a limit is reached, it is the exception alone that reveals to us this "law" from which it also constitutes the unusual and necessary deviation. It seems then, in novelistic literature, and perhaps in all literature, that we could never recognize the rule except by the exception that abolishes it.
> (*Book* 109)

To the extent that the identity of the genre depends on complying with a norm, where the norm is the potentially transgressible limit, the logic of genre is played out in the dialectics of affirmation and negation of this norm enshrined as law. According to Jacques Derrida, the law of genre simultaneously poses an identity and a repetition because genre is only manifested by the proliferation of works that in turn affirm an identity with regard to genre and difference among them. Derrida then wonders if there might not be at the heart of the law of genre a principle of contamination and if "the condition for the possibility of the law were the *a priori* of a counter-law, an axiom of impossibility that would confound its sense, order and reason?" ("Law" 222). Nevertheless, whether every transgression confirms the rule, or whether there is a counterlaw principle existing in every law, the point is that genres are a social reality, they function as literary institutions, and every institution is a coordinate that as such has a guiding purpose. What, then, are the genres that *Disquiet* affirms and transgresses, those with which it shares a family air and that permit its intelligibility as a work, as literature,[2] and as an exceptional case?

The Book of Disquiet *before the Three Traditional Genres*

If we ask ourselves about the literary genres employed by Pessoa, the usual response would be lyric, narrative—short stories like "O banqueiro anarquista" ("The Anarchist Banker")—and theater, where his static drama *O marinheiro* (*The Mariner*) stands out. We might add a host of different kinds of texts, ranging from journalistic articles and pamphlets to studies in aesthetics, politics, religion, and other matters unquestionably of interest to specialists but of debatable literary status. What is beyond doubt, however, is that *Disquiet* comes under the heading of great literature although it cannot be assimilated into any of the three main genres. In spite of this, there is still a temptation to seek similarities with the genres of the triad—drama, narrative, and lyric—because of their authority as guarantees of literarity.[3] From the standpoint of reception, might it not be argued that its fragments are akin to prose poems, as suggested by Adelto Gonçalves and by Raúl Romero and René P. Garay? Does it not tell the minimal story of a man without attributes, along the lines of the modernist tendency to reduce the novelistic peripeteia, as Antonio Tabucchi, Thomas J. Cousineau, and Jackson maintain?[4] Or perhaps we are pondering a dramatic unfolding instead, as Lopes postulates? Affinities with the traditional genres seem to be raised in the work itself too, by virtue of the modernist self-referentiality I mentioned above. One reads in *Disquiet*: "Um romance é uma historia do que nunca foi, e um drama é um romance dado sem narrativa. Um poema é a expressão de idéas ou de sentimentos em linguagem que ninguem emprega, poisque ninguem falla em verso" ("A novel is a history of what never was, and a play is a novel without narrative. A poem is the expression of ideas or feelings in a language no one uses, since no one speaks in verse"; *Desassossego* 489; *Disquiet* 436).[5] And it is not unusual to find the enunciative voice interpreted in a generic key: "Sou uma figura de romance por escrever" ("I'm a character in a novel as yet unwritten"; *Desassossego* 417; *Disquiet* 367) and "Sou bocados de personagens de dramas meus" ("I am bits of characters from my own dramas"; *Desassossego* 99; *Disquiet* 60).

As we shall see, whether by affirmation or transgression, the three traditional genres constitute one of the main keys to a generic reading of *Disquiet*. Why so much insistence on thinking about such a particular work in this key? Because tradition has established that literature is indisputably constituted by lyric, drama, and narrative in their different subgenres, to the point of their coming to be conceived of as natural. Nevertheless, this is a modern point of view. Aristotle, the first theorist of literary genres, did not take lyric into account, because in his view it was not an imitative genre. According to Jean-Marie Schaeffer, the central problem of the theory of genres is the need for a prior distinction between literary and nonliterary language (*Qu'est-ce* 8–10). As the material—language—is the same in both cases, a specific criterion of distinction must be introduced. Aristotle opted for mimesis or fiction as the differentiating feature. Deemed to be a nonmimetic expression, lyric remained excluded from the realm of poetry, the name given, until about the eighteenth century, to what we now call literature (R. Williams 46; Widdowson 31–33). Nevertheless, the Renaissance and Romanticism claimed the poetic status of forms like the ode, the elegy, and the sonnet, which then came to form a third genre alongside the two great imitative genres—tragedy and the epic poem—under the joint heading of lyric poetry. The French theorist Gérard Genette explains that there were only two ways to promote its poetic dignity: "The first one is to uphold, while somewhat expanding, the classical dogma of *mimesis* and strive to show that that type of statement is still, in its own fashion, an 'imitation.' The second and more radical way is to break with the dogma and proclaim the equal poetic dignity of a nonrepresentational utterance" (*Architext* 28). In the first case, the imitative dimension of lyric expression is upheld. If the monologue of an epic or tragic character can express emotions that are clearly fictitious, since there is no person behind them, why is an analogous imitation not possible in poetry? In the second case, the dignity of lyrical forms is claimed in the name of the romantic theory of disinterested beauty and the autotelism of art. Although they are theoretically mutually excluding, these two structural definitions of literature, as Todorov calls them, have coexisted ever since and have been linked together. This brief historical overview has served, first, to criticize the naturalization of the three traditional genres and, second, to identify fiction as the dominant criterion in any definition of literature. It is not possible to understand the genre-based ascriptions to which *Disquiet* is submitted without taking the triad's historical authority into account.

Dignifying a Misty Literature

As I have said, Pessoa worked with the three great genres but also with many others of less clearly defined literary status. In a letter to Mário Beirão dated 1 February 1913, he confessed that he was writing "versos ingleses, portugueses, raciocínios, temas, projectos, fragmentos de coisas que não sei o que são, cartas que não sei como começam ou acabam, relâmpagos de críticas, murmúrios de metafísicas. . . . Toda uma literatura, meu caro Mário, que vai da bruma—para a bruma—pela bruma" ("English verses, Portuguese verses, reasonings, themes, projects, fragments of things that I don't know what they are, letters that I don't know how they begin or end, flashes of criticism, murmurs of metaphysics. . . . An entire literature, my dear Mário, which comes from the mist—to the mist— through the mist"; *Correspondência 1905–1922* 79). We could conjecture that many of these "fragments of things" would end up forming part of some editions of *Disquiet*. As Jerónimo Pizarro notes, from its first posthumous appearance, the book suffered an inflation that meant it swallowed up a good part of Pessoa's writings that did not fit into the traditional genres: "A partir da década de 1990, o *Livro do Desasocego* tornou-se uma espécie de arca em que foram sendo 'depositados' novos escritos; era 'O Grande Livro', e tudo o que Pessoa escreveu . . . parecia ter cabimento nessas páginas" ("After the 1990s, *Livro do Desasocego* became a kind of trunk in which new writings were 'deposited'; it was 'The Great Book,' and everything that Pessoa wrote . . . seemed to fit into those pages"; "Apresentação" 7). Hence, dignifying the misty literature of *Disquiet* cannot be alien to attempts to add a fourth category to the triadic system, one that is able to find space for "didactic genres" (following Diomedes), "argumentative genres" (following ancient rhetoric), or the so-called "literatures of the self" that have been upheld since the end of the Second World War. It would not be nonsensical to place *Disquiet* alongside genres with some kind of family air, like autobiography, confession, essay, the diary, or the epistle, although its elusive nature always ends up transgressing their genre laws. The problem with establishing a fourth category is usually the miscellaneous nature of its results and the internal division with regard to its literarity, since not all didactic and argumentative genres would easily be subsumed into literature. Nevertheless, this instability is the consequence of extending the sphere of literarity, which occurred with the weakening of classical poetry and rhetoric and the emergence of style as a literary criterion. And the fluctuation of the limits of literature clashes with the stability of the traditional genres.

Two interesting proposals would allow the inclusion of Pessoa's misty literature in the sphere of literary genres. The first is "the *conditionalist* theory of literariness" proposed by Gérard Genette in *Fiction and Diction* (5). According to Genette, there are two criteria and two regimes of literarity. The criteria are fiction and diction. In the Aristotelian tradition, all mimetic representation— all fiction—is literature. This tradition is complemented by romantic poetics, which identifies style and formal beauty—diction—as another criterion of literarity. The two regimes upheld by Genette are the constitutive, which determines what text is literary, and the conditional, which asks when a text is literary. The constitutive regime consolidates the traditional genres: drama and narrative, which are fiction, and lyric, which is diction. Genette's proposal is that this constitutive regime should be complemented by a conditional regime that allows, in certain circumstances, consideration as literature of all writing of a style that does not correspond with the three great genres—"diction in prose." In terms of this proposal, *Disquiet* could conditionally be included in the broad genre of diction in prose.

The second proposal entails a complete reshaping of the whole system. In *The Logic of Literature*, Käte Hamburger discusses the Aristotelian principles from a phenomenological perspective and suggests that distinguishing between the classes of discourse should be done on the basis of the relationship between the subject of enunciation—which she calls the I-origin—and the enunciated. According to Hamburger, we have three kinds of discourse. On the one hand, there are the nonliterary ones, in which the I-origin is real, and on the other, we find fictitious discourses, in which the subject of the enunciation is simulated, as in the cases of narrative and drama. Lyric, as might be imagined, once again presents problems: it is not a fictional discourse, yet it constitutes an undeniable part of literary art. Hamburger, however, inscribes lyric in a third group of discourses, together with literatures of the self, which she calls existential. In Hamburger's view, existential discourses are those that present a real I-origin but whose enunciate does not deal with the world but rather retreats back into the subject of the enunciation, which becomes the core theme of the enunciate. In this, they differ from nonfictional discourses. They have no utilitarian purpose and do not seek any function in reality but concentrate on one's own subjectivity. It would seem that *Disquiet* has found a place as a genre here, alongside both lyric and the so-called literatures of the self, because there is no doubt that its main theme is the problematic status of the subject. Taking a fragment of the work almost randomly from among many similar ones, we read, "Que ha em tudo isto senão eu? Ah, mas o tedio é isso, é só isso. É que em tudo isto—céu, terra, mundo,—o que ha em tudo isto não é senão eu!" ("What is there in all this but myself? Ah, but in that and only that lies tedium. It's the fact that in all this— sky, earth, world—there is never anything but myself"; *Desassossego* 476; *Disquiet* 424). If one accepts Hamburger's thesis, Pessoa's work as a whole is inscribed mainly in the existential genres, leaving for the fictional genre just a few short stories and his incursions into theater.

As we can see, Genette's and Hamburger's approaches suggest ways of thinking about literary genres beyond the Aristotelian distinction between literary art and the other verbal discourses. Inscribing *Disquiet* in a conditional poetics or an existential genre functions as long as we consider that the work is not fictional. But what happens when we are confronted with the fact that fragments of the work describe actions that never occurred, supposedly experienced by a subject of the fictitious enunciation?

The Dilemma of Fiction: Between the Lyric and the Autobiographical Self

The question about the degree of fictionalization of the subject in the phenomenon of heteronymism[6] has consequences in attributing a genre to *Disquiet*. David Jackson takes this further by suggesting that heteronymism results from Pessoa's experimentation with genre: "Stylistic alteration preceded and propitiated his 'trunk full of people,'" in such a way that "the rewriting and rethinking of Western literary traditions in the work of Fernando Pessoa involves the question of genre as much as it does that of personality and authorship. The 'drama of persons,' the theme that has dominated critical readings, extends as well to a 'drama of genres'" (15). It is therefore essential to focus on the status of the instance of enunciation in relation to the different existential genres that, following Hamburger, we might associate with *Disquiet*, from poetic prose to literatures of the self. One of the work's many self-referential moments would seem to confirm this multiple ascription. In it, a corpus with which the work is related is evoked: "Em Pascal: ◊ Em Vigny: Em ti ◊ Em Amiel, tão completamente em Amiel: ◊ . . . (outras frases) . . . Em Verlaine, nos simbolistas, ◊ Tanto doente como eu . . . Nem o privilegio de uma pequena originalidade de doença . . . Faço o que tantos antes de mim fizeram . . ." ("In Pascal: . . . In Vigny: In you . . . In Amiel, so completely in Amiel: . . . In Verlaine, and the symbolists . . . All of them as sick as me . . . I do not even have the privilege of even a hint of originality in my sickness . . . I do what so many others before me did"; *Desassossego* 94–95; *Disquiet* 56).[7]

Critics have seen a family air among fragments of the work and the prose poem of the symbolist tradition (Gonçalves; Romero and Garay). There is no lack of arguments for this thesis, especially regarding the writings from between 1913 and 1920 that were originally attributed to Vicente Guedes and are identified in the Pizarro edition as the first phase of the book. This is a corpus of an aestheticist tone, full of symbolist commonplaces. The proximity between lyric and prose would be confirmed by the mention in the author's notes for any future editions of poems that Pessoa had previously planned to include in *Disquiet* and that did, in fact, appear in the first edition of 1982 (Pessoa, *Desassossego* 465; *Disquiet* 426–27). Needless to say, the irruption of poetic prose occurred in a turn-of-the-century context as resistance to the automatization of versified lyric. Indeed, Pessoa himself came to consider it as the third evolutionary stage of Western poetry in his preface to Luís Pedro's book *Acrónios*. According to this text, after a first, quantitative stage of Greco-Latin poetry and a second, syllabic stage based on verse, accentuation, and rhyme, a rhythmic stage was reached in which "se reduz a poesia, tamsòmente, a uma prosa com pausas artificiaes, isto é, independentes das que são naturaes em todo discurso e nelle se indican pela pontuação" ("poetry is reduced to mere prose with artificial pauses, which is to say, independently of those that are natural in all discourse and indicated by punctuation"; Pessoa, "Prefacio" 5). This idea has its correlate in *Disquiet*, where an excess of formal constriction of versified lyric is lamented and poetic prose is advocated:

> Como a música, o verso é limitado por leis rítmicas, que, ainda que não sejam as leis rígidas do verso regular, existem todavia como resguardos, coacções, dispositivos automáticos de opressão e castigo. Na prosa falamos

livres. Podemos incluir ritmos musicais, e contudo pensar. Podemos incluir ritmos poéticos, e contudo estar fóra dêlles. Um ritmo ocasional de verso não estorva a prosa; um ritmo ocasional de prosa faz tropeçar o verso.

(Pessoa, *Desassossego* 397)

Like music, poetry is bound by rhythmic rules, which, although they are not the rigid rules of regular meter, do still exist as controls, constraints, automatic mechanisms of oppression and punishment. In prose we can speak freely. We can include musical rhythms and yet still think. We can include poetic rhythms and yet still exist outside them. An occasional poetic rhythm does not get in the way of prose, but an occasional prosaic rhythm can cause poetry to stumble.   (*Disquiet* 347–48)

But the relations between *Disquiet* and lyric go far beyond a desire for classification since they squarely situate us before the conundrum of the status of the subject of the enunciation, and this, as we have seen, is a problem that has pursued lyric since the origins of the theory of literary genres and has conditioned its literary legitimacy.

To understand the tensions between the lyrical subject and the empirical subject, we need to go back to the philosophical debates of the first third of the nineteenth century. In the processes whereby the German Romantics dignified lyric, the genre system fell into the domain of aesthetics. Poetry ceased to be a mere question of forms and themes to be understood in terms of the relationship between subjective and objective. According to this conception, lyric poetry was mainly considered subjective, dramatic poetry objective, and epic poetry objective-subjective. G. W. H. Hegel's *Aesthetics: Lectures on Fine Art* consolidated the subjective conception of lyric linked with the personal and intimate. The romantic view of lyric as an expression excluding fiction and presupposing the transparency of the subject has been enormously influential through to the present day. However, as Dominique Combe explains, another postulate coexisted with exaltation of the artist's ego, namely that of the poet's dissolution into the cosmic totality, an idea embraced by authors from Schelling to Novalis. This line was taken up by Friedrich Nietzsche in *The Birth of Tragedy from the Spirit of Music* in order to reinterpret the distribution of genres in the aesthetic opposition between the lyricism of Dionysian inebriety and the epic of Apollonian form. This new conception offered the possibility of conceiving a lyrical ego dissolved in the universal and thus overcoming the opposition between subjective and objective. In Combe's view, the encounter at the end of the nineteenth century between this theory of the Dionysian subjectivity of post-Romantic philosophy and the practice of depersonalization of symbolist poetry assured the diffusion of a "lyrical self" separate from the life of the poet. Recall the voluntary impersonality of Charles Baudelaire's poetry, Arthur Rimbaud's "I is another," and the poet's illocutionary disappearance in Mallarmé (Combe 44–45).

The phenomenon of heteronymism and thematization of the depersonalization of the self as practiced by Pessoa could be considered as the exacerbation
of this tradition.[8] Irene Ramalho-Santos connects this question with the Nietzschean gesture I have just mentioned (*Atlantic Poets* 13–14). Indeed, she goes
so far as to confirm the fictional status of the entire Pessoan enunciation: "the
poet's most complex fictional gesture of *self-objectivation*, that is to say, of *othering* himself . . . while keeping intact the fiction of the integral subject, or self-
same persona (Pessoa), as precisely what it is also: a fiction (or *objective mask*)"
(*Atlantic Poets* 2–3).[9] As we read in the *Ultimatum* manifesto, the notion that
we possess a personality separate from the others is described as "uma ficção
theologica" ("a theological fiction"; *Obra completa de Álvaro de Campos* [2014]
415; *Selected Prose* [2001] 218). Nevertheless, Santos situates both fictions in the
domain of lyric: "two major lyrical fictions—the author-as-work-as-one-and-self-
same, on the one hand, and the fragmentary nonauthor-as-other(s) (heteronyms),
on the other" (*Atlantic Poets* 3). The opposite option would also apply: an explanation of *Disquiet*, if not in an openly biographical key, at least as an expression of
the emotional and intellectual repercussions of a lived experience.[10] To this end,
one can invoke affirmations like those of Pessoa's famous letter of 13 January 1935
to Casais Monteiro, in which he says that Soares is "um semi-heteronymo porque, não sendo a personalidade minha, é, não differente da minha, mas uma
simples mutilação della" ("a semi-heteronym because even though he is not my
own personality, he is not so much different from myself as he is a mere distortion of that personality"; *Eu sou* 560; *Selected Prose* [2001] 573), or when
he inscribes the genesis of heteronymism in a psychiatric disorder. Yet,
whether we endow heteronymism with a fictional dimension or give credit to
its pathological origin, we are doing no more than going round and round the
problem of literary referentiality and the tension between literature and biography. The famous opening quartet of the poem "Autopsychography" offers a dialectical way out:

> O poeta é um fingidor
> Finge tão completamente
> Que chega a fingir que é dor
> A dor que deveras sente.   (*Poesia: Antologia mínima* 95)

> The poet is a faker
> Who's so good at his act
> He even fakes the pain
> Of pain he feels in fact.   (*A Little Larger* 314)

We find a theoretical exposition of this position in Karlheinz Stierle, for whom
the lyrical subject neither coincides with the empirical subject nor is merely fictional but, rather, is constituted as a problematic subject in search of its identity
and whose only authenticity resides in this search:

There is little interest in knowing whether this configuration originates in an autobiographical datum, whatever it might be, or in a fictional constellation. The authenticity of the lyrical subject resides not in its effective homologation (or vice versa) but in the articulated possibility of a problematic identity of the subject, reflected in the problematic identity of the discourse. (436)

Combe raises another possibility: "the lyrical subject is not opposed so much to the empirical subject, by definition outside literature and language, as it is to the autobiographical subject which is the literary expression of this empirical subject" (50). Without leaving the representational sphere, we have shifted the problem from one extreme to another of the existential genres, from lyric to writings of the self.

Indeed, the so-called literatures of the self tend to occupy a priority position in all genre identification of *Disquiet*. In Pizarro's words, the book "started off as a kind of postsymbolist diary influenced by conventional nineteenth-century diaries and confessions, but it ended up as the diary of a fictitious person" ("Editor's Note" xvii), while David Jackson suggests that "the accumulation of inner thoughts . . . places the 'Book' within the traditions of the philosophical diary, the novel of self-realization, or confessional memoirs, whether they be in biographical or fictional form" (163). References to the writing itself as autobiographical or as a diary—for example, "Este livro é a autobiographia de quem nunca existiu" ("This book is the autobiography of someone who never existed"; Pessoa, *Desassossego* 37; *Disquiet* 6), or "Parecerá a muitos que este meu diario, feito para mim, é artificial de mais" ("It will seem to many people that this diary of mine, written solely for myself, is too artificial"; *Desassossego* 148; *Disquiet* 106)—and the many appeals to memory and mentions of Amiel would seem to confirm that this set of forms constitutes the ideal model to which Pessoa tends, although it may be an object of transgression, or the end result may fail:

> Invejo—mas não sei se invejo—aquelles de quem se póde escrever uma biographia, ou que podem escrever a propria. Nestas impressões sem nexo, nem desejo de nexo, narro indifferentemente a minha autobiographia sem factos, a minha historia sem vida. São as minhas Confissões, e, se nellas nada digo, é que nada tenho que dizer. (*Desassossego* 283)

> I envy—although I'm not sure if envy is the right word—those people about whom one could write a biography, or who could write their autobiography. Through these deliberately unconnected impressions I am the indifferent narrator of my autobiography without events, of my history without a life. These are my Confessions and if I say nothing in them it's because I have nothing to say. (*Disquiet* 229)

The approaches to the genre specificity of autobiography—which would apply to the two different memoir and confessional genres—revolve around the status of the narrator. In his influential *Le pacte autobiographique*, Philippe Lejeune suggests a theory of narrative genres that does not depend on fictionality but on pragmatic agreement about what the text "does," founded not so much in literary tropes as in acts of speech. Autobiography derives its genre identity from a contract between author and reader, the "autobiographical pact" according to which the author promises the reader that the persons of narrator and character are one and the same as that of the empirical author. According to Lejeune's theory, the tension between literature and referent is not problematic. Paul de Man's position is the opposite, since he conceives of the representation of identity as an effect of a narrative convention that does not require the biographical reference. In the case of autobiography, the dominant rhetorical figure is prosopopoeia, which consists of

> the fiction of an apostrophe to an absent, deceased or voiceless entity, which posits the possibility of the latter's reply and confers upon it the power of speech. Voice assumes mouth, eye and finally face, a chain that is manifest in the etymology of the trope's name, *prosopon poien*, to confer a mask or a face (*prosopon*). Prosopopoeia is the trope of autobiography, by which one's name . . . is made as intelligible and memorable as a face. Our topic deals with the giving and taking away of faces, with face and deface, *figure*, figuration and disfiguration.   ("Autobiography" 926)

What de Man proposes is that there is no prenarrative, empirical, and referential self, for this is always the arbitrary result of the story of life. Hence, every autobiography consists of the creation of a voice for the person who does not have one, like a mask that hides what does not belong to the scene and has no form beyond that which the mask confers. Conscious of the rhetorical game of disfiguration of his writing, Pessoa—or any of his masks— asserts his nonexistence beyond writing: "Sou, em grande parte, a mesma prosa que escrevo. Desenrolo-me em periodos e paragraphos, faço-me pontuações, e, na distribuição desencadeada das imagens, visto-me, como as creanças, de rei com papel de jornal . . . Tornei-me uma figura de livro, uma vida lida" ("I am, for the most part, the very prose that I write. I shape myself in periods and paragraphs, I punctuate myself and, in the unleashed chain of images, I make myself king, as children do, with a crown made from a sheet of newspaper . . . I've become a character in a book, a life already read"; *Desassossego* 387; *Disquiet* 338). After this long inquiry into the Pessoan enunciation in terms of genre, going from the lyrical self to autobiographical prosopopoeia, one sees that *Disquiet* rejects Hamburger's distinction between fictional and existential literary genres and likewise refuses to come into literature though the back door as diction in prose, only conditionally literary, as Genette would have it.

The Book of Disquiet *as a Fragmentary Essay*

There is still one last genre assignment to examine. Paulo de Medeiros (*Pessoa's Geometry*) submits that heteronymism is not a decisive element in *Disquiet* and that its status as a masterpiece of Western modernism does not in any way depend on that. Yet disregarding heteronymism has consequences for genre. If we leave aside the problem of the fictional status of the enunciation and focus on formal, thematic, and epistemological questions, the essayistic dimension of the book is immediately manifested. An inclination for this option means either excluding *Disquiet* from the domain of literature or redefining the system of genres and the place the essay might occupy within it. When invoked as a fourth genre, the essay tends to be helpful in accommodating all literature that does not easily fit into the triad. Some writers even present the essay as the laboratory of all writing, the "matrix of all generic possibilities" (Bensmaïa 124), or as the result of a weakening of formal features: "a refuge for certain functions and certain effects after the weakening of the structure of recognized genres (a diary that loses its chronological composition, a letter that is no longer addressed, a treatise that relaxes its forms of argumentation)" (Macé 140). Both proposals seem tailor-made for genre designation of the whole potential corpus of *Disquiet*, from its most elaborated fragments to its draft versions.

Yet it is also legitimate to see in them a formal and epistemological intention relating them to the more radical aspects of the essay.[11] With this, I refer to writing that is heir to Michel de Montaigne, found in the reflective horizon of classic texts by Lukács ("On the Nature") and Adorno ("Essay as Form"), among others. These authors coincide in indicating that the essay challenges the separation, consolidated throughout the nineteenth century, between the aesthetic experience and the cognitive experience and that it does not bow before the requirements of art, the demands of science, or the stipulations of philosophy, hence the difficulty of its classification. On the one hand, the essay is not fiction and neither does it create anything new, although the fact of its corresponding to a subjective expression could mean that it is confused with art. On the other hand, it does not establish positive or objectifiable knowledge, as science requires, and neither does it follow any method or construct a system of thought, as philosophy has done, at least until Hegel. Nevertheless, the essay has a formal and epistemological vocation.[12]

Its most outstanding epistemological features are its nonsystematicity and reflexivity, which is why the essay rejects all objectifiable truth and instead proposes a partial and provisory knowledge. Conscious of the finiteness of the subject, it stakes its validity on perspectivism and retreats to the instance of enunciation as an act of critical awareness. Recall that, after having declared the project of painting himself, Montaigne ends up confessing in the third volume of *Essays* that "now the lines of my painting do not go astray, though they change and vary . . . I cannot keep my subject still. . . . I do not portray being; I portray passing" (740). The exercise of reflexivity links the essay with the existential genres. But while, in these, the self is the thematic nucleus of the work, in the essay the self is not an object but the dialectical pole of reflection allowing clarification of the perspective.

The most characteristic formal feature of the essay is its fragmentary nature, which impedes organic development of the work. According to Lukács, unlike literary works, which conclude in accordance with an internal logic, the essay ends unexpectedly, in a way that departs from the course it has taken. Its central procedure is interruption (14). Adorno considers that this apparently arbitrary gesture is more honest and aware than organic endings, which, simulating a false naturalness, are equally or more arbitrary ("Essay as Form" 164–65). In the realm of Pessoan criticism, Ramalho-Santos has presented this procedure as a poetic device that would be expressed through heteronymism as an interruption of the illusion of the instance of enunciation and would extend throughout Pessoa's work (*Atlantic Poets* 237). But interruption is, above all, a feature of all provisional writing, of the draft, of the essay, especially in its more radical modality, which is what Schlegel achieved with the fragments published in the journals *Lyceum* and *Athenäum*. Santos, Medeiros, and Gago, among other critics, have offered convincing arguments about the relationship of *Disquiet* and Schlegel's fragments.

In Schlegel, interruption attains an epistemological dimension since it prevents claims of knowledge of a totality. The fragment, independently of its length, is always part of something bigger that, however, is not accomplished. The procedure Schlegel employs to indicate this impossibility is irony. Fragment 42 in *Lyceum* expresses it as follows:

> There are ancient and modern poems that are pervaded by the divine breath of irony throughout and informed by a truly transcendental buffoonery. Internally: the mood that surveys everything and rises infinitely above all limitations, even above its own art, virtue, or genius; externally, in its execution: the mimic style of an averagely gifted Italian *buffo*.
> (*Philosophical Fragments* 5–6)

Schlegel invokes a mask of commedia dell'arte—the Italian *buffo*—which at any point in the work can interrupt the narrative illusion to address the public. The rhetorical trope corresponding to this is the parabasis, a term used by Schlegel and paired by Paul de Man (*Aesthetic* 178) with the anacoluthon—whose interruption is more of a syntactic order. From within the rhetoric, these two figures have the power to crack open its representation. Through the parabasis, the work has a way out toward what it is not, signaling an exteriority it does not have but that, structurally, it bears in mind. Irony is thus a kind of conceptual parabasis, asymptotically pointing to the totality toward which the fragment is oriented, which can only be negatively obtained, as an absence.

Furthermore, irony forces us to suspend all certainties about the self and its capacity to know and know itself. Not surprisingly, Schlegel mentions Socrates in fragment 108, which Pessoa himself could have written: "Socratic irony is the only involuntary and yet completely deliberate dissimulation. . . . In this sort of irony, everything should be playful and serious, guilelessly open and deeply hidden" (*Philosophical Fragments* 13). Already at the founding of the essay genre, Montaigne had radicalized Socratic irony with his famous motto "Que sçais-je?" (477), which means "What do I know?" but sounds like "What do I essay?" In this series, which could culminate with *Disquiet*, Pessoa includes Francisco Sanches: "A ironia é o primeiro indício de que a consciência se tornou consciente. E a ironia atravessa dois estádios: o estádio marcado por Sócrates, quando disse 'sei só que nada sei', e o estádio marcado por Sanches, quando disse 'nem sei se nada sei'" ("Irony is the first indication that consciousness has become conscious, and it passes through two stages: the stage reached by Socrates when he said 'I only know that I know nothing,' and the stage reached by Sanches, when he said 'I do not even know that I know nothing'"; *Desassossego* 411; *Disquiet* 361).[13]

In the parabasis—or in its conceptual correlate, irony—we may have found the predominant rhetorical procedure in *Disquiet*. All the book's key notions are enunciated as totalities that are incomplete or in a constant process of disintegration, starting with the very unity of the finished work: "por que escrevo eu este livro? Porque o reconheço imperfeito. Sonhado seria a perfeição; escrito, imperfeiçoa-se; porisso o escrevo" ("[s]o why am I writing this book? Because I recognize that it is imperfect. Were I to dream it, it would be perfection; the mere fact of writing makes it imperfect, which is why I am writing it"; *Desassossego* 71; *Disquiet* 35). Irony, which has its sentimental correlate in *saudade*, impregnates the entire work, bringing about the mutual interaction of its dual referential and fictional status. Irony, too, is the hallmark of reflexivity through which a subject is invoked as a totality that only emerges as absence:

> E eu, verdadeiramente eu, sou o centro que não ha nisto senão por uma geometria do abysmo; sou o nada em torno do qual este movimento gyra, só para que gyre, sem que esse centro exista senão porque todo o circulo o tem. Eu, verdadeiramente eu, sou o poço sem muros, mas com a viscosidade dos muros, o centro de tudo com o nada à roda.
>
> (*Desassossego* 417)

> And I, I myself, am the center that exists only because the geometry of the abyss demands it; I am the nothing around which all this spins, I exist so that it can spin, I am a center that exists only because every circle has one. I, I myself, am the well in which the walls have fallen away to leave only viscous slime. I am the center of everything surrounded by the great nothing.   (*Disquiet* 367)

Irony allows us to place on the same level the different types of interruption presented by the fragments of the work: that which answers to the author's will (as in the fragments published in his lifetime), that resulting from abandonment of writing because of external causes, and that caused by limitations of material support, revealed in the inner separation of some passages and in the overall interruption of the work. Irony functions as an element of the fragments that is at once disintegrating and cohesive since the interruption occurs not only in the blank spaces between them but also inside the writing itself, expressed as a constant parabasis. In brief, it seems that parabasis, a theatrical resort made transcendental by Schlegel, could provide the key to the book's genre, if not for the fact that both parabasis and irony call into question any possibility of attributing a genre to *Disquiet*, any possibility of classification:

> Os classificadores de coisas, que são aquelles homens de sciencia cuja sciencia é só classificar, ignoram, em geral, que o classificavel é infinito e portanto se não pode classificar. Mas o em que vae meu pasmo é que ignorem a existencia de classificaveis incognitos, coisas da alma e da consciencia que estão nos intersticios do conhecimento.   (*Desassossego* 472)

> Generally speaking, the classifiers of the world, those men of science whose only knowledge consists in their ability to classify, are ignorant of the fact that what is classifiable is infinite and therefore unclassifiable. But what amazes me most is that they know nothing of the existence of certain unknown classifiable categories, things of the soul and the consciousness that live in the interstices of knowledge.   (*Disquiet* 420)

Genre Unity and Diversity in The Book of Disquiet

Probably the most common expression in all the attempts to characterize the genre of *Disquiet* is that of an "unclassifiable" work. As we've seen, the opposite is true, for the work's lack of genre definition makes it extremely classifiable. The matter rests on the criteria we adopt: what the frontiers of genre are, what the level of abstraction of its pertinent features is, and, above all, what its explanatory model is. Hence, any attribution of genre to *Disquiet* is legitimate as long as the basic assumptions are made explicit. When this does not occur, the most likely outcome will be, as a result of inertia, a biological paradigm considering works as closed organic units, an approach that has dominated genre theory in the West ever since Aristotle (Rollin 130). This turns the discourse on genre into an ontological discussion because, on the one hand, the work is reified, and, on the other, it is referred to a transcendental exteriority, which is the genre (Schaeffer, "Du texte" 184). This paradigm also clears the way for the prejudice that genres are mutually exclusive, when we've seen that not all genre labels have the same status since they tend to depend on different criteria (semantic, formal, modal, pragmatic, and so on). Even when considered at the same level, different segments of a work can potentially belong to different genres (Schaeffer, *Qu'est-ce* 70). Schaeffer calls this associative faculty of texts 'genericity.'

From this standpoint, genre does not follow a logic of belonging but of participation. And, as we have seen, *Disquiet* participates in different genres in accordance with the criteria we choose as pertinent.

Here is a final proposal: Why not include the problem of genre in the discussion about the unity of *Disquiet*? For Pizarro, the efforts to guarantee unity and cohesion in the work are, apart from being ideological, impossible, since "não existe uma edição 'definitiva', entre outros motivos, para além dos humanos e dos comerciais, porque a incerteza e a multiplicidade estão na sua origem" ("there is no 'definitive' edition, among other reasons, besides human and commercial ones, because uncertainty and multiplicity are at its origin"; "Ansiedade" 292). Yet, in Foucault's analysis, in modernity the conception of oeuvre has been based on its unity and its limitation (Foucault, "What"). The regulatory function of this unity has been the author. When the figure of the author enters into crisis, this function does not disappear but is displaced.[14] This has been the drift of the work in the last few decades, summed up by Silvestre in the formula "Pessoa = Trunk = Archive = Digital." What the formula aims to summarize is that:

> A partir de certa altura, que podemos situar na década de 80, Pessoa começa a ser não o metanome mas cada vez mais um deíctico para um espólio metonimicamente indexado a uma arca. A transformação do espólio em arquivo, por meio dos trabalhos de instituições competentes para o efeito, ocupa as décadas posteriores, até à digitalização actual, que encerra um processo *historicamente necessário*, a partir do momento em que se lançam os trabalhos da edição crítica, mas não sem efeitos sobre a própria constituição daquilo que é hoje um Pessoa-Arquivo.   (87)

> From a certain point, which we can situate in the 1980s, Pessoa starts to be not a metaname but, increasingly, a deictic for a legacy metonymically indexed to a trunk. The transformation of the legacy into an archive through the work of institutions equipped for this purpose occupies the subsequent decades until today's digitalization, which closes a *historically necessary* process from the moment when the critical edition is launched, but not without effects on the very constitution of what is today a Pessoa-Archive.

The last incarnation of *Disquiet* is the *Arquivo LdoD: Arquivo Digital Colaborativo do Livro do Desassossego*, developed and hosted at the University of Coimbra. It brings together the facsimiles of the entire corpus of *Disquiet*, the authorial testimonies, and the four most representative editions (Coelho, Cunha, Zenith, and Pizarro). It thus enables ecdotic and genetic consultation and offers a history of the different publishers' versions, as well as the possibility of many reading itineraries (Portela 358). But so far, it appears that there has been no exploration of the potential of this tool for inquiring into the problem of the genre of the work, which, as we have just seen, is one of the dimensions of both its unity and its diversity. First, together with the ecdotic and genetic dimension of the archive, it would be possible to implement the perspective of the authorial genre regime,[15] which consists of establishing the repertoire of genres available at the time of writing the fragments. Starting from Pessoa's own testimonies, as well as mentions of specific works and the types of text found in the facsimile corpus, it would be possible to reconstruct the horizon of expectations with which he worked and to establish a multiple set of genre references he might have counted on, whether it was to adopt them or to transgress them. According to Hans Robert Jauss, "a masterwork is definable in terms of an alteration of the horizon of the genre that is as unexpected as it is enriching; the genre's prehistory is definable in terms of a trying and testing of possibilities" (94). Second, the social dimension of the archive, which is what Portela calls the publishing history of the work, could be complemented by the history of the successive and various attributions of genre made by critics, which, moreover, have explicitly or implicitly determined the different publishing criteria. Finally, the archive's virtual dimension, which is what Portela calls the variety of interactive tours of the work offered by the *Arquivo* to users, could be complemented by the readerly genre regime, consisting of the ability of each reader or critic to associate the work with others to which it bears some resemblance. As Jauss wrote, the "horizon of the expectable is constituted for the reader from out of a tradition or series of previously known works, and from a specific attitude, mediated by one (or more) genre and dissolved through new works" (79). In this sense, and according to Schaeffer's perspective, unlike authorial genericity, which remains closed, readerly genericity leaves all classification permanently open because no text can determine the possible subsequent affinities that future readers might establish with a literary corpus that is continually expanding and being modified. Hence, nobody can know how many ascriptions can be made to *Disquiet*, how many will follow criteria that are above suspicion today, or if some of them will achieve a certain institutional stability, to such a point that the genre mists that have been discussed in this text will remain as a remote, eccentric anecdote.

NOTES

1. All translations not otherwise attributed are my own.

2. *Literature* is a complex, controversial term. For an overall view, see Widdowson.

3. I use this term in the sense given to it by the Russian formalists and as employed by Gérard Genette, as I mention below.

4. Jackson suggests three genre traditions for the *Livro*: the philosophical diary, confessional memoirs, and the novel of self-realization: "Authorship by a narrative 'personality,' or heteronym in the case of Guedes, enhances the fictional potential of the 'Book' as a novel comparable to others of the period" (163).

5. The editions cited throughout this essay are the *Livro do desassossego*, edited by Jerónimo Pizarro and published by Tinta-da-china, and *The Book of Disquiet*, translated by Margaret Jull Costa, edited by Pizarro, and published by New Directions.

6. On the genesis and meaning of the term *heteronymism*, see Pizarro (*Fernando Pessoa* 34–47).

7. In the cited edition, the diamond indicates a blank space left by Pessoa.

8. Another perspective would be linking *Disquiet* with symbolism through the Mallarmé-style resonances of "O Grande Livro como dizem os francezes" ("what the French call the Great Book"; *Desassossego* 271; *Disquiet* 218).

9. Here, Santos is playing at linking the Nietzschean mask with the etymology of the poet's name, which, in Latin, as Octavio Paz pointed out, meant "mask" of the kind used by Roman actors ("El desconocido de sí mismo" [Joaquín Mortiz] 133).

10. This is the influential poetic theory of Wilhelm Dilthey, who links lyric with the poet's *Erlebnis* ("lived experience"). On the concept of *Erlebnis*, see his *Introduction to the Human Sciences*. On the relationship between *Erlebnis* and lyric, see Dilthey, *Poetry and Experience*.

11. Medeiros (*Pessoa's Geometry*) rightly highlights the need for a philosophical perspective as a procedure for reading the fragmentary dimension of *Disquiet*.

12. Rui Sousa has documented the interest shown by Pessoa in this kind of writing in the mid-1910s, when *Disquiet* was first planned. Pessoa had a French edition of Montaigne's *Essays* in his personal library but engaged more actively with a skeptical book of essays entitled *Quod Nihil Scitur* (*That Nothing Is Known*), published by the Portuguese humanist Francisco Sanches in 1581 (R. Sousa, "Michel de Montaigne" 28, 93).

13. On Pessoa's interest in Sanches, see R. Sousa ("Michel de Montaigne").

14. The decisive action of the different editors on the corpus of *Disquiet* is a demonstration of this displacement.

15. I use Schaeffer's concepts of "authorial regime" and "readerly regime" (*Qu'est-ce* 147–55).

Mensagem: The Ideas behind a Poetic Vision

Onésimo T. Almeida

Fernando Pessoa published only one book, *Mensagem* (*Message*), during his life-time and did so solely at the insistence of António Ferro, a sort of ideologue of the Salazar regime. As director of the secretariat for national propaganda, Ferro essentially created a literary contest in order to render the penurious poet some financial assistance. *Mensagem*, however, at less than one hundred pages, was disqualified from consideration as a book and was ultimately awarded a special prize created ad hoc (Barreto, "*Mensagem*").

Though *Mensagem* is not Pessoa's only controversial work, none has provoked more debate. At the time of publication, criticism of the volume and its ideology was silenced by Portugal's censorship regime, which continued for decades after-ward to make use of the book by taking it out of context. To help address the many misreadings, misappropriations, and misunderstandings of *Mensagem*, and to gain relevant insights into Pessoa's ideological background, it is important to revisit this work.

During Pessoa's lifetime, opinions about the book were circulated through-out the country, albeit not all in written form. José Blanco has outlined in clear strokes the ideological breadth shining through in the two analyses known and published during the poet's life ("*Mensagem*"). In them, one can easily detect the two trends flagged by Blanco: the strict nationalist reading, which views the book "politicamente . . . como uma peça do ressurgimento de Portugal através do Estado Novo" ("politically . . . as a piece of the resurgence of Portugal through the New State"; 74),[1] and another that calls for a much more profound reading of the work, as much in relation to the "message" contained within as to the work's form. Of the critiques from sectors of the opposition to the regime that circu-lated at the time we have primarily indirect knowledge because of a lack of pub-lished texts. In a telling example, published only four years after the death of the poet, Augusto da Costa proposes to continue the development of a thesis defended in four earlier articles, claiming to demonstrate that Fernando Pessoa was a "poeta e escritor nacionalista" ("poet and nationalist writer"; 1).[2] In the beginning of that article, Vitorino Nemésio is the only name cited among those who supposedly mocked *Mensagem* as "mediocre," but, judging by Costa's reasoning, the critique within those lines aimed even to the left of Nemésio. Some of the most significant passages are excerpted below:

> "Medíocre," um livro de Fernando Pessoa, tão louvado pelos "valores humanos"[†] a-propósito de versos assinados por "heterónimos"? O caso seria extraordinário, se não tivesse explicação fácil. Nos versos assinados por "heterónimos" Fernando Pessoa podia ser até génio, porque não era político; ao passo que nos poemas que constituem a *Mensagem*, assinados pelo seu próprio nome, Fernando Pessoa é poeta nacionalista, mais do que nacionalista, "imperialista português." Para cumulo, o livro foi premiado pelo Secretariado da Propaganda Nacional! Poderiam os "valores humanos," nestas circunstâncias, achar admirável a *Mensagem*? Não podiam. . . . Estamos perante um caso patente de escamoteação político-literária. Elevam ás culminancias da glória os "heterónimos" a-políticos de Fernando Pessoa; ignoram sistemáticamente ou rebaixam até á mediocridade a obra nacionalista que Fernando Pessoa deixou assinada pelo seu nome. Dizer que um poeta nacionalista tem talento, é 100% contra a ética comunistoide: [para tal ética] os "valores humanos" fazem quási exclusivamente política contra a Nação. Política literária, que é uma política como qualquer outra.
>
> † Alusão eufemística e irónica à oposição, que se reclamava deles defensora.

(Costa 1)

> "Mediocre," a book by Fernando Pessoa, so praised by the "human values"[†] on account of verses signed by "heteronyms"? The case would be extraordinary, if there were not an easy explanation. In the verses signed by "heteronyms," Fernando Pessoa may even be a genius, because he was not political; whereas in the poems that constitute *Mensagem*, signed with his own name, Fernando Pessoa is a nationalist poet, more than nationalist, "Portuguese imperialist." To cap it off, the book was honored by the Secretariat of National Propaganda! Could the "human values," in these circumstances, find *Mensagem* admirable? They could not. . . . We are before a patent case of a political-literary cover-up. They elevate to the apex of glory Fernando Pessoa's apolitical "heteronyms"; they systematically ignore or demote to mediocrity the nationalist work that Fernando Pessoa left signed with his own name. To say that a nationalist poet has talent is 100% against the communist-leaning ethics: [for such ethics] "human values" are almost exclusively about politics against the Nation. Literary politics, which is politics like any other.
>
> † A euphemistic and ironic allusion to the opposition, which claimed to be defenders of such values.

It becomes obvious that *Mensagem* was interpreted from the start by the two extremes of the political spectrum as a nationalist work, with the difference being that one faction claimed the work as its own and the other rejected the work for the same reason—having read it as ideologically amenable to the regime to which that faction was opposed. In one form or another, then, nearly all criticism understood *Mensagem* to be a nationalist poem, but with the approval of some and the reproach of others. The critics who pointed to or suggested other readings did not provide substantial enough reasons to free the book from the political categorization that gripped it from the outset.

The abolition of censorship in Portugal after the 25 April Revolution made possible the publication of unpublished works by Pessoa that in no way conformed to the prevailing vision of the poet's political ideology. Jorge de Sena, who in 1960 had brought to light in a newspaper a sequence of three Pessoan anti-Salazar poems (*Estado de São Paulo*),[3] published them in Portugal soon after the revolution (*Diário popular*, 6 June 1974). Since then, the possibility of openly debating the issue and the gradual appearance of new pieces of information[4] have made it clear that there was, on the part of Pessoa, a considerable distancing with regard to the Salazar regime, as had occurred already with regard to the Republic (Bernardino).

By bringing to light some more unpublished works from Pessoa's estate, Teresa Rita Lopes publicly demonstrated that the poet's nationalism diverged from the strict interpretations that the left as much as the right made of it. In Pessoa there was a sui generis character, designated by himself as "nacionalismo cosmopolita" ("cosmopolitan nationalism"; *Pessoa Inédito* 312–13).[5]

Very recently, António Valdemar published a short article in which he speaks of significant conversations with two national political figures—Mário Soares, the leader of the Socialist Party and later president of the Republic, and Álvaro Cunhal, the leader of the Communist Party. Soares did not consider Pessoa one of his author-mentors, but, on a trip aboard the training ship *Sagres* and in direct contact with the sea, he decided to reread *Mensagem* and built up some affection for it, detecting in the work a "simbólica" ("symbolic") systematization of the history of Portugal. He even reacted to Valdemar's insistence on associating the book with European fascism (Valdemar 8). Cunhal was unbending: "A Mensagem é um momento contraditório na obra de Pessoa. . . . É uma obra fraquíssima, porque Pessoa quis conformar a obra poética com a mensagem política. E o resultado é que a obra poética fracassou completamente. A *Mensagem*—insistiu—é um fracasso" ("The message is a contradictory moment in the work of Pessoa. . . . It is a very weak work, because Pessoa tries to align the poetic work with the political message. And the result is that the poetic work failed completely. *Mensagem*—he insisted—is a failure"; Valdemar 8).

This suggests that the comprehension and reception of Pessoa's book did not appreciably change over half a century. How then can we redefine the ideology of *Mensagem* and situate it within the Pessoan ideology and worldview?

Before we proceed, perhaps it would be useful to define our terms. *World-view* is understood here as the background coordinates of the view that one has of oneself, of the universe, and of one's place within it. The term *ideology* has a more limited scope: it encompasses that area of the worldview in which ethical convictions in general, and political convictions in particular, are concentrated and conjoined.[6]

The elements present in *Mensagem* do not in themselves suffice to communicate the underlying Pessoan ideology in the work. It is fundamental in this analysis to keep in mind everything that Pessoa wrote about the work, about Portugal, and about politics. Of even greater import, it is crucial to frame those ideological convictions within the vaster background of the Pessoan worldview, particularly Pessoa's aesthetic conceptions and beliefs about the role of myth, of poetry, and of poets. After that, one must situate the resultant framework of Pessoa's worldview in general, which is an especially complex task, given the multiplication of Pessoa's "I" in heteronyms. Although it is impossible to accomplish such a large endeavor in the limited space of this introduction, I offer a summary of the explanation that I developed first in *Mensagem: Uma tentativa de reinter-pretação* (*Message: An Attempt at Reinterpretation*) and further in various essays collected in the book *Pessoa, Portugal e o futuro* (*Pessoa, Portugal, and the Future*).

Pessoa concerned himself seriously with the state of decadence in which Portugal found itself. The experience of having lived a considerable part of his childhood and adolescence exposed to English culture must have sharpened his perception of difference and accentuated his feelings of obligation in relation to his homeland, encouraging a dream of contributing to a national resurgence. Convinced that the pessimistic and defeatist attitude that predominated in Portugal would never lead to the construction of anything, he proposed to elaborate a plan that, put into practice, would instill a dynamic, positive, and creative attitude in the nation.

Influenced by Thomas Carlyle (see Cavaco), Pessoa conceived of a society in which an aristocracy of heroes, among whom the poet was the greatest, would play the role of the engine in the evolutionary process of a people: "the highest degree of imagining is that of a poet, it is in poetry that we are going to search for the soul of the race" (Pessoa, "Nova poesia" 69). He embraced the philosophy of Henri Bergson as a backdrop: creativity is attained when in a state of continuous tension produced through an assumption of the past that projects us to a profoundly superior, spiritual future of broad horizons (see, e.g., Bergson, *Évolution* and *Énergie*).

Familiar with the myth of the general strike proposed by Georges Sorel as a means to free oneself from decadent inactivism, Pessoa would have adapted the idea to the Portuguese case but followed the model closely. The new myth should have popular roots (thus Pessoa's having sought out Sebastianism[7] and the bases of nationalism elaborated by the Portuguese Renaissance[8]). It should point to an imminent, near future, although the exact period may neither be known nor defined. The myth should be described in vague and mysterious terms, so as to appeal to the people—hence the fog, the utilization of hermetic symbolism, and the myth's formulation at the highest point of intersection between symbol, word, and idea, all in the form of expression that corresponds to Pessoa's conceptions of poetry. It does not matter that the mythical future is unattainable, since in the dynamic process of reaching for it, one can operate, create, and carry out acts that would be impossible without that tension. The idea of recovering the Quinto Império, or Fifth Empire—an equally "national" myth—is thus transformed into a spiritual empire so as to appear possible yet simultaneously unattainable.[9] Not even Pessoa believed that a new material empire would be a good ideal for the country.

The project of constructing this new national myth had two components: one theoretical, which over the years Pessoa elaborated in a fragmentary fashion, writing down countless sociological reflections about Portugal; the other component was the presentation of the myth to the Portuguese in general, expressed in the superior form of poetic art—the only form capable of touching not just reason but the feeling of the people—which would come to be realized in *Mensagem*.

Finally, Pessoa holds a special concept of myth, which happens to be the same as Sorel's and that no one else in all of history used. For both writers, instead of being fixated on the past, the myth is totally projected on the future, existing as an agent in the process of its fulfillment, pointing to the path for the truth that is being constructed or serving to point to that path, even if it is still shrouded in fog. Pessoa's attitude toward the concept of truth reflects an epistemological conception that dates back to Blaise Pascal and the pragmatists, such as William James. Traditionally, the concept of truth had divided philosophers between defenders of truth as correspondence (Aristotelian) and defenders of truth as coherence (Platonic); each approach applied only to past and present matters. Neither position is informative with regard to the future—that is, to events that have not yet occurred. Further, human beings can alter the course of events. They can make choices and force themselves to achieve determined objectives. Although they may not reach these objectives in their totality, such an attitude places human beings in a position of being able to accomplish something. Human beings can influence the future, that which is going to be true; hence Pessoa speaks about truth as choice.

A key of interpretation is valid when it permits the explanation of the fundamental elements that make up a problem. The reading suggested above appears to provide that possibility. It would explain Pessoa's description of himself as a "sebastianista racional" ("rational Sebastianist"; A. Monteiro and Blanco, *Poesia* 228) as well as how one would understand his conception, expressed in the poem "Ulisses" ("Ulysses") in *Mensagem* itself, that "[o] mito é o nada que é tudo" ("[a] myth is nothing—yet it's all"; Pessoa, *Poetry: Minimal Anthology* 167).

Moreover, it makes it unnecessary to take everything that *Mensagem* says about the Fifth Empire or about Sebastian literally, and the poet himself need not appear to have intended to be the reincarnation of the king.

The Pessoan myth presents all these elements that make up the myth in Sorelian terms, and in the light of this model, there is no need to continue to interpret them literally. Nor, much less, must one pick apart their content, since the mysterious character of what is going to happen and the uncertainty of the time in which it will be realized are the pivotal psychological factors and the sine qua non of the myth's effectiveness. Pessoa was too Bergsonian to boast of the right to indicate a plan or to describe the future. What was important in his view was to restructure one's energies in a creative tension, whatever form that tension took, to get out of the retrogressive, unproductive, and decayed nihilism in which the country found itself.

These conceptions of the myth as a rational construction and of the truth as choice appear to me to have fundamental implications in Pessoan hermeneutics, above all because they reveal a much more articulated worldview than that suggested by an entire discourse of fragmentation. Attentive reading of Pessoa's philosophical writings leaves his position about the problem of truth clear: he explicitly defends a pragmatically constructed truth.[10]

If these pieces of the puzzle are correctly fitted together, then the connections between Pessoa's worldview and his political ideology no longer suffer from incoherent misfittings. And thus disappears a Gordian knot: the admirers of Pessoa grappled with recognizing the genius of the heteronyms and understanding the orthonymous Pessoa, who seemed to have become entangled in a narrow and backward nationalism and visionary delusions. If this is true, it is once again Pessoa himself who best outlines his ideological profile, in his famous autobiographical note from 30 March 1935:

> Ideologia política: Considera que o sistema monárquico seria o mais próprio para uma nação organicamente imperial, como é Portugal. Considera, ao mesmo tempo, a Monarquia completamente inviável em Portugal. Por isso, a haver plebiscito entre regimes, votaria, embora com pena, pela República. Conservador do estilo inglês, isto é, liberal dentro do conservantismo, é absolutamente anti-reaccionário. . . .
>
> Posição patriótica: Partidário de um nacionalismo místico, de onde seja abolida toda a infiltração católico-romana, criando-se, se possível for, um sebastianismo novo, que substitua espiritualmente, se é que no catolicismo português houve alguma vez espiritualidade. Nacionalista, que se guia por este lema: "Tudo pela Human idade; nada contra a Nação."
> (Barreto, "A chamada 'nota autobiográfica'" 515, 517)[11]

> Political ideology: He considers that the monarchical system would be most fitting for an organically imperial nation, as Portugal is. He considers, at the same time, the Monarchy completely unviable in Portugal. Therefore,

if there were a plebiscite between systems of government, he would vote, although sadly, for the Republic. Conservative in the English style, that is, liberal within conservatism, and absolutely anti-reactionary. . . .

Patriotic position: Adherent to a mystic nationalism, from where all Roman Catholic infiltration will be abolished, creating, if at all possible, a new Sebastianism, which would replace it spiritually, if it is in Portuguese Catholicism that there was once spirituality. Nationalist that guides himself by this motto: "Everything for Humanity; nothing against the Nation."

This reading does not intend to insinuate that the trajectory of Pessoa's political ideology was linear. An extremely subtle spirit, Pessoa exposed himself to every kind of idea, transforming all of them through the sieve of his analysis.[12] He constructed and broadened his unique vision of the world throughout his whole life, with hesitations, ambiguities, and even errors, later corrected or retracted, in his reading of some political events, as in the case of the pamphlet *O interregno: Defeza e justificação da dictadura militar em Portugal* (*The Interregnum: Defense and Justification of the Military Dictatorship in Portugal*). His project for Portugal likewise took shape over the years. Initially not knowing quite where he was going, he learned year after year where he did not want to go.[13] If at different moments in the political history of his time it is possible to find Pessoa more reactionary or more liberal, taken together his political positions reveal a remarkable consistency. They are in accord with the quoted ideological classification that the poet makes of himself. If this is so, whatever the practical translation of expressions like "cosmopolitan nationalism"[14] may be, it does not seem defensible in any way to continue to attach it ideologically to the political regime that "awarded" him recognition for his *Mensagem*.

As I have attempted to demonstrate, my proposed reading of *Mensagem* as a myth understood in the light of the possible influence of Bergson and, above all, of Sorel, for whom the myth of the general strike would constitute the fundamental pillar, may help us understand the why of Fernando Pessoa's insistence on the role of the poet and of poetry as messenger of the myth and mobilizer of the spirit of the people, the only way of acting on the Portuguese mentality to make Portuguese society emerge from its inactive pessimism.[15] Believing that the national myth with popular roots—Sebastianism—would act to transform the collective mentality, Pessoa created the expression "rational Sebastianism"—almost an oxymoron—conscious of the *fabricated* character of that myth but aware and convinced of its potential, provided the myth were expressed in poetic form and adorned with countless aesthetic effects that would impart the necessary strength to act upon readers.

In the light of the Sorelian conception of the myth, the diverse pieces of the puzzle surrounding *Mensagem* seem to complement each other in a coherent whole. Yet when I published my first book about *Mensagem* in 1987, I still did not possess any proof that Pessoa was, in fact, acquainted with the work of Sorel, nor did I have any knowledge that any critic had suggested this influence. Only the reading of Pessoa's texts about myth had made me associate him with the pages of Sorel's *Refléxions sur la violence* (*Reflections on Violence*). Thanks to a referral by José Blanco, Francisco Peixoto Bourbon, the youngest of the circle of friends with whom Pessoa met at the Café Montanha, confirmed in our subsequent correspondence that the poet knew of and admired Sorel's thought. Bourbon himself had published an article in a small regional newspaper that referred to Pessoa's appreciation for the French thinker. I took note of that connection in detail in the essay "Pessoa, a *Mensagem* e o mito em Georges Sorel" ("Pessoa, *Mensagem* and Myth in Georges Sorel"; 211–22), later included in my book *Pessoa, Portugal e o futuro*, in which I include additional evidence from manuscripts found in the Pessoan estate by Jerónimo Pizarro.

Bourbon generously responded to my inquiry about Pessoa and Sorel in his first letter, dated 6 November 1987: "De uma coisa pode desde já estar certo: Fernando Pessoa conhecia a obra de Georges Sorel que em certos pontos lhe merecia concordância e apreço" ("Of one thing you can henceforth be certain: Fernando Pessoa was acquainted with the work of Georges Sorel who, in certain points, merited accord and appreciation").[16] Some days later, Bourbon added that my "raciocínio está cem por cento certo" ("rationale is one hundred percent certain"; 6 Dec. 1987), attaching a photocopy of an article he had published the previous year in the newspaper *O Comércio de Gaia* (*Gaia's Commerce*), where he had made affirmations that were in complete accord with those that I had proposed in my text.

Lacking, nonetheless, was an explicit reference to Sorel's name on Pessoa's part. The tireless Bourbon did not give up on writing to all those whom he suspected could furnish clues. A few days later, I received another letter from him with a photocopy of a fragment (BNP/E3, 133G-49), in which the poet had noted, together with two other books, "G. Sorel: *Les illusions du progrès*" ("G. Sorel: *The Illusions of Progress*"). In addition, in a letter of 20 February 1988, Bourbon opened up other perspectives to me that were intimately related to the Bergson-Sorel line:

> [J]ulgando que me valorizava um dia declarei a Fernando Pessoa que era cartesiano cem por cento. Com grande surpresa e decepção minha, levei uma corrida em pêlo.
>
> Segundo me recordo e a memória me não atraiçoa Fernando Pessoa declarou-me que Descartes era, infelizmente, um dos filósofos mais superficiais e mais nocivos. Teria sido como que o pai espiritual dos enciclopedistas e de Augusto Comte, que o saudoso poeta não suportava. . . .
>
> Declarou então que um dos pontos que lhe merecia pleno aplauso na obra de Georges Sorel era a forma como ele havia demonstrado que "Pascal havia vencido Descartes." Que o pensamento de então [ou seja, de há meio século] estava profundamente influenciado pelas ideias de Pascal e de Bergson. Que a derrota de Descartes representava, sem dúvida, a derrota

do racionalismo e por racionalismo ele entendia o intelectualismo da época. Mas na vitória de Sorel havia para ele um ponto fraco: a vitória do sindicalismo com que Fernando Pessoa de forma alguma concordava. Tinha mesmo profundo desprezo por sindicalistas, a quem chamava sub-gente.

Fiquei na íntima convicção que Bergson havia conseguido traçar como que uma linha divisória entre o que é inerte e o que é vivo e que a ciência e a fé poderiam daí para o futuro coexistir como dois princípios absolutos. Que a razão se torna imbecil e impotente, por profundamente incompetente quando se permite ultrapassar o físico para invadir a metafísica, a que Fenando Pessoa tinha em tanto apreço, quer a moral e o aspecto religioso. Aí seria o único e exclusivo domínio da fé segundo Pascal, do *mito* segundo Sorel, e da intuição segundo Bergson.

Em conclusão, Fernando Pessoa tinha pleno conhecimento da obra de Sorel, pelo menos parcialmente, mas dada a sua maneira apaixonada de ser e o apreço em que tinha Sorel, por alguns pontos das suas especulações filosóficas, é difícil admitir que além da obra em que ele entendia que Pascal havia vencido Descartes, não procurasse devorar toda a obra publicada até à data de Sorel.

[T]hinking that it would earn me some respect, one day I declared to Fernando Pessoa that I was a hundred percent Cartesian. To my great surprise and disappointment, I received a tongue-lashing.

According to what I recall, if my memory does not betray me, Fernando Pessoa declared to me that Descartes was, unfortunately, one of the most superficial and most detrimental philosophers. He would have been like the spiritual father of the encyclopedists and Augusto Comte, whom the late poet could not stand. . . .

He then declared that one of the points that deserved full acclaim in the work of Georges Sorel was the way in which he had demonstrated that "Pascal had defeated Descartes." That the thought then [that is, half a century ago] was profoundly influenced by the ideas of Pascal and Bergson. That the fall of Descartes represented, no doubt, the fall of rationalism, and by rationalism he understood the intellectualism of the time. But in Sorel's victory there was, for him, a weak point: the victory of syndicalism with which Fernando Pessoa in no way agreed. He really had a profound disdain for syndicalists, whom he called sub-people.

I remained intimately convinced that Bergson had managed to draw a dividing line between what is inert and what is alive and that science and faith could from then to the future coexist as two absolute principles. That reason becomes imbecile and impotent, in the sense of profoundly incompetent, when it is allowed to surpass the physical to invade metaphysics, of which Fernando Pessoa had such appreciation, be it morality or religious aspects. There it would be the single and exclusive domain of faith according to Pascal, of *myth* according to Sorel, and of intuition according to Bergson.

In conclusion, Fernando Pessoa had full knowledge of the work of Sorel, at least partially, but given his passionate way of being and the appreciation he had for Sorel, for some points of his philosophical speculations, it is difficult to accept that besides the work in which he understood that Pascal had defeated Descartes, he did not seek to devour all the published work until Sorel's time.

All this is so coherent with itself and with the Fernando Pessoa that appears to me behind *Mensagem*! This anti-Cartesian attitude and admiration for Pascal are entangled with the concept of pragmatic truth that became fundamental for Pessoa. The idea that although we do not know what is going to happen, we can influence what is going to happen and can thus in some way choose the future by betting on our preferences culminates in the entire project of *Mensagem*.

Equipped with all this information about the ideas underlying the Pessoa concept, we may here consider a core poem from *Mensagem*, "Ulisses," in which the term *mito* ("myth") arises followed by a sort of definition:

> O mito é o nada que é tudo.
> O mesmo sol que abre os céus
> É um mito brilhante e mudo—
> O corpo morto de Deus,
> Vivo e desnudo.
> Este que aqui aportou,
> Foi por não ser existindo.
> Sem existir nos bastou.
> Por não ter vindo foi vindo
> E nos criou.
> Assim a lenda se escorre
> A entrar na realidade,
> E a fecundá-la decorre.
> Em baixo, a vida, metade
> De nada, morre.   (Pessoa, *Mensagem* 25)

> A myth[17] is nothing—yet it's all.
> The very sun that crowns the sky,
> A muted myth too bright to pall—
> It's God's dead body hung on high,
> Alive and bared for all.

> The one who wandered here ashore,
> By not existing, came to live.
> His nonexistence served us more.
> Not having come, he came to give—
> To form the nation's core.

Just so, the legend's potent theme
Recasts the real, the story told,
Till none can tell a gap or seam.
But half of nothing, life, less bold,
Ends here—the lesser dream.   (*Poetry* 167)

    Of all the authors I have consulted on the subject of myth, from Thomas A. Sebeok, Mircea Eliade, Claude Lévi-Strauss, and G. S. Kirk to Joseph Campbell, Karen Armstrong, and Bruce Lincoln, none of them include any view of myth as future and as active on the course of events as Pessoa and Sorel did. With regard to the future, we can say that Pessoa was postmodern insofar as he believed himself to be a construct, resulting in the idea that the past neither should nor could be taken as a model for the future. Although the poet used in his rationally constructed myth the model of the grandeur of the Portuguese past, he did not repeat it purely and simply but rather employed it as an incentive in order to help strengthen the belief in the possibility of returning from obscurity to build something grandiose.

    That is to say, in this sense Pessoa was not a postmodernist except in his inaction or incapability of taking action. In his worldview it was clear that, in the meaninglessness of the postmodern world, we are left with the possibility of creating sense for ourselves. If the great majority of people behave according to myths, the elites are those who produce sense, who move forward by creating myths (future truths are all myths, and rational Sebastianism is only one of them) and indicating pathways. Those pathways that he, Pessoa, never had the emotional will to follow. Notwithstanding, he managed to see them very far, illuminated by the brilliance of his ingenious intelligence. Pessoa, in his orthonym, is not exclusive, but he is Pessoa. And he is a brilliant construction, philosophically grounded. It is not worth obscuring it or, because he is an aristocrat of the spirit, to give up trying to unravel the complex pieces of the seemingly enigmatic puzzle he created and maintained throughout his life as part of the complex plural network he also built around him.

    I hope the quotation that follows leaves clear that it is not I who is putting ideas in Pessoa's head; rather, I am merely detecting them:

Há só uma espécie de propaganda com que se pode levantar o moral de uma nação—a construção ou renovação e a difusão consequente e multímoda de um grande mito nacional. De instinto, a humanidade odeia a verdade, porque sabe, com o mesmo instinto, que não há verdade, ou que a verdade é inatingível. O mundo conduz-se por mentiras; quem quiser despertá-lo ou conduzi-lo terá que mentir-lhe delirantemente, e fá-lo-á com tanto mais êxito quanto mais mentir a si mesmo e se compenetrar da verdade da mentira que criou. Temos, felizmente, o mito sebastianista, com raízes profundas no passado e na alma portuguesa. Nosso trabalho é pois

mais fácil; não temos que criar um mito, senão renová-lo. Comecemos por
nos embebedar desse sonho, por o integrar em nós, por o incarnar. Feito
isso, cada um de nós independentemente e a sós consigo, o sonho se der-
ramará sem esforço em tudo que dissermos ou escrevermos, e a atmosfera
estará criada, em que todos os outros, como nós, o respirem. Então se dará
na alma da Nação o fenómeno imprevisível de onde nascerão as Novas Descobertas, a Criação do Mundo Novo, o Quinto Império. Terá regressado a
casa El-Rei D. Sebastião.

        (Pessoa, *Sobre Portugal* 254–55 [BNP/E3, 125B-36^r])[18]

There is only one type of propaganda with which one can raise the morale
of a nation—the construction or renovation, and the resulting and diverse
diffusion, of a great national myth. By instinct, humanity hates the truth,
because it knows, with the same instinct, that there is no truth, or that the
truth is unattainable. The world conducts itself by lies; whoever wants to
wake the world up or lead it will have to lie to it deliriously, and will do so
with all the more success by lying to themselves and convincing themselves of the truth of the lie created. We have, happily, the Sebastianist
myth, with deep roots in the past and in the Portuguese spirit. Our work is
thus easier; we do not have to create a myth but rather to renew one. Let's
begin by getting ourselves drunk on that dream, by integrating it into ourselves, by incarnating it. Having done that, each one of us independently
and alone with ourselves, the dream will spill out effortlessly into everything that we say or write, and the atmosphere created will be one in which
all others like us breathe the dream. Then there will arise in the spirit of
the nation the unforeseeable phenomenon from which were born the New
Discoveries, the Creation of the New World, the Fifth Empire. King
Sebastian will have returned.

Pessoa unfurled himself in fragments that are hardly manageable in a single
portrait. Nonetheless, we should not forget, as everything in him was intentional
and rethought (many times even calculated), that he signed much writing with
his own name. An inability to reduce oneself to a singular portrait should not be
considered abnormal. It is, incidentally, very normal for a person to be polyhedral.
A modern human being's personality easily decenters itself in folds and labyrinths
at times incoherent or arduously reconciled without that process destroying the
central nucleus of that personality. As a matter of fact, no one is absolutely
coherent. If Pessoa is an extreme case of fragmentation, that does not mean that
he did not have his center. One might venture that, if we want to know what an
individual's actual beliefs are, all we have to do is note what makes them blush
while in conversation—or what irritates them, we could put forward. Pessoa had
moments in which he became irritated and was even moved to publicly defend
his profound convictions. About other facets of his life, he may not have

become publicly irritated, but there are signs that he blushed privately, despite his reticence and silences.

It is true that the heteronymic constellation does not permit us to paint a portrait of Pessoa with a firm brush. The contours will always be faded, osmotic, and, above all, made up of many crisscrossed lines. I do not believe, however, that we can find sufficient evidence in the heteronyms for us to unfurl the portrait completely, exaggerating the multiplication of likeness. There exists a difference between the contrary and the contradictory. In fact, Pessoa's contradictions are not as extensive as they are sometimes purported to be. Note as well that over the years Bernardo Soares resembles Pessoa himself more and more, and even Álvaro de Campos loses his distinctive features and becomes more like his creator. In the long run, the heteronyms end up being much more one another's cousins and relatives based on Pessoa, who clearly emerges from within the labyrinth of his writings, despite the contours that make up that diffuse snarl that his devotees know well.

Until the end of his life, Pessoa maintained his singular sense of "rational Sebastianism, holding that what was necessary to mobilize the Portuguese mentality and to free it from the depressive and pessimist state in which it found itself was a belief in the myth of *Mensagem*. Abulic and incapable of civic or political intervention in the second phase of his existence, and divided as well by the multiple visions of the world that he maintained simultaneously, he lived all those realities nearly exclusively in his brain. Therefore, *Mensagem* ended up being something like what Mahatma Gandhi is said to have answered when asked what he thought of Western civilization: "It would be a good idea."

Pessoa would nourish this good idea of his until the end of his days.

NOTES

A portion of this essay was written in Portuguese and published in *Observatório da língua portuguesa* in 2022. It was translated into English for this volume by Kevin Ennis.

1. English translations not otherwise attributed are by Kevin Ennis.

2. A photocopy of this text was furnished to me by Luís Amaro, whom I sincerely thank.

3. Sena maintained his anonymity.

4. Among these, three volumes by Pessoa (*Sobre Portugal; Da República; Ultimatum*) stand out along with the exposition catalog *Fernando Pessoa: O último ano* (*Fernando Pessoa: The Last Year*); see also Pessoa, *Santo António*; J. Sousa. A collection of Pessoa's political writings was put together in Pessoa, *Contra Salazar*; see also Pessoa, *Sobre o fascismo*.

5. Lopes later published *Pessoa por conhecer*.

6. The concept of ideology has a long history of confusion and misunderstanding. Recently, it has become very common to use the term in the sense of worldview. Because

of the existence of two distinct and analytically separate realities—worldview and ideology—the two concepts are maintained herein. The theoretical justification of this use is given elsewhere; see Almeida, *Concept of Ideology*.

7. Sebastianism is a messianic belief rooted in Portuguese history and folklore, centered on the return of King Sebastian of Portugal, who disappeared during the Battle of Alcácer Quibir in 1578. According to the myth, King Sebastian would return one day to save Portugal in its darkest hour, leading the nation to a glorious resurgence. This belief became a symbol of hope and national renewal during periods of crisis and decline in Portuguese history.

8. Pessoa distances himself explicitly from the nationalism of Teixeira de Pascoaes, although he recognizes the importance of reconstituting the fundamental elements of Portuguese culture manifested since Luís de Camões and of passing through Antero de Quental and António Nobre to Pascoaes. For Pessoa's "synthetic nationalist, . . . there is not, specifically, a national soul; there is only a national direction" (*Da República* 224).

9. The Fifth Empire is a concept in Portuguese cultural and spiritual thought that envisions a utopian future where Portugal leads a new global empire based not on territorial conquest but on spiritual and intellectual values. Rooted in the ideas of Camões and later expanded by Pessoa, the Fifth Empire represents the culmination of human history, where wisdom, culture, and spirituality reign supreme. It is often associated with a messianic vision of Portugal's destiny as a guiding light for humanity.

10. I developed this theme in the essay "Pessoa e verdade(s)," later included in my book *Pessoa, Portugal e o futuro*.

11. See also Barreto, "Salazar"; E. Lourenço and Oliveira 20–22.

12. The idea that constantly shines through in Pessoa's criticism is that the author is conscious of transcending his own influences, although he assimilates and transforms many of them because they serve his objectives.

13. Indeed, Pessoa's thought is almost always affirmed in a negative manner. He appears to know what he does not want better than what he does want.

14. See Seabra, where the narrow interpretation of Pessoa's nationalism is convincingly rejected. See also Blanco's succinct but precise Note in A. Monteiro and Blanco, 251–55.

15. We may ask ourselves if Pessoa maintained throughout his lifetime this conception of poetry as a potential spiritual mobilizer. Probably not, although nothing written that is known to us makes us suppose that he abandoned it. It seems indubitable that for years he maintained this conviction as a given. In the final phase of his life, the doubts about each one of his certainties intensified and multiplied, as did the abulia that he confessed made him incapable of taking action or carrying out everything that he recognized as important. In a letter to Adolfo Casais Monteiro, who gently rebuked the publication of *Mensagem*, Pessoa assumes his nationalist side without reservation: "Sou, de facto, um nacionalista mystico, um sebastianista racional. Mas sou, àparte isso, até em contradicção com isso, muitas outras coisas. E essas coisas, pela mesma natureza do livro, a *Mensagem* não as inclue" ("I am, in fact, a mythic nationalist, a rational Sebastianist. But I am, aside from that, and even in contradiction with that, many other things. And those things, by the same nature of the book, *Mensagem* does not include"; A. Monteiro and Blanco 228–30).

16. The disagreements Pessoa has with Sorel do not have anything to do with Sorel's conception of myth but strictly with his socialist views.

17. I believe the translation should be "the myth," not "a myth."

18. This interview was first published in the *Jornal do Commercio e das Colonias* (*Journal of Commerce and Colonies*), curiously on the historic date of 28 May 1926.

The "Great Book," Caeiro, and Pessoa's Theory of Poetry

Irene Ramalho-Santos

In "The Art of Rumination: Pessoa's Heteronyms Revisited," I refer to *Livro do desassossego* (*The Book of Disquietude*) as Pessoa's "book of ruminations" (see also Ramalho-Santos, "Arte").[1] It was my way of putting in writing what I had been suggesting for some time and wish to explore further in this essay: that the *Livro* holds the theory of Pessoa's poetic practice. Throughout those sprawling, fragmentary texts that Pessoa never put together as a book (which does not mean that a book does not exist),[2] the *Livro* constructs a poetic subject that ends up not existing, whether silently hiding behind a poetics of absence or boisterously exploding into a poetics of excess—heteronymic multiplicity as the other side of not existing, or being nobody.[3] It is proper to this absented poetic subject to say nothing, and that is precisely how he ends up saying all there is to be said—about us and the world—in verse, in prose, and in the prose of his poems.

Livro do desassossego is "o Grande Livro que diz que somos" ("the Great Book that says we are"), as Teresa Sobral Cunha (Pessoa, *Desassossego* [Relógio d'Água] 325) first read the difficult manuscript recently redeciphered by Jerónimo Pizarro (Pessoa, *Desassossego* [Tinta] 271).[4] Here is how Pizarro now reads the passage in question, a handwritten addition to a curious typescript on cleanliness and uncleanliness, to which I will return: "Partir da Rua dos Dourados para o Impossível . . . erguer-me da carteira para o Ignoto. . . . Mas isto interseccionado com a Razão—o Grande Livro como dizem os franceses" ("To depart from Rua dos Douradores for the Impossible . . . rise from my desk for the Unknown. . . . [B]ut *intersected* by Reason, the Great Book, as the French say"; *Desassossego* [Tinta], frag. no. 211, p. 271; *Disquiet* [New Directions], frag. no. 206, p. 218; emphasis added). "Interseccionado" ("intersected") cannot but bring to mind Pessoa's major modernist isms: *paùlismo* ("swampism"), *sensacionismo* ("sensationism"), and *interseccionismo* ("intersectionism"), the third of which he once described as rather a "method" than a movement (Ramalho-Santos, *Atlantic Poets* 162). Whether as method or movement, in 1914 Pessoa was planning an anthology of intersectionism (*Antologia do Interseccionismo*); at about the same time, while he and Mário de Sá-Carneiro were discussing the "intersection of literature and politics," Pessoa dropped the name of a new ism that apparently never went beyond the privacy of Pessoa's exchange with Sá-Carneiro but that becomes very interesting in the context of this essay: *Caeirismo*.[5]

The *grand livre* ("great book") of the French is *le grand livre de comptabilité*, the credit-and-debit ledger of boss Vasques's firm of business transactions with the world first "discovered" by the Portuguese. In other words, *le grand livre* of the French is, in good commercial Portuguese, *o Razão*, the book of accounts that it is the assistant bookkeeper Bernardo Soares's responsibility to keep. It seems to me, therefore, that when Pessoa thought of the *grand livre* of the French and capitalized *Razão* (as Pizarro shows), he forgot to replace the "a" introducing "razão" with the *o* that should introduce "Razão." This is precisely what Richard Zenith does starting with his ninth edition of the *Livro*, suggesting that it is difficult to distinguish *a* from *o* in the scribbled addition (see Pessoa, *Desassossego* [Assírio e Alvim; 2013], frag. no. 42, p. 81; 517 un).[6] Zenith is right, of course, that Pessoa wanted Bernardo Soares's ledger to resonate with reason and all the faculties of reason, not least the imagination. Or perhaps it would suffice to say, after Wallace Stevens, "true imagination," convening "intelligence" and "memory," as "the sum of our faculties" (Stevens 61). After all, Bernardo Soares's Book of Accounts lives on the same street ("Rua dos Douradores") as the "livro casual e meditado" ("casual, meditated book") that the poet goes on writing all along with the same "cuidado e indifferença" ("care and indifference"; Pessoa, *Desassossego* [Assírio e Alvim; 1998] frag. no. 13, p. 55; my trans.).[7] The interesting thing is that the "livro estúpido" ("stupid book") of "impressões diarias" ("random impressions"; *Desassossego*, frag. no. 442, p. 390–91; *Disquiet* [New Directions] frag. no. 297, p. 307) and the ledger interrupt each other. One of the fragments (*Desassossego*, frag. no. 409, pp. 365–66; *Disquiet*, frag. no. 413, pp. 438–39) actually relates that, on a particular day, Bernardo Soares "subitamente" ("suddenly") found himself alone in the "escritório" ("office"). He was enjoying his solitude, fully immersed in memory, daydreaming, and imaginings, when this "solidão espairecida" ("amused solitude") was interrupted by the sudden arrival of one of the employees. "Vida normal" ("normal life") restored, the assistant bookkeeper picked up the "caneta esquecida" ("forgotten pen") to resume his work on the ledger. The pen retrieved from its forgetfulness in "devaneio" ("reverie")[8] to resume ledger work is also the subjectless pen that materializes the poet's "dream writing" in the textual space of the "casual, meditated book." After all, the two books intersect in the *escritório*, literally, in Portuguese, the scene of writing (*escrita*).[9] It is at the intersection of these two books that what I call the book of ruminations emerges, the great book that speaks us all as it speaks the world— and speaks the poet by theoretically grounding him, even if in absentia. Thus, even if a misreading, Teresa Sobral Cunha's reading continues to make sense: at the intersection, the Great Book is the book "that says we are" ("que diz que somos").

Paulo de Medeiros argues forcefully that *Livro do desassossego* is "uma das mais importantes tentativas de teorizar a condição humana na modernidade" ("one of the most important attempts at theorizing the human condition in modernity"; *O silêncio* 157).[10] *O silêncio das sereias*, a title Medeiros borrows from Franz Kafka (*Das Schweigen der Sirenen*, or *The Silence of the Sirens*), shows that the *Livro* puts Pessoa alongside many other modernist authors in the Western tradition, Kafka foremost among them, who anxiously question the very idea of modernity and that of the human condition as "modern." We might even say that Pessoa's Bernardo Soares / assistant bookkeeper, no less than Kafka's Gregor Samsa / traveling-salesman-turned-"ungeheures Ungeziefer" ("monstrous insect") in *The Metamorphosis*, is a metaphor of the human condition in modernity (Kafka, *Verwandlung* 9; *Metamorphosis* 3). Medeiros also suggests that the poets' questioning of modernity and the human condition in modernity is inextricably linked to how they envision their own relation to writing. This is not exclusive to modernity. Though modernist poets, like Wallace Stevens, for example, or Pessoa, excelled at it, metapoetry was not an invention of modernism. Two centuries earlier, Hölderlin wondered in the elegy "Brot und Wein" ("Bread and Wine"), "[W]ozu Dichter in dürftiger Zeit?" ("[W]hat are poets for in destitute times?"; 30). We could even visit a more distant time and remote place, invoke the pre-Columbian poet Nezahualcoyotl, and give voice to the Nahuatl poet's anxiety about the impossibility of speaking "true words" and so letting flowers, feathers, and stones say the unsayable (see also Ramalho-Santos, "America in Poetry"). "What is writing for?" the works of many of our modernist poets cry out, whether explicitly or implicitly, in a centerless time of abysmal unknowns, ambiguous progress, senseless wars, somber emptiness, major insignificances, unsettling alienation, bourgeois ambitions, formless individualities, oppressive inequalities, noisy unanimities, suffocating commonalities, hypocritical solidarities, and fake moralisms.

Pessoa is no exception: he is also troubled by the purpose of writing. *Livro do desassossego*, Medeiros argues, "deve ser lido como uma grande e ininterrupta indagação sobre o que significa ser-se escritor" ("should be read as a large and uninterrupted inquiry into what it means to be a writer"; *O silêncio* 148). Eduardo Lourenço, the critic who has written compelling pages about the *Livro* as an existential *cri de coeur*, has described the work as "escrita como des-existência" ("writing as the opposite, or other side, of existence").[11] I would like to push Lourenço's and Medeiros's insights a little further and suggest that, more than theorizing the human condition in modernity by inquiring about the impossible task of the writer, *Livro do desassossego* theorizes the poet—and the very act of *poeming* itself.[12] It does so by absenting the poet from writing. Theoretically, the poet gives precedence to the poem by absenting himself.[13] Once the poem is written and the work done, the writer is no longer there; indeed, it seems that the poet was never there at all: "Sou, em grande parte, a mesma prosa que escrevo" ("I am, in large measure, the very prose I write"; Pessoa, *Desassossego*, frag. no. 193, p. 200; *Disquiet*, frag. no. 316, p. 338); "Tornei-me uma figura de livro" ("I have become a figure in a book"; *Desassossego*, frag. no. 192, p. 201; *Disquiet*, frag. no. 316, p. 338); "Sou bocados de personagens de dramas meus" ("I am bits of characters of my own plays"; *Desassossego*, frag. no. 495, p. 442; *Disquiet*, frag. no. 54, p. 60);[14] "Quero ser uma obra de arte" ("I want to be a work of art"; *Desassossego*, frag. no. 114, p. 139; *Disquiet*, frag. no. 29, p. 31); "Sou uma figura de romance por escrever" ("I am a character in an unwritten novel"; *Desassossego*, frag. no. 262, p. 258; *Disquiet*, frag. no. 337, p. 367); "ser a página de um livro" ("to be the page of a book"; *Desassossego*, frag. no. 31, pp. 66–68; *Disquiet*, frag. no. 218, p. 231). The page of the book is the "pessoa própria" ("the proper person/Pessoa"; *Desassossego*, frag. no. 259, pp. 254–55; *Disquiet*, frag. no. 326, p. 351) into which the writer delights in losing himself and letting his not-being-himself be cuddled by sensuous, siren-like words and vibrant images.

Álvaro de Campos's memorable characterization of Fernando Pessoa's nonexistence has been repeated many times: "Fernando Pessoa . . . não existe, propriamente falando" ("Properly speaking, Fernando Pessoa does not exist").[15] In an introduction for a projected edition of *Livro do desassossego* that circumstances prevented him from bringing to light, Jorge de Sena wrote some very illuminating pages on Fernando Pessoa's "ciência de não-ser" ("science of not-being"; Sena, "Introdução" 181).[16] My emphasis, however, is different from his. Since I am particularly interested in understanding Pessoa in *Livro do desassossego* as the theorist of his poetic practice, I start out by paraphrasing Álvaro de Campos— *theoretically speaking, the poet does not exist*—and then go on to suggest that this phrase of mine sums up Pessoa's theory of poetry. Pessoa's oeuvre as a whole, with its mirror games of properly nonexisting *pessoas*, already points in this direction, as Sena so brilliantly shows. I would like to argue further that, from the *Livro*'s viewpoint, the nonexisting persons prefigure the theoretically nonexisting poet. As "pessoas-livros" ("people-books"; Pessoa, *Páginas íntimas* 101), the heteronyms make up the prosthetic poet that Soares keeps insisting does not exist or is a makeshift nothing: "Sou postiço" ("I am artificial"; *Desassossego*, frag. no. 30, p. 65; *Disquiet*, frag. no. 353, p. 381), the writer declares in one of the sketches, this "aesthetics of artificiality" (as identified in *Desassossego*, frag. no. 114, pp. 138–39; *Disquiet*, frag. no. 29, pp. 31–32) promptly creating the aesthetically other-of-the-poet—the poem, writing, poetry itself. This is, I think, how Pessoa reads Rimbaud's paradox in his famous *voyant* letter (to Georges Izambard, 13 May 1871, and Paul Demeny, 15 May 1871): "Je est un autre" ("I is an other"; Rimbaud 304–05). The poet's radical other is poetry. As such, Pessoa's poet is *estrangeiro* ("foreign"; Pessoa, *Desassossego*, frag. no. 83, pp. 112–13; frag. no. 86, p. 115; see also "Lisbon Revisited (1926)" [*Obra completa de Álvaro de Campos* 184–86]), *transeunte* ("passer-by"; frag. no. 208, pp. 213–14; see also "Lisbon Revisited (1926)"), *translato* ("translated"; frag. no. 31, pp. 66–68; see also "Cruzou por mim" [*Obra completa de Álvaro de Campos* 339–42]), *intruso* ("intruder"; frag. no. 429, pp. 381–82), *hóspede* ("guest"; frag. no. 429, pp. 381–82), *intervalo* ("interval"; frag. no. 204, pp. 210–11), and *entre-sou* ("betweenness"; frag. no. 281, pp. 271–72). That is to say, the poet (not the empirical human being—Pessoa—to whom all the credit must ultimately be given) is "nothing," the nothing that Álvaro de Campos so beautifully materializes in "Tabacaria" ("Tobacco Shop") by postulating not poetic immortality (a topos widely sung in the Western tradition) but poetic mortality: "[O Dono da Tabacaria] morrerá e eu morrerei. / Ele deixará a tabuleta, eu deixarei versos /

A certa altura morrerá a tabuleta também, e também os versos" ("[The Owner of the Tobacco Shop] will die and I will die. / He will leave the signboard, and I will leave poems. / After a while the signboard will also die, and also the poems"; *Obra completa de Álvaro de Campos* 204). The poet's realization of his absolute nonexistence and being no one comes to the writer in the *Livro* in a flash: "Cheguei hoje, de repente, a uma sensação absurda e justa. Reparei, num relâmpago íntimo, que não sou ninguém. Ninguém, absolutamente ninguém" ("I arrived today at an absurd yet precise sensation. I realized, in an inner flash, that I am no one. Absolutely no one"; *Desassossego*, frag. no. 262, p. 257; *Disquiet*, frag. no. 337, p. 367). The radical solitude of the poet's being-nothing comes across poignantly in a passage of the *Livro* depicting the pariah-like status of an utterly forlorn human being: "Nunca tive alguém a quem pudesse chamar 'Mestre.' Não morreu por mim nenhum Cristo. Nenhum Buda me indicou um caminho. No alto dos meus sonhos nenhum Apolo ou Atena me apareceu, para que me iluminasse a alma" ("I have never had anyone I could call 'Master.' No Christ died for me. No Buddha showed me the way. In my grandest dreams, no Apollo or Athena ever appeared to enlighten my soul"; *Desassossego*, frag. no. 461, p. 406; *Disquiet*, frag. no. 160, p. 165).

We might even say that the fact that Bernardo Soares is not allowed to write poems—which does not mean that there is no poetry in *Livro do desassossego*— is one more piece of evidence that, theoretically speaking, "the poet" does not exist—which is also the reason why Alberto Caeiro, the "master," must die while, in a sense, contradicting or challenging the assistant bookkeeper. Furthermore, Caeiro, doubly nonexisting because he is already "dead," continues to make poems appear.[17]

While all the major heteronyms make subtle or indirect appearances in the *Livro* as nonexisting poets (Ricardo Reis perhaps less so),[18] Alberto Caeiro is actually explicitly invoked and reread, and a couple of lines from poem VII of *O guardador de rebanhos* (*The Keeper of Sheep*) are quoted as providing an "inspiration" and a "liberation":[19]

> Releio passivamente, recebendo o que sinto como uma inspiração e um livramento, aquelas frases simples de Caeiro, na referência natural do que resulta do pequeno tamanho da sua aldeia. Dali, diz ele, porque é pequena, pode ver-se mais do mundo do que da cidade; e por isso a aldeia é maior que a cidade . . .
>
> > "Porque sou do tamanho do que vejo
> > E não do tamanho da minha altura."
>
> Frases como estas, que parecem crescer sem vontade que as houvesse dito, limpam-me de toda a metafísica que espontaneamente acrescento à vida. Depois de as ler, chego à janela sobre a rua estreita, olho o grande céu e os muitos astros, e sou livre como um splendor alado cuja vibração me estremece no corpo todo.

"Sou do tamanho do que vejo!" Cada vez que penso esta frase com toda a atenção dos meus nervos, ela me parece destinada a reconstruir consteladamente o universo. "Sou do tamanho do que vejo!" Que grande posse mental vai desde o poço das emoções profundas até às altas estrelas que se reflectem nele, e, assim, em certo modo, ali estão.

E já agora, consciente de saber ver, olho a vasta metafísica objectiva dos céus todos com uma segurança que me dá vontade de morrer cantando. "Sou do tamanho do que vejo!" E o vago luar, inteiramente meu, começa a estragar de vago o azul meio-negro do horizonte.

Tenho vontade de erguer os braços e gritar coisas de uma selvajaria ignorada, de dizer palavras aos mistérios altos, de afirmar uma nova personalidade larga aos grandes espaços da matéria vazia.

Mas recolho-me e abrando. "Sou do tamanho do que vejo!" E a frase ficame sendo a alma inteira, encosto a ela todas as emoções que sinto, e sobre mim, por dentro, como por sobre a cidade por fora, cai a paz indecifrável do luar duro que começa largo com o anoitecer.

(Desassossego, frag. no. 46, p. 80)

I passively reread, welcoming what I feel as an inspiration and a liberation, those simple lines by Caeiro referring to what naturally results from the smallness of his village. From there, he says, because it is small, you can see more of the world than from the city, hence the village is larger than the city . . .

> "Because I am the size of what I see
> And not the size of my height."

Lines like these, which seem to crop up regardless of any will to say them, cleanse me of all the metaphysics I spontaneously add on to life. After reading them, I go to my window overlooking the narrow street, look at the sky and all the stars, and feel free in a winged splendor whose vibration makes my whole body shiver.

"I am the size of what I see!" Each time I think of this phrase with the attention of all my nerves, it seems to me to be destined to reconstruct the universe constellatedly. "I am the size of what I see!" What mental power goes from the well of deep emotions to the high stars reflected on it and which, somehow, are there too.

Actually, aware that I can see, I look at the vast objective metaphysics of all the skies with a certainty that makes me want to die singing. "I am the size of what I see!" And the vague moonlight, all my own, begins to spoil with vagueness the horizon's half-black blue.

I feel [the urge to raise] my arms and shout things of unknown savagery, to speak words to the high mysteries, to assert a new and vast personality before the wide spaces of empty matter.

But I collect myself and calm down. "I am the size of what I see!" And the phrase becomes my entire soul, I lean all the emotions I feel against it, and upon me, inside, as upon the city, outside, there falls the indecipherable peace of the harsh moonlight that begins to spread as the night falls.

(*Disquiet*, frag. no. 227, pp. 241–42)

In this long quotation I would like to highlight two images: cleanness ("asseio") and constellations. The fragment clearly suggests that Caeiro cleanses the speaker in the *Livro* "of all the metaphysics [he] spontaneously add[s] on to life." This line of thinking will force me to go back to fragment 42 (which begins, "Não compreendo senão como uma espécie de falta de asseio . . ." ["Only as a kind of lack of cleanness do I understand . . ."]; *Desassossego* frag. no. 42, p. 81; *Disquiet*, frag. no. 206, pp. 217–18) as well as to "o Razão" and from there to Caeiro's poems. There we encounter constellations, for Caeiro, like the starry sky, appears endowed with the astral power to preside over the whole universe; what fragment 46 suggests Caeiro's phrase ("I am the size of what I see") is supposed to do, literally, is to "reconstruct the universe constellatedly" ("reconstruir consteladamente o universo"), the unusual adverb pointing to the importance of astral influence on life on earth. But it is not so much Pessoa's well-known interest in astrology that concerns me here; it is rather his use of the astral image of constellations as self-sufficient, poetry-like forms (or vice versa).

Besides "consteladamente" ("in the manner of constellations" or "the way constellations work"), *Livro do desassossego* has several instances of the use of the verb *constelar* ("constellate"), whether in the specific sense of having to do with astrology, as in the phrase "constelado destino" ("constellated destiny"; *Desassossego*, frag. no. 389, p. 350; *Disquiet*, frag. no. 89, p. 103); in simple reference to the starry night, as in "a grande noite vagamente constelada" ("the vast, vaguely constellated night"; *Desassossego*, frag. no. 50, p. 83; *Disquiet*, frag. no. 358, p. 386); or meaning "adorning, decorating," as in "constelar de novas flores ou de novos astros os campos ou os céus" ("constellating the fields or the skies with new flowers and new stars"; *Desassossego*, frag. no. 27, p. 63; *Disquiet*, frag. no. 296, p. 306). In a particularly striking fragment (*Desassossego*, frag. no. 110, p. 136), the verb is used reflexively ("constelo-me" ["I constellate myself"]; *Disquiet*, frag. no. 256, p. 271), with the result that the writer seems to disappear in astral infinity as if part of a constellation. I am tempted to see here Caeiro (as in *Desassossego*, frag. no. 46, p. 80) reconstructing his own universe constellatedly. This line of thinking leads me once again to Caeiro's poems, this time with a special reference to *Poemas inconjunctos* (*Inconjunct Poems; Obra Completa de Alberto Caeiro* 85–120) and the theoretical implications of such an apparently strange title.[20]

But first let me comment briefly on fragment 42 and that apparent afterthought rashly scribbled at the end of the previously existing typescript. Or perhaps it was just a sudden thought Pessoa wanted to register for future use. Some readers have indeed assumed that those scanty three lines do not belong there. Leyla Perrone-Moisés, for example, does not include them in her edition

of the *Livro* (see Pessoa, *Desassossego* [Editora Brasiliense] 86–87).[21] I sympa-
thize with this view. I myself had doubts once. On my old copy of Zenith's first
edition I, too, scribbled in the margin early on, "[D]oesn't seem to 'belong' here."
Although I have never erased the comment (as part of the history of my understanding of the *Livro* and Pessoa in general), my old perplexity is long gone. The
desire manifested in those final, earnestly penciled words I would call immortal
longings that yet do not let go of mortality; they are rather intersected, by way
of the concrete reality of Vasques's ledger, with the chaotic, unpleasant dirtiness
so graphically described in the previous paragraphs. Animal images of filth, slim-
iness, danger, and death combine to picture the sorry human condition in
modernity as existing in little less than a pigsty, however metaphorical. At the
same time, though, the tropes on "lavar o destino" ("washing destiny") and
"mudar de estar" ("changing being-there"), though suggesting multiple ways of
being, the heteronyms immediately coming to mind, point above all to the
process of purification that Maurice Blanchot's essay on "le droit à la mort" ("the
right to death"; "Littérature"; "Literature") presents as a condition of writing.

By articulating such images and concepts as cleanness ("asseio") and unclean-
ness ("desasseio") with others, like life, existence, destiny, powerlessness, consciousness and unconsciousness, nothingness, and death, the typed text of
fragment 42 suggests itself as an excellent example of how the *Livro* theorizes
the human condition in modernity. The brief handwritten passage added at the
end, however, with its focus on the intersecting Great Book, sheds a new, meta-
poetical light on the writing previously reported: "escrevo nos vidros, no pó do
necessário, o meu nome em letras grandes, assinatura quotidiana da minha
escritura com a morte" ("I write on the windowpanes, on the dust of necessity,
my name in capital letters, daily signature on my compact with death"; *Desassossego*, frag. no. 42, pp. 76–77; *Disquiet*, frag. no. 206, pp. 217–18). The writer
of these dark lines does not exist, does not live, and does not die, simply because
he is "não-ele" ("not-him"). The empty space of his (not) being-there is the all
properly named the nothing. Such a nonbeing doesn't even have the right to
death. Or perhaps, as Blanchot would put it, it is "l'œuvre" ("the work") that
"n'est finalement plus capable de mourir" ("is no longer capable of dying"), thus
offering the writer "la dérision de l'immortalité" ("the mockery of immortality";
"Littérature" 328; "Literature" 340). The paradoxes of "mays" and "musts" and
"power" at the close of Emily Dickinson's "My Life had stood—a Loaded Gun"
(J754/Fr764) speak eloquently to the complex intersections of life and art with
which Blanchot deals in this essay.[22] The (modernist) scribbler of the *Livro*, by
constructing his own nonexistence, offers a far more somber view of "the mockery
of immortality": "Quem vive como eu não morre: acaba, murcha, desvegeta-se"
("Whoever lives like me does not die: he ends, withers, devegetates").

Blanchot's essay is useful for reading Pessoa's work as a whole. In fact, it sounds
at times, implausibly, as if written with multiple Pessoas in mind: the writer as
several people in one ("Littérature" 303; "Literature" 312), the poet becoming
other ("Littérature" 305; "Literature" 314), and writing condemning the poet to

a life that has nothing to do with real life ("Littérature" 328; "Literature" 340). My understanding of Pessoa's poetic theory, however, is not the Mallarméan one, so well articulated by Blanchot, that the poet disappears by becoming his poem; my understanding of Pessoa's theory of poetry, as I have been suggesting, is that the Pessoan poet is theoretically nonexistent. Caeiro, who makes the assistant bookkeeper want to die singing his line, "I am the size of what I see," is cleansed of all metaphysics—that being perhaps why he returns "virginity" to Álvaro de Campos[23]—and becomes the nonpoet purified into absolute seeing: "Eu nem sequer sou poeta; vejo" ("I am not even a poet; I see"), says Caeiro-of-the-clear-gaze in a poem from *Poemas inconjunctos* ("A espantosa realidade das coisas" ["The amazing reality of things"]; *Obra completa de Alberto Caeiro* 91). Before turning to *Poemas inconjunctos*, I wish to go over the condition of the poet in *O guardador de rebanhos*.

Poem I of *O guardador de rebanhos* traces what I just called the "condition" of the poet—that is to say, the condition of being a nonpoet: he doesn't want to be a poet ("Ser poeta não é uma ambição minha" ["Being a poet is not my ambition"]), and he doesn't really write poems, black on white ("Escrevo versos num papel que está no meu pensamento" ["I write poems on a piece of paper in my mind"]). All he wants is to be found in his nonpoems as "qualquer coisa natural" ("something natural"; *Obra completa de Alberto Caeiro* 32). Of course, there is a poet in *O guardador de rebanhos*—"Alberto Caeiro"—but it is a poet always on the verge of undoing himself; a poet intent on learning how to unlearn, on cleansing himself of learning, so as to be able merely to see; a poet eager to unwrap himself and be, not "Alberto Caeiro" (i.e., a poet), but a human animal produced by nature (57; poem XXVI); a poet prone to falling sick (49–50; poem XV); a poet who writes only the prose of his verses (58–59; poem XXVIII) and lets poetry come forth like flowers (64; poem XXXVI). In many of the poems of *O guardador de rebanhos*, we can hear Pessoa's denunciation of romantic sentimentalism as a way of being *not a poet*. A good example is precisely poem XXVIII, just mentioned, where Caeiro discredits poets that commit the sin of pathetic fallacy by ascribing feelings to flowers, souls to stones, and ecstasies in the moonlight to rivers. Or poem X, where only the keeper of sheep knows what the wind really says, not the passerby supposedly hearing memories and longings (47–48). Better still is poem XXXII, about "um homem das cidades" ("a city man"), whose preaching of social justice leaves Caeiro wondering about rural sounds *not being like* the bells of little chapels summoning flowers and brooks to mass (61–62).

"A minha poesia é natural como levantar-se o vento" ("My poetry is as natural as wind rising"; 49), the last line of Caeiro's poem XIV, sums up the theory of Pessoa's poetless poetry: *poiesis* without *poietes*, as is clearer in poem XXXVI, inveighing against poets that strain themselves in their making in order to be artists because they don't know how to bloom (64). Eduardo Lourenço once said that Caeiro's poetry hankers after a silence prior to the word (*Pessoa revisitado* 43). Could this be what Pessoa was thinking of when he came up with

"Caeirism"? To be sure, "Caeiro" is not a nature poet, not even in the manner of Francis of Assisi. Although Francis may have been an inspiration of sorts to the Pessoan persona, he "astonishes" Caeiro negatively in one of his "inconjunct poems" for loving things without even looking at them ("Leram-me hoje S. Francisco de Assis" ["I was read Saint Francis today"]; *Poemas completos* 133; *Poemas de Alberto Caeiro* 87; *Obra completa de Alberto Caeiro* 70).

What I am suggesting is that "Caeiro" is not a "something" poet, or an "anything" poet. "Caeiro" is a *poetry poet*. This is how I understand the phrase that proclaims "Caeiro" "o poeta do ovo de Colombo" ("the poet of Columbus's egg"; *Obra completa de Alberto Caeiro* 246; see also 281).[24] His utterly original, deceivingly "easy" poems, like the line that so struck Bernardo Soares ("Sou do tamanho do que vejo" ["I am the size of what I see"]), "seem to crop up regardless of any will to say them." No human making could have produced Caeiro's poems. They are like constellations. Sometimes, they offer themselves *not in conjunction*. That is what *inconjunct* means in astronomy:[25] celestial bodies that, by reason of their positions, do not affect one another. They may be part of a constellation, but they are not in conjunction: they are "inconjunct poems."

Thanks to Ivo Castro, we know now that Pessoa put together *O guardador de rebanhos* as a cycle with extremely great care (Pessoa, *Poemas de Alberto Caeiro* 7–25, 263–64). The set of forty-nine poems survived as such, in spite of many gestures of revision on the individual poems, even after publication, and has come down to us in that form in all the editions, even if the various modern editors use different individual choices amongst Pessoa's post-print variants.[26] A beautiful constellation, I would call *O guardador de rebanhos*. In a letter to Gaspar Simões of 25 February 1933, commenting on his intention of publishing his complete poems, Pessoa also seemed to consider *O pastor amoroso* (*The Shepherd in Love*) as another cycle. *Poemas inconjunctos*, however, he had not yet collected ("não tenho reunidos"), nor was he sure when he could do it, since the poems required revisions that were not merely "verba" ("verbal") but rather "psicológica" ("psychological") as well (*Obra poética* 707). The rest of Caeiro's work Pessoa considered mere "posthumous" fragments, or so he had Ricardo Reis write in one of this heteronym's many reflections on Caeiro (*Obras em prosa* 126). Reis goes on to say of Caeiro that, after *O pastor amoroso*, his sensibility and intelligence pale and his work is not the same. Once *O guardador de rebanhos* was written, Reis concludes, nothing seems to justify the (inconjunct) poems.

It is true, as Reis argues, that the imaginary of the *Poemas inconjunctos* is largely the same as that of *O guardador de rebanhos*, though on a more somber note, referring more darkly to death and dying. But the privileging of mere seeing is still there, as in the poem quoted above, "A espantosa realidade das coisas" ("The amazing reality of things"; *Obra completa de Alberto Caeiro* 91), where the poet claims not to be a poet and just to see; or the poet's insistence on the poetic necessity of always seeing for the first time in "Creança desconhecida e suja brincando á minha porta" ("Unknown and dirty child playing at my door"; *Obra completa de Alberto Caeiro* 106); or the importance of looking without opinion, which is another way of "merely" seeing, in "Entre o que vejo de um campo e o que vejo de outro campo" ("Between what I see of a field and what I see of another field"; *Obra completa de Alberto Caeiro* 110). The topos of sickness also crops up in *Inconjunct Poems*, rather more insistently, as if confirming Reis's opinion about Caeiro's diminished powers after *O guardador de rebanhos* and *O pastor amoroso*: "Estou doente. Meus pensamentos começam a estar confusos" ("I am sick. My thoughts begin to be confused"; *Obra completa de Alberto Caeiro* 98); "Mas por que me interrogo, senão porque estou doente?" ("But why do I question myself if not because I am sick?"), in "Seja o que for que esteja no centro do mundo" ("Whatever it is that is at the center of the world"; *Obra completa de Alberto Caeiro* 100); "Estive doente um momento" ("I was sick for a while"), in "Pétala dobrada para traz da rosa que outros diriam de velludo" ("Back-folded petal of the rose others say is of velvet"; *Obra completa de Alberto Caeiro* 107). This last example cannot but remind the reader of the poems in *O guardador de rebanhos* in which Caeiro *is not a poet*, as opposed to those sentimental poets that ascribe meaning and feeling to things. And yet the poet of *Poemas inconjunctos* never makes himself totally absent, as we saw happen in *O guardador de rebanhos*. There is even a poem in which the poet fails to perform his theory of disappearing into only seeing. He speaks of things while (he confesses) he should merely see them, without thinking and regardless of time or space ("Vive, dizes, no presente" ["Live, you say, in the present"]; *Obra completa de Alberto Caeiro* 112). The poet of *Poemas inconjunctos* is never in a hurry, because the sun and the moon are never in a hurry either ("Não tenho pressa: não a teem o sol e a lua" ["I am in no hurry: nor are the sun and the moon"]; *Obra completa de Alberto Caeiro* 111[27]). Likewise, perhaps, Pessoa never hurried back to these poems—constellated with sun, moon, and stars as some of them are—to put them in conjunction and make a real constellation out of them.

Ivo Castro says that devoted readers of Pessoa are still a long way off from a "padronizada" ("standardized") edition of *Poemas inconjunctos* (Pessoa, *Poemas de Alberto Caeiro* 263). I wonder, would Pessoa really want one? Or could he ever have verified a "standard" edition? Assuming their posthumous condition and the risk of fragmentariness, as Ricardo Reis suggests, Caeiro's "inconjunct poems" are like deconstellated stars (Bernardo Soares would say), or stars out of conjunction (I say); or, elaborating on Blanchot, they are stars of disaster intimating "le limite de l'écriture" ("the limit of writing")—the fragment-poem in abeyance or interrupted (*Écriture* 17; *Writing* 7). After all, if the poet does not exist, theoretically speaking, "todos os poemas são sempre escriptos no dia seguinte" ("all the poems are always written the next day"; *Obra completa de Álvaro de Campos* [2014] 225)—by being read.[28]

NOTES

1. Except where I specify otherwise, I quote from Richard Zenith's first edition of 1998, providing fragment numbers paired with page numbers, and from the 2017 translation of *The Book of Disquiet*, by Margaret Jull Costa, edited by Jerónimo Pizarro and published by New Directions. (I have explained elsewhere why I prefer *desassossego* rendered as "disquietude," Zenith's first choice as well. See Pessoa, *Disquietude*; Ramalho-Santos, "Tail.")

2. For a thorough description of the disquieting nonexistence of *Livro do desassossego*, see Pizarro, "Muitos desassossegos."

3. José Gil first spoke of *Livro do desassossego* as Pessoa's "laboratório poético" ("poetic laboratory"). He reads the *Livro* as the active locus of poetic experimentation but not of theoretical thinking. Pessoa theorizes "preferably in other places," Gil adds, "journal articles, projects of prefaces, letters." He is right, but my argument in this essay is that the *Livro*'s poetic experimentation implicitly weaves a (poetless) theory of poetry. See Gil, *Fernando Pessoa* 13.

4. Sobral Cunha immediately identified in this passage the clear reference to the ledger ("o Razão"). All translations, unless otherwise attributed, are my own.

5. *Antologia do Interseccionismo* is mentioned in a letter to Armando Côrtes-Rodrigues, 4 October 1914; *Caeirismo* in the draft of a letter to Sá-Carneiro (28 July 1914?). See Pessoa, *Sensacionismo* 348–53.

6. Zenith has also silently corrected some lapses since his first edition.

7. For "Rua dos Douradores" as the "home" of both "life" and "art," see Pessoa, *Desassossego*, frag. no. 9, p. 53; *Disquiet*, frag. no. 343, pp. 373–74.

8. "Devaneio" throughout the *Livro* suggests poetic creativity. I wonder if, when he translated it as "reverie," Zenith had also in mind Emily Dickinson's poem that begins, "To make a prairie it takes a clover and one bee" (Dickinson, Transcription; J1755/Fr1779).

9. See Derrida, "Freud": "The 'subject' of writing does not exist if we mean by that some sovereign solitude of the author. The subject of writing is a system of relations between strata: of the Mystic Pad, of the psyche, of society, of the world. Within that scene the punctual simplicity of the classical subject is not to be found" (113). The phrase "dream writing" is Derrida's (87). The pen is, of course, part of Freud's "Mystic Pad."

10. See also Medeiros's *Pessoa's Geometry of the Abyss*.

11. See E. Lourenço, "Poética" 105. Note how the critic's thinking cleverly plays with existence-as-desistance.

12. *Poeming* refers to the act of creating or engaging with poetry in a broad sense—not just writing a poem but embodying the poetic process, becoming a vessel for poetry. It emphasizes the dynamic, active nature of poetry in the *Livro do desassossego*, whose text theorizes not just the content of poetry but the very act of living and breathing poetry, even to the point of the poet's own disappearance from the act of writing.

13. I am speaking here of a male poet, but great women poets often choose to absent themselves as well. Emily Dickinson, for example, absents herself exceptionally well into "possibility" ("I dwell in Possibility"; J657/Fr466).

14. In his first edition, Zenith gave an alternative version in the MS: "Sou uma personagem de dramas meus" ("I am a character of my own plays"). Pizarro prefers, as do I,

"bocados de personagens" ("bits of characters") as more in tune with the fragment's musings on the "pulverization of personality," clearly pointing to the heteronymic explosion (*Desassossego* [Tinta], frag. no. 54, pp. 98–99). Zenith later makes the same choice (Pessoa, *Desassossego* [Assírio e Alvim; 2013] 445).

15. In a text first published by Teresa Rita Lopes, *Pessoa por conhecer* 413.

16. My arguments here relate more to the fragments of what Sena calls the last phase of the *Livro*—that is to say, sketches dated roughly from 1929 onward of a work definitely ascribed to Bernardo Soares.

17. José Gil has written some very interesting pages on the philosophical meaning of "the death of Caeiro" (*Cansaço* 37–68). I am concerned here with its poetic meaning.

18. But see the Reis-like mode in *Desassossego*, frag. no. 236, pp. 234–35: "Não se subordinar a nada" ("To submit to nothing"; Pessoa, *Disquiet*, frag. no. 283, p. 293).

19. It is curious that Caeiro, the "master" of them all, should appear as the most prominent heteronym in a *Livro* that calls masterhood into question. Manuel Gusmão sensed (but did not explore) the importance of Caeiro's explicit presence in *Livro do desassossego* very early on. See Gusmão's fine reading of Caeiro in his *A poesia de Alberto Caeiro* (25–27).

20. Perhaps because it seemed to suggest the idea of poems not part of a "set" (*conjunto*, a word spelled by Pessoa as "conjuncto"), this title has been long established in Pessoan scholarship as *Poemas inconjuntos*, even though "inconjunto" is not a proper Portuguese word. Although I do not usually favor keeping Pessoa's often erratic orthography in modern, readerly editions, it will be clear later on why I recommend always keeping Pessoa's spelling in this case. I first reflected on the astronomical and astrological implications of *Poemas inconjunctos* in "Being Blind, Being Nothing, Being a Poet: Emily Dickinson 'Reads' Fernando Pessoa": "Pessoa called these Caeiro poems *Poemas inconjunctos*, I suspect, because he did not see them as in conjunction with *O guardador de rebanhos* (*The Keeper of Sheep*) or *O pastor amoroso* (*The Shepherd in Love*). Since in the Portuguese language 'inconjunto' does not register as a proper word to mean the opposite of *conjunto* ('set, ensemble'), Pessoa, who spelled both words 'conjuncto' and 'inconjuncto,' must be borrowing his meaning from the English word *inconjunct*. In English, *inconjunct* means 'celestial bodies lacking conjunction,' and that is probably how Pessoa wanted these poems to be read. Not as 'assorted poems,' 'miscellaneous poems,' or 'uncollected poems,' as translators and critics often have it, and not as poems not part of a set ('conjunto'), but rather as poems lacking conjunction: 'inconjunct poems.' These poems are out of shepherd orbit, so to speak, and yet they are somehow still part of the same constellation."

21. Curiously enough, however, Perrone-Moisés immediately follows the said fragment with another one that also mentions "o Razão" intersected with reverie: "Tenho diante de mim as duas páginas grandes do livro pesado" ("I have before me the two large pages of the heavy book"; Pessoa, *Desassossego*, frag. no. 5, p. 49; *Disquiet*, frag. no. 187, p. 198).

22. I offer a reading of Dickinson's poem in "Narcissus in the Desert."

23. Campos offered a response to Caeiro in his "Notas para a recordação do meu Mestre Caeiro" ("Notes to Remember My Master Caeiro"): "o efeito em mim foi receber de repente, em todas as minhas sensações, uma virgindade que não tinha tido" ("the effect on me was suddenly to receive, in all my sensations, a virginity I had not had before"; Pessoa, *Obras em prosa* 108).

24. Garcez shows that the originality of Caeiro's poetry consists in its dealing skillfully with its own dependence on and independence from the Western tradition of nature poetry in its articulations with religiosity, both Western and Eastern. To her mind, the phrase "Caeiro é o poeta do ovo de Colombo" ("Caeiro is the poet of Columbus's egg") means that Caeiro is the poet of the obvious (140).

25. The term is no longer widely used in astronomy; it is now practically circumscribed to astrology.

26. Pizarro and Patricio Ferrari, while keeping the *The Keeper of Sheep* intact, give sequential numbers to all the poems, the first poem of *O pastor amoroso* being number 50. The editors come up with a total of 115 (conjunct or inconjunct?) poems (Pessoa, *Obra completa de Alberto Caeiro* 31–120).

27. Pizarro edited this verse as part of a briefer version of the same poem (Pessoa, *Obra completa de Alberto Caeiro* 439).

28. Cf. Pessoa, *Obra poética* 376.

The Political Poetry of Álvaro de Campos: At the Margin of the Margin

Sofia de Sousa Silva

To my brother-in-law, Bayard Marques Palmeiro, in loving memory

In the long reception that the work of Fernando Pessoa has enjoyed among Portuguese poets since the beginning of its publication by the Ática publishing house in the 1940s, there has been room for many tributes, appropriations, and citations. But there has also been room for more or less subtle criticism of the poet. And there seems to be a common denominator in those harsh assessments. Among the poets, Sophia de Mello Breyner Andresen, who dedicated several poems to the creator of the heteronyms, resorts on more than one occasion to the expression "non-lived" to speak of Pessoa. In the poem "Cíclades" ("Cyclades"), Pessoa is "esquartejado pelas Fúrias do não vivido" ("quartered by the Furies of the non-lived"; Andresen, *Obra poética* 651). In "Fernando Pessoa," Pessoa invokes "a presença já perdida" ("his already lost presence") and says that he was "como as ervas não colhidas" ("as the unpicked grass"; Andresen, *Livro sexto* 62; *Log Book* 48–49),[1] as if, in him, life and work opposed each other and the choice was always in favor of work, in detriment to life and, perhaps above all, to love (see F. Lourenço, "O não vivido"; Martins, "Passo muito depressa"; S. Silva, "A vida verdadeira"). Jorge de Sena speaks of "artifice" and "pride" concerning the creation of the heteronyms, ultimately defined as "faking" (in allusion to Pessoa's definition of the poet as a faker in "Autopsicografia" ["Autopsychography"; *Poesia: Antologia mínima* 95]), which he regards as a kind of absence of the individual. To faking Sena opposes his own notion of testimony, with which he identifies poetry and by means of which it is up to poetry to effectively change the world (Sena, Preface). According to Sena, "faking" can only educate the spirit but cannot change it. Mário Cesariny, an exponent of late Portuguese surrealism, in "Louvor e simplificação de Álvaro de Campos" ("Praise and Simplification of Álvaro de Campos"), substitutes "o paquete que entra" ("the incoming steamer"), which is "com a Distância" ("with the Distance"; *Obra completa de Álvaro de Campos* [2014] 73; *A Little Larger* 166), for a simple everyday boat to Barreiro, an unglamorous region on the outskirts of Lisbon, as if willing to bring Campos to a historical present. A few years later, Cesariny, in a book about Pessoa entitled *O Virgem Negra* (*The Black Virgin*), not only alludes to the poet's corpse—found intact and darkened while the body was being transported to the Jerónimos Monastery in Lisbon many decades after his death—but also stresses the sparing eroticism of the poetry of Pessoa's more well-known heteronyms and imagines a truly sexual encounter among them.

Even one of the finest interpreters of Pessoa, Eduardo Lourenço, refers to the poet's "sexualidade branca" ("white sexuality"; *Pessoa revisitado* 117) and employs terms such as "Noite" and "Exílio" ("Night" and "Exile"; *Poesia e metafísica* 163) to speak of the time of Pessoa, almost as if in a defense of the poet. In a theoretical text introducing the neorealist movement, Rui Monteiro explains, "[A] geração que ora surge continua a de [18]70, aproveita muito da do Orfeu, e sendo a sua herdeira cultural, opõe-se a ambas" ("[T]he generation that now arises continues that of the [18]70s, makes use of much of that of *Orpheu*, and being their cultural heir, opposes both"). From the generation of the 1870s, the movement inherited the desire for intervention in reality, which is understood socially. Nonetheless, according to Monteiro, "a realidade parcelar" ("partial reality"), being the object of attention of the nineteenth-century writers, is "deformadora" ("deforming"). What interests the new generation is "total reality" ("realidade total"). Later on, he explains that "a substituição do individual pelo social" ("the substitution of the individual with the social") is what separates the new generation from *Orpheu* and *Presença*—literary magazines then considered as two sides of the same modernism ("Razões" 53). Also in the scope of neorealism, even in a poem such as "Arte poética" ("The Art of Poetry") by Mário Dionísio, which seems so indebted to the poetry of Álvaro de Campos with its references to the factory, to automobiles, to the city, and even to the tobacco shop, the final verses say, "A poesia está na luta dos homens / Está nos olhos abertos para amanhã" ("Poetry is in the struggle of men / It is in the eyes open to tomorrow"; Dionísio, *Poesia completa* 57).

The belief in "men" and in their "struggle" could not lie further from Álvaro de Campos when he writes:

> Não: tudo menos ter razão!
> Tudo menos importar-se com a humanidade!
> Tudo menos ceder ao humanitarismo!
> (*Obra completa de Álvaro de Campos* [2014] 340)

> No: anything but having good reasons!
> Anything but caring about humanity!
> Anything but giving in to humanitarianism!   (*A Little Larger* 267)

Behind these more or less veiled objections, there seems to be unease with the manner in which the poetry of Pessoa, or much of it, faced the historical issues of its time. At the outbreak of the First World War, an ode by Ricardo Reis—"Os jogadores de xadrês" ("The Chess Players")—summons readers to be as the players who remain impassive before the imminent arrival of the warrior who has already slaughtered their families and will soon kill them (*Obra completa de Ricardo Reis* 106–09). Álvaro de Campos, for his part, often places himself deliberately apart from morality and against society.

Though Campos is sometimes read as a defender of modernity and an enthusiast for modern times, there is more subtlety and complexity than appears at first glance in his relation to this time, which is still our own, and to the place of poetry in it.

The Desire for Freedom

Placing himself confidently in the realm of art, apart from morality and science, in "Ode triunfal" ("Triumphal Ode"), one of the poems with which he introduces himself to readers in the poetry magazine *Orpheu*, in 1915, Campos praises all that still scandalizes our hearts to this day:

> A maravilhosa belesa das corrupções políticas,
> Deliciosos escândalos financeiros e diplomáticos,
> Agressões políticas nas ruas,
> E de vez em quando o comêta dum regicídio
> Que ilumina de Prodígio e Fanfarra os céus
> Usuais e lúcidos da Civilisação quotidiana!
> Notícias desmentidas nos jornais,
>
> . . . .
> Como eu vos amo a todos, a todos, a todos,
>
> . . . .
> Ah, como todos os meus sentidos teem cio de vós!
> (*Obra completa de Álvaro de Campos* [2014] 50–51)

> The dazzling beauty of graft and corruption,
> Delicious financial and diplomatic scandals,
> Politically motivated assaults on the streets,
> And every now and then the comet of a regicide
> Lighting up with Awe and Fanfare the usual
> Clear skies of everyday Civilization!
> Fraudulent reports in the newspapers,
>
> . . . .
> How I love all of you, every last one of you!
>
> . . . .
> Ah, how all my senses lust for you!   (*A Little Larger* 155–56)

One may read these verses with irony, and maybe several readers have done so because it is a way to withstand the discomfort provoked by such words. But to read it with irony is to soften the poignancy of Campos.

In "Ode triunfal," just as in "Ode marítima" ("Maritime Ode") and in several other poems by Campos, the place that the poet claims for himself is at the margin of social life. To his "vida sentada, estática, regrada e revista" ("seated, static, orderly and repetitive life"; *Obra completa de Álvaro de Campos* [2014] 84; *A Little Larger* 176) the poet contrasts his desire to break with civilization and even with the human condition:

> Eu queria ser um bicho representativo de todos os vossos gestos.
> Um bicho que cravasse dentes nas amuradas, nas quilhas,

Que comesse mastros, bebesse sangue e alcatrão nos convezes,
Trincasse velas, remos, cordâme e poleâme,
Serpente do mar feminina e monstruosa cevando-se nos crimes!

(*Obra completa de Álvaro de Campos* [2014] 88)

I'd love to be an animal that would embody all your acts,
That would sink its teeth into the hulls and keels,
That would eat masts, drink blood and tar on ship decks,
Chew sails, oars, ropes and pulleys—
A monstrous, female sea-serpent gorging on your crimes!

(*A Little Larger* 180)

The thinking that emerges from these verses does not clearly identify with any political, moral, or scientific current, with any given association toward a common interest. Instead, it tirelessly states its independence, telling us: "Deixem-me em paz!" ("Leave me alone!"; *Obra completa de Álvaro de Campos* [2014] 176; *A Little Larger* 216)—not because the author is a subjective poet but because he will not condone the social order. He will not adapt: "Não! Só quero a liberdade! . . . Não me vistam as camisas de força das maneiras!" ("No! All I want is freedom! . . . Don't make me dress up in the straitjacket of manners!"; *Obra completa de Álvaro de Campos* [2014] 256–57; *Collected Poems* 93). It is necessary to lend our ears to this.

Exerting his freedom and independence in relation to the values that guide social life at the beginning of the twentieth century, the poetry of the heteronym Álvaro de Campos teaches us that what should be expected of art is something else: it is that which finds no place in the world ruled by work, by profit, by the idea of progress, by good manners, patriotism, or conformity. His poetry lets flourish violent impetuses and expresses masochistic desires and destructive impulses. It gives voice to what human beings repress in order to be able to live in society (Freud, *Civilization and Its Discontents*). It is the space of transgression (Bataille), the space that fits that which would have dire outcomes should it surface in social life. It goes on to criticize modern technical civilization, the dehumanization of the individual, the use of calculation to assess what cannot be calculated. Campos's work is a kind of anti-education.[2]

In his criticism of modernity at the beginning of the twentieth century, Pessoa/Campos shows that the West is a power that uniformizes and annihilates differences and singularities. The "Opiário" ("Opiary"), a poem by the young Álvaro de Campos, already unveils his disenchantment with the contemporary world:

Eu acho que não vale a pena ter
Ido ao Oriente e visto a Índia e a China.
A terra é semelhante e pequenina
E há só uma maneira de viver.   (*Poesia: Antologia minima* 219)

To sail East to see China and India
Wasn't worth it after all.
There's only one way of living,
And the earth's the same, and small.   (*A Little Larger* 148)

The European technical mentality has expanded to other continents since the fifteenth century, and instead of opening itself to the new, it has exterminated, enslaved, catechized, and homogenized. In the same vein, José de Almada Negreiros, also a poet from *Orpheu*, wrote "The Hate Scene" (dedicated to Álvaro de Campos):

Tu, que te dizes Homem!
. . . .
Tu, qu'inventaste as Ciências e as Filosofias,
as Políticas, as Artes e as Leis,
e outros quebra-cabeças de sala
e outros dramas de grande espectáculo . . .
Tu, que aperfeiçoas sabiamente a arte de matar . . .
Tu, que descobriste o cabo da Boa-Esperança
e o Caminho-Marítimo da Índia
e as duas Grandes Américas.
e que levaste a chatice a estas terras.
e que trouxeste de lá mais Chatos p'raqui
e qu'inda por cima cantaste estes Feitos . . .
Tu, qu'inventaste a chatice e o balão,
e que farto de te chateares no chão
te foste chatear no ar,
e qu'inda foste inventar submarinos
p'ra te chateares também por debaixo d'água.
Tu, que tens a mania das Invenções e das Descobertas
e que nunca descobriste que eras bruto,
e que nunca inventaste a maneira de o não seres . . .
Tu consegues ser cada vez mais besta
e a este progresso chamas Civilização!   ("A cena do ódio" 59)

You, who call yourself Man!
. . . .
You, who invented Science and Philosophy,
Politics, the Arts and Law,
and other salon brainteasers
and other wanton dramatics . . .
You, who conscientiously perfect the art of killing.
You, who discovered the Cape of Good Hope
and the Sea-Route to India

and the two Great Americas,
and took dullness to these Lands
and brought Dullards back
and to cap it all wrote cantos of such Deeds . . .
You, who invented dullness and the balloon,
and tired of dulling yourself on the ground marooned
took dullness into the air,
and even invented submarines
so you could take dullness underseas . . .
You're obsessed with Inventions and Discoveries
and yet you've never discovered you're a beast,
and yet you've never invented a way of not being one . . .
Instead you manage to become more bestial by the day
And you call such progress Civilisation!   ("The Hate Scene" 60)

Besides the criticism of a West that annihilates differences, Campos shares with Almada Negreiros the disillusion with ideas that modernity has consecrated, such as the notion of progress. In "Ode triunfal," often regarded as an exaltation of modern life, he says:

Ah, e a gente ordinária e suja, que parece sempre a mesma,
Que emprega palavrões como palavras usuais,
Cujos filhos roubam às portas das mercearias
E cujas filhas aos oito anos—e eu acho isto belo e amo-o!—
Masturbam homens de aspecto decente nos vãos de escada.
A gentalha que anda pelos andaimes e que vai para casa
Por vielas quase irreais de estreiteza e podridão.
Maravilhosamente gente humana que vive como os cães
Que está abaixo de todos os sistemas morais,
Para quem nenhuma religião foi feita,
Nenhuma arte criada,
Nenhuma política destinada para eles!
Como eu vos amo a todos, porque sois assim,
Nem imorais de tão baixos que sois, nem bons nem maus,
Inatingíveis por todos os progressos,
Fauna maravilhosa do fundo do mar da vida!
              (*Obra completa de Álvaro de Campos* [2014] 54)

Ah, and the ordinary, sordid people who always look the same,
Who use swearwords like regular words,
Whose sons steal from grocers
And whose eight-year-old daughters (and I think this is sublime!)
Masturbate respectable-looking men in stairwells.
The rabble who spend all day on scaffolds and walk home

On narrow lanes of almost unreal squalor.
Wondrous human creatures who live like dogs,
Who are beneath all moral systems,
For whom no religion was invented,
No art created,
No politics formulated!
How I love all of you for being what you are,
Neither good nor evil, too humble to be immoral,
Impervious to all progress,
Wondrous fauna from the depths of the sea of life!

(*A Little Larger* 158)

Technical progress has not been followed by progress in the ways of living; freedom and justice are not available for the poor. On the contrary, "the ordinary, sordid people" seem to be always the same. Their wrongdoing is coauthored by "respectable-looking men" and accepted by the rest.

In "Triumphal Ode," Campos repeatedly expresses a near-erotic attraction to machines, yet he also reveals that the individual operating the machine is akin to a pack animal, in a way that foreshadows Chaplin's *Modern Times*. It is dehumanization promoted by industrialization. In a sudden break, a stanza between parentheses comes to say:

(Na nora do quintal da minha casa
O burro anda à roda, anda à roda,
E o mistério do mundo é do tamânho disto.
Limpa o suor com o braço, trabalhador descontente. . . .)

(*Obra completa de Álvaro de Campos* [2014] 54)

(The donkey goes round and round
The water wheel in my yard,
And this is the measure of the world's mystery.
Wipe off your sweat with your arm, disgruntled worker. . . .)

(*A Little Larger* 158–59)

The water wheel, powered by an animal that incessantly repeats the same turning movement, an archaic technology, coexists with factories and the large European capitals. The poem quickly passes from the donkey that goes round to the disgruntled worker, who also lives like this inside a modern factory.

In "Lisbon Revisited (1923)," Campos affirms his disdain for science, which modernity has elevated to replace God after his death as the ultimate organizing and justifying principle of life. Being a naval engineer, according to the biography Pessoa gave him, Campos places technique in a very restricted role and claims for himself madness and the right to it:

Sou um technico, mas tenho technica só dentro da technica.
Fóra d'isso sou doido, com todo o direito a sel-o.
Com todo o direito a sel-o, ouviram?
Não me macem, por amor de Deus!
(Obra completa de Álvaro de Campos [2014] 175)

I'm a technician, but my technique is limited to the technical sphere,
Apart from which I'm crazy, and with every right to be so.
With every right to be so, do you hear?
Leave me alone, for God's sake!   (*A Little Larger* 216)

His independence also defies the most common social expectations:
"Queriam-me casado, fútil, quotidiano e tributável?" ("You want me to be
married, futile, predictable and taxable?"; *Poesia: Antologia minima* 277; *A
Little Larger* 216), he asks, in a sad summary of modern life: marriage by convention, the everyday deprived of the extraordinary, work that brings nothing
new to the world but still generates income and is taxed. It is the bourgeois
dream that has produced many victims.

In "Ode maritima," Campos defines modern life as a "vida sentada, estática,
regrada e revista" ("seated, static, orderly and repetitive life"; *Obra completa de
Álvaro de Campos* [2014] 84; *A Little Larger* 176) in which there is no room for
creativity or novelty outside of art.

The same Campos who is capable of such violent verses as those in "Ode maritima" and in "Ode triunfal" denounces the deathly character of modernity and
its wars. This 1916 poem is a kind of funereal prayer for the dead of the First
World War:

Por aqueles, minha mãe, que morreram, que caíram na batalha . . .
Dlôn—ôn—ôn—ôn . . .
Por aqueles, minha mãe, que ficaram mutilados no combate
Dlôn—ôn—ôn—ôn . . .
Por aqueles cuja noiva esperará sempre em vão . . .
Dlôn—ôn—ôn—ôn . . .
Sete vezes sete vezes murcharão as flores no jardim
Dlôn—ôn—ôn—ôn . . .
E os seus cadáveres serão do pó universal e anónimo
Dlôn—ôn—on—on . . .
E eles, quem sabe, minha mãe, sempre nos amem, com esperança . . .
Loucos, minha mãe, loucos, porque os corpos morrem e a dor não
    morre . . .
Dlôn—dlôn—dlôn—dlôn—dlôn—dlôn . . .
Que é feito daquele que foi a criança que tiveste ao peito?
Dlôn . . .
Quem sabe qual dos desconhecidos mortos aí é o teu filho
Dlôn . . .

Ainda tens na gaveta da cómoda os seus bibes de criança . . .
Ainda há nos caixotes da dispensa os seus brinquedos velhos . . .
Ele hoje pertence a uma podridão órfã *somewhere in France.*
Ele que foi tanto para ti, tudo, tudo, tudo . . .
Olha, ele não é nada no geral holocausto da história
Dlôn—dlôn . . .
Dlôn—dlôn—dlôn—dlôn . . .
Dlôn—dlôn—dlôn—dlôn . . .
Dlôn—dlôn—dlôn—dlôn—dlôn—dlôn . . .

(Obra completa de Álvaro de Campos [2019] 171–72)

For those, mother, who have died, who have fallen in battle . . .
Dong—dong—dong—dong . . .
For those, mother, who have been mutilated in combat
Dong—dong—dong—dong . . .
For those whose bride will wait forever in vain . . .
Dong—dong—dong—dong . . .
Seven times seven times will the flowers in the garden wilt
Dong—dong—dong—dong . . .
And their corpses will belong to the universal and anonymous dust
Dong—dong—dong—dong . . .
And those, who knows, mother, will always love us, with hope . . .
Madmen, mother, madmen, because bodies die and pain does not . . .
Dong—dong—dong—dong—dong—dong . . .
What has become of he who was the child that you had on your breast?
Dong . . .
Who knows which of the unknown fellows there is your son
Dong . . .
You still have his child bibs in the chest of drawers . . .
There are still his old toys in boxes in the pantry . . .
He now belongs to an orphan rottenness *somewhere in France.*
He who was so much to you, everything, everything, everything . . .
Look, he is nothing in the general holocaust of history
Dong—dong . . .
Dong—dong—dong—dong . . .
Dong—dong—dong—dong . . .
Dong—dong—dong—dong—dong—dong . . .

The poem certainly dialogues with "Le dormeur du val" ("The Sleeper in the Valley"), by Rimbaud (*Complete Works* 46–47), but in Campos the room given to affection is greater; the individual is identified by the love that others have for him, just as in his poem "Aniversário" ("Birthday"; *Obra completa de Álvaro de Campos* [2019] 262–64) and even in the poem "O menino de sua mãe" ("The Boy of His Mother"; *Poesia: Antologia mínima* [2018] 77–78), by Pessoa.

Campos's gaze is all-encompassing, embracing both society's darkest realities—like child exploitation and violent tendencies—and the marginalized expressions of nonnormative sexualities. He extends compassion to individuals, regardless of the societal judgments that surround them, while simultaneously highlighting the absurdity of everyday life. And he pauses to cry over the dead. His extreme freedom is a lesson that is not easy to deal with even now, in a time of intense social demands (however different from those in his days). The young reader of Campos often wants to adjust him to the sensibilities of our time and wishes to see him condemn the crimes, the corruption, and the child abuse.

Against Futurism

The singular posture of Campos in the face of modernity is also revealed in his attitude toward Italian Futurism, which he nears at a certain moment. A poem says:

> O binómio de Newton é tão belo como a Vénus de Milo.
> O que há é pouca gente para dar por isso.
>
> (Álvaro de Campos)
>
> 6666———666666666———666666666666666
>
> (O vento lá fora)   (*Obra completa de Álvaro de Campos* [2019] 373)

> Newton's binomial theorem is as beautiful as the Venus de Milo.
> What happens is that few people realize it.
>
> (Álvaro de Campos)
>
> whoooosh———whoooooooooosh———whooooooooooooooosh
>
> (The wind outside)

In the "Futurist Manifesto," published in 1909 in the Parisian newspaper *Le Figaro*, the Italian poet Marinetti says, "A racing car whose hood is adorned with great pipes, like serpents of explosive breath—a roaring car that seems to ride on grapeshot is more beautiful than the Victory of Samothrace" (89). The verse of the engineer Campos establishes a direct relation to Marinetti's sentence, but the Winged Victory of Samothrace is replaced by another sculpture from ancient Greece, the Venus de Milo, goddess of love and beauty, and the "roaring car" gives way to a work of thought, to something that cannot be grasped by the hands: Newton's binomial theorem. In addition, the degree of comparison changes. For Marinetti, the automobile is more beautiful than one of the most beautiful sculptures of antiquity, the Winged Victory of Samothrace; for Campos, Newton's binomial theorem is as beautiful as one of the other most beautiful sculptures conserved by the ancient Greeks. These differences demonstrate how the futurism of Campos is different from that of Marinetti, for it does not wish to abolish the past but rather is capable of recognizing beauty both in the past and in the present, both in art and in science, both in what is tangible and in what is intangible. And Campos prefers beauty and wisdom to war.[3]

The signature of the heteronym divides the poem into two parts, as if the first stanza were signed by Campos and the other by the wind. As a disciple of Alberto Caeiro, Campos learns to see and hear nature, but by training, he is a thinking man. His initial verse encompasses art and science, the most elevated productions of the human spirit, but there is something with respect to which he himself cannot speak, and he needs to allow it to speak for itself: the wind.

Understanding the Political Dimension

One of the best-known among Pessoa's poems in the spirit of opposition to society is perhaps the "Poema em linha recta" ("Poem in a Straight Line"). In it, Pessoa defines Campos, the heteronym into which he says he has put "toda a emoção que [ele] não [dá] nem a [si mesmo] nem à vida" ("all the emotion that [he does] not give either to [himself] or to life"; *Cartas entre Fernando Pessoa e os directores* 253) as someone much different from his contemporaries. He presents himself as someone who embodies all that is considered ugly or embarrassing in his time. If we made a list of the adjectives that the poet claims for himself, in contrast, we would see which values were considered positive in his contemporary society. The portrait of an age is thus composed.

About this poem, Cleonice Berardinelli writes:

> Denegrindo exageradamente a sua imagem, mas ao mesmo tempo estranhando que só ele seja 'vil e errôneo nesta terra'; chamando aos outros príncipes e semideuses mas perguntando-se 'onde há gente no mundo', a que visará o poeta? Como classificar este poema excepcional, senão como um texto dominado pela ironia, talvez sarcasmo, com que Álvaro de Campos traça o retrato impiedoso da sociedade à qual pertence, mas de que condena a hipocrisia?   (Pessoa, *Obras em prosa* 420–21)

> Exaggeratingly denigrating his image, but at the same time finding it strange that he is "the only one on earth who's ever wrong and despicable," calling the other princes and demigods but asking himself, "Where in the world are there people?," what would be the poet's aim? How to classify this exceptional poem other than as a text dominated by irony, perhaps sarcasm, with which Álvaro de Campos draws the unsparing portrait of the society to which he belongs, but whose hypocrisy he condemns?

In the poem "Esta velha angústia" ("This Old Anguish"), Campos writes: "Se eu pudesse crêr num manipanso qualquer— / Jupiter, Jehova, a Humanidade — /

Qualquer serviria" ("If only I could believe in a fetish— / Jupiter, Jehovah, Humanity— / Any at all would do for me"; *Obra completa de Álvaro de Campos* [2014] 297; *A Little Larger* 143–44). He knows that the idea of humanity, worshiped by the disciples of the philosopher Auguste Comte, creator of positivism, is also a fiction, for there is no humanity but only human beings, all of whom are different. He criticizes any idea of homogenization, and there resides the truly political character of his poetry. The "homem vulgar" ("other [ordinary] person"; *Desassossego* [Tinta] 254; *Disquiet* [New Directions] 202) who so horrifies Bernardo Soares, author of *The Book of Disquiet* (a work that has great affinity with the poetry of Campos), the "é o Esteves sem metafísica" ("Esteves, who is without metaphysics"; *Poesia: Antologia mínima* 291; *Collected Poems* 18), a character in the poem "Tabacaria" ("The Tobacco Shop"; *Poesia: Antologia mínima* 285–91), the man who corresponds without reflection to the tasks that society attributes to him, is the precursor of the Nazi officer Adolf Eichmann, whose trial in Israel prompted the philosopher Hannah Arendt to reflect upon the "banality of evil:"

> Adolf Eichmann went to the gallows with great dignity. . . . He was in complete command of himself, nay, he was more: he was completely himself. Nothing could have demonstrated this more convincingly than the grotesque silliness of his last words. He began by stating emphatically that he was a *Gottgläubiger*, to express in common Nazi fashion that he was no Christian and did not believe in life after death. He then proceeded: "After a short while, gentlemen, we shall all meet again. Such is the fate of all men. Long live Germany, long live Argentina, long live Austria. I shall not forget them." In the face of death, he had found the cliché used in funeral oratory. Under the gallows, his memory played him the last trick; he was "elated" and he forgot that this was his own funeral. It was as though in those last minutes he was summing up the lesson that this long course in human wickedness had taught us—the lesson of the fearsome, word-and-thought-defying banality of evil.   (*Eichmann* 252)

Evil is not necessarily the work of monsters but of those who suspend their capacity to think and reflect, who do not place themselves in the place of others, and who only express themselves through clichés. Evil can even be the work of the self-proclaimed "good citizen," as can be seen today. The antidote to authoritarianism requires the capacity to think for oneself; the defense of the unique; the possibility of welcoming strangeness, failure, and doubt in oneself; the use of a language that is not propaganda; and the defense of what has no place in a social order dominated by utility. And most of all, it requires the freedom of art.

In *The Human Condition*, Hannah Arendt makes a distinction between politics and society. The social is the junction of atoms, of uniformized elements, which is why social studies can be based on statistical data and methods:

It is the same conformism, the assumption that men behave and do not act with respect to each other, that lies at the root of the modern science of economics, whose birth coincided with the rise of society and which, together with its chief technical tool, statistics, became the social science par excellence. Economics—until the modern age a not too important part of ethics and politics and based on the assumption that men act with respect to their economic activities as they act in every other respect—could achieve a scientific character only when men had become social beings and unanimously followed certain patterns of behavior, so that those who did not keep the rules could be considered to be asocial or abnormal.   (41–42)

Contrary to statistics, which, as Arendt shows, is born together with the pre-dominance of the social, politics presupposes the fact that each human being is different from the other, there being no uniformity. According to this distinc-tion, neorealist poetry would be not political but social poetry, in which human beings are often elements in a chain:

Eu e tu
elos da mesma cadeia
grãos da mesma seara
pedras da mesma muralha!   (Namorado 39)

Me and you
links in the same chain
grains from the same harvest
stones from the same wall!

In the poetry of Campos, individuals are not defined by their social position; rather, each one is a singularity. Instead of the idea of a spokesperson for the masses, the poet is someone who stages impotence, anguish, nostalgia for child-hood, violence, sexuality. It is from his independent place that he speaks out against the world, embraces impulses that can have no place in social life, dis-plays contradictions and miseries that are not reduced to social explanations, and explores new meanings of language.

At the end of this journey, it is worth asking whether poetry can remain so independent from the social discourse as we know it. With the immense human-itarian and environmental crises that our time has been witnessing, it is almost natural that we expect poetry to help give answers to our restlessness. It is almost natural that we want Pessoa or Campos to justify himself. It is almost natural that we expect poets to say what we want to hear, that their words keep us company in our struggle for a world that is anti-patriarchal, anti-racist, respectful of the environment, and ultimately more just.

But has poetry, throughout its long tradition, served solely as a mirror of society? I consider what might have happened if the medieval Galician-Portuguese troubadours had written only *cantigas de amor* ("love songs"), which conformed to the courtly ideals and hierarchical structures of their time, emphasizing chivalric love and the subordination of the lover to a noble lady. We would not know of the immense richness and variety of the *cantigas de amigo* ("friendship songs") and their testimony of the persistence of the pagan and Islamic elements in Iberian culture even as Christian rulers gained control of the region during the thirteenth and fourteenth centuries.

One of the risks of reducing poetry to a mere vehicle for social movements can be seen in the context of the Islamic State (ISIS), where art is co-opted to serve violent ideologies. A 2015 article published in *The New Yorker* reflects on the poetry produced in this context and introduces a little-known fact: its extreme prestige among jihadists.

> Analysts have generally ignored these texts, as if poetry were a colorful but ultimately distracting by-product of jihad. But this is a mistake. It is impossible to understand jihadism—its objectives, its appeal for new recruits, and its durability—without examining its culture. This culture finds expression in a number of forms, including anthems and documentary videos, but poetry is its heart.   (Cresswell)

Instrumental music is prohibited by ISIS, but poetry on the contrary is affirmed and embraced for its propagandistic possibilities. But it is not just any poetry that fulfills this role:

> The views expressed in jihadi poetry are, of course, more bloodthirsty than anything on "Sha'ir al-Milyoon" [a poetry contest on television]: Shiites, Jews, Western powers, and rival factions are relentlessly vilified and threatened with destruction. Yet it is recognizably a subset of this popular art form. It is sentimental—even, at times, a little kitsch—and it is communal rather than solitary. Videos of groups of jihadis reciting poems or tossing back and forth the refrain of a song are as easy to find as videos of them blowing up enemy tanks. Poetry is understood as a social art . . .
>   (Cresswell)

It seems relevant to us that poetry appreciated in this context is to be read aloud and not in silence. It aims to consolidate a group with common objectives, to strengthen bonds. Criticism, doubt, hesitation, and failure are not welcome in it.

Commenting on the article published in *The New Yorker*, the Brazilian writer Bernardo Carvalho writes:

> O jihadismo . . . rejeita tudo o que na modernidade ocidental define a grande poesia, a começar pela polissemia, pela ambiguidade, pela ironia e

pelo humor. O sentido militante precisa ser manifesto, unívoco e literal. A militância substitui a dúvida pela palavra de ordem e o cético pelo crente. Um dos versos citados no artigo diz: "Acabou a era de submissão ao descrente."

Jihadism . . . rejects all that in Western modernity defines great poetry, beginning with polysemy, ambiguity, irony, and humor. The militant meaning must be manifest, univocal, and literal. Militancy has substituted doubt with catchphrases and the skeptic with the believer. One of the verses quoted in the article says: "The age of submission to the unbeliever is over."

And the writer concludes:

Ao se servir da poesia como instrumento doutrinário e de propaganda, o jihadismo acaba nos dando mais uma lição: ele explicita, por oposição, o valor profundamente político da poesia que o senso comum considera inócua, aquela "que não serve para nada", a poesia que se lê sozinho e que celebra a dúvida, a ambiguidade, a ruptura e a possibilidade de interpretação (a inteligência) do leitor. Primeiro, porque ela trata de um mundo real (e não de uma fantasia mítica) e depois, porque, ao cantar singularidades e subjetividades, não pretende impor regras, nem limites nem fronteiras a ninguém.

By making use of poetry as an instrument of indoctrination and propaganda, jihadism ends up giving us another lesson: it explains, through opposition, the profoundly political value of the poetry that common sense considers innocuous, that "which serves for nothing," the poetry that is read alone and that celebrates doubt, ambiguity, rupture, and the possibility of interpretation (intelligence) on the part of the reader. First, because it concerns a world that is real (and not a mythical fantasy) and then because, by singing of singularities and subjectivities, it does not intend to impose rules, or limits, or boundaries on anyone.

Perhaps the contrast with jihadist poetry teaches us the truly political importance of the "poetry of solitude" (Paz, "Poesía de soledad") of Campos. His turning his back on morality and society, his desire for freedom from social conventions, his anti-education, his criticism of the naivety of the notion of progress, and even his embracing of the human, in all of its dimensions, weaknesses, dreams, restlessness, and doubts, as well as of the possibilities and failure of language, constitute a manner of being plural and anti-totalitarian. Perhaps the poetry of Campos gives us, his readers, a task: to rethink the demands of good behavior that we so often make of our contemporary poets. It is worth asking ourselves whether this attitude is not, on our part, authoritarian and intolerant.

Perhaps we should ask ourselves whether we want to entangle our poets and artists in a social web, condemning their work to immediatist obligations, and whether we are not somehow reproducing the colonial mindset of Western Europe in its encounter with other cultures. Perhaps we should instead consider whether it is worth ensuring that the social world does not stifle poetry and art— and their freedom.

NOTES

Translated by Marco Alexandre de Oliveira. All translations from the Portuguese are by the translator except where otherwise attributed.

1. The line alludes to the poem "Escripto num livro abandonado em viagem" ("Written in a Book Abandoned in Travel"), by Álvaro de Campos, whose final verse says, "Fui, como hervas, e não me arrancaram" ("I was as the weeds and they never tore me out"; Pessoa, *Obra completa de Álvaro de Campos* [2014] 206; *Collected Poems* 22).

2. I reconsider here the reading made in S. Silva, *Reparar brechas*.

3. I reconsider here the reading made in S. Silva, *Fernando Pessoa* 40.

Bringing Pessoa into the Philosophy Curriculum

Jonardon Ganeri

Departments of philosophy—at least those in the anglophone university system in the United States, the United Kingdom, Canada, Australia, and even India—have until recently been breathtakingly conservative, if compared with other departments in the humanities, with respect to the curriculum. It has generally been the case that the work of only a very small group of philosophers (the familiar luminaries in the historical "canon," such as Aristotle, Immanuel Kant, David Hume, John Locke, René Descartes, and a very few others), as well as the contemporary writings of a very small subset of authors, has been considered worth teaching. There have been attempts to diagnose the reasons for the strange phenomenon that a discipline that prides itself on thinking freely about the deepest and most universal issues of human concern should have so restricted itself to the ideas of a small number of white European men (Norden; see also Ganeri, "Taking"; Levine), but recent encouraging signs point to a new recognition of the need to diversify the discipline, to expand the curriculum with the inclusion of a much greater variety of voices and experiences, without thereby discarding or sidelining the traditional canon (Schwitzgebel). There is a growing insistence on the vital contribution that women have made in the history of philosophy (projectvox.org); there are urgent demands that the tremendously rich philosophies of India, China, and Africa be able to inform the way the discipline conceives of itself (Ganeri, "Why Philosophy"); and the philosophical voices of Indigenous peoples too demand to be heard (Maffie). The challenges that this opening up of the field presents, as well as ways to negotiate them, have been discussed in a recent series of essays on the blog of the American Philosophical Association, including "So you want to teach some Indian philosophy" (Ganeri), "So you want to teach some Chinese philosophy" (Lai), and "So you want to teach some Islamic philosophy" (Adamson). These essays address all the standard arguments put out by those who wish to resist diversification in the discipline, and I will not repeat those arguments and their rebuttal here.

Instead, this essay makes a case for the incorporation of Fernando Pessoa in the teaching of philosophy, especially in courses in the philosophy of mind. I believe that Pessoa's writings and ideas constitute an immensely valuable addition to a philosophy of mind curriculum at both undergraduate and postgraduate levels; indeed, I would go further and say that his ideas are revolutionary and cannot afford to be overlooked. Admittedly, the most typical reaction I get when I say this to my colleagues in philosophy is "Fernando who?" But I have also noticed that another reaction is surprisingly common: "Oh, yes, I love Pessoa!" Pessoa is, it turns out, the secret passion of surprisingly many of my colleagues. To them I say, have the courage of your convictions: bring Pessoa out of the shadows and into your undergraduate and graduate teaching.

There are now a good number of excellent recent teaching materials in English about Pessoa and his philosophy. Among monographs, I recommend Paulo de Medeiros's *Pessoa's Geometry of the Abyss*, Jerónimo Pizarro's *Fernando Pessoa: A Critical Introduction*, and my own *Virtual Subjects, Fugitive Selves: Fernando Pessoa and His Philosophy* and *Fernando Pessoa: Imagination and the Self*. The overview essays I have found helpful to philosophy students include those by Jerome Boyd Maunsell, John Frow, and Rehan Visser. Finally, a new collection is a very valuable resource: *Fernando Pessoa and Philosophy: Countless Lives Inhabit Us*, edited by Bartholomew Ryan, Giovanbattista Tusa, and Antonio Cardiello, as is Ryan's new monograph *Fernando Pessoa*.

The most obvious, but also the most superficial, difficulty with introducing Pessoa into a course on philosophy is that he does not write the way philosophers are expected to. That is to say, he does not write conventional essays with a thesis, an argument, a consideration of counterarguments, and a conclusion—the sort of essay that might be published in *The Philosophical Review* or *The Journal of Philosophy*. Neither can *The Book of Disquiet* be described as a monograph in philosophy in any conventional sense. In his youth, Pessoa did attempt to write essays in the style of conventional philosophy, in English and in Portuguese, and these have, very helpfully, recently been collected and published (*Philosophical Essays*). But I hope I shall be forgiven if I say that they are not very good. This simply wasn't where Pessoa's genius, and his brilliance, lay, and the conventional philosophical essay format afforded no scope at all for the writer to develop his ideas and to engage in philosophical self-exploration. To those who wish to bring Pessoa into the curriculum of a philosophy course, my advice would be to avoid those mementos of extreme juvenilia.[1]

Pessoa's philosophical genius is to be found instead in his later work, his heteronymic poetry and his antinovel *The Book of Disquiet*. One has therefore to train students how to read these Pessoan texts philosophically, for they will have little or no experience in how to go about it, and up to this point in their philosophical education they will not have gained the necessary skills. A promising place to begin in their new education as philosophical readers is with Søren Kierkegaard, the great Danish existentialist. Kierkegaard is hardly ever himself granted a seat at the table of the canon, but he is taught often enough for there to have been plenty of exposure to his style of writing in pseudonyms as well as good teaching materials about Kierkegaard's use of pseudonym. A Pessoan heteronym is not a pseudonym, but the materials that have been developed to aid instructors who want to teach Kiekegaard are also valuable when it comes to Pessoa, and Kierkegaard's work is sufficiently similar to Pessoa's for Kierkegaard to serve as a "fifth column" in the project of bringing about change in philosophy teachers' understanding of what they ought to be doing—change enough for them to be able to see why Pessoa should be included.

One key element of learning thus to approach Pessoa is this: in the case both of Kierkegaard and Pessoa, the deep interplay between literary form and philosophical content is absolutely central, as is the idea of reading as protreptic, a way to transform the student's understanding and vision, not merely a vehicle for a data transfer from teacher to student. Students need to be taught to see the philosophy *in* a work of literature, something a standard education in philosophy leaves them utterly unequipped to do. So, in particular, the use of literary tropes like irony, the double, and the literary mask themselves have philosophical purposes and are not "only" literary devices.[2]

Another key element in getting students to the point that they are able to read and appreciate Pessoa as a philosopher is training in the long history of first-personal thought experiments. Pessoa is rarely explicit, but it seems evident that his approach to philosophical inquiry belongs in a tradition that stretches back through Descartes and Augustine to Avicenna and perhaps further. For these thinkers, casting philosophical inquiry in a first-personal form was essential to the nature of the discovery they sought to make. When students are taught the *First Meditation*, they are told that the method of radical doubt involves putting themselves in the same position Descartes is in, sitting in his study in front of the fire. The *cogito* is a performance each one of us makes for ourselves, and that is essential to its ability to demonstrate that this is so (B. Williams). Students are much less likely to be taught Avicenna's "flying man" thought experiment, and there is no evidence that Pessoa himself knew about it, but this too is an essentially first-personal mode of philosophizing. In it, each of us is invited to imagine ourselves created in midair, and without any sensory or even proprioceptive experience. Avicenna says that even then you imagine yourself as being present to yourself, and so that there is a type of self-awareness that is independent of sensation (Adamson and Benevich). Turning to Pessoa, his very technique, which he describes as one of cultivated "dreaming"—that is to say, of directing imagining of and simulating alternative sensoria—is a method of first-personal inquiry (Pessoa, *Disquiet* [Penguin] 405). With Pessoa, however, the appropriately cultivated first-personal "dreamer" makes discoveries about subjectivity and the self that far outstrip those of Avicenna and Descartes.

Having introduced students to the deep constitutive ties between literary form and philosophical content, and having educated them in the role of first-personal techniques in philosophical inquiry, it is finally possible to acquaint them with Pessoa's work. Here, of course, the new concept one wishes to introduce them to is the concept of the heteronym, and in my experience the best place to begin is with Pessoa's letters, written in the final year of his life, where he comes as close as he ever does to speaking somewhat less than ironically about his life work.[3] My approach in teaching heteronymy has been to seek out real-world examples, which I have found in performers' use of their own name as a stage name, in the self-portraiture of the painter Yasumasa Morimura, and in Afrofuturism's use of a multitude of "machine names" (see Ganeri, *Virtual Subjects* 14–15, 31–32). The examples can be multiplied, and indeed as Pessoa is increasingly taught in the classroom, I am confident that instructors will find plenty of fresh examples of their own of heteronymy "in the wild." When students have got an intuitive handle on the concept, and perhaps not until then, one can move on to reading the heteronymic poems (Pessoa, *A Little Larger* and *Fernando Pessoa & Co.*). A technique I have found works well is to first describe the particular experiential style associated with each of the three heteronyms, Alberto Caeiro, Álvaro de Campos, and Ricardo Reis, and then ask students to interpret the poems as embodiments and expressions of ways of seeing the world according to those different styles of feeling. Some of the poems are, of course, philosophical master classes in their own right, quite apart from the heteronymic apparatus.

At this stage, if the class is a more advanced one in the philosophy of mind, one can discuss in a more analytical fashion the implications of heteronymy for the philosophy of self (I do this in my graduate class but not with my undergraduate students). A range of contemporary writers on the philosophy of mind can easily be brought into dialogue with Pessoa at this point; I have concentrated on J. J. Valberg and Mark Johnston, but options abound. There are, moreover, many theoretical applications of the concept of heteronymy in the philosophy of mind, from issues to do with the individuation of subjects, the structure of the field of experience, and the existence of other minds to the role of simulation in empathy. The very concept of a subject of experience seems, in the work of Pessoa, to be disambiguated and deepened. Bringing Pessoa into dialogue with contemporary thinkers like Galen Strawson and Dan Zahavi promises to be extremely fruitful on both sides.

According to Strawson, the self is a transient subject of experience, lasting at best a very few moments, and he has no good way to articulate what it is for each of these transient selves to be "another I" of me. Pessoa illustrates this idea through his concept of diachronic heteronymy when he writes in a famous poem, "Não sei quantas almas tenho. / Cada momento mudei" ("I don't know how many souls I have. / I've changed at every moment"; *Poemas de Fernando Pessoa (1921–1930)* 197; *Selected Prose* [2007] 243), and when he asserts in a letter, "Sendo assim, não evoluo, VIAJO. . . . Vou mudando de personalidade" ("And so I do not evolve, I simply JOURNEY. . . . I continuously change personality"; *Cartas entre Fernando Pessoa e os directores* 266; *Selected Prose* [2007] 263). Here Pessoa's use of the first person is subtle and precise: it is I who have many souls, and it is I who continuously change selves.

Zahavi provides an account of what he calls the "minimal self," a self consisting in brute reflexive for-me-ness. He writes that it is a "first-personal mode of givenness" and is that by virtue of which experience is "lived through" by me and not merely occurrent within me. So for-me-ness is said to be "an invariant dimension of phenomenal character" and "the categorical basis of our capacity for first-person thought" (Zahavi and Kriegel 49). This self-representation theory of subjectivity draws its inspiration from the work of twentieth-century French and German phenomenology. It is the reflexive theory that what for-me-ness consists in is an experience self-representing itself. The idea that for-me-ness consists in phenomenal self-disclosure is certainly an important and powerful one, but it is, from a Pessoan perspective, inconsistent with a fundamental datum about conscious experience, the discovery of heteronymic subjectivity. If for-me-ness consists in brute self-representation, then no distinction can be made between the for-me-ness associated with Caeiro and the for-me-ness associated with Reis. We need more than reflexivity: what we need is the idea that there are distinct invariant ways of feeling indexed to distinct subjects. Whereas Jean-Paul Sartre, for example, refers only to the idea of prereflective consciousness as the basis of the notion of ego, Pessoa's vocabulary is richer, exploiting and exploring a phenomenological notion of heteronymy and associated concepts.

Insofar as heteronymic subjectivity challenges other accounts of the very nature of subjectivity, I would actually go so far as to venture that Pessoan phenomenology should be recognized as a distinct and highly original strand of the European phenomenological tradition. Put simply, the trouble with reflexivist theories of subjectivity is that they are attenuated, meaning that they do not permit a phenomenological distinction to be drawn between one subject and another. It would be as if the members of a group of people each affirmed that their own country was the best and we were expected to identify their actual nationalities from these bare reflexive affirmations. For-me-ness is indeed "the categorical basis of our capacity for first-person thought," but just for that reason it cannot consist in reflexive self-representation. Pessoa writes, more interestingly, that

[a] unica maneira de teres sensações novas é construires-te uma alma nova. Baldado esforço o teu se queres sentir outras cousas sem sentires de outra maneira, e sentires de outra maneira sem mudares de alma. Porque as cousas são como nós as sentimos—ha quanto tempo julgas tu saber isto e não o sabes?—e o unico modo de haver cousas novas, de sentir cousas novas é haver novidade no sentil-as."   (*Desassossego* [Tinta] 141–42)

[t]he only way to experience new sensations is to build yourself a new soul. All your efforts will be in vain if you want to feel other things without yourself feeling in a different way, and to do so without a change of soul. Because things are as we feel them—how long have you thought you knew

this without actually knowing it?—and the only way to have new things, to feel new things, is to find a new way of feeling them."

(Disquiet [New Directions] 100)

Subjects of experience are now not barely reflexive acts of self-presentation but manners of feeling, and there are as many manners of feeling as there are I's.

Returning to Pessoa's writings, the greatest challenge, perhaps, is how to teach *The Book of Disquiet*. The very fact that this is not a book by any conventional understanding of that term is both a problem and an opportunity. Simply to assign it as a reading is not likely to be beneficial, because, while students do love reading *The Book of Disquiet*, it is hard for them to know what they are meant to learn in the course of doing so. My strategy to date has been to ask students to become archaeologists among the fragments. I will introduce them to a particular idea and ask them to come back with fragments—or sketches, as we might term the pieces of text—that speak to that idea or theme. For example, the various scattered remarks about attention collectively constitute a very interesting perspective on this hotly contested topic in the philosophy of mind. It seems too that there are many opportunities here to create student-centered exercises involving the selection and reordering of sketches, inviting students to compose their own sequences in ways that develop a philosophical theme. (A software tool whereby the numbered sketches in the English translations could be rearranged to complement an amazing digital resource, the *LdoD Archive* [ldod.uc.pt], would be of benefit here.) In reconstructing chains of fragments, somewhat as if they were memories, students can be introduced to the idea of the narrative sense of self and the extent to which that is itself a work of fictional creation.

Coming from a background in South Asian philosophy, I find the possibility of a dialogue between his philosophy of the subject and South Asian explorations of selfhood especially fascinating. My approach here, which works well in the classroom, has been to retrieve especially difficult puzzles in the history of the philosophy of self from different philosophical traditions—South Asian, Chinese, Islamic—and then to ask whether Pessoa's exceptionally rich and original theory can help us to solve them. I have shown how to do this in my book *Virtual Subjects, Fugitive Selves: Fernando Pessoa and His Philosophy*.

To give one of my favorite examples, there is a famous parable about a butterfly in the Taoist classic the *Zhuangzi*, which reads as follows:

Once Zhuang Zhou dreamt he was a butterfly, fluttering about joyfully just as a butterfly would. He followed his whims exactly as he liked and knew nothing about Zhuang Zhou. Suddenly he awoke, and there he was, the startled Zhuang Zhou in the flesh. He did not know if Zhou had been dreaming he was a butterfly, or if a butterfly was now dreaming it was Zhou. Surely, Zhou and a butterfly count as two distinct identities! Such is what we call the transformation of one thing into another.   *(Zhuangzi* 21)

What is the nature of the relationship between Zhou the dreaming subject and Zhou whom the butterfly dreams of being, a subject within the butterfly's dream? The parable has been studied and pondered for centuries. But we have only to remember that among Pessoa's heteronyms there is a special one, the orthonym "Fernando Pessoa himself." Says Pessoa,

> Fernando Pessoa's writings belong to two categories of works, which we may call orthonymic and heteronymic. The heteronymic works of Fernando Pessoa have been produced by (so far) three people's names—Alberto Caeiro, Ricardo Reis, and Álvaro de Campos. . . . If these three individuals are more or less real than Fernando Pessoa himself is a metaphysical problem that the latter—not privy to the secret of the Gods and therefore ignorant of what really is—will never be able to solve.
>
> (*A Little Larger* 3)

The "Zhou" who is the subject of the butterfly's dream, we can now see, is an orthonym of the "Zhou" who is dreaming of being a butterfly, and then—provided only that we have a sound philosophical account of heteronymy and thus of orthonymy—the puzzle is solved.

In general, the final part of a philosophy of mind course could well look for applications of Pessoa's philosophy to problems in the philosophy of mind. It goes without saying that problems to do with identity, its fragmentation or unity, will be especially amenable to such an approach. This will lead the class, perhaps, to issues in contemporary social and political philosophy, where the topic of identity assumes greatest prominence. How should one think of oneself when one's identity is increasingly multiplex and intersectional? How should one survive in a society in which one has many radically distinct identities—online and in person, at home and at work, in public and in private—a society in which, more particularly, one is subject to constant and invasive surveillance? Perhaps studying Pessoa will be able to teach all of us new and better ways to live.

NOTES

1. Ryan notes in a review of the volume that this project by the teenage Pessoa "was abandoned early on and has no original ideas or insights other than thinking through some of the philosophers referred to throughout the fragments and notes, most especially Kant and Schopenhauer, with hints of Plato, Spinoza and Nietzsche" ("Notebooks" 320).

2. For explorations of a range of affinities between Pessoa and Kierkegaard, see Lourenço, "Kierkegaard e Pessoa ou as máscaras do absoluto" and "Kierkegaard e Pessoa ou a communicação indirecta"; Ryan, "Into the Nothing."

3. Especially "Letter to Adolfo Casais Monteiro, 13 January 1935." Pessoa prefers to use the abstract noun "heteronymism" (*heteronimismo*), rather than "heteronymy"; see Pizarro, *A Critical Introduction* 34.

Reframing Writerly Identity with the Works of Pessoa and Other Modernist Poets

Meghan P. Nolan

The Portuguese poet Fernando António Nogueira Pessoa posthumously exposes the visceral reality of his life through a work of presumed fiction. In the first major section of *The Book of Disquiet*, Pessoa's semi-heteronym,[1] Bernardo Soares, writes:

> Tudo quanto tenho feito, pensado, sido, é uma somma de subordinações, ou a um ente falso que julguei meu, por que agi d'elle para fóra, ou de um peso de circumstancias que suppuz ser o ar que respirava. Sou, neste momento de vêr, um solitario subito, que se reconhece desterrado onde se encontrou sempre cidadão. No mais intimo do que pensei não fui eu.
>
> (Pessoa, *Desassossego* [Tinta] 289)

> All that I've done, thought or been is a series of submissions, either to a false sense of self that I assumed belonged to me because I expressed myself through it to the outside, or to a weight of circumstances that I supposed was the air I breathed. In this moment of seeing, I suddenly find myself isolated, an exile where I always thought I was a citizen. At the heart of my thoughts I wasn't I.
>
> (*Disquiet* [Penguin] 39–40; see also *Disquiet* [New Directions] 236)

In this moment, Soares has a sudden realization that he cannot possibly claim the "self" that he has long since viewed as his own. Soares explains that he has relied upon this perception as a stable and sound externalization of his inner intent, one that he has perhaps over-familiarized through declarations of the "I." However, like most who dare to ponder this prospect, Soares quickly discovers that there is no definitive or graspable entity, and it is through this intense awareness that he also reveals the stark truth of the man behind the curtain—that corporeal being through which his words are irrefutably filtered—a poet who takes this frightening realization for its full worth. For in the wake of this apprehension, Pessoa does not scramble to pin down an identifiable self; rather, he decides to live completely within that experience of great uncertainty and to expand upon it . . . exponentially.

Pessoa's interests, like those of many writers, lie primarily within the art and conception of writing itself. A very deliberate poet, Pessoa approaches this pursuit through an incessant need to fracture the self into scores of disparate parts, and as much as these writerly personas could be considered inspirational by-products, to Pessoa, they are an absolute necessity of his invention. As Soares indicates, intent is at the heart of all expressions of individual identity, and so I argue that it is only when examining Pessoa's oeuvre within the context of writerly identity and the linguistic constraints to which he (and others) must adhere that the reader is able to fully appreciate this intentionally mystifying initiative and see its usefulness as a functional writing hermeneutic. Since Pessoa is not the only modernist poet to tackle these ideals, we must also situate his work in relation to the other poets of his time who explore similar linguistic identity tropes— each of whom circumvents the primary problems of writerly identification.

That is to say, Fernando Pessoa and his renowned anglophone peers, W. B. Yeats, T. S. Eliot, and Ezra Pound, each tackle linguistic constraints in relation to the individual through the meticulous practice of an identity fragmentation that Maud Ellmann refers to as "the poetics of impersonality." Each of these poets represents the extremes of a poetic self-division that strives for matchless ambiguity. Yeats is the Originator, the earliest modernist fragmentor to intentionally diffuse himself in this way through several well-defined personas like Sherman, Howard, Robartes, and Aherne (Nolan 58). Eliot is the Liberator, who brings modern fragmentation to a vast readership through his publication of *The Waste Land*. Pound is the Editor, who strives to perfect the technique through an indeterminable number of revisions of the impersonal aesthetic in his exhaustive cantos (and through his proofing of both Yeats's and Eliot's works). Pessoa is the Master because of the sheer intensity of his fragmentation, which seems to border the impossible more than any other. His practice of fracturing the self into 136 different personas is often viewed as a brand of haphazard deconstruction or, worse yet, categorized casually as a personality disorder on the basis of media stereotypes, however, this type of identity rupture through writing is an intentional move that goes far beyond the desire to simply inhabit multiple speech genres at once and toward the more detailed mechanics or performances of identification found in diverse (and necessary) displays of poetic similitude—the very methods of resemblance that poets utilize in order to emotionally connect with their readers. Accordingly, this brand of fragmentation can facilitate useful discussions in composition and literature classrooms regarding the construction and analysis of writerly identity within literary works and one's own writing when viewed as a complex expression of two concurrent but separate modes of language transfer: first, as the exemplification of the ways in which individuals truly convey themselves (i.e., through multiplicity, linguistic and otherwise) and, second, as the manifestation of various entry points to poetic connectivity for readers of divergent backgrounds. Namely, the works of modernist poets, particularly those of Pessoa, can directly help students build an awareness of their own writerly identities and better understand (and develop) those personal fragmented performances they already enact.

Unraveling Linguistic Habitus with Poetic Similitude

In order for students to recognize and engage with personal multiplicity on this level, some overarching linguistic limitations must be addressed first, as social and institutional ideals are consistently determined through a multifaceted process of linguistic regulation—a process Pierre Bourdieu denotes as "linguistic habitus," or those dispositions that generate normative practices, perceptions, and attitudes governed by learned models of speech and writing (Bourdieu and Thompson 12–17). *Habitus* implies that social norms not only ensure standardization but also subsequently ostracize those who do not buy in through stringent censorship. In other words, those who do not function within the specified linguistic norms of a given community, genre, or sphere are considered to be eccentric, a trait that G. W. F. Hegel indicates is undesirable insofar as "the community can only maintain itself by suppressing the spirit of individualism" (Butler, *Antigone's Claim* 36). Collective judgments are also steeped in an unhealthy preoccupation with seeing the individual as a stable or linear entity despite the reality of universal flux.

One of Pessoa's lesser-known fictitious authors weighs in on this exact ideal. The Baron of Teive is Pessoa's only aristocratic heteronym, and he has little to show for his existence other than a single manuscript said to be published after his own suicide. But Teive gets to the heart of the normative issue at hand when he writes, in some of his most thoughtful prose,

> Não é no individualismo que reside o nosso mal, mas na qualidade d'esse individualismo. E essa qualidade é elle ser estatico em vez de dynamico. Damo-nos valor por o que pensamos em vez de que por o que fazemos. Esquecemos que o não fizemos, não o fomos; que a primeira funcção da vida é a acção, como o primeiro aspecto das coisas é o movimento.
>
> (Pessoa, *Educação* 43)

> Our problem isn't that we're individualists. It's that our individualism is static rather than dynamic. We value what we think rather than what we do. We forget that we haven't done, or been, what we thought; that the first function of life is action, just as the first property of things is motion.
>
> (*Education* 18)

In this selection, Teive asserts that humans should, and often do, desire to separate themselves from normative mandates, yet there is fault to be found in the distinct lack of productive action toward this goal. Much like his aforementioned heteronymic kin, Teive finds the common immobile perception of self extremely problematic and therefore prescribes deliberate progress for all aspects of the individual. Thus one develops the capacity to make one's actual and perceived selves more dynamic or versatile as opposed to adhering to expected performative standards. Heteronymism is positioned as a valuable means of self-conceptive action—as a way for writers to possibly sidestep the obligations associated with what Teive believes to be the primary problem of individualism. But, as Hegel suggests, the apparent idiosyncrasy of such an impersonal approach to writing also simultaneously raises greater social concerns.

Consequently, there are many safeguards that writers of all kinds must put in place in order to ensure the acceptance of their work as valuable or worthy commodities, because as both Bourdieu and Mikhail Bakhtin discern, every utterance has a perceived value or capital that is not much different from that of currency. In the light of this, Judith Butler proclaims that each writer must make sure that they are properly addressing or "playing to" their audience through a process she refers to as "giving an account of oneself" (*Giving*). Interestingly, this sense of accountability is intrinsic to language models, because, as the sociologist Erving Goffman contends, all communications are very much like theatrical performances where one party is vying for the other's approval (*Forms, Presentation*). This tendency leads to a sort of "primordial rule" of communication: The writer or speaker is always accountable to their audience because the audience determines the worth of the messenger's statements and in turn their personal value as well. It is in these terms that "Pound hints that the writer is marooned in language, rather than authenticated by his verse" (Ellmann 1),[2] and if this is true, then the genuineness of poetic quality becomes questionable; worse yet, it renders Pessoa a most serious offender.

An authenticity issue arises almost immediately for novice readers of Pessoa, who perceive, particularly when they are introduced to his writings through his primary heteronyms, that very little of his writing is attributed to himself. As a result, readers ultimately question the trustworthiness of a poet who uses voices in excess—voices he himself deems distinctly separate from that of his own but for which he at times still feels personally responsible (Kotowicz 65). Through the verse of Álvaro de Campos, it would appear as if Pessoa tries to assure the reader otherwise:

> Sim, sou eu, eu mesmo, tal qual resultei de tudo,
> Especie de accessorio ou sobrecelente proprio,
> Arredores irregulares da minha emoção sincera,
> Sou eu aqui em mim, sou eu.
> > (*Obra completa de Álvaro de Campos* [2014] 265)

> Yes it's me, I myself, what I turned out to be,
> A kind of accessory or spare part of my own person,
> The jagged outskirts of my true emotion—
> I'm the one here in myself, it's me.   (*A Little Larger* 240)

But this glimmer of possibility that Pessoa may in fact be in there somewhere is further complicated and quickly dispelled, as Richard Zenith notes: "Not even in the Portuguese poetry written under Pessoa's own name will we find a unified, integrated, natural voice" (Pessoa, *Fernando Pessoa & Co.* 27). This sheer magnitude of heteronymic expression complicates the situation to an uncomfortable degree, because the intangibility of Pessoa's corpus as a whole can be misconstrued as inauthentic as well.[3] Still, the works of the heteronyms demand a type of engagement beyond that of the standard poetic fare (i.e., poetry not so closely entangled with the identity of the poet), for their authors do not claim to have wisdom beyond their means or seek to elevate humanity through their writings; rather, they long to expose the irrationality of linguistic limitations. They often do this through flagrant paradox, thus broaching ethical concerns that can be traced back to sixteenth-century poetics, as in Philip Sidney's claim that the poet's purpose is to affirm ethical edicts through his works; more important, it is the way in which a poet does this through his verse that makes him unique. Unlike Friedrich Nietzsche, who centuries later averred that "only the poet who could lie would be able to tell the truth" (G. Monteiro, *Man Who Never Was* 29), according to Sidney, the poet does not lie, because he has no need to; the poet simply reports that which is true. Sidney also proposes that poetry itself (and therefore the poet) holds humanity's purest intentions, because the work and its author act as an ethical mirror (Sidney 35–36). As Eliot points out, "giving moral instruction" is in fact the main aim of didactic poetry (*On Poetry* 4). Part of morality is also an assumed honesty and integrity in the actual words that the writer produces—the poet, especially held in as high a regard as he is, should be a sort of over-reliable narrator of all that is and not just one who simply reports ethically.

It is in this vein that in *The Order of Things* the French theorist Michel Foucault declares that the poet's fundamental function is principally to use language in order to find and define similarities between subjects. Foucault asserts that the poet's primary role is to identify and communicate through complex resemblances, a skill that surpasses those in normal language usage (50). This concept of similitudes, he later explains, is rooted in the sixteenth-century conventions of discourse—namely, *convenientia* (convenience), *aemulatio* (emulation), analogy, and sympathy. However, he also provides the key to fully understanding the poet's innate antithesis—the madman (cf. Pessoa, *Escritos*), who, according to Foucault, acts in direct opposition to the poet in his use of a proliferating resemblance that fails to reinforce compulsory order. He then advances this point by contending, "The poet brings similitude to the signs that speak it, whereas the madman loads all signs with a resemblance that ultimately erases them" (Foucault, *Order* 50). Eliot, too, weighs in on this idea of the madman, and Maria de Lurdes Sampaio observes that *The Waste Land* itself is truly an exemplification of his insistence that the poet must endure a sort of self-sacrifice through "'a continual extinction of personality'" (278). But even he resumes his distinction that the poet must consciously direct his readers toward connections of fresh feelings, and claims, "That is the difference between the writer who is merely eccentric or mad and the genuine poet" (*On Poetry* 9). Through their learned assessments, these writers (quite wittingly, I suspect, in the case of Foucault in particular, since he is uncannily aware of such incessant and doubling binds) have squarely situated the distinguished figure of the poet within the very criteria that all writers must face: all writers must play to their audience in order to legitimize, and they must do so within the bounds of "moral" standards, because the only way to become the authority on a subject is to gain widespread acceptance. Therefore, the poet must abide by another essential rule—thou shalt not use similitude in a way that is not immediately accessible or easily communicable to others—lest he be considered insane. (It is worth noting that the converse also applies: the poet should not use similitude in a manner that is too ordinary or predictable, lest he be considered a fraud.) And so it is through this estimation of the madman that the poetic and philosophical works of Pessoa and his immediate contemporaries must be approached.

While avid readers of Pessoa revel in his mastery of all aspects of similitude, in Foucault's estimation, Pessoa's work is problematized (particularly for inexpert readers) because of the sheer intricacy and proliferation of poetic parallels that too often seem to result in contradictory statements (e.g., the lack of or late assignment of authorship for some works) that create such a colossal plethora of inconsistencies that without deeper inspection, they in essence appear to eradicate one another. However, Jerónimo Pizarro makes clear that heteronymism is "the construction of other authorial figures and, to this extent, less a phenomenon close to madness than a technique or method of composition of other authors, that is, a vertiginous creation of alter egos by an *ego* . . . , which, instead of denying its multiplicity, seeks to live with it and make the most of it" (*Fernando Pessoa* 35). Additionally, Bakhtin contends that because language is simply a kind of social phenomenon forever dependent and changing along with the factors of its histories, such doubleness in prose is essentially prefigured into its discourse. In an excerpt from the introduction to a Spanish anthology of Fernando Pessoa's work, the Mexican poet and diplomat Octavio Paz champions this principle:

> El poeta inocente es un mito pero es un mito que funda a la poesía. El poeta real sabe que las palabras y las cosas no son lo mismo y por eso, para restablecer una precaria unidad entre el hombre y el mundo, nombra las cosas con imágenes, ritmos, símbolos y comparaciones. Las palabras no son las cosas; son los puentes que tendemos entre ellas y nosotros.
> (Ferrari, "Fernando Pessoa" 224)

> The innocent poet is a myth, but a cover-up myth of poetry. The real poet knows that words and things are not the same, and that in order to establish a facade of unification between man and the natural world he is required to name things such as imaginations, rhythms, symbols and comparisons [similitudes]. The words themselves are not the things; they are the bridges that stretch between them and us.[4]

Paz examines the inherent ruse of poetry: the poet is distinctly aware of the separation between words and things but intentionally uses words to represent things as a way to bridge gaps in comprehension. And as the manipulator of language, he must make difficult decisions about how to position that which is not real within reality. In this sense, the poet regularly functions within paradox, and it is well within his right to do so, because in order to make those complex connections for others (as Eliot and Foucault so mandate), the poet must attempt constant contradiction through language usage itself. In the first few stanzas of poem XXVII, originally from the collection *O guardador de rebanhos* (*The Keeper of Sheep*), Pessoa's heteronym Alberto Caeiro confirms the paradoxical nature of poetic language:

> Só a Natureza é divina, e ella não é divina . . .
> Se ás vezes fallo d'ella como de um ente
> É que para fallar d'ella preciso usar da linguagem dos homens
> Que dá personalidade ás cousas
> E impõe nome ás cousas.
> Mas as cousas não teem nome nem personalidade:
> Existem, e o céu é grande e a terra larga,
> E o nosso coração do tamanho de um punho fechado . . .
>
> (*Obra completa de Alberto Caeiro* 265)

> Only Nature is divine, and she is not divine . . .
> If I sometimes speak of her as a person
> It's because I can only speak of her by using the
> language of men,
> Which imposes names on things
> And gives them personality.
> But things have no name or personality:
> They just are, and the sky is vast, the earth wide,
> And our heart the size of a closed fist . . .   (*A Little Larger* 30)

In this selection, Caeiro too points to the contradictory nature of language itself as a communicative trope by distinguishing the difference between the words and the things they represent. Therefore, both Paz and Pessoa suggest that paradox does not inherently undermine authenticity or the poet's obligation to honesty, unless we are willing to fully deconstruct the binary structures of language as an institution. In addition to this, Eliot notes, most poets frequently (and easily) utilize three voices as well. The poet freely bounces between: speaking to himself, addressing the audience, and dialoguing as a character through his verse. Furthermore, because the poet uses his own version of written language, he can never be completely absent from his impersonalized endeavors. The physical act of writing externalizes memory, and therefore halts the flow of the current autobiographical self, but, as Pound suggests, it thus naturally highlights the inborn division of the self (Ellmann 63). All these ideas combine to show the real beauty of the "impersonal" as a poetic trope.

Pessoa greatly exceeds modernist expectations in his poetry, precisely because he appears to provide a valuable demonstration of Foucault's madman, or one who "fulfills the resemblance that never ceases to proliferate" (Foucault, *Order* 50). In Pessoa's works this "madness" manifests in the form of mounting similitudes that seem to negate the overarching purpose of poetry in that they disqualify the very experience employed for poetic connection. We see this dilemma play out in the poetics of Pessoa's heteronyms time and again. For instance, Caeiro attempts to connect to the reader through those previously discussed classical modes of similitude required of the poet, only to stumble on the fundamental inadequacies of his own language:

> Quem me dera que a minha vida fosse um carro de bois
> Que vem a chiar, manhaninha cedo, pela estrada,
> E que para de onde veiu volto depois
> Quasi á noitinha pela mesma estrada.
> Eu não tinha que ter esperanças—tinha só que ter rodas . . .
> A minha velhice não tinha rugas nem cabello branco . . .
> Quando eu já não sevia, tiravam-me as rodas
> E eu ficava virado e partido no fundo de um barranco.
> Ou então faziam de mim qualquer coisa differente
> E eu não sabia nada do que faziam de mim . . .
> Mas eu não sou um carro, sou diferente,
> Mas em que sou realmente differente nunca me diriam.
>
> (*Obra completa de Alberto Caeiro* 50–51)

> If only my life were an oxcart
> That creaks down the road in the morning,
> Very early, and returns by the same road
> To where it came from in the evening . . .
> I wouldn't have to have hopes, just wheels . . .
> My old age wouldn't have wrinkles or white hair . . .
> When I was of no more use, my wheels would be removed
> And I'd end up in a ditch, broken and overturned.
> Or I'd be made into something different
> And I wouldn't know what I'd been made into . . .
> But I'm not an oxcart, I'm different.
> But exactly how I'm different no one would ever tell me.
>
> (*A Little Larger* 26)

Using analogy, Alberto Caeiro likens his existence to that of an oxcart in a wish that his life could only be as simple as the utilitarian object; he subsequently expresses frustration at the lack of a viable explanation for the essential difference between himself and the object, yet the reader gets the feeling that this heteronym knows that the answer to his own question is firmly rooted in language itself. As physical matter, both man and object are essentially constituted of the same microscopic components, and the philosophizing of Caeiro's fellow heteronym Charles Anon suggests it is the "soul" that separates human from object (Pessoa, *Philosophical Essays* 60). However, the oxcart, like all objects, requires a being with a soul (in this case either ox or human) to fulfill or initiate its purpose. This ready-made distinction is thus slightly obfuscated because it requires additional distinction between Caeiro and the unmentioned ox (who also, arguably, possesses this element of "soul"). Further deliberation reveals a better distinction to be Caeiro's use of language itself as a means of differentiation—as it underpins human understanding of not only the self but also the world and emotional reaction. After all, it is human language (and not that of the ox or any other) that forces the presumption of the self through the distinction of "'I am' statements and other indications of permanence" (Nolan 55).

According to Caeiro's poem, the essence of humanity requires this mode of communication not only as a means of connection and identification but primarily in order to justify and judge its own existence. Unlike Caeiro, the oxcart and the ox have no need (or ability) to defend themselves, nor are they dependent upon language as a means of situating themselves in relation to each other and to other things, and so when either breaks down or deteriorates it does so without compunction. The same cannot be said of their hominid converse, as Caeiro's poetic musing is in and of itself a critical display of that human condition of language—the poem is a complicated expression of the self wherein the language used to identify it also expresses common judgments of its existence, such as the wish to defy the perceived negative effects of aging, the need to escape the burdens of human thoughts through "hopes," and a desire to be transformed into something that does not have these linguistic liabilities (i.e., the oxcart). In this perfect example of yet another similitude—sympathy—Caeiro's poetic sentiment overrides singular attribution, because it is an expression that can presumably be shared by large numbers of people. This assertion is problematic, however, because the words themselves are not enough for the reader to be able to competently empathize with Caeiro's strange desire for inanimacy (especially considering that most writerly efforts are usually spent personifying such objects poetically and otherwise). Remarkably, if we now return to Foucault's definition of the poet, the answer to this reader-oriented conundrum is readily apparent.

Pessoa's propagation of similitude (and its successive erasure) is a very deliberate choice. Despite Foucault's interpretations, Pessoa's crime is not found in a rejection of analogy, for Pessoa and the heteronyms use poetic resemblance quite frequently and astutely. The first line of one of his poems even declares, "Ah, tudo é símbolo e analogia!" ("Ah, everything is symbol and analogy!"; *Poemas dramáticos* 76; my trans.). For that matter, he does not lose control of that mechanism either, for even in Pessoa's extreme deconstruction there is at the center of it all the heart of a poet. As Robert Crawford expresses, the modern poet is a scholar who applies the wealth of his academic knowledge to his creative works, "[c]omplicating and teasing us beyond the normal texture of English . . . [and] hinting at new ways of being a modern poet. Self-consciously sophisticated and primitive at once . . ." (68). Pessoa performs as a sort of super-poet, then, a role he wittingly takes on to become the rightful successor to

"Portugal's great bard Luís de Camões" (Kotowicz 18). His extreme written version of creationism, although undoubtedly contradictory, is not something to be viewed as separate from the poetic agenda; rather, it should be located at the outermost pole of its expression.

Feeling in a New Language

For students to fully grasp the significance of such nuances in and through poetic identity, they also must appreciate that Pessoa and the other modernist fragmentors, more than any other group of poets, have managed to harness the full potential of the aforesaid paradox in relation to written identity performance, as they often eschew language barriers through acts of appropriation as well. It is clear that although the modernist fragmentor is enacting a purpose of the poet rarely fulfilled, he is not truly a madman in Foucauldian terms, for his attempts to transcend linguistic limitations (as those of Pessoa above) prove that his goals adequately incorporate those of the poetic archetype as opposed to counteracting them. With that aside, Foucault plainly states that the poet's is an "allegorical role; beneath the language of signs and beneath the interplay of their precisely delineated distinctions, he strains his ears to catch that 'other language,' the language, without words or discourse, of resemblance" (Foucault, *Order* 50). It is that other language surrounding the more common written expressions of similitude that is most important to fragmentation, because "[t]he [modernist] poet here is using not so much a language as a linguistic spectrum that, for some moments at least, problematizes . . . the notion of a 'native language'" (Crawford 64). Similitude, even in its most common forms (i.e., analogy, metaphor, sympathy, etc.), is not actually substantiated in the transmission of words at all; rather, its meaning is derived from raw feeling.

Modernists like Pessoa embrace the chaos of a multifaceted existence as natural, and so theirs is a masterful practice reliant upon the delicate balance of knowledge both academic and experiential for two reasons: so that it does not collapse under its own weight and so that their complex acts of the impersonal will be communicable at all (even if minutely). One means of accomplishing this is through Eliot's concept of emotive connectivity, through which they combine their scholarly understanding of various cultures with their personal experiences of them, and this cultural bifurcation is what appears to attract each to the practice of written fragmentation in the first place. Each modernist poet examined herein has experience both living and studying abroad: Pound and Eliot both had extended periods as expatriates in England; Yeats bounced between Ireland and England; and Pessoa lived in South Africa as a child and later had a short stint in England himself before returning to Portugal. All four thus naturally inhabit Eliot's ideal of feeling in multiple languages at once. There are times when the resulting modernist linguistic mash-ups can seem excessive (as in Pound's cantos, where one is frequently confronted with a multitude of languages in a single poem). Yet one important motivation for their adoption of several non-native dialects is undoubtedly that most of the time they are themselves appropriations and extensions of the practice of fragmentation.

Yeats often uses Latin for emphasis, as in the title "Ego Dominus Tuus." These words, originally spoken to Dante in a dream by a personified version of Love (*Vita nova* 3), are meant to foreground the atmosphere of the conversation that follows, but they can be loosely translated to English in one of two ways: either "I am your master" or "I am your lord." Neither approximation accurately expresses the presence of the perceived dominant life force in the poem. However, by using the Latin phrasing, Yeats preserves the intended sentiment as best he can while simultaneously satisfying the modernist proclivity for intertwining history with the movement's purpose in regard to fragmentation. Pound turns to the classics in order to further his identity appropriations as well. In canto IV, he transports the reader to the era of ancient myth through his intentional use of Latin in selected dialogue as he refers to the myth of Itys, borrowing a line from Horace's *Odes*. Although "Et ter flebiliter" (Pound 13) easily translates to "And thrice with tears" (Terrell 12), the poet chooses to deliver the line in Latin because it would lose its authenticity and historical grounding through translation. Likewise, at the end of the first stanza of "The Fire Sermon" in *The Waste Land*, Eliot exclaims: "*Et, O ces voix d'enfants, chantant dans la coupole!*" (line 202). This line has a multilayered significance, referencing several non-English works. According to Michael North, it is meant to echo the last line of the French poet Paul Verlaine's sonnet "Parsifal," which itself is a paraphrase of a line from Richard Wagner's German opera of the same name (Eliot, *Waste Land* 12). By choosing the French instead of an English translation, Eliot maintains an initial connotation that is readily accessible for those who are willing to engage; the reader can also assume that it is a sentiment the author believes is best expressed in French.

Fluent in English, French, and Portuguese, Pessoa naturally transcends the linguistic limitations of experience on an individual level. Like Pound, he translates the works of other poets, and, as Sampaio notes, "Although there is no confession by Pessoa that translation might be a mask or a process of depersonalization, one may infer this from some of his plans to translate the elected poets (such as Shakespeare's works)" (280). But, as the consummate fragmentor, he pushes the exercise even further than his modernist contemporaries in that his globally positioned fictitious authors are said to be multilingual as well. While Pessoa and the majority of the heteronyms are residents of Portugal's capital city, Lisbon, or the surrounding countryside, in the Pessoa universe there are many fictitious authors who live and write more variably. For instance, France is home to the poet and satirist Jean Seul de Méluret; Pessoa's English poets and writers Thomas Crosse and Frederick Wyatt—the latter "a slant allusion to the English poet Sir Thomas Wyatt" (Foley 67)—reside in London along with their essayist counterpart Horace James Faber; and Alexander Search maintains the American viewpoint as a short story writer and poet (see Pessoa, "Very Original

Dinner"). Through these characters, Pessoa does not fall into the trap of catering to a specified audience; instead he creates a vast performance of multivalence that grants access points for readers of various backgrounds and temperaments. Not only does he believe in the crossing of languages (and writing genres) through personas of various cultures; he also has several alter egos who are themselves polyglots, like Gaudencio Nabos, a journalist who knows several languages and reports in both English and Portuguese, as well as the translator heteronyms: Charles James Search (brother to Alexander), Claude Pasteur, and Vicente Guedes, who are acknowledged as the authors responsible for interpreting the works of their fellow personas.[5] Some of the heteronyms even show an ability to feel in a language other than those they speak, as demonstrated by the primary heteronym Álvaro de Campos. Through Campos, Pessoa fully explores the possibilities of communicating in one language and feeling in another, because despite the fact that his poems are written in Portuguese and French, Campos hints at those sentiments he feels only through English by assigning corresponding English titles to his works (G. Monteiro, "Fernando [Antonio Nogueira] Pessoa" 6).

This is a complicated endeavor. The reader can never completely comprehend the process of experiencing emotions across different languages—a process mediated by fragmentation—by simply evaluating the poet's words on the page. All they can do is emulate the performance or compare the author's written experience to their own, and neither course is completely satisfactory. Poets' words are often deemed meaningless without feeling—and poets' feeling valued according to their ability to express it to others—hence modernist poets like Pessoa are overtly aware of the interdependence of feeling and word. The heteronym Ricardo Reis argues that it is words that give reality to feeling:

> Outros com lyras ou com harpas narram,
>   Eu com meu pensamento.
> Que, or meio de musica, acham nada
>   Se acham só o que sentem.
> Mais pesam as palavras que, medidas,
>   Dizem que o mundo existe.
>
> (*Obra completa de Ricardo Reis* 164)

> Others recount with lyres or harps;
>   I convey through my thoughts.
> He who seeks only in music
>   Discovers nothing beyond his feelings.
> Words hold more weight when, carefully crafted,
>   They affirm that the world exists.   (trans. by eds.)

This persistent bond between words and feeling is further complicated because within the practice of fragmentation it can be extremely difficult to suss out distinctions between the modernist poet's own voice and that of his creations.

Although the personas' poetics are meant to be viewed as individual, there is no question that some of their traits are intentionally and unintentionally akin to those of the poet himself. Eliot believed that this happens because

> [t]he author may put into that character, besides its other attributes, some trait of his own . . . [s]omething perhaps he never realized in his own life, something of which those who know him best may be unaware, something not restricted in transmission to characters of the same temperament, the same age, and, least of all, of the same sex.   (*On Poetry* 102)

There is no hard line of separation when it comes to the divided self; hence the sheer magnitude of alternate writing identities combined with the three voices of the poet-self can easily become overwhelming and confusing for any reader (in addition to which perhaps a majority of readers encounter Pessoa in translation).

With that said, modernist fragmentors, like Pessoa, do not require us to revel in their personal performances of self-division; rather, they beg us to be a party to our own, because the personal nature of fragmentation renders the poet's experience moot unless we are willing to step outside those boundaries ourselves. Walter Benjamin proclaims in his essay "The Task of the Translator" that every translator must be a poet in order to convey "that which lies beyond communication in a work" (*Selected Writings* 253), and since interpretation must be undertaken from the audience's perspective, as readers we must entirely commit to that charge. We should not only strive to experience things through another language or culture as the modernists do (or at least attempt to scrutinize our bilingual and multilingual performances if applicable), but we owe it to ourselves to experiment with our own methods of written identity fragmentation, because the act of dividing the self into various written personas can be beneficial for all writers, regardless of skill level, genre, or inclination. This practice can be challenging, particularly because of the aforementioned issues of authenticity, unless we view it in the light of a more familiar genre.

As previously discussed, it is difficult for the average person to garner sincere connection through extreme displays of the impersonal, so perhaps each modernist fragmentor's approach may be best understood as the equivalent of another, more widely accepted performance of written multiplicity . . . that of the dramatic play. The acts of fragmentation discussed herein share many of the same components of a play, even beyond those theatrical attributes of language detailed by Goffman. That is because, at its core, the impersonal aesthetic is an inscrutable production that reveals the conflict of individualism in relation to a multitude of linguistic and societal constructs; its plot varies depending on the personas' backgrounds and how and when the reader drops in on each character in relation to the others.

In practice, this mutable performativity is always at the front of the fragmentor's mind. Pessoa, for example, refers to his heteronymism as "drama-em-gente" ("drama-in-character"), and this phrase, which he might have taken from the English poet Robert Browning, is meaningful in two major senses: Pessoa, as George Monteiro has said, is "interested in the drama that [comes] from within individuals, and he [is] interested in the imaginary dramatic world created through the interactions among the members of his group of imagined poets" ("Fernando [Antonio Nogueira] Pessoa"). He elucidates this play-like staging of his personas in a letter dated 20 January 1935, in which he also credits his own inner dramatist, rather than his innate poet-self, with the orchestration of the greater heteronymic dialogue:

> O que sou essencialmente—por traz das mascaras involuntarias do poeta, do raciocinador e do que mais haja—é dramaturgo. O phenomeno da minha despersonalização instinctiva, a que alludi em minha carta ante-rior, para explicação da existencia dos heteronymos, conduz naturalmente a essa definição. Sendo assim, não evoluo, VIAJO. . . . Vou mudando de per-sonalidade, vou (aqui é que póde haver evolução) enriquecendo-me na capacidade de crear personalidades novas, novos typos de fingir que com-prehendo o mundo, ou, antes, de fingir que se póde comprehende-lo.
>
> (*Cartas entre Fernando Pessoa e os directores* 266)

> What I am essentially—behind the involuntary masks of poet, logical rea-soner and so forth—is a dramatist. My spontaneous tendency to deperson-alization . . . naturally leads to this definition. And so I do not evolve, I simply JOURNEY. . . . I continuously change personality, I keep enlarging (and here there is a kind of evolution) my capacity to create new charac-ters, new forms of pretending that I understand the world or, more accu-rately, that the world can be understood. (*A Little Larger* 273)

To Pessoa it is important to inhabit as many identities as possible with a play-wright's keen sensibility because it is a way of trying to understand the binds that constrain the individual in the world at large and subsequently to attempt to communicate that vast struggle to a readership. In true modernist fashion, he also paradoxically expresses that this impersonal stance provides a way for him to grapple with the fact that such matters can never truly be understood at all. Thus, he describes his compound performance of fragmentation as the evo-lution of the self—an unpredictable journey that frees him (and by proxy his audi-ence) of stilted beliefs and unnecessary parameters.

It is within Eliot's perspective on the verse play that another justification for viewing modernist depersonalization in this way emerges. In his lecture "The Three Voices of Poetry," Eliot makes it clear that, as in a stage play, each frag-mented persona must have his own set of detailed characteristics in order for the ascription of various poetic verse styles to be construed as authentic, and because the voice of the poet-self is naturally limited, the poet must use an abundance of these personas in order for his language to reach the "intensity" necessary for extending its own boundaries (*On Poetry* 100). These ideas, developed thirty-one years after the publication of *The Waste Land*, are undoubtedly fueled by Eliot's own practice of the impersonal, and his assessment, along with Pessoa's, suggests that in order to fulfill his duty to the audience, the poet must also extend his role to that of a conscious director of personas, delicately balancing the performances of those contradictory identities within the greater creative work. With that said, even with the best direction one hindrance remains: genuine sympathy through written language alone is impossible—there are no accurate descriptors for such coexisting entities, nor are there verbs that indicate simultaneous states of being. This is why the reader, who is subjected to a given experience solely through written expositions, can never fully grasp modernist fragmentation through traditional means of language consumption alone.

Modernist fragmentors endeavor to expand upon and challenge the ways in which we often think about and perceive writerly identification as a whole, and the pure strength of their impersonal aesthetic is that it does not force the singularity of individualism or sensation upon its readers—it merely provides a framework for circumventing common linguistic identity traps. I have noted elsewhere that "poetic fragmentation offers logical context for this mode of analysis, as it is the intentional division of the self in writing in order to interrogate interrelated social conventions such as identity, language, culture, politics, and more" (Nolan 54). As Robert Crawford writes, "If words are among our greatest possessions, then poetry is language operating at its limits, and pointing the way beyond. In it imagination and articulation fuse at their highest intensity" (1). Through their poetics, Pessoa and his contemporaries (Eliot, Pound, and Yeats) each exemplify a new way of being that teaches us to welcome flexibility with open arms. Fragmenting the self may seem eccentric, outdated, or out of the ordinary at best, but truthfully it is not as unusual a concept in today's society as one might think. The online sphere makes possible the creation of such personas with great ease, as social media platforms like *Facebook*, *Instagram*, *LinkedIn*, *Twitter*, and other Internet forums present us with several avenues for alternate writing identities of our choosing, whether real or fictional. And so, to help students build an awareness of their own writerly identities and those of literary figures, we can and should look to the modernist poets, because they provide a way for us to better understand and evolve those fragmented performances we already enact.

NOTES

1. According to Jerónimo Pizarro, Pessoa "invented the most recent meaning of 'heteronym'" (*Fernando Pessoa* 34). Pessoa referred to his three primary writerly personas (Alberto Caeiro, Álvaro de Campos, and Ricardo Reis) as heteronyms, while Soares is designated as a semi-heteronym; Pizarro and Richard Zenith each clarify that the designation was an intentional decision on the poet's part in order to emphasize the extreme difference between the background, education level, socioeconomic status, and profes-

sion of each of the heteronyms, who are meant to be viewed and read as completely separate individuals. Pessoa states as much in his "Tábua bibliográphica" (Pizarro, *Fernando Pessoa* 42). Interestingly, the heteronyms are acquainted with one another, and their meetings are documented through their individual works.

2. Ellmann and the other sources cited in the discussion below use masculine pronouns for the figure of the poet, as does the remainder of this essay, in the light of the fact that the poets under discussion are male.

3. A great deal of Pessoa's work was written on napkins, envelopes, and other marginalia, and completed works were sometimes not filed under the proper name or were not labeled with an author at all.

4. In the cited article, Ferrari analyzes the margin notes of Pizarnik (a well-known Pessoa reader) in Paz's 1962 anthology *Fernando Pessoa: El desconocido de sí mismo*. The selected passage is my own translation of Paz's original text from the introduction, as the article and the passage both appear entirely in Spanish.

5. These rudimentary descriptions of the personas are derived from research in Zenith's introduction to *Fernando Pessoa & Co.: Selected Poems*, Rita Patrício and Pizarro's preface to Pessoa's *Obras de Jean Seul de Méluret*, and Anne Terlinden's book *Fernando Pessoa: The Bilingual Portuguese Poet*. However, Pizarro and Ferrari's *Eu sou uma antologia: 136 autores fictícios* presents a much more comprehensive breakdown of all of Pessoa's 136 fictitious authors.

EDITING

From Meta-Editing to Virtual Editing: The *LdoD Archive* as a Computer-Assisted Editorial Space

Manuel Portela

As both conceptual and technical artifact, the *LdoD Archive*, a collaborative digital archive of Fernando Pessoa's *Livro do desassossego* (*The Book of Disquiet*), contains an innovative model for the literary acts of reading, editing, and writing. Re-creating the textual and fictional universe of *The Book of Disquiet* according to ludic principles of textual manipulation, the *LdoD Archive* fosters new reading, editing, and writing practices. Its programmed features can be used in multiple activities, including leisure reading, study, analysis, advanced research, and creative writing. Through the integration of computational tools in a simulation space, it brings together textual production, textual reception, and textual analysis in its experimentation with the procedurality of the digital medium. This experiment is based on a complex ecology of models, programs, tools, algorithms, and interfaces whose end result can be described as an open-ended evolutionary textual environment that fully incorporates user interaction (Portela and Rito Silva; *Arquivo LdoD*; Portela, "Simulación").

This essay addresses the editorial component of the *LdoD Archive*, showing first how its representational dimension takes the form of a meta-edition—that is, an edition that has been designed as a comparative micro- and macrorepresentation of other editions. I then show how this representational dimension is turned into a simulation dimension when the encoded textual units from the various expert editions are freely used as building blocks of the virtual editions. I argue that this dynamic computer-assisted simulation space is an attempt to embody the performativity of the editorial act itself. The editorial focus of the *LdoD Archive* thus shifts retroactively from each particular expert edition to the archive of the *Book* as a series of autograph documents, from each particular expert edition to other expert editions as possible and actual versions of the *Book*, and from those two focuses to any number of potential textual arrangements. The continuous unediting and reediting through the programmed functionalities of the platform instantiates the very processuality of editing.

From Edition to Meta-Edition

One of the goals of the *LdoD Archive* is to show Pessoa's *Book* as a network of potential authorial intentions and a conjectural construction of its successive editors. Our digital representation of the dynamics of textual and bibliographical variation depends on both XML encoding of variation sites (deletions, additions, substitutions, variants, paragraph and text divisions, etc.), metatextual information concerning authorial and editorial witnesses (date, order, heteronym, etc.), and a data model that fosters multiple perspectives and exploratory interactions with the textual materials at different scales. While TEI-XML markup may be considered as a critical apparatus on its own, it is through algorithmic analysis, visualization tools, and graphical interface that users are able to critically engage with the dynamics of variation in authorial and editorial witnesses.

Our data model for the textual archive and the strategies adopted for encoding all the authorial and editorial witnesses are aimed at providing comparability among all the authorial or editorial versions of each text, including their relative position within each edition of the book. Instead of following a digital scholarly editing model based on the bibliographic practice of the "definitive" critical edition that subsumes and transcends earlier editions, the *LdoD Archive* is designed according to meta-editorial principles. The purpose of the meta-edition is to offer a critical probe into four editions as actual forms of the *Book* whose textual embodiment results from four distinct sets of editorial principles and criteria. Through comparison and manipulation, the editorial interface has been designed to emphasize the hypothetical constructedness of the *Book* rather than a single version of the work. Thus, each historical version is seen as the contingent result of specific editorial interventions among a network of versions.[1]

Pessoa's *Livro do Desassossego* is an unfinished book project. Pessoa wrote more than five hundred texts meant for this work between 1913 and 1935, the year of his death. The Portuguese National Library has catalogued 722 sheets as belonging to the *Livro*, of which 374 are typescripts, while 348 are manuscripts. Some of them are written on recto and verso. Only twelve texts from the *Livro* were published by Pessoa in literary magazines. Texts explicitly assigned by Pessoa to the *Livro* contain the annotation "L. do D." However, there are more than two hundred texts without the "L. do D." annotation that also belong (or have been judged by editors to belong) to the *Livro*.

The first edition of this book was published only in 1982, and another three major versions have been published since then. This first edition, in two volumes (reprinted only once, in 1997), was edited by Jacinto do Prado Coelho, with textual transcriptions by Maria Aliete Galhoz and Teresa Sobral Cunha. Three major editions have been published since then. These were edited, respectively, by Cunha in 1990–91, by Richard Zenith in 1998, and by Jerónimo Pizarro in 2010. Those four major editions (of which Cunha, Zenith, and Pizarro remain in circulation) have been the basis for most other editions in circulation, both in Portuguese and in translation.[2] Thus the expert editions included in the *LdoD Archive* are the main critical editions published between 1982 and 2012.[3]

The total set of fragments in each edition has varied either because new texts have been discovered in Pessoa's archive, or because editors have decided to include or exclude particular texts. Another reason for variation originates in the fact that some documents have been interpreted as one single text or as more than one text. The number of fragments in the editions that we have encoded for the *LdoD Archive* is as follows: the edition by Coelho contains 520 fragments; the 2008 revised edition by Cunha, 748 fragments; the 2012 revised edition by Zenith, 514 fragments; and the edition by Pizarro, 586 fragments. Those four editions were selected as representative because they were the latest versions of each edition when we began encoding the files for the *LdoD Archive* in 2012. The 1982 edition is the only one that has not changed, since its editor died in 1984. The other three editions have continued to undergo a number of small changes (in the corpus, in the transcription, in the ordering of texts), although they have maintained their basic structure and principles of organization.

As it exists today, the *Livro* may be characterized as a set of autograph (man-uscript and typescript) fragments, mostly unpublished at the time of Pessoa's death, which have been transcribed, selected, and organized into four different editions, implying various critical and genetic interpretations of what constitutes this book. Editions show five major types of variation: variation in readings of particular passages, in selection of fragments, in division of texts, in the texts' relative position within the book, and also in heteronym attribution.[4] The first authorial persona for the *Livro* was Vicente Guedes, but Pessoa later reassigned the work to Bernardo Soares, a persona he described as a "semi-heteronym" in the well-known letter to Adolfo Casais Monteiro about the genesis of the het-eronyms (13 January 1935).[5] Although the authorial personas behind the *Livro* tend not to be viewed as full heteronyms, heteronym attribution has been an important function in structuring the editions of the work. An alternative view holds that Bernardo Soares was intended as literary character who is outside Pes-soa's heteronymic constellation of fictional authors (Martins, "*Livro*").

Those editorial instantiations have given material expression to four different models of constructing the *Livro*. We could summarize this history as follows: the first model (the edition by Coelho) orders fragments according to a combi-nation of thematic and chronological proximity; the second model (the edition by Cunha) distinguishes between two periods of composition and their respec-tive heteronyms (Guedes and Bernardo Soares) while strengthening the discur-sive unity of the fragments within each part, for example, by removing text numbering and by rearranging the internal structure of a certain number of more fragmentary texts; the third model (the edition by Zenith) considers the production of Bernardo Soares as the main axis of the work and anchors the remaining fragments so that Soares's voice becomes predominant, relegating the set of early large texts by Guedes to a final section; finally, the fourth model (the edition by Pizarro) produces a critical and genetic reconstruction based on the documented or inferred chronology of the composition of fragments, thus bringing the order of the *Livro* closer to its archival order.[6]

An analysis of their editorial introductions and diachrony of publication demonstrates how editions compete against each other in order to legitimize their particular ways of constructing the *Book* from Pessoa's textual archive. This fight for validation of textual form also reflects the commercial dynamics of competition in the book market. In other words, variations in the *Book*'s internal textual form depend not only on the explicit criteria and literary models invoked by the editors of each edition but also on a set of implicit socioliterary factors. The almost immediate publication of new revised editions for each of the three major editions whenever a new reincarnation of the book appears on the market highlights this dynamic of competition for the cultural and financial capital of the work.

Editors' particular interpretation of what *The Book of Disquiet* is or should be inscribes their editorial intentionality on the selection and organization used to access authorial intentionality. This means that the transition from the transcription of the documents to the macroscale of their bibliographic structure is also produced with a certain conjunction of the ideas of *book*, *The Book of Disquiet*, and *Pessoa*. Editorial interpretations concerning the nature of the *Book* as a work, including notions about its place in the literary economy of Pessoa's entire oeuvre, function as organizing principles for each version of the *Book*. Pizarro, for instance, highlights the work's protean dimension, referring to the double origin of autograph texts, which correspond to two moments of distinct intentionality and style, associated first with the heteronym Vicente Guedes and later with the semi-heteronym Bernardo Soares. He also refers to the polyphony of Pessoa's other heteronymic voices, many of which seem to converge within the *Book* in its later moment of composition. The metamorphic character of the work is further testified by the incommensurability between the four major editions published since 1982 (Pizarro, "Os muitos desassossegos"). Zenith considers the fragment as a literary form and not as a mere contingency of the incompleteness of the writing process. For him, the fragment is adequate to the internal logic of the *Book*, and his edition explores the hypothesis of presenting the work as a novel narrating the inner life of Soares (Zenith, "*Livro*"). Different ways of conceiving the work thus correspond to different models of editorial construction.

Microvariations and Macrovariations

The meta-editorial perspective described above is a way of modeling the textual dynamics that determine the transformation of documents into books. The *Book* takes shape through interpretative acts that have selected, transcribed, and organized its texts according to specific conceptions of the work. Understood as a particular textual form based on autograph witnesses, the *Book* becomes the expression of an editorial project that has inscribed itself into the work's archive. The encoding of the network of variations across the editions, on the one hand, and the relations between them and the autograph witnesses, on the other, makes the textual form of each edition available for algorithmic processing. Editions become machine-readable qua editions—that is, as specific interventions in the work's textual archive. The editorial process itself is primed through a series of analytical and comparative tools. Critical editions in print are electronically edited according to a digital rationale of a second-order representation of a first-order representation.

Hans Walter Gabler, Elena Pierazzo ("Rationale" and *Digital*), and other editors see in the digital edition the possibility of returning the work and the text to the document, which suggests an identification between text and document that would suspend the interpretative intervention of the editor. This theoretical perspective is favored by the possibility of facsimile representation of high-resolution images of the original witnesses, which could thus be objectified without the mediation of a transcription. The growing number of documentary digital editions is a consequence of this technical production context. However, as Peter Robinson claims, the separation between text and document is inherent in the act of reading itself, since marks inscribed on a surface become legible forms only through an interpretive act. It is the performance of reading that transforms the marks of the document (that is, inscriptions on a given surface) into the text (that is, a set of signifiers that imply questions of intentionality, agency, authority, and meaning), and it is also through the act of reading that the text is projected onto the unstable and changing horizon of the work.

The movement from document to text and from text to work contains an inverse movement (from work back to document) through which a certain idea of the work inscribes itself in the form and organization of the text as inferred from the documents. Editing Pessoa's centrifugal and reticular body of unpublished work is an especially acute experience of the productive function of reading in activating the force fields that allow one to move back and forth from document to text to book to work. The *LdoD Archive* embodies an understanding of the nature of textual semiosis as process involving self and object in a continuous and interdependent process of meaning production through acts of reading that can also be expressed through acts of editing.

From a theoretical standpoint, the concept *document* is used to describe the object containing the original inscriptions. In the *LdoD Archive*, the document is represented by the digital image of manuscripts, typescripts, and printed autographs. The concept *text* refers to the document after an act of reading takes place. To the extent that transcription is also a reading act, the result of any transcription would be a text. In the *LdoD Archive* the text is represented by the topographic transcription of autograph documents and by the textual transcription of the four selected editions. Finally, the concept of *book* refers to the diverse forms of *The Book of Disquiet*—that is, to a particular selection and organization of texts into a bibliographic whole.

The Editions interface contains a complex representation that brings together the microscale of textual transcriptions based on the documents and the macroscale of editorial arrangements based on each expert's editorial intervention toward a totality of a bibliographic structure (fig. 1). On the right-hand side, a bibliographic visualization of the relative position of the transcribed text in each expert edition is provided. "Minha alma é uma orchestra occulta" ("My soul is a hidden orchestra"; Pessoa, *Desassossego* [Tinta] 41; *Disquiet* [New Directions] 7) has been divided into five different texts in Coelho (27, 78, 259, 357, and 437), corresponding to text 15 in Cunha, text 310 in Zenith, and text 1 in Pizarro. Textual transcriptions can also be compared against one another, and all points of variation (orthography, choice of variants, divergent readings, punctuation, paragraph division, text division) are highlighted (fig. 2). From the point of view of the data model, editorial witnesses become part of a network of versions. Interactors can move from each edited book to another edited book or to the work's archive, that is, the text can be represented as unedited or reedited in another version of itself.

By placing digital facsimiles in the context of topographic transcriptions, the *LdoD Archive* enables users to experiment with the transit from document to text and from text to document. Situating both facsimile and topographic transcription in the context of the experts' editions, the *LdoD Archive* shows several possible transitions from text to book and from book to text. To the extent that each text of each edition is contextualizable in an archive of authorial and editorial witnesses, it is the very process of construction of text from document and of book from text that the genetic and social dimensions of the *LdoD Archive* place in evidence. The construction of the book—as the product either of an unfulfilled self-editing authorial act or of a series of third-person editorial acts—becomes an instantiation of the conceptual and material process of identity and

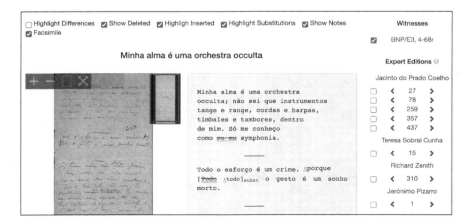

Figure 1. Screen capture of the Editions interface displaying a digital facsimile image, a topographic genetic transcription, and four macrovariations.

Minha alma é uma orquestra oculta

Minha alma é uma orquestra oculta; não sei que instrumentos tangem e rangem, cordas e harpas, timbales e tambores, dentro de mim. Só me conheço como sinfonia. ――――――― Todo o esforço é um crime porque todo o gesto é um sonho morto. ――――――― As tuas mãos são rolas presas. Os teus lábios são rolas mudas (que aos meus olhos vêem arrulhar). Todos os teus gestos são aves. És andorinha no abaixares-te, condor no olhares-me, águia nos teus êxtases de orgulhosa indiferente. É toda ranger de asas, como dos □, a lagoa de eu te ver. Tu és toda alada, toda □ ――――――― Chove, chove, chove... Chove constantemente, gemedoramente, □ Meu corpo treme-me a alma de frio... Não um frio que há no espaço, mas um frio que há em ver a chuva... Todo o prazer é um vício, porque buscar o prazer é o que todos fazem na vida, e o único vício negro é fazer o que toda a gente faz.

Minha alma é uma orchestra occulta

Minha alma é uma orchestra occulta; não sei que instrumentos tangem e rangem, cordas e harpas, timbales e tambores, dentro de mim. Só me conheço como symphonia. ――――――― Todo o esforço é um crime, porque todo o gesto é um sonho morto. ――――――― As tuas mãos são pombas presas. Os teus labios são rolas mudas. (que os meus olhos vêem arrulhar). Todos os teus gestos são aves. És andorinha no abaixares-te, condôr no olhares-me, aguia nos teus extases de orgulhosa indifferente. É toda ranger de azas, como dos □, a lagoa de eu te vêr. Tu és toda alada, toda □ ――――――― Chove, chove, chove... Chove constantemente, gemedoramente, □ Meu corpo treme-me a alma de frio... Não um frio que ha no espaço, mas um frio que ha em eu ser o espaço... ――――――― Todo o prazer é um /vicio/, porque buscar o prazer é o que todos fazem na vida, e o unico vicio negro é fazer o que toda a gente faz.

Figure 2. Screen capture of the Editions interface displaying the comparison of the textual transcription in Zenith and Pizarro for witness BNP/E3, 4–68r.

difference that enables text and book to emerge from a series of inscriptional marks and metamarks and from the acts of reading and interpreting those marks and metamarks.

As mentioned above, representation of the dynamics of variation in the *LdoD Archive* involves the consideration of two distinct levels. One is the level of microvariations—that is, variations that are internal to the fragments, such as authorial revisions, editorial readings of particular passages, or orthographic variants that resulted from reforms in spelling conventions.[7] The other is the level of macrovariations, or variations that are external to the fragments, such as the inclusion and sequencing of fragments as well as heteronym attribution. In other words, the first type of variations results in a given textual form for each fragment or piece of writing, while the second type results in a given book structure for the entire corpus. How are these micro- and macrovariations represented in the *LdoD Archive*? How are authorial revisions and editorial variants marked and visualized in ways that enable readers to understand the writing and editorial processes at the scale of both textual form and book structure?

Transcriptions of the authorial and editorial textual forms are treated as variants for encoding purposes (fig. 3). The <rdg> TEI element stands for reading and is used to represent both authorial and editorial microvariations (within the TEI body) and macrovariations (within the TEI header). The editions and authorial sources are referred through the "wit" attribute. Additionally, a structured

```
▼<app>
  ▼<rdg wit="#Fr279.WIT.MS.Fr279a.338 #Fr279.WIT.ED.CRIT.C1 #Fr279.WIT.ED.CRIT.Z
    Minha alma é uma
    ▼<app type="orthographic">
       <rdg wit="#Fr279.WIT.MS.Fr279a.338 #Fr279.WIT.ED.CRIT.P #Fr279.WIT.ED.CRIT
       <rdg wit="#Fr279.WIT.ED.CRIT.SC #Fr279.WIT.ED.CRIT.Z">orquestra</rdg>
    </app>
    <lb ed="#Fr279.WIT.MS.Fr279a.338"/>
    ▼<app type="orthographic">
       <rdg wit="#Fr279.WIT.MS.Fr279a.338 #Fr279.WIT.ED.CRIT.P #Fr279.WIT.ED.CRIT
       <rdg wit="#Fr279.WIT.ED.CRIT.SC #Fr279.WIT.ED.CRIT.Z">oculta;</rdg>
    </app>
    não sei que instrumentos
    <lb ed="#Fr279.WIT.MS.Fr279a.338"/>
    ▼<app type="substantive">
       <rdg wit="#Fr279.WIT.MS.Fr279a.338 #Fr279.WIT.ED.CRIT.C1">tange e range,</
       <rdg wit="#Fr279.WIT.ED.CRIT.Z #Fr279.WIT.ED.CRIT.P #Fr279.WIT.ED.CRIT.SC"
    </app>
    cordas e harpas,
    <lb ed="#Fr279.WIT.MS.Fr279a.338"/>
    timbales e tambores, dentro
```

Figure 3. Excerpt from the XML-TEI encoding of the fragment "Minha alma é uma orchestra occulta" (BNP/E3, 4–68r). All sites of variation across the witnesses and across the editions have been marked up.

hierarchical nomenclature is used to identify witnesses, for instance, the value #Fr279.WIT.MS.Fr279a.338 denotes an authorial source (MS) witness (WIT) identified by "Fr279a.338" of fragment 279 (Fr279), where 279 is an arbitrary number that identifies a particular XML file within the *LdoD Archive* system. This same identifier is used for referring the textual transcriptions in the four expert editions (#Fr279.WIT.ED.CRIT.C, #Fr279.WIT.ED.CRIT.Z, #Fr279 .WIT.ED.CRIT.SC, and #Fr279.WIT.ED.CRIT.P). Thus, in this instance, the same abstract entity (Fr279) can have five textual expressions, one of which is a topographic transcription of the autograph witness, while the other four are transcriptions of the editorial transcriptions of the autograph witness.[8] Transcriptions of authorial sources and of editorial sources become part of a constellation of microvariations.

We may say that the representation of the genetic dimension takes place in the context of the work's socialized dimension, while the work's editorial forms can be perceived in the context of its genetic history. Revision processes in the autograph materials as well as variants and variations in editorial readings are encoded in the same XML file in a way that allows for both a single view of each autograph or editorial witness and comparative views of multiple witnesses (see figs. 1 and 2, above). At the level of the header, each TEI file contains the metatextual information required for comparing bibliographical features, such as "L. do D." markers in Pessoa's papers, the numerical sequence of fragments in each edition, the date of composition, or other metatextual attributes.

In the *LdoD Archive*, visualization of variations takes place at the general level of the graphical user interface and within textual transcriptions. The user is allowed to move within each (authorial or editorial) textual witness and across different textual witnesses. This navigational strategy allows readers to see revision sites within authorial witnesses and to generate comparisons between any two, three, four, five, six, or seven witnesses—that is, up to three authorial witnesses and up to four editorial witnesses.[9] Authorial witnesses can be compared against one another but also against their editorial versions, and vice versa: editorial witnesses can be compared against each other but also against their source documents. Our topographic transcription represents four types of spatial marks in the autographs: line breaks (using the <lb> element), spacing between paragraphs (using the <space> element), dividing rulers (using the <pb> element), and revision sites (using the @place attribute on <add>). The main goal of the topographic transcription is to facilitate the side-by-side reading of the facsimile and its transcription.

This ability to examine the microvariations in the textual form of each fragment across the database of witnesses is further contextualized, at the level of macrovariations, by the possibility of navigating within the bibliographical sequence offered by each scholarly edition. Buttons for showing revision sites (deletions, additions, and substitutions) and buttons for comparing transcriptions against the digital facsimiles of authorial witnesses allow users to move across all layers of variation from within a single screen. The right-hand menu provides immediate visualization of the relative position of each fragment within any given expert edition of the *Book*, while the footer provides other metatextual information (concerning a heteronym attribution or "L. do D." mark, for instance). One-to-one or one-to-many comparisons between the *LdoD Archive*'s own transcription and the four editions are also supported. This principle also applies to each and all expert editions.

Microvariations across textual transcriptions and macrovariations across bibliographical structures in the work's genetic and editorial archive are displayed through a network of shifting perspectives. This network allows users of the *LdoD Archive* to see Pessoa's writing process and his changing and variable plans for the *Livro*. At the same time, readers become aware of the conjectural nature of the editorial solutions of the expert critical editions for producing a structured textual and bibliographical form out of a half-finished and fragmentary work. Further micro- and macrovariations will result from the archive's socialization of editorial and authorial acts of production at the virtual level, opening up the work's existing archive to future appropriations and transformations.

From Meta-Edition to Virtual Edition

Expert editions—accessible through the Editions interface—correspond to historically existing forms of the book, each of which transcribes, selects, and orders texts according to a set of criteria that aim to produce a book as an instantiation of the "work." Virtual editions—created by users through the Virtual interface—will be other possible (temporary or persistent) ways of producing the *Book* (or simply a particular collection of texts) in the context of the collaborative and dynamic functionalities offered by the *LdoD Archive*. Each expert version of the *Book* is the historical embodiment of a particular idea about the work, while each virtual editing of the *Book* is a way of experiencing the process of moving from text to book to work. The fact that most virtual editions by nonexperts will only engage with a small sample of the fragments is in itself a reiteration of the *LdoD Archive*'s procedural and unfinished dimension. The process of editing rather than the edited object has become the center of the system.

Besides using TEI XML encoding and programming to re-create the history of the editorial dynamics, the *LdoD Archive* also explores the simulative potential of the digital medium as a space for virtualizing the *Book* in ways that enable users to experiment with the processes of editing in relation to this work. Experts and nonexperts collaborate by making and annotating their own editions. Editorial interventions can take two forms: selecting and ordering fragments as part of a user-defined virtual edition and annotating selected fragments through tags and glosses, including the development of taxonomies. Each of these types of intervention can also make use of computer-generated editing, since the selection, ordering, and annotation can be algorithmically performed. These machine-generated editions and taxonomies can be worked upon by a human editor in a collaborative process. Collaboration in the *LdoD Archive* thus describes both the machine-assisted processes and the social collaboration by various users. This interactive feature of the archive is further enhanced by search and navigation functions that allow a strong integration between the closed set of scholarly materials and the open virtual editing additions.

"Mallet," for instance, is a virtual edition based on the corpus of the Pizarro edition, whose taxonomy has been algorithmically generated (ldod.uc.pt/edition/acronym/LdoD-Mallet). The topic generation software Mallet was used for generating thirty categories after performing 1,500 iterations on the corpus. Each category was named with the three most relevant words of the generated topic, resulting in topics such "nevoa leve frio" ("mist light cold"), "noite dia luz" ("night day light"), "sonho cousas sonhos" ("dream things dreams"), or "vida ser alma" ("life being soul"). Fragments were associated to their category if the percentage was higher than eleven percent. Given that Pizarro's edition has sequenced the texts according to their dates of composition, the way the categories are attached to particular texts provides a glimpse into the persistence or emergence of topics over time. Those generated topics could become the basis of another virtual edition, in which the topic modeling of the fragments might be used for defining theme-based clusters or sequences. They could also be used as the source for defining a more complex and refined taxonomy. Both operations—sequencing texts or recategorizing texts according to automated analyses—are examples of the range of interactions provided by the platform, from the machine-assisted human edition to the human-assisted machine edition.

A different example is provided by the "Jacinto Prado Coelho—Annotated Edition" (ldod.uc.pt/edition/acronym/LdoD-JPC-anot). The production of this edition was also used as a test of the virtual editing tools of the platform, including both the strictly textual—selecting, adding, deleting, rearranging, tagging, glossing—as well as the collaborative and administrative tools (figs. 4 and 5). This virtual edition uses the same selection and ordering of texts as the printed Coelho edition of 1982, to which a taxonomy was added based on the two indexes of the original edition: "Ideographic Index" (Pessoa, *Desassossego* [Ática], 2: 275–77) and "Index of Cited Authors" (2: 279–80). It was developed by nine virtual editors, under the coordination of Rita Catania Marrone, in May 2017. The taxonomic associations resulting from the original indexing provide us with a global visualization of the thematic rationale of that first critical edition, which grouped most of the texts from the book according to fifty-six constellations of topics and subtopics.

Additional examples of virtual editing include theme-based anthologies of selected texts, such as the "Daydreaming Machine" virtual edition (ldod.uc.pt/edition/acronym/LdoD-Medial), which is presented as follows:

> This edition contains selected texts from the *Book of Disquiet*. All texts include references to different types of media technologies (typewriter, printing, lithography, gramophone, photography, film, radio) either in relation to the practice of writing or in relation to sensation and perception. For example: "Those who can write are those who know how to see their dreams with sharp clarity (and do so) and to see life as they see dreams, to see life immaterially, taking pictures of it with reverie's camera, which is insensible to the rays of what's heavy, useful and circumscribed, such things yielding nothing but a black blur on the photographic plate of the soul" (BNP/E3, 7-35-36, translation by Richard Zenith). "I'm an ultrasensitive photographic plate. All details are engraved in me out of all proportion to any possible whole. The plate fills up with nothing but me. The outer world that I see is pure sensation. I never forget that I feel" (BNP/E3, 9-49, translation by Richard Zenith). "And it is then, in the middle of life's bustle, that my dream becomes a marvellous film" (BNP/E3, 2-79r, translation by Richard Zenith). "On rainy days his talking never became mournful, and he would cry out—sure of his shelter—a constant sentiment that hovered in the sadness like a phonograph before its time" (BNP/E3, 2-89 3-2, translation by Richard Zenith).

The participatory affordance of the digital medium has two major aspects: an environment for collaboration and social interaction, on the one hand, and the possibility of marking material changes at the level of code, on the other. Material changes can be marked up in the XML encoding or as new data and metadata generated by users' interaction with the archive, which are stored in the database. These features of networked computational media have been used to redesign the digital archive as a dynamic environment for editorial experimentation. A scholarly remediation of *LdoD* according to tested principles of electronic philology becomes part of a larger interactive environment where editing

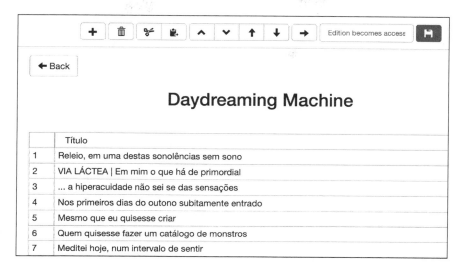

Figure 4. Screen capture from the "Daydreaming Machine" virtual edition displaying a row of textual editing tools for searching, selecting, adding, deleting, cutting, pasting, saving, and moving texts.

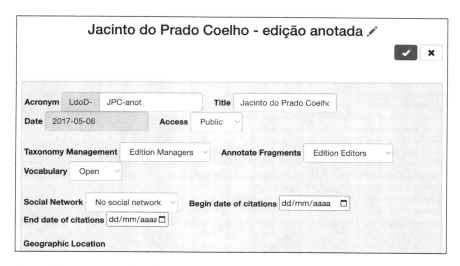

Figure 5. Screen capture from the "Jacinto do Prado Coelho—Annotated" virtual edition displaying administrative tools used to define an edition's properties, add editors to an edition, and grant them editorial or administrative permissions.

practices around *The Book of Disquiet* are socialized within the digital medium itself. Aggregation of genetic and editorial witnesses according to criteria defined by readers occurs within a virtual space that allows users to make their own critical annotations. Representation of textual form and textual transmission is complemented by simulatory experiments with editing processes and bibliographic structures.

Exploding the Book: Editing as Process

Critical editing approaches to *The Book of Disquiet* have attempted to capture or, more accurately, to reconstruct the unity of authorial intention on the basis of textual and documentary evidence. Their unstated aim is to turn the projective and conjectural unity of the edition into a continuation of the authorial project, as inferred from the "L. do D." texts and from the work's metatexts—that is, Pessoa's notes and plans for the *Book*. Acknowledging the changing nature of authorial intentionality at different moments, and the open-endedness necessarily resulting from the work's unrevised and unstructured incompleteness, the editions have to make their own intentionality stand in as a surrogate for an elusive final textual form. The problem of organizing the *Book* thus becomes a problem of dealing with the unruly and undisciplined material manifestations of acts of writing for a work in progress whose major feature is the fragment, whether as a finished, self-contained unit or as an unfinished and unrevised draft.

By definition, editing *The Book of Disquiet* is an obsessive process of suturing textual pieces in ways that minimize their constitutive fragmentariness, even if many texts and documents in the corpus are bound to resist any seamless integration. Acts of editorial surgery cannot but fail to efface themselves, since text, book, and work (and, to a certain extent, some of the documents themselves) have always to be postproduced.[10] The purpose of the meta-editing and virtual editing perspective in the *LdoD Archive* is to redirect our focus to the seams and sutures in order to see how each edition is sewing its own version of the book into some coherent form. Thus, an opposite heuristic to the integrative mode of print editions becomes imaginable: the text can be explored even more radically so that all textual pieces are nothing more than a constellation of fragments.

Literary materiality can be remade according to the modularity of digital materiality. Texts can be factorialized in their permutations. Not only loose sheets collected in envelopes or strung together in the autograph archive can be subject to further disintegration; the posthumous print editions themselves can also be torn apart and critically fragmented. Once autographs and expert editions have been explored in this way, then the processuality through which an editorial act begins to take shape can perhaps be simulated and enacted. Each transcription and each book emerges within a series of possible instantiations of their form through the process whereby the act of editing performs itself as a choreography of readings and interpretations that inscribe themselves in the work's archive and in its socialized forms.

So, what is a fragment in the *LdoD Archive*? A fragment is a modular textual sequence, and it constitutes the basic unit of composition of the *LdoD Archive*. Most textual sequences of the *Book* are also independent material units, since they are written in single loose sheets (or small groups of loose sheets) without a defined relative ordering. The fragments encoded in the *LdoD Archive* correspond to the sum of all texts that were considered as belonging to or associated with the *Book* in the four critical editions, including those texts that are published as an appendix or annex to the main text. All fragments of the *LdoD Archive* are also textual units of the *Book* according to at least one of the editions. As they metamorphose into digital objects, textual units meant for the *Book* turn into computational fragments whose modularity also reflects their new medium.

The structure of the *LdoD Archive* places all the fragments at the same relative distance from one another—that is, with the same modularity index. However, in the editions, not all textual units have the same degree of relative independence, since there are groups of texts that are closer to each other, either because they are part of a larger textual unit or because of thematic or chronological proximity. Thus the textual units of the editions have different indexes of modularity, as there are groups of texts that are closer to one another. This is the main difference between a text as a unit within a given edition (or in the authorial archive) and a fragment as a unit within the *LdoD Archive*.

The modular organization of the fragments (i.e., their placement at the same relative distance from each other) in the *LdoD Archive* is a precondition for the comparison and virtualization of the editions to be processed in the open way envisioned by our model. This stressing of the modular fragmentariness of the *Book* in the *LdoD Archive* is a critical tool for opening up this work's potential for reading, editing, and writing to new interventions. The critical distortion introduced by our data model—which is the major support of the dynamic features of the *LdoD Archive*—gives technical expression to a digital rematerialization of documents, texts, and work beyond bibliographic models. The *Book* is not an entirely freely remixable assemblage of loose fragments, but the radial and heterarchical configuration of its units in the *LdoD Archive* allows us to simulate authorial projectuality and editorial projectuality as processes for imagining the work as book and the document as text. By using the modularity of the digital medium as a critical probe into the modularity of the *Book*, the *LdoD Archive* becomes a computer-assisted simulation of the processual nature of editing.

NOTES

1. For a review of the *LdoD Archive* as a new kind of digital critical edition, see Barbosa and Pittella.

2. For a detailed editorial history of all the works by Fernando Pessoa, see Pizarro, *Mediación editorial* 29–90.

3. These editions may be found, respectively, at ldod.uc.pt/edition/acronym/JPC, ldod.uc.pt/edition/acronym/TSC, ldod.uc.pt/edition/acronym/RZ, and ldod.uc.pt/edition/acronym/JP.

4. In 2015, Teresa Rita Lopes edited a new version of the work, titled *Livro(s) do desassossego*, in which she adds thirty-five texts by Barão de Teive (another heteronym by Pessoa) to the corpus of texts attributed to Vicente Guedes and Bernardo Soares. Although most scholars will disagree with the addition of the textual corpus by Barão de Teive, this edition is yet another demonstration of the continuous nature of the authorial and editorial forms of the work, reinforcing, to a certain extent, the theoretical justification for the virtual editing dynamic functionalities in the *LdoD Archive*.

5. The letter is transcribed at ldod.uc.pt/fragments/fragment/Fr722/inter/Fr722_WIT _ED_CRIT_C.

6. For an analysis of the editions focused on the return to the archive as fostered by digital media, see Silvestre. Pessoa's incomplete and changing editorial plans for the *Livro* have been closely examined by Sepúlveda.

7. A reformed orthography was introduced in Portugal during Pessoa's lifetime (1911), but Pessoa continued to write according to the earlier spelling conventions. In their editions of the *Livro*, Coelho and Pizarro follow Pessoa's orthography, while Cunha and Zenith have modernized Pessoa's spelling according to contemporary Portuguese orthography, which was used by convention until 2012. The adoption of a new reformed orthography in that year means that further spelling variations are being added to the latest editions of the *Livro*. In the *LdoD Archive*, all spelling variations in both authorial sources and editorial transcriptions have been marked up.

8. For a detailed discussion of the *LdoD Archive*'s encoding template, see Rito Silva and Portela. This article explains how the software architecture supports the traditional process of TEI encoding with the added function of dynamically extending the versions of *The Book of Disquiet* on top of a TEI representation.

9. For most fragments there is only one extant witness for the autograph text, either a manuscript or a typescript. However, there are a few instances in which there are two or three autograph versions (such as a manuscript, typescript, and published version or two typescript versions).

10. Although there is a core of about five hundred texts that all editors agree belong to the *Book*, a significant number of texts either are not included in the corpus of a specific edition or are included only in the appendix. There is also a small group of texts whose internal structure or whose unity is difficult to determine.

Editing Pessoa's "Radical Scatters"

John Pedro Schwartz and Jerónimo Pizarro

In 1988, Luiz Fagundes Duarte called for the evolution of the "crítico textual" ("textual critic") into a "crítico textual genético" ("genetic textual critic"), who would assemble, organize, and study all the papers containing a given text with the aim of laying bare the author's process of composition. Genetic criticism, he wrote, should present "uma especie de cometa com a sua cauda" ("a kind of comet with its tail"). The head of the comet would consist of the fixed text, whether finished—that is, published and in circulation—or "virtual"—that is, a text "que *poderia ter vindo a sê-lo*" ("that *could have come to be such*"; 170).[1] The tail of the comet would then be the genetic apparatus.

Duarte's rationale ushered in a shift in Fernando Pessoa studies from literary criticism aimed at interpreting a fixed text to genetic criticism bent on studying a text in relation to all the material that the author added, transformed, or rejected in the course of composing it. This development bore fruit in Portugal with a project to publish critical editions of Pessoa's works, a project sponsored by the Imprensa Nacional–Casa da Moeda and led by a group of editors, including Duarte, known as the "Equipa Pessoa." Two works in 1990 inaugurated the project: *Poemas de Álvaro de Campos*, edited by Cleonice Berardinelli, and *Editar Pessoa*, an introductory collection of essays by the coordinator of the team, Ivo Castro. The trade in critical editions has continued with the Colecção Pessoa (Pessoa Collection) created by the Lisbon publisher Tinta-da-china in 2013. In short, Duarte's call succeeded in shifting critical attention from the head to the tail of Pessoa's comet.

Pessoa's archive at the National Library of Portugal contains a wealth of both genetic material and virtual texts. Naturally, such wealth drives the ongoing trend toward genetic criticism in Pessoan studies. Over the past two decades that trend has converged with the increasing sophistication of electronic editing tools, resulting in the launch of seven digital platforms dedicated to Pessoa's works and the manuscripts at their base. Yet this "Transformação Digital" ("Digital Transformation") of Pessoa's archive, like the broader wave of genetic criticism that envelops it, has focused almost exclusively on fixed texts (Aldabalde and Pittella 103). Expanding the focus is necessary because the archive also boasts a trove of fragmentary texts that bear no direct connection to those texts that have dominated scholarly attention. The trove consists of no fewer than fourteen folders—133 to 133N—filled with more than a thousand documents. Pessoa scholars, even those of genetic stock, have long neglected these fragments, regarding them as islands of a vast textual continent. To fill this gap, we propose extending Duarte's appeal for archival study—hitherto limited to genetic material and virtual texts—to embrace those documents that bear Pessoa's "radical scatters." Such is the term that Marta L. Werner uses to refer to the fragmentary texts—materially discrete and inherently autonomous—composed by Emily Dickinson in the final decades of her life. The study of Pessoa's isolated fragments forms a logical extension of the critical refocusing from the head (the fixed text) to the tail (the genetic material) of Pessoa's archive.

We begin our study by considering two examples of manuscript study centered on the archives of Jorge Luis Borges and Herman Melville, the first involving print books and the second an electronic archive. Looking at these examples helps us imagine possible approaches to editing Pessoa's fragmentary texts. Next, we examine Werner's fascinating work with Dickinson's late manuscripts—work that has been issued in both an electronic archive and a print edition, each containing dozens of facsimiles, transcriptions, and annotations. Werner's scholarship demonstrates the kinds of critical-genetic methods that scholars can use to study Pessoa's overlooked manuscripts—dating, describing, transcribing, classifying, and interpreting. We then consider some of Pessoa's fragments, reproducing and transcribing them, interpreting them in relation to other texts, and exploring the potential links among writing, materials, and media. Finally, we suggest a model for teaching students how to study Pessoa's radical scatters in the context of a single-author course. In short, this essay makes the case for both the analysis and the presentation of Pessoa's fragmentary texts. A critical and editorial enterprise, it amounts at the same time to a pedagogy, for it can and should be carried out by students and scholars alike.

Working with Borges's and Melville's Manuscripts

Two recent examples of manuscript study can be instructive for scholars interested in working with Pessoa's fragmentary texts. The first concerns Borges and consists of four books: *How Borges Wrote*, by Daniel Balderston, and *Poemas y Prosas breves* (*Poems and Short Prose Works*), *Ensayos* (*Essays*), and *Cuentos* (*Stories*), a collection of three volumes of facsimiles of Borges manuscripts with introductions, typographical transcriptions, and commentaries, edited by Balderston and María Celeste Martín. At the end of the first volume, Martín explains that their transcriptions "son más cercanas al documento original de lo que sería una transcripción diplomática normal, y son denominadas 'fac-similes tipográficos' en que el formato y el espaciado (interlinear, entre palabras e incluso entre letras) siguen con exactitud el manuscrito del autor" ("are closer to the original document than a normal diplomatic transcription would be, and they are called 'typographic facsimiles,' in which the format and the spacing [interlinear, between words and even between letters] exactly follow the author's manuscript"; Borges, *Poemas* 133).

Another suggestive example of manuscript study is the *Melville Electronic Library: A Critical Archive* (melville.electroniclibrary.org/index.html). A work in progress, the MEL aims at creating a set of scholarly digital editions of Melville's works, treating each work as a "fluid text," that is, "any written work that exists in multiple versions resulting from authorial, editorial, or adaptive revision"

(Bryant). These editions will collate extant print editions, highlight variants, and display revision narratives explaining each change. Editing tools will also enable MEL editors to provide textual notes and contextual annotations, with links to images and data—including facsimiles of manuscripts and diplomatic transcriptions—in the MEL archive. Readers can draw down passages from the editions and use images and data selected from the archive to generate scholarly and pedagogical projects of their own.

An electronic library boasts several advantages over print versions of facsimiles, transcriptions, and annotations of a writer's manuscripts. The archive gives users direct access to the MEL's entire collection of digital images and texts. Search engine tools offer a classification of the digitized materials that a print book simply cannot duplicate. The MEL's Projects section is conceived as "a workspace in which visitors can draw upon images and texts in our Archive and Editions sections to create new scholarship, pedagogy, and classroom assignments." Finally, the very nature of fluid texts makes them particularly suited to digital editions. In fact, the MEL editors argue, "All written works are fundamentally fluid texts." The problem lies with readers' difficulty in gaining access to the multiple versions of written works—a problem "best addressed through digital editing" (Bryant). In short, the MEL appears to be spearheading the "Digital Transformation" of Melville's archive, in parallel with that of Pessoa's.

Working with Dickinson's Fragmentary Texts

Werner's electronic archive of Dickinson's fragments, launched in 2010, is entitled *Radical Scatters: Emily Dickinson's Late Fragments and Related Texts, 1870–1886* (radicalscatters.unl.edu). The archive consists of eighty-two documents bearing over one hundred fragmentary texts composed by Dickinson in the final decades of her life. It also includes associated texts drawn from the writer's oeuvre. In addition to the primary materials organized for electronic search, the archive features indexes of the documents in the archive arranged by type, libraries of codes and search paths, a library of Dickinson's "hands," bibliographical and critical glosses on the fragments and related texts, and an appendix of the earliest printed sources of Dickinson's fragments. The combination of methods and digital tools "make possible the study of macrogenetic phenomena (i.e., phenomena occurring across the documents in the archive) and the analysis of microgenetic details (i.e., the salient features of individual documents)" (Werner, "Woe").

Werner distinguishes between two main types of fragments. "Autonomous" fragments, properly so called, have no direct links to other poems or letters in Dickinson's oeuvre, at least none that are now retrievable. By contrast, "trace" fragments connect to a larger "constellation" of poems, letters, or drafts among Dickinson's papers. "Again, and again," Werner writes, "as if poems, letters, and fragments communicated telepathically, a line or phrase from a fragment re-appears, often altered, in the body of a poem, a message, or even another fragment."

The special nature of these "trace" fragments lies in their being simultaneously both open and resistant to incorporation into other texts. They are "neither residents nor aliens, neither lost nor found" ("Woe"). The ambivalence of "trace" fragments in effect qualifies Hans-Jost Frey's idea that a fragment is neither a whole nor a part, and as such it remains resistant to closure.

Werner has created thirty-five document constellations that take as their starting points Dickinson's "trace" fragments among the primary texts featured in the archive. The constellations also show the texts to which the fragments are related. To take the briefest example, constellation 3 contains just two documents—a fragment bearing the text "Grasped by / God—" and a transcript of a poem in which the phrase reappears in altered form as "grasped of God" ("Document Constellations"). Such constellations are endlessly centrifugal, and Werner's work represents but a first attempt at charting the relations among documents. As she states, the document constellations may be extended in two different ways. They may be extended to represent the complex relations among all the documents in the constellations. They may also be extended to represent the complex relations between these documents and all the documents that make up Dickinson's oeuvre. The first might be characterized as an expansion of the constellation in terms of density, the second as an expansion in terms of size.

Werner's innovative approach to Dickinson's radical scatters carries four major implications for textual scholars of Pessoa. First, the neglected materials in an archive gain new status through the demonstration of the critical and analytical operations they lend themselves to. Those radical scatters properly considered "autonomous" derive literary value and scholarly interest from their very discontinuity and instantaneity. Those deemed to be "trace" fragments, and so included in a constellation, call for critics to explore their ever-expanding relations both with the other documents in the constellation (density) and with all the other documents in the writer's oeuvre or archive (size). The latter expansion forces a recasting of the archive in cometary terms different from those laid down by Duarte. Duarte conceived of the tail of a comet as consisting exclusively of genetic material. He neglected to consider the relations that "trace" fragments might bear with genetic material and, by extension, with the fixed text. An understanding of these potential relations allows us to embrace these particular fragments, together with genetic material, within the sweep of the comet's tail.

Second, the emphasis shifts from editing fixed texts to constellating fragments and associated texts. In fact, tracing the links between avant-texts, inter-texts, and post-texts, on the one hand, and a larger constellation of poems, letters, and drafts among a writer's papers, on the other, is paradigmatic of all textual criticism, which by its very nature combines editing with interpretation. Since the publication of Jerome McGann's *A Critique of Modern Textual Criticism* in 1983, textual theory has witnessed a shift away from final authorial intentions and the single authoritative text to the concept of historically contingent and equally valid "versions."[2] The editorial work of selecting, dating, ordering, transcribing, annotating, and formatting a text constitutes not a value-free presentation of that text but rather a premise-laden interpretation of it. Aligned with this shift in textual and editorial theory is the abovementioned concept of "fluid texts," distinguished by its sociological view of the "work" as "the energy a culture (represented by writers, editors, adaptors) puts into delivering 'versions' associated with an originating title into the public sphere, over time" (Bryant).

The concept of versions might be extended to include constellations. This form of revision assembles the multiple versions of a line or phrase from a fragment as it reappears, often altered, in the body of some other writing of the author, including that of another fragment. It aims to reveal the author's repurposing of a given line or phrase from a fragmentary text. With the changes in purpose or context come changes in the meaning of the line or phrase. The focus here is synchronic; after all, a group of stars displaying a recognizable pattern constitutes a synchronic formation. At the same time, the constellation of fragments and associated texts lends itself to diachronic study, as a line or phrase may be seen to transform over time or to catalyze the composition of another text. The interpretive challenges involved in assembling, organizing, comparing, and contrasting fragmentary texts make forming constellations a miniaturized and more extreme form of textual editing, one that can prove instructive for textual scholarship at large. Conversely, textual editing itself can be considered a type of constellating practice. After all, the MEL's editing of Melville's fluid texts consists of gathering, ordering, and annotating their authorial, editorial, and adaptive revisions. It consists, that is, of constellating their multiple versions.

Third, the emphasis shifts from only editing fixed texts to also editing constellatory fragments "[n]ever prepared for publication," in Werner's words, "perhaps never even meant to be read by anyone other than the scriptor herself" ("Woe"). Now, it should be noted that in Pessoa's case the distinction between fixed texts and constellatory fragments breaks down. The roughly thirty thousand manuscripts that Pessoa left in two trunks upon his death—both the source material for all his posthumously published texts and the radical scatters alike—were all perhaps "never prepared for publication." They might all be "private writings," or "texts produced for the eyes of their author or another individual person," as defined by João Dionísio, a member of the Equipa Pessoa, in a volume on personal writings and textual scholarship (*Private*). Pessoa's case aside, the object of Werner's study is not conceived as stable and unitary, nor is it regarded, as in recent editorial theory, as a particular text bound by a finite sequence of versions. Rather, analysis centers on the relations between a line or phrase from a fragmentary text and associated texts. It is important to recall that these relations are ever-expanding, both in terms of density and size.

Fourth, the multiplication of these relations to embrace all the documents in a writer's oeuvre, and not just those of a particular constellation, makes it possible to imagine the constellation as extending past the very boundaries of that oeuvre. Indeed, we might even think of one writer's radical scatters in conjunction with those of other writers; that is, we might even think of constellations of archives. To help us do so, it is necessary to briefly examine the notion of a "constellation," a critical concept increasingly popular within literary studies. Mads Thomsen has defined the search for constellations as a mode of analysis that sees patterns in world literature through the shared properties of works often distant in time and space (4). Irene Ramalho-Santos has read Pessoa as part of a constellation of Anglo-American modernist poets, ranging from Whitman to Crane and Rich, who share an imaginary based on the Atlantic world system (*Atlantic Poets*). As far back as 1982, Thomas MacFarland used the concept to challenge Harold Bloom's rivalry-based theory of influence (*Western Canon*). Rather than focus on "strong" poems and their juxtapositions, MacFarland concentrated on the cross-cultural patterns formed by philosophical systems, novels, and journals, as well as by such "astral debris" as "dispersed metaphorical clusters," "emotional solar winds," and "cosmic rays of doctrine."

MacFarland's scrutiny of "the streamings of this variegated astral matter" in his discernment of cross-cultural patterns parallels Duarte's genetic emphasis on the tail of the cometary archive (433). Their shared attention to neglected literary material is analogous to Werner's editorial work with Dickinson's manuscripts, Balderston's with Borges's, and the MEL's with Melville's. To form a constellation of the radical scatters of different writers, then, is to see, in the fragmentary texts of their archives, patterns based on shared properties or relations. To find these patterns one might ask the following questions: How might Dickinson, Pessoa, Borges, and Melville share an aesthetic of the fragment? What similarities might be detected in their compositional processes? Are their fragments equally unpublished or considered equally unpublishable? Might the relations binding the fragments with associated texts in one author's archive be compared with those relations in another author's archive? In other words, do types of associative relations held in common across archives exist? To read Pessoa's fragmentary manuscripts in conjunction with those of other writers might reveal unexpected patterns worthy of critical consideration.

In short, Werner's work with radical scatters challenges the unexamined priority of fixed texts and genetic material over fragmentary texts by redirecting scholarly focus to the latter. Indeed, her work represents a further stage in the evolution of criticism called for by Duarte—from the textual critic to the genetic textual critic and on to the critic of fragmentary texts.

The Performative Aspect of "Posthumography"

Craig Saper has coined the term "posthumography" to designate the neglected genre of posthumously published texts—papers, letters, incomplete monographs, documents, and ephemera. According to Saper, there is always a performative aspect to posthumous publication that views texts as historically discrete entities to be reproduced in facsimile: "When the artist or writer is no longer 'around,' then others will have to 're-perform' the works. That performance now involves storage, retrieval, and reissuing in digital or other forms, all of which attempt to recreate the experience of reading the original text." The shift in editorial theory made it clear that the editorial process must never be regarded as a transparent window onto the text.[3] Saper builds on this insight to argue that, in the age of digital editions, archives, and facsimiles, the editorial process often involves layers of technological intervention that call for exposure and analysis. The critical aim is to prevent these layers from becoming naturalized to the point of invisibility and also to prevent both editors and readers from lapsing into naivete regarding the reproduction of the previously unpublished or unpublishable parts of an archive. Digital editing no more offers a transparent window onto the text than print publishing does.

Indeed, Saper's critique of the performative aspect of "posthumography" inspires questions relevant to the publication of radical scatters, whether online or in print. How does the facsimile differ from the original despite the "performance" copying both the media and the materials? How do different supports (paper vs. computer screen) shape the text differently? What are the respective affordances and limitations of a digital archive and a print book (a question we began answering above)?

Working with Pessoa's Fragmentary Texts

An in-depth exploration of the contents of folders 133 to 133N—classified as "Produções breves" ("Brief Productions")—yields a trove of fragments ranging from schemas, aphorisms, short fictions, and poems to drafts, notes, quotations, and esoteric writings. Figure 1 shows a "trace" fragment in that a keyword—really, a key figure or image—from the fragment reappears, altered, in another text by Pessoa. A transcription of the fragment is as follows:

> Arethusa da alma
> vãe ter a um
> mar qualquer
>
> Arethusa of the soul
> will flow into
> whatever sea

In Greek mythology, Arethusa was a nymph and a daughter of Nereus. Pursued by the river god Alpheus, the Nereid fled from her home in Arcadia through a passage under the sea and emerged as a freshwater fountain on the island of Ortygia in Syracuse, Sicily. It is tempting to read this fragment as an adumbration of Pessoa's literary ideology of sensationism, with its pantheistic call "Sentir tudo de todas as maneiras" ("To feel everything in every way"; *Prosa: Antologia mínima* 103). Just as Arethusa, transformed into a stream, will flow into whatever sea, so Pessoa's soul, depersonalized, will enter into anyone's thoughts and feelings.

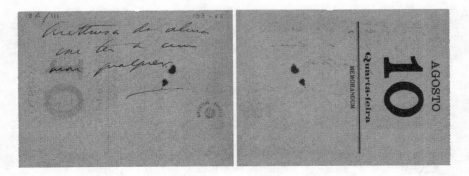

Figure 1. Calendar page. Circa 1910. Biblioteca Nacional de Portugal, Lisbon, BNP/E3, 133–85.

Pairing the fragment with a poem from 1930, entitled "Arethusa," enriches the meaning of both texts. The poem hews closely to the mythological figure and her coursing flight beneath the sea, even likening Arethusa to a sea-born Venus. True to his paganistic belief both in a fixed order of things and in a force anterior to the gods, Pessoa casts Arethusa's onward flow as obedient to the "inclin[ation]" of fate. At the same time, the poem reads like a metaphor for the esoteric tradition of reincarnation. Arethusa's "careful self" or "soul" passes through the "corporal dark of earth" out into the "light" (*Poesia inglesa* 498).

Both the poem's riverine and its subterranean imagery may owe something to Samuel Taylor Coleridge's "Kubla Khan," "Where Alph, the sacred river, ran / Through caverns measureless to man / Down to a sunless sea" (55). The difference is that Alph debouches into a "sunless sea," or "a lifeless ocean," whereas Arethusa, more optimistically, emerges upon "the lone rocks," bared to the "light" and "clasp[ed]" by the sea. In Pessoa's fragment, the contrast between "sunless sea" and "whatever sea" is equally stark. These kindred contrasts gain significance in the context of Pessoa's 1934 essay "O homem de Porlock" ("The Man from Porlock"), in which Pessoa presents his theory of the fragment.[4] In this brief work, Pessoa meditates on the interruption of Coleridge's composition of "Kubla Khan" by the unexpected visit to his home of a man from Porlock. The interruption is famously responsible for the poem's fragmentary character, split into a beginning and an end. Pessoa finds that all artists experience internally an unexpected visit from "the man from Porlock"; all artistic creation suffers an "interrupção fatal . . . d'aquella pessoa externa que cada um de nós tem em si" ("fatal interruption . . . of that external person each one of us carries within"). In consequence, what artists leave behind is but "fragmentos do que não sabemos que seja," "o princípio e o fim de qualquer coisa perdida" ("fragments of something unrecognizable," "the beginning and the end of whatever lost thing"; "Homem" 8). For Pessoa, then, the fragmentary character of "Kubla Khan" is paradigmatic of all poetic creation.

Now, if every poem is a fragment, then every fragment might be considered a potential poem: the status of "Arethusa" as a fragment raises the possibility that "Arethusa of the soul will flow into whatever sea" is a poem. More importantly, the juxtaposition of both Arethusa texts with "Kubla Khan" brings out the contrast between the continuous course of the creative soul, emblematized by the mythical figure, and the interrupted process of all artistic creation, epitomized by Coleridge's poem. Arethusa is able to cover the length of her subterranean journey because she symbolizes the soul, or self, idealized by sensationism. The ideal poet of sensationism can girdle the globe uninterruptedly, absorbing every artistic influence and experiencing every sensation along the way. In her unobstructed flow Arethusa resembles the child, unencumbered by internal visitors, that in his essay Pessoa wishes he as an artist could be. No man from Porlock surprises the Arethusan soul; no fatal interruption besets her coursing flight. In his essay Pessoa argues that every poem is a fragment of what could have been but never came to be—"a mesma expressão da nossa alma" ("the very expression of our soul"; "Homem" 8). In both fragment and poem Arethusa's completed voyage serves as a metaphor for just this total expression of the artist's soul. In effect, the Arethusa texts function as the flip side to "Kubla Khan"—they represent the creative integrity that inevitably lapses into interrupted creation. Paradoxically, Pessoa's fragmentary text on Arethusa speaks of the same closure that as a fragment it resists.

Finally, the poem's imagery of a "second birth," coupled with the line "These captive waves that shall be free" (*Poesia inglesa* 498), recalls Pessoa's prophecy of a resurgent Lusitania that would spread its cultural, spiritual values—in contrast to Britannia's militaristic, material values—around the globe.

Read in the light of the poem, the fragment "Arethusa of the soul will flow into whatever sea" now appears to prefigure both Pessoa's pantheistic sensationism and his call for a Portuguese empire so spiritually influential that it would claim not just the Atlantic, where once its fleet held sway, but indeed "whatever sea." Adding weight to this reading is the fact that in 1910 Pessoa began work on *Portugal*, a series of cantos dealing with national history that would later develop into *Mensagem* (*Message*). In fact, Pessoa wrote fragments from *Portugal* on pages torn from the same calendar that supplied the page on which he composed the Arethusa fragment. As Nicolás Barbosa and colleagues argue, "*Portugal* parece um projecto que, numa primeira fase, ocupou dois meses de 1910: 'Agosto-Setembro'" ("*Portugal* appears to be a project that, in its early phase, occupied two months in 1910: 'August-September'"; 11[7] EN-71[r]). "Isto é, um projecto posterior aos meses de Abril, Maio, Junho e Julho desse ano, que são os meses das pequenas folhas destacadas de um calendário e utilizadas para escrever alguns fragmentos" ("That is to say a project dating to after April, May, June, and July of that year, which are the months of the small pages torn from a calendar and used to write several fragments"; 80). If the Arethusa fragment indeed dates to 1910—especially if it dates to August of that year (the month from which the fragment's page was torn)—then a strong case could be made that in that cryptic line Pessoa was pondering a theme from *Portugal*.

In presenting our next constellation, we build on the pioneering work on radical scatters within Pessoa studies. In 2011, Patricio Ferrari reassessed the role of marginalia in the creation and development of the pre-heteronyms and in Caeiro's literary production ("On the Margins"). In the same year, Jerónimo Pizarro and Ferrari examined the notes that Pessoa made on dust jackets from his book collection in order to determine the relationship between the annotations and the contents. They found that the dust jackets had not merely served as a material support but that the poet had often used the surfaces to record both his reactions to the books and the ideas and writing plans they inspired. At the same time, there exists another possible approach to studying the notes, as the authors indicated but chose not to pursue: "the *marginalia* can be studied as such within the framework of a broader study of the fragment and its role in Pessoa's prose writing" (61). To study the fragment *as* a fragment—that is the ultimate task of the critic of radical scatters.

The constellation takes as its core two fragments of the dust jacket of one of Pessoa's books, as shown in figure 2. The quotation on document 104A-54 ("if to . . . is a fool," with the annotation "p. 203. Greenwood") is taken from one of the two books by G. G. Greenwood owned by Pessoa and now housed in the Casa Fernando Pessoa in Lisbon, both dealing with the "problem" of Shake-

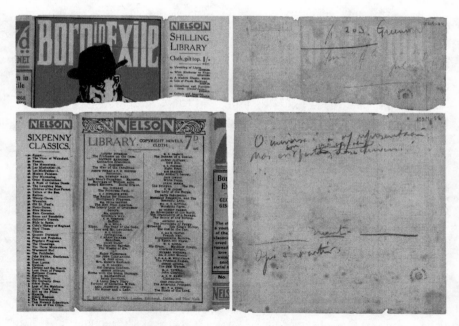

Figure 2. Dust jacket. Gissing, George. *Born in Exile*. Thomas Nelson and Sons, 1910. Biblioteca Nacional de Portugal, Lisbon, BNP/E3, 104A-54 and 133M-88. Casa Fernando Pessoa, Lisbon, CFP 8-220.

speare's authorship.[5] On document 133M-88, Pessoa has written, "O universo é a m[inha] representação / mas eu [↑ sou] parte [↑ do todo, corpo e alma] desse universo" ("The universe is m[y] representation / but I [↑ am] part [↑ of the whole, body and soul] of that universe"), "<u>Eremita</u>," and "Agir é mentir" ("To act is to lie"). "<u>Eremita</u>" is an allusion to Pessoa's short story "O Eremita da Serra Negra," or "O Eremita" ("The Hermit of the Black Mountains," or "The Hermit"). A close analysis of these marginalia would first seek connections between each of them and the contents of Gissing's novel. A second, more promising move would explore possible relations among the Greenwood quotation, the two fragmentary texts, and the story themselves. Indeed, the story and the second fragmentary text share the theme of the futility and falsity of action, in light of the uncertainty of knowledge and the impossibility of belief. Finally, analysis would investigate the links between each of the marginalia and associated texts in Pessoa's oeuvre. For example, both the line "The universe is m[y] representation" and the line "To act is to lie" express ideas that Pessoa revisited throughout his career. Again, Pessoa's interest in the question of Shakespeare's authorship was closely related to the development of his heteronymic system, as Pizarro and Ferrari have demonstrated (63–67). An alternative approach would be to group this document in a constellation—of a material sort—with other dust jackets of books by Gissing found in Pessoa's archive, shown in figures 3 and 4. Written on the back cover of *The Odd Women* is "Shakespeare não dá o vago, da-o como o subtil" ("There is no vagueness in Shakespeare that he does not render as subtlety"; fig. 3). On the dust jacket of an edition of *The Tempest* found in his library, Pessoa wrote, "An air of symbol and allegory drifts over the whole piece, which the atmosphere of magic enveloping it both heightens and hints at."[6] The connections among the Shakespeare-related marginalia in these three dust jackets call for the sort of study that a critic of fragmentary texts would pursue.

"Autonomous" fragments, too, merit consideration. Consider the example in figure 5. The fragment reads, "Ter opiniões é estar vendido a si-mesmo. Não ter opiniões é existir. Ter todas as opiniões é ser poeta" ("To have opinions is to sell out to oneself. Not to have opinions is merely to exist. To have every opinion is to be a poet"). A translation of this text was mistakenly included in the Penguin edition of *Livro do desassossego* (*The Book of Disquiet*). In fact, the fragment was attributed to Álvaro de Campos in another textual witness (cf. Pessoa, *Obra completa de Álvaro de Campos* [2014] 708). Properly regarded as "autonomous," the fragment was at one time considered to form part of a fixed text. These shifts in both attribution and status show how easily an otherwise independent text can lend itself to linkage with other heteronyms or other texts.

Such linkage bears further illustration. The fragment perfectly encapsulates sensationism, with its dual emphasis on depersonalization and cosmopolitanism. Indeed, the lines recall similar ones that Pessoa used to define his literary ideology, such as these from 1915: "Ter opiniões é não sentir. Todas as nossas opiniões são dos outros" ("To have opinions is not to feel. All our opinions come from other people"; *Prosa: Antologia mínima* 51). The same critical concern

Figure 3. Dust jacket. Gissing, George. *The Odd Women*. Thomas Nelson and Sons, 1907. Biblioteca Nacional de Portugal, Lisbon, BNP/E3, 14⁵-96. Casa Fernando Pessoa, Lisbon, CFP 8-221.

appears in these lines from Álvaro de Campos's 1923 leaflet "Aviso por causa da moral" ("Notice Regarding Morality"): "Ser novo é não ser velho. Ser velho é ter opiniões. Ser novo é não querer saber de opiniões para nada" ("To be young is not to be old. To be old is to have opinions. To be young is not to want to know about opinions at all"; *Obra completa de Álvaro de Campos* [2014] 429).[7] In fact, the fragment belongs to this corpus of texts, a corpus that could easily be expanded to include dozens of instances in which Pessoa articulates his views on impersonality and universality, whether in a literary or sociological context. Also linking this fragment to these and other texts are Pessoa's grammatical and stylistic tendencies toward simple copular sentences, negative definition, syllogism, and aphorism. Even independent fragments, then, can be linked,

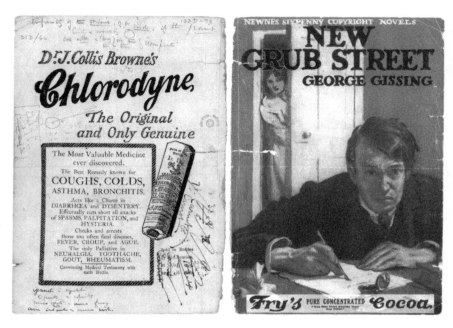

Figure 4. Dust jacket. Gissing, George. *New Grub Street*. George Newnes, 1926. Biblioteca Nacional de Portugal, Lisbon, BNP/E3, 133D-98.

thematically or formally, with other texts in a writer's oeuvre to form a different sort of constellation than the linguistic one envisioned by Werner. In this particular synchronic constellation both the idea and the form of the fragmentary text reappears, recast, in other writings by Pessoa.

Our notion of a constellation of documents arranged on the basis of a shared theme or form extends Werner's concept of a constellation created on the basis of a shared line or phrase. The point is that most "autonomous" fragments lend themselves to association with other texts in a writer's oeuvre. According to Werner, "autonomous" fragments may form the nucleus of a lost or unwritten poem or text or, alternatively, a breakaway line from a poem, a letter, or another composition not yet identified, or a brief but complete pensée, a passage destined for incorporation into another composition, perhaps a letter or a longer meditation—to list just some of the possibilities that Werner names ("Document Constellations"). As our demonstration makes clear, "autonomous" fragments, whatever their status, stand to gain meaning when read in the context of an author's whole oeuvre.

Consider figure 6, an example both of a fragment that hovers somewhere between "trace" and "autonomous" and of a constellation as thematic as it is linguistic. The transcription is "retiro-me ao silencio" ("I withdraw into silence"). "Silencio" is one of Pessoa's favorite words. Indeed, the line links up with a bundle

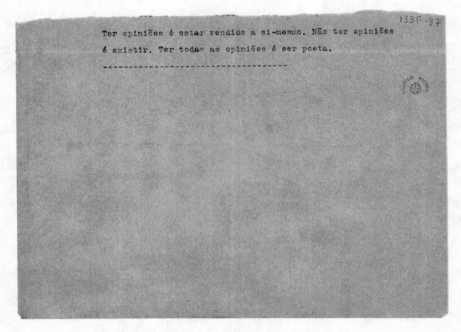

Figure 5. Fragment. Circa 12 Nov. 1930. Biblioteca Nacional de Portugal, Lisbon, BNP/E3, 133F-87^r.

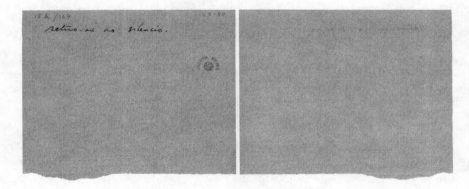

Figure 6. Fragment. Circa 1914. Biblioteca Nacional de Portugal, Lisbon, BNP/E3, 133-88.

of recurring themes in Pessoa's oeuvre—the disbelief in the value of action, the retreat from human society, the shrinking from physical contact with things, and the abstraction of dreamscapes. Ultimately, these themes reflect Pessoa's poetic embrace of the "abyss," his metaphor for the groundlessness of being, knowing, and personal identity. The consequent misfit between a given philosophical vocabulary and the reality of the self and the world that it purports to express or represent leads the poet precisely to "withdraw into silence."[8] Pessoa's drama *Fausto*, his poem "Abdicação" ("Abdication"), Álvaro de Campos's poem "Vem, Noite antiquíssima e idêntica" ("Come, Night, most ancient and unchanging One"), and the decadent passages in *The Book of Disquiet* come readily to mind in connection with this brief text.[9] One passage in particular is text 71, in which the author of *The Book of Disquiet* describes the country refuge of his mind as a "retiro verde" ("verdant retreat"; *Desassossego* [Tinta] 125), noted for its "academia vegetal dos silêncios" ("vegetal academy of silences").

Linking the Textual with the Material

The materiality of the documents bearing Pessoa's radical scatters forms an additional point of interest, one that lends itself to a different sort of editing project than the online archive. Here again, Werner leads the way in finding critical value in manuscripts long considered a minor aspect of a writer's oeuvre. Her electronic edition of Dickinson's late fragments, *Radical Scatters*, has its counterpart in her print edition of Dickinson's late writings, *The Gorgeous Nothings: Emily Dickinson's Envelope Poems*. The book presents fifty-two late "envelope fragments"—most of them stanzas or sentences that often emerge as the beginnings or endings of poems or, alternatively, find their place in letters Dickinson wrote between 1864 and 1885—collected by Werner. Chronologically ordered, facsimiles of the envelope fragments are reproduced in actual size and full color, front and back. They are juxtaposed with drawings by the book's coeditor, Jen Bervin, that outline the shape of the envelopes, into which are inserted transcriptions of the Dickinson texts inscribed on the envelopes.

Gorgeous Nothings assumes a close connection between the materiality of the envelope and the text inscribed thereon. So tight is the linkage that one critic has referred to the envelope poems as "thing-poems" (Arsić). In her preface to the book, Susan Howe considers them a cross between poetry and visual art. Bervin writes, "When Dickinson approached her composition space to write, she was reading and responding to her materials." Accordingly, "[t]o represent a Dickinson poem accurately in print," it is necessary, she declares, quoting Jerome McGann, "'to accommodate our typographic conventions to her work'" (11).

Note Bervin's emphasis on the editors' accommodation of the media and materials to those of Dickinson. By contrast, a Saper-influenced approach would highlight the ways that the typographic conventions inevitably fall short of accommodating the original work. Certainly, the fact that *Gorgeous Nothings* focuses on the materiality of Dickinson's envelope poems influenced the editors' decision to publish them in print rather than online, as Werner did with the poet's radical scatters. The insertion of the transcriptions into drawings in the shape of the envelopes points to a desire to lend the aura of the original to what is clearly Werner's intervention. Naive though the "performance" may be, *Gorgeous Nothings* surely illustrates some of the affordances of a print edition over an electronic one.

Werner's work raises a host of questions for scholars of Pessoa's fragmentary texts. Might it be possible to establish a similarly close connection between the message and the medium? Note that these media include hotel stationery, office stationery, calendars, and scraps of paper as well as envelopes. What is the relationship here between textuality and materiality? Is there a link between what Pessoa writes with and on, and what and how he writes? Might some of Pessoa's manuscripts constitute experiments with visual form? Pessoa often mixes both writing materials and fragments within the same document. He also frequently draws boxes or line segments to divide the compositional space. Do these writing habits follow a logic worth exploring? How significant are the line breaks in the fragmentary texts cited above? For example, is "Arethusa da alma / vãe ter a um / mar qualquer" a line of prose or a pair of hexasyllables (the second one split into two)? How might the internal divisions of the writing surfaces shape Pessoa's expression? Is Pessoa responding to the material, or does the material simply offer a neutral space in which to write?

Teaching Pessoa's Fragmentary Texts

In addition to both an electronic and a print edition, Pessoa's radical scatters call for classroom study, especially as a module within a broader course devoted to the author. In this scenario, students could prepare to examine Pessoa's fragments by reading, earlier in the course, a variety of Pessoa's works—whether written in English, Portuguese, or French—with the aim of achieving familiarity with his major themes. The module proper could begin by steeping students in textual and editorial theory, the theory of constellations (as against the theory of influence), the theory of "posthumography," and the theory of radical scatters. Students could also read the three textual and critical introductions that Werner provides on her website: "'Most Arrows': Autonomy and Intertextuality in Emily Dickinson's Late Fragments," "'A Woe of Ecstasy': On the Electronic Editing of Emily Dickinson's Late Fragments," and "Dickinson's Late Hand." Students could carefully examine Werner's constellations, noting how the reappearance of a phrase in altered form gives the different documents a textual coherence.

Students could then be introduced to a selection of Pessoa's fragments in facsimile, made digitally available by the professor. Students could be initiated into the mysteries of both transcription and the physical description of writing media and materials. Students could be asked to interpret the fragments, as far as possible, in the context of their readings of Pessoa's works, as in our demonstrations above. In effect, students could form constellations of fragments and related texts in the author's oeuvre on the basis of formal or thematic similarity—or even of material similarity, as in the example of the Gissing dust jackets above. Ideally, students could also create linguistic constellations of the kind envisioned by Werner, associating "trace" fragments with other writings by Pessoa as they appear there in altered form. Finally, students could be asked to ponder the links between what and how Pessoa wrote, on the one hand, and the media and materials he used, on the other. To prepare them to consider these links, instructors could assign selected readings from Werner's *Gorgeous Nothings*.

One important lesson that students could learn is that many seemingly isolated fragments, when read in the context of the author's oeuvre, lend themselves to connection with other texts. The more students know about Pessoa—the module should be the final one of the course—the more they will be able to associate a given fragment with other writings by the author. Context shapes the meaning of a text; it follows that a writer's oeuvre molds the meaning of a fragment. Werner divides fragments into two kinds—"autonomous" and "trace." Yet it would be more accurate to state that fragments fall along a spectrum from the "autonomous" through the "resonant" to the "trace." Indeed, the majority of Pessoa's fragments lie within the "resonant" middle range.

Duarte argued that "[o]s materias recusados são quase tao importantes como os que permaneceram: a solidez dos últimos (que são o efeito) assenta na virtualidade dos primeiros (que funcionam como causas), e estes não deixam de estar presentes naqueles" ("the rejected materials are almost as important as those that were retained: the solidity of the latter [the effect] is based on the virtuality of the former [the cause], and the former continue to be present in the latter"; 170). A similar relation to that between rejected and retained materials obtains between fragments—especially, "resonant" ones—and fixed texts. As Werner argues, fragments are "symptoms of the processes of composition, data—aleatory, contingent—of the work of writing" ("Woe"). To rephrase Duarte, the product of composition depends on the process, and the process continues to be present in the product. The study of radical scatters, then, is ultimately inseparable from—is continuous with—the study of fixed texts. Such is the final, important lesson that students could learn in a module devoted to Pessoa's fragmentary texts.

Pessoa's thousand-plus fragmentary texts, contained in folders 133 to 133N, clamor for assembly, organization, reproduction, transcription, and annotation, whether in the form of an electronic archive like *Radical Scatters* or the MEL or of a print edition like that of Dickinson's envelope poems or the volumes on Borges's manuscripts. They call equally for pedagogical application. The classroom study of Pessoa's radical scatters would not first require their scholarly publication but only their digital facsimile and circulation. Students could lead the way in constellating and commenting on Pessoa's fragmentary texts. Indeed, a classroom project might even take the form of collaborating with professionals on the creation of a digital archive or a digital edition.[10] The MEL enables visitors to assemble and sort materials and generate projects that will be added to the MEL platform, so student-led electronic editing projects can easily be envisioned.

Many "trace" fragments have been salvaged by genetic critics and included in the Critical Edition of the Works of Fernando Pessoa. Werner's editorial commentary on each of her constellations has its rough counterpart in the genetic rationales that these critics include at the back of their editions. Yet Pessoa's fourteen folders' worth of radical scatters have never seen publication on their own—have never been accorded their editorial due. The fragments merit such treatment because of their many-sided critical value—as constellatory fragments both "trace" and "resonant," as documents of the materiality of composition, and as "symptoms of the processes of composition." With the increasing sophistication of electronic editing tools, both the reproduction and the online and print publication of Pessoa's fragments are now possible. An electronic archive would contribute to the "Digital Transformation" of Pessoa's archive, while both it and a print publication would continue the scholarly work begun on the handwritten notes on Pessoa's dust jackets. With the completion of the Critical Edition a decade ago, now is the time to shift attention to the tail of Pessoa's cometary oeuvre.

NOTES

1. All translations in this essay are ours.

2. See Bornstein (1–16) for an excellent summary of these developments in editorial and textual theory.

3. The same point was made by Pizarro (*Mediación*).

4. See *Prose: Minimal Anthology* for a complete translation of "O homem de Porlock" ("The Man from Porlock").

5. Scans of these books, displaying Pessoa's marginalia, are available for download at bibliotecaparticular.casafernandopessoa.pt/index/aut/G/greenwoodgg.htm.

6. A scan of the book, displaying Pessoa's marginalia, can be downloaded at biblio tecaparticular.casafernandopessoa.pt/8-507/1/8-507_item1/index.html?page=145.

7. See *Prose: Minimal Anthology* for a complete translation of "Aviso por causa da moral" ("Notice Regarding Morality").

8. See Schwartz, "Rendering the Formless," for a discussion of metaphysical ground lessness in *Fausto*.

9. See *Poetry: Minimal Anthology* for a translation of both "Abdicação" ("Abdication"; 33) and "Vem, Noite antiquíssima e idêntica" ("Come, Night, most ancient and unchanging One"; 231–35).

10. The *Zooniverse* is one platform that offers features that would be helpful for this type of project.

NOTES ON CONTRIBUTORS

Onésimo T. Almeida is professor at Brown University. He teaches the intellectual and cultural history of Portugal in the Department of Portuguese and Brazilian Studies and has been department chair for more than a decade. Author of two dozen books, he is coeditor of various journals and book series. He is a member of various academies, including the Portuguese Academy of Sciences, and doctor honoris causa from the University of Aveiro, Portugal.

Steffen Dix is author or editor of several books, book chapters, and articles in international peer-reviewed journals. Currently, he is assistant professor of European studies at the Universidade Aberta in Lisbon. Since early 2021, he has been a research fellow at the Research Centre for Global Studies at the same university. His research interests include European modernism and the religious history of Europe, especially secularization and the relationship between religion and modernity.

Jonardon Ganeri is Bimal K. Matilal Distinguished Professor of Philosophy at the University of Toronto. His books include *Virtual Subjects, Fugitive Selves: Fernando Pessoa and his Philosophy* (2020), *Fernando Pessoa: Imagination and the Self* (2024), *Classical Indian Philosophy* (2020), *Attention, Not Self* (2018), *The Lost Age of Reason: Philosophy in Early Modern India 1450–1700* (2020), *The Self: Naturalism, Consciousness, and the First-Person Stance* (2012), *The Concealed Art of the Soul* (2012), *Semantic Powers* (1999), *Philosophy in Classical India: The Proper Work of Reason* (2001), *Identity as Reasoned Choice: The Reach and Resources of Public Reason in South Asia* (2013), and *Inwardness: An Outsider's Guide* (2021).

António Ladeira is associate professor of Lusophone literatures at Texas Tech University, where he is the coordinator of the Portuguese program. His research interests include gender (and masculinity) topics in Lusophone literatures, literatures of the Portuguese diaspora in the United States and Canada, and contemporary Portuguese poetry. He was a visiting researcher and Fulbright scholar at the University of São Paulo with a project on Clarice Lispector and has published books of his own poetry and collections of short stories. He edited, with Yudith Rosenbaum and Eliane Fittipaldi, *Personagens de Clarice: Figurações do humano e do não-humano em obras de Clarice Lispector* (2023).

Paulo de Medeiros is professor of modern and contemporary world literatures in the Department of English and Comparative Literary Studies of the University of Warwick. His research centers on critical theory and Luso-Brazilian narrative with a focus on the interrelations between politics and literature as well as on postcolonial issues. He has recently published two monographs: *Pessoa's Geometry of the Abyss: Modernity and the Book of Disquiet* (2013) and *O Silêncio das Sereias: Ensaio sobre o Livro do Desassossego* (2015). He received the PEN Portugal Prize for essays (ex aequo) for the latter in 2016. He is one of the editors of *Pessoa Plural*. One of his current book projects concerns the idea of a postimperial Europe.

Meghan P. Nolan is assistant professor of English and chair of the Sam Draper Honors Program at Rockland Community College, State University of New York. She is a persona studies scholar and multigenre writer who focuses on fragmented perceptions of self-hood and written identities through academic works, fiction, nonfiction, and poetry. She is the author of the poetry collection *Stratification* (2008), and her essays have recently been published in *Persona Studies*, *Thread*, *The 100 Greatest Detectives*, *Exquisite Corpse: Studio Art–Based Writing in the Academy*, *Transnational Crime Fiction*, and *Mean Streets: A Journal of American Crime and Detective Fiction*.

Bernat Padró Nieto is associate professor in literary theory and comparative literature at Universitat de Barcelona, where he is one of the founding members of the research group Comparative Literature in the European Intellectual Sphere. He has been visiting professor at Universidad de la República in Uruguay, guest lecturer at University Eötvös Loránd in Budapest and at Humboldt University of Berlin, visiting researcher at Université Bordeaux Montaigne, and visiting scholar at New York University. His areas of research are comparative literature, periodical studies, and intellectual history in Latin America and the Iberian Peninsula. He edited the volumes *Qui Acusa? Figures de l'intellectual europeu* (2015), *I Convenció Ciutadana sobre la Universitat Catalana* (2017), and *Circuits perifèrics de literatura* (2024).

Jerónimo Pizarro is professor at the Universidad de los Andes, Colombia, where he holds the Camões Institute Chair in Portuguese studies. He edited the *Livro do desassossego* (2010) and *The Book of Disquiet* (2017) and is the author of *Fernando Pessoa: A Critical Introduction* (2021). He is the editor of Colecção Pessoa at Tinta-da-china and the editor in chief of *Pessoa Plural: A Journal of Fernando Pessoa Studies*. In 2013 he won the Eduardo Lourenço Prize.

Manuel Portela directs the PhD program in materialities of literature at the University of Coimbra. He is the author of *Literary Simulation and the Digital Humanities: Reading, Editing, Writing* (2022) and *Scripting Reading Motions: The Codex and the Computer as Self-Reflexive Machines* (2013), the general editor of *LdoD Archive: Collaborative Digital Archive of the Book of Disquiet* (2017–24; coedited by António Rito Silva), and one of the contributors to *The Bloomsbury Handbook of Electronic Literature* (2017). He has published widely on digital literature and digital editing, including articles in *Digital Humanities Quarterly*, *Digital Scholarship in the Humanities*, *Umanistica Digitale*, *Leonardo Electronic Almanac*, *Electronic Book Review*, *Textual Cultures*, and *Variants*.

Irene Ramalho-Santos is professor emerita of English, American studies, and feminist studies at the Faculty of Letters, University of Coimbra, where she was coordinator of doctoral programs in those three fields until September 2011. Between 1998 and 2018, she was an international affiliate of the Department of Comparative Literature at the University of Wisconsin, Madison, where she taught regularly as a visiting professor. She is the author of *Atlantic Poets: Fernando Pessoa's Turn in Anglo-American Modernism* (2003), *Fernando Pessoa e outros fingidores* (2021), and *Fernando Pessoa and the Lyric: Disquietude, Rumination, Interruption, Inspiration, Constellation* (2022). She has published extensively, both in Portuguese and in English, on various topics in English language literature and culture as well as on American studies, comparative literature, poetic theory, cultural studies, and feminist studies.

Ellen W. Sapega is professor in the Department of Spanish and Portuguese at the University of Wisconsin, Madison. Her publications include articles and book chapters on

Portuguese modernism, memory, visual culture, and commemoration since the late nineteenth century and on the contemporary Portuguese novel. She has published two monographs, *Ficções Modernistas* (1992) and *Consensus and Debate in Salazar's Portugal* (2008), and is currently working on a book on visual and literary representations of Lisbon during the late twentieth and early twenty-first centuries.

John Pedro Schwartz is associate professor of English at the American University of Malta. His books *Poetry: Minimal Anthology* (2020) and *Message* (2022) offer rhymed and metered translations of poems by Fernando Pessoa. He sits on the editorial board of the journal *Pessoa Plural: A Journal of Fernando Pessoa Studies* and has published scholarly articles on James Joyce, Henry James, Virginia Woolf, Jorge Luis Borges, and Pessoa as well as on the interstices of composition, media, and museum studies. He has coedited two books, *Archives, Museums and Collecting Practices in the Modern Arab World* (2012) and *TransLatin Joyce: Global Transmissions in Ibero-American Literature* (2014).

Sofia de Sousa Silva is associate professor at Universidade Federal do Rio de Janeiro. She has completed postdoctoral research at Universidade do Porto and currently collaborates with its Instituto de Literatura Comparada Margarida Losa. She is the author of *Fernando Pessoa: Para descobrir, conhecer e amar* (2016). At the publisher Bazar do Tempo, she coordinates Atlântica, a series dedicated to modern and contemporary Portuguese poetry, and edited the series volume *Aqui estão as minhas contas: Antologia poética de Adília Lopes* (2019).

WORKS CITED

Adamson, Peter. "So You Want to Teach Some Islamic Philosophy?" *Blog of the APA*, 19 Apr. 2021, blog.apaonline.org/2018/09/03/so-you-want-to-teach-some-islamic-philosophy.

Adamson, Peter, and Fedor Benevich. "The Thought Experimental Method: Avicenna's Flying Man Argument." *Journal of the American Philosophical Association*, vol. 4, no. 2, summer 2018, pp. 147–64.

Adorno, Theodor W. "The Essay as Form." *New German Critique*, no. 32, spring-summer 1984, pp. 151–71.

———. *Negative Dialectics*. 1973. Translated by E. B. Ashton, Routledge, 2004.

———. *Negative Dialektik*. 1966. Edited by Rolf Tiedemann, *Gesammelte Schriften*, vol. 6, Suhrkamp Verlag, 2013.

Adriano, Carlos. "Biografia de Fernando Pessoa escrita por Richard Zenith sai em inglês." *Quatro cinco um: A revista dos livros*, 1 July 2021, www.quatrocincoum.com.br/br/resenhas/poesia/vidas-fingidas.

Agamben, Giorgio. *"What Is an Apparatus?" and Other Essays*. Stanford UP, 2009.

Aldabalde, Taiguara Villela, and Carlos Pittella. "A trajetividade do Pessoa digital." *Património Cultural e Transformação Digital*, edited by Fernando Ilharco et al., Universidade Católica Editora, 2018, pp. 102–30.

Allegro, Isabel. "'O gesto e não as mãos': A figuração do feminino na obra de Fernando Pessoa: Uma gramática da mulher evanescente." *Revista colóquio/letras*, nos. 140–41, Apr. 1996, pp. 17–47, coloquio.gulbenkian.pt/cat/sirius.exe/issueContentDisplay?n=140&p=17&o=p.

Almada Negreiros, José de. "A cena do ódio." Cardiello et al., pp. 57–72.

———. "The Hate Scene." Translated by Jethro Soutar. Cardiello et al., pp. 58–73.

Almeida, Miguel Vale de. *Senhores de si*. Fim de Século, 2000.

Almeida, Onésimo T. *The Concept of Ideology: A Critical Analysis*. 1980. Brown University, PhD dissertation.

———. *Mensagem: Uma tentativa de reinterpretação*. Secretaria Regional de Educação e Cultura, 1987.

———. "Pessoa, a *Mensagem* e o mito em Georges Sorel." *Actas do IV congresso de estudos pessoanos*, Fundação Eng. António de Almeida, 1991, pp. 211–22.

———. "Pessoa e verdade(s)—ou a crítica do abuso de leituras herméticas." *Encontro internacional sobre Fernando Pessoa*, edited by Isabel Fundação Calouste Gulbenkian, 1990, pp. 195–203.

———. *Pessoa, Portugal e o futuro*. Gradiva, 2014.

Andresen, Sophia de Mello Breyner. *Livro sexto*. Assírio e Alvim, 2014.

———. *Log Book: Selected Poems*. Translated by Richard Zenith, Carcanet, 1997.

———. *Obra poética*. Assírio e Alvim, 2015.

Arendt, Hannah. *Eichmann in Jerusalem*. 1963. Penguin Books, 2006.

————. *The Human Condition*. 1958. 2nd ed., U of Chicago P, 1998.

Armstrong, Karen. *A Short History of Myth*. Canongate, 2005.

Arquivo LdoD: Arquivo digital colaborativo do Livro do desassossego. Edited by Manuel Portela and António Rito Silva, Centro de Literatura Portuguesa da Universidade de Coimbra, 2017, ldod.uc.pt/.

Arsić, Branka. "Thing-Poems: On Marta Werner's and Jen Bervin's *The Gorgeous Nothings*: Emily Dickinson's Envelope Poems." *The Journal of Nineteenth-Century Americanists*, vol. 3, no. 2, fall 2015, pp. 236–47.

Badiou, Alain. "The Age of the Poets." *The Age of the Poets: And Other Writings on Twentieth-Century Poetry and Prose*, translated by Bruno Bosteels, Verso Books, 2014, pp. 1–20.

————. *Handbook of Inaesthetics*. Translated by Alberto Toscano, Stanford UP, 2005.

Bakhtin, Mikhail Michajlovič. *Speech Genres and Other Late Essays*. U of Texas P, 1999.

Balderston, Daniel. *How Borges Wrote*. U of Virginia P, 2018.

Balso, Judith. *Affirmation of Poetry*. Translated by Drew Burk, Univocal, 2014.

————. *Pessoa, the Metaphysical Courier*. Translated by Drew Burk, Atropos Press, 2011.

Il banchiere anarchico. Directed by Giulio Base, Sun Film Group, 2018.

Barbosa, Nicolás, and Carlos Pitella. "The Website of Disquiet: The First Online Critical Edition of Fernando Pessoa." *Pessoa Plural: A Journal of Fernando Pessoa Studies*, no. 12, 2017, pp. 725–32, https://doi.org/10.7301/Z07S7KZD.

Barbosa, Nicolás, et al. "*Portugal*, o primeiro aviso de *Mensagem*: 106 documentos inéditos." *Pessoa Plural: A Journal of Fernando Pessoa Studies*, no. 17, spring 2020, pp. 76–229, https://doi.org/10.26300/djfd-kf82.

Barreto, José. "António Ferro: Modernism and Politics." Dix and Pizarro, pp. 135–54.

————. "Apresentação." *Sobre o fascismo, a ditadura militar e Salazar*, edited by Barreto, Tinta-da-china, 2015, pp. 7–47.

————. "A chamada 'nota autobiográfica' de Fernando Pessoa de 30 de março de 1935." *New Insights into Portuguese Modernism from the Fernando Távora Collection*, special issue of *Pessoa Plural: A Journal of Fernando Pessoa Studies*, edited by Ricardo Vasconcelos, no. 12, fall 2017, pp. 502–20, https://doi.org/10.7301/Z0RV0KXN.

————. "Fernando Pessoa: Germanófilo ou aliadófilo? Um debate com João de Barros que não veio a público." *Pessoa Plural: A Journal of Fernando Pessoa Studies*, no. 6, 2014, pp. 153–215, https://doi.org/10.7301/Z0K64GJW.

————. "A *Mensagem* de Fernando Pessoa e o prémio do SPN de 1934." *Pessoa Plural*, no. 14, fall 2018, pp. 289–329. *Brown Digital Repository*, https://doi.org/10.26300/eray-jf59.

————. *Misoginia e anti-feminismo em Fernando Pessoa*. Ática, 2011.

————. "Salazar and the New State in the Writings of Fernando Pessoa." Pizarro and Dix, *Pessoa*, pp. 168–214, www.jstor.org/stable/41105310.

Bataille, Georges. *Literature and Evil*. Translated by Alastair Hamilton, Penguin Books, 2012.

Beck, Ulrich, and Edgar Grande. *Das kosmopolitische Europa: Gesellschaft und Politik in der Zweiten Moderne*. Suhrkamp Verlag, 2004.

Benjamin, Walter. *Illuminations*. Edited by Hannah Arendt, translated by Harry Zohn, Schocken Books, 1968.

———. *Selected Writings, 1913–1926*. Edited by Marcus Bullock and Michael W. Jennings, Belknap Press, 2004. Vol. 1 of *Selected Writings*.

———. "Theses on the Philosophy of History." Benjamin, *Illuminations*, pp. 253–64.

———. "Über den Begriff der Geschichte." *Gesammelte Schriften*, by Benjamin, vol. 1.2, edited by Rolf Tiedemann and Hermann Schweppenhäuser, Suhrkamp Verlag, 1980, pp. 691–704.

Bensmaïa, Réda. *Barthes à l'essai: Introduction au text réflechissant*. G. Narr, 1986.

Bergson, Henri. *L'énergie spirituelle*. Félix Alcan, 1920.

———. *Évolution créatrice*. Félix Alcan, 1920.

Bernardino, Teresa. "Fernando Pessoa e a República." *Diário de Notícias*, 26 June 1988.

"Biblioteca Particular Fernando Pessoa." *Casa Fernando Pessoa*, 2022, bibliotecaparticular.casafernandopessoa.pt/index/index.htm.

Birmingham, David. *A Concise History of Portugal*. 3rd ed., Cambridge UP, 2018.

Blanchot, Maurice. *The Book to Come*. Translated by Charlotte Mandell, Stanford UP, 2003.

———. *L'écriture du désastre*. Gallimard, 1980.

———. "Literature and the Right to Death." Translated by Lydia Davis. *The Work of Fire*, translated by Charlotte Mandell, Stanford UP, 1995, pp. 300–44.

———. "La littérature et le droit à la mort." *La part du feu*, by Blanchot, Gallimard, 1949, pp. 293–331.

———. *The Writing of the Disaster*. Translated by Ann Smock, U of Nebraska P, 1995.

Blanco, José. *Fernando Pessoa, esboço de uma bibliografia*. Imprensa Nacional–Casa da Moeda, 1983.

———. "Fernando Pessoa's Critical and Editorial Fortune in English: A Selective Chronological Overview." Pizarro and Dix, *Pessoa*, pp. 13–32.

———. "A *Mensagem* e a crítica do seu tempo." Lourenço and Oliveira, pp. 69–74.

———. *Pessoana*. Assírio e Alvim, 2008. 2 vols.

Bloom, Harold. *Genius: A Mosaic of One Hundred Exemplary Creative Minds*. Warner Books, 2002.

———. *The Western Canon: The Books and School of the Ages*. Penguin, 1994.

Borges, Jorge Luis. *Cuentos*. Edited by Daniel Balderston and María Celeste Martín, Borges Center, U of Pittsburgh, 2020.

———. *Ensayos*. Edited by Daniel Balderston and María Celeste Martín, Borges Center, U of Pittsburgh, 2019.

———. *Poemas y prosas breves*. Edited by Daniel Balderston and María Celeste Martín, Borges Center, U of Pittsburgh, 2018.

Bornstein, George, editor. *Representing Modernist Texts: Editing as Interpretation*. U of Michigan P, 1991.

Botto, Antonio. *As canções de António Botto*. Ática, 1975.

Bourbon, Francisco Peixoto. "Evocando Fernando Pessoa." *O Comércio de Gaia*, 11 Mar. 1986.

Bourdieu, Pierre. *Masculine Domination*. Stanford UP, 2001.

Bourdieu, Pierre, and John B. Thompson. *Language and Symbolic Power*. Harvard UP, 1991.

Brady, Leo. *From Chivalry to Terrorism: War and the Changing Nature of Masculinity*. Alfred A. Knopf, 2003.

Bréchon, Robert. *Étrange étranger: Une biographie de Fernando Pessoa*. Christian Bourgois, 1996.

———. *L'innombrable: Un tombeau pour Fernando Pessoa*. Christian Bourgois, 2001.

Bru, Sascha, et al. "Borderless Europe, Decentring Avant-Garde, Mosaic Modernism." *Europa! Europa? The Avant-Garde, Modernism and the Fate of a Continent*, edited by Bru et al., De Gruyter, 2009, pp. 3–17.

Bryant, John. "Editing Fluid Texts." *Melville Electronic Library*, 2021, melville .electroniclibrary.org/editing-fluid-texts.

Butler, Judith. *Antigone's Claim: Kinship between Life and Death*. Columbia UP, 2000.

———. *Giving an Account of Oneself*. Fordham UP, 2005.

"Calendario Portugal 1988—Cafe Delta. Cafes." *Todocoleccion*, 2021, en .todocoleccion.net/calendars-old/calendario-portugal-1988-cafe-delta -cafes~x51002509.

Camões, Luís Vaz de. *The Lusiads*. Translated by Landeg White, Oxford UP, 2008.

Campbell, Joseph. *The Mythic Dimension: Selected Essays 1959–1987*. Edited by Anthony Van Couvering, HarperCollins Publishers, 1997.

Cardiello, Antonio, et al., editors. *Nós, os de "Orpheu" / We, the "Orpheu" Lot*. Boca—Palavras que Alimentam, 2015.

Carvalho, Bernardo. "Os bardos da hora." *Blog IMS*, 10 June 2015, blogdoims.com.br/ os-bardos-da-hora/.

Castro, Ivo. *Editar Pessoa*. Imprensa Nacional–Casa da Moeda, 1990.

Castro, Mariana Gray de. *Fernando Pessoa's Modernity without Frontiers: Influences, Dialogues, Responses*. Tamesis, 2013.

———. *Fernando Pessoa's Shakespeare: The Invention of the Heteronyms*. Critical, Cultural and Communications Press, 2016.

Cavaco, Gilbert. *Mensagem: Esoterismo e ideologia em Fernando Pessoa*. 1979. New York U, PhD dissertation.

Cavalcanti Filho, José Paulo. *Fernando Pessoa: A Quasi Memoir*. Translated by Filipe Faria, Mimesis International, 2019.

———. *Fernando Pessoa: Uma quase-autobiografia*. Record, 2011.

Cesariny, Mário. "Louvor e simplificação de Álvaro de Campos." *Nobilíssima visão*, Assírio e Alvim, 1991, pp. 64–73.

———. *O virgem negra: Fernando Pessoa explicado às criancinhas naturais e estrangeiras*. 2nd ed., Assírio e Alvim, 1996.

Chartier, Roger, editor. *¿Qué es un texto?* Círculo de Bellas Artes, 2006.

Coleridge, Samuel Taylor. "Kubla Khan." *"Christabel," "Kubla Khan: A Vision," "The Pains of Sleep."* London, 1816, pp. 55–58. *Google Books*, play.google.com/books/reader?id=aMkNAAAAQAAJ&pg=GBS.PA54&hl=en.

Combe, Dominique. "La référence dédoublée: Le sujet lyrique entre fiction et auto-biographie." *Figures du sujet lyrique*, edited by Dominique Rabaté, PU de France, 1996, pp. 39–64.

Conversa Acabada. Directed by João Botelho, V. O. Filmes / Rádio e Televisão de Portugal, 1981.

Costa, Augusto da. "Fernando Pessoa e os 'valores humanos.'" *Diário da Manhã*, 19 Nov. 1938.

Cousineau, Thomas J. *An Unwritten Novel: Fernando Pessoa's* The Book of Disquiet. Dalkey Archive Press, 2013.

Crawford, Robert. *The Modern Poet: Poetry, Academia, and Knowledge since the 1750s.* Oxford UP, 2004.

Crespo, Ángel. *La vida plural de Fernando Pessoa.* Seix Barral, 1988.

Cresswell, Robyn, and Bernard Haykel. "Battle Lines." *The New Yorker*, 1 Jun. 2015, www.newyorker.com/magazine/2015/06/08/battle-lines-jihad-creswell-and-haykel.

Croce, Benedetto. *Aesthetic as Science of Expression and General Linguistic.* Translated by Douglas Ainsile, Noonday Press, 1920.

Cronk, Nicholas. "Voltaire's Incomplete Works (and Why They Will Stay That Way)." *Early Modern French Studies*, vol. 43, no. 2, 2021, pp. 222–39. *Taylor and Francis Online*, https://doi.org/10.1080/20563035.2021.1902197.

Dante Alighieri. *Vita nova.* 1295. Edited by M. Barbi, Letteratura italiana Einaudi, 1932, www.bibliotecassredentore.it/wp-content/uploads/2020/12/Vita-nuova-di-Dante-Alighieri.pdf.

Dejung, Christof, et al. *The Global Bourgeoisie: The Rise of the Middle Classes in the Age of Empire.* Princeton UP, 2019.

Derrida, Jacques. "Freud and the Scene of Writing." Translated by Jeffrey Mehlman. *Yale French Studies*, no. 48, 1972, pp. 74–117.

———. "The Law of Genre." Translated by Avital Ronell. *Modern Genre Theory*, edited by David Duff, Pearson Education, 2000, pp. 219–31.

Dickinson, Emily. *The Gorgeous Nothings: Emily Dickinson's Envelope Poems.* Edited by Marta L. Werner and Jen Bervin, New Directions, 2013.

———. "I dwell in Possibility." Circa 1862. Harvard U, Houghton Library, Cambridge, Massachusetts, packet 19, fascicle 22. *Emily Dickinson Archive*, www.edickinson.org/editions/19/image_sets/9922.

———. "My Life had stood—a Loaded Gun." Circa 1862–64. Harvard U, Houghton Library, Cambridge, Massachusetts, packet 24, fascicles 40 and 34. *Emily Dickinson Archive*, www.edickinson.org/editions/2/image_sets/12170834.

———. Transcription of "To make a prairie it takes a clover." Edited by Mabel Loomis Todd, 1896. Amherst College, Amherst, Massachusetts, Archives and Special Collections, box 16, folder 10. *Amherst College Library Digital Collections*, acdc.amherst.edu/view/EmilyDickinson/ma00167-16-10-00097.

Dilthey, Wilhelm. *Introduction to the Human Sciences*. Edited by Rudolf J. Makkreel and Frithjof Rodi, Princeton UP, 1989.

———. *Poetry and Experience*. Princeton UP, 1985.

Dionísio, João, editor. *Private: Do (Not) Enter: Personal Writings and Textual Scholarship*. Special issue of *Variants: The Journal of the European Society for Textual Scholarship*, no. 8, 2012.

Dionísio, José Amaro. "Pessoa 'fast-food.'" *Expresso*, 18 June 1988, pp. 53R–55R.

Dionísio, Mário. *Poesia completa*. Imprensa Nacional–Casa da Moeda, 2016.

Dix, Steffen, and Jerónimo Pizarro, editors. *Portuguese Modernisms: Multiple Perspectives in Literature and the Visual Arts*, Legenda, 2011.

Döblin, Alfred. *Berlin Alexanderplatz*. Suhrkamp Verlag, 1980.

Duarte, Luiz Fagundes. "Texto acabado e texto virtual ou a cauda do cometa." *Revista da Biblioteca Nacional*, 2nd series, vol. 3, no. 3, Sept.-Dec. 1988, pp. 167–81.

"Editorial." *Blast*, no. 2, July 1915.

Eksteins, Modris. *Rites of Spring: The Great War and the Birth of the Modern Age*. Houghton Mifflin, 1989.

Eliade, Mircea. *Aspects du mythe*. Gallimard, 1963.

Eliot, T. S. *On Poetry and Poets*. Farrar, Straus and Giroux, 2009.

———. *The Waste Land*. Edited by Michael North, W. W. Norton, 2000.

Ellmann, Maud. *The Poetics of Impersonality: T. S. Eliot and Ezra Pound*. 2nd ed., Harvard UP, 1988.

"Espólio Fernando Pessoa." *Biblioteca Nacional de Portugal*, 2008, purl.pt/1000/1/.

Estado de São Paulo, 20 Aug. 1960, acervo.estadao.com.br/linha-do-tempo/.

"Fernando Pessoa." *In Our Time*, BBC, 3 Dec. 2020, www.bbc.co.uk/programmes/m000q0yj.

Ferrari, Patricio. "Fernando Pessoa y Alejandra Pizarnik: Escritos, marginalia y otros apuntes en torno a la metrica y al ritmo." *Bulletin of Spanish Studies*, vol. 88, no. 2, 2011, pp. 221–48.

———. "On the Margins of Fernando Pessoa's Private Library." *Luso-Brazilian Review*, vol. 48, no. 2, 2011, pp. 23–71.

Filme do Desassossego. Directed by João Botelho, Ar de Filmes, 2010.

Foley, Stephen Merriam. "Pessoa's Wyatt." *Pessoa Plural: A Journal of Fernando Pessoa Studies*, no. 10, fall 2016, pp. 66–75, https://doi.org/10.7301/Z0PR7T5P.

Foucault, Michel. *The Order of Things: An Archaeology of the Human Sciences*. Vintage Books, 1994.

———. "What Is an Author?" *Textual Strategies: Perspectives in Post-structuralist Criticism*, edited by Josué V. Harari, Cornell UP, 1979, pp. 141–60.

Freud, Sigmund. *Civilization and Its Discontents*. Translated by James Strachey, Hogarth Press, 1930.

Frey, Hans-Jost. *Interruptions*. State U of New York P, 1996.

Frias, Aníbal. *Fernando Pessoa et le quint-empire de l'amour: Quête du désir et alter-sexualité*. Petra, 2012.

Frier, David G., editor. *Pessoa in an Intertextual Web: Influence and Innovation.* Legenda, 2012.

Frow, John. "'A Nonexistent Coterie': Pessoa's Names." *Affirmations: Of the Modern,* no. 1, 2013, pp. 196–213, affirmationsmodern.com/articles/83/.

Gabler, Hans Walter. "Theorizing the Digital Scholarly Edition." *Literature Compass,* no. 7, 2010, pp. 43–56.

Gago, Carla. "Interstícios: O fragmento em Fernando Pessoa." *A arca de Pessoa: Novos ensaios,* edited by Steffen Dix and Jerónimo Pizarro, Imprensa de Ciências Sociais, 2007, pp. 229–42.

Ganeri, Jonardon. *Fernando Pessoa: Imagination and the Self.* Oxford UP, 2024.

———. "So You Want to Teach Some Indian Philosophy?" *Blog of the APA,* 27 Apr. 2021, blog.apaonline.org/2018/10/08/so-you-want-to-teach-some-indian -philosophy.

———. "Taking Philosophy Forward." *Los Angeles Review of Books,* 20 Aug. 2018, lareviewofbooks.org/article/taking-philosophy-forward.

———. *Virtual Subjects, Fugitive Selves: Fernando Pessoa and His Philosophy.* Oxford UP, 2021.

———. "Why Philosophy Needs Sanskrit, Now More Than Ever." *Comparative Philosophy and Method: Contemporary Practices and Future Possibilities,* edited by Steven Burik et al., Bloomsbury Academic, 2022, pp. 139–58.

Garcez, Maria Helena Nery. *Alberto Caeiro: "Descobridor da natureza"?* Centro de Estudos Pessoanos, 1985.

"Gato Fedorento." *Wikipédia: A enciclopédia livre,* Wikimedia, 1 June 2023, pt .wikipedia.org/wiki/Gato_Fedorento.

"Gato Fedorento Big Brother Grandes Portugueses." *YouTube,* uploaded by Joao Vital, 19 Aug. 2013, www.youtube.com/watch?v=mED3hHK84E4.

Genette, Gérard. *The Architext: An Introduction.* Translated by Jane E. Lewin, U of California P, 1992.

———. *Fiction and Diction.* Translated by Catherine Porter, Cornell UP, 1993.

Gil, José. *Cansaço, tédio, desassossego.* Relógio d'Água, 2013.

———. *O devir-eu de Fernando Pessoa.* Relógio d'Água, 2010.

———. *Fernando Pessoa ou a metafísica das sensações.* Relógio d'Água, [1987?], pp. 1–28.

———. *Fernando Pessoa ou la métaphysique des sensations.* Éditions de la Différence, 1988.

Giménez, Diego. "¿Una novela no escrita?" *Pessoa Plural: A Journal of Fernando Pessoa Studies,* no. 6, fall 2014, pp. 276–78, https://doi.org/10.7301/Z0J67FDH.

Goffman, Erving. *Forms of Talk.* U of Pennsylvania P, 1981.

———. *The Presentation of Self in Everyday Life.* Doubleday, 1990.

Gonçalves, Adelto. *Fernando Pessoa: A voz de Deus.* Editora da Universidade Santa Cecília, 1997.

Guerreiro, Ricardina. *Do luto por existir: A melancolia de Bernardo Soares à luz de Walter Benjamin.* Assírio e Alvim, 2004.

Gusmão, Manuel. *A poesia de Alberto Caeiro.* Editorial Comunicação, 1986.

Hamburger, Käte. *The Logic of Literature.* Translated by Marilynn J. Rose, Indiana UP, 1973.

Hegel, G. W. F. *Aesthetics: Lectures on Fine Art.* Translated by Thomas Malcom Knox, Oxford UP, 1975. 2 volumes.

Hölderlin, Friedrich. "Arbeitsreinschrift im Homburger Folioheft." *Hölderlins Elegie "Brod und Wein" oder "Die Nacht,"* edited by Wolfram Groddeck, Stroemfeld, 2012, pp. 301–05.

Howe, Susan. Preface. *The Gorgeous Nothings: Emily Dickinson's Envelope Poems,* by Emily Dickinson, edited by Marta L. Warner and Jen Bervin, New Directions, 2013, pp. 6–7.

O ídolo. Directed by Pedro Varela, Blanche Film, 2021.

Jackson, K. David. *Adverse Genres in Fernando Pessoa.* Oxford UP, 2010.

Jameson, Fredric. *The Modernist Papers.* Verso Books, 2007.

———. *A Singular Modernity: Essays on the Ontology of the Present.* Verso Books, 2002.

Um jantar muito original. Directed by Leandro Ferreira, produced by RTP / Marginal Filmes, 2021.

Jauss, Hans Robert. "Theory of Genres and Medieval Literature." *Toward an Aesthetic of Reception,* translated by Timothy Bahti, U of Minnesota P, 2005, pp. 76–109.

Jennings, Hubert D. *Fernando Pessoa, the Poet with Many Faces: A Biography and Anthology.* Edited by Carlos Pittella, Tinta-da-china, 2019.

Johnston, Mark. *Surviving Death.* Princeton UP, 2010.

Kafka, Franz. *The Metamorphosis.* Translated by Susan Bernofsky, edited by Mark M. Anderson, Norton Critical Edition, W. W. Norton, 2016.

———. *The Trial.* Translated by Idris Parry, Penguin, 2015.

———. *Die Verwandlung.* Edited by Vladimir Nabokov, Fischer, 1986.

Kennan, George F. *The Decline of Bismarck's European Order: Franco-Russian Relations, 1875–1890.* Princeton UP, 1979.

Kimmel, Michael. "Masculinity and Homophobia." *Theorizing Masculinities,* edited by Harry Brod and Michael Kaufman, Sage, 1994, pp. 119–41.

Kirk, G. S. *Myth: Its Meaning and Functions in Ancient and Other Cultures.* Cambridge UP, 1970.

Klobucka, Anna, and Mark Sabine, editors. *Embodying Pessoa: Corporeality, Gender, Sexuality.* U of Toronto P, 2007.

———. "Pessoa's Bodies." Klobucka and Sabine, *Embodying Pessoa,* pp. 3–36.

Kotowicz, Zbigniew. *Fernando Pessoa: Voices of a Nomadic Soul.* Shearsman Books, 2008.

Lai, Karyn. "So You Want to Teach Some Chinese Philosophy?" *Blog of the APA,* 27 Apr. 2021, blog.apaonline.org/2018/10/22/so-you-want-to-teach-some-chinese-philosophy.

Lancastre, Maria José de. *Fernando Pessoa: Uma fotobiografia.* Imprensa Nacional–Casa da Moeda, 1981.

Lanier, Douglas. "Shakespeare™: Myth and Biographical Fiction." *The Cambridge Companion to Shakespeare and Popular Culture,* edited by Robert Shaughnessy, Cambridge UP, 2007, pp. 93–113.

Leith, Mrs. Disney [Mary Charlotte Julie]. *The Boyhood of Algernon Charles Swinburne*. Chatto and Windus, 1917.

Lejeune, Philippe. *Le pacte autobiographique*. Seuil, 1975.

Levine, Peter. "The Lack of Diversity in Philosophy Is Blocking Its Progress." *Aeon*, 11 Nov. 2021, aeon.co/ideas/the-lack-of-diversity-in-philosophy-is-blocking-its -progress.

Lévi-Strauss, Claude. *Myth and Meaning*. Schocken Books, 1978.

Lewis, Pericles, editor. *The Cambridge Companion to European Modernism*. Cambridge UP, 2001.

Lincoln, Bruce. *Theorizing Myth: Narrative, Ideology and Scholarship*. Chicago UP, 1999.

Lisbon Story. Directed by Wim Wenders, Roadmovies Filmproduktion, GmbH / Madragoa Filmes, 1994.

Lopes, Teresa Rita. *Pessoa por conhecer*. Estampa, 1990. 2 vols.

Lourenço, Eduardo. *Fernando, Rei da nossa Baviera*. Imprensa Nacional–Casa da Moeda, 1986.

———. *Here on Douradores Street: Essays on Fernando Pessoa*. Edited and translated by Ronald W. Sousa, Gávea Brown, 2010.

———. "Kierkegaard e Pessoa ou a comunicação indirecta." Lourenço *Fernando*, pp. 121–44.

———. "Kierkegaard e Pessoa ou as máscaras do absoluto." Lourenço, *Fernando*, pp. 97–109.

———. *Pessoa revisitado: Leitura estruturante do drama em gente*. Inova, 1973.

———. *Poesia e metafísica: Camões, Antero, Pessoa*. Sá da Costa, 1983.

———. "Uma poética do silêncio (A propósito do L. do D.)." *O lugar do anjo*, by Lourenço, Gradiva, 2004, pp. 103–09.

Lourenço, Eduardo, and António Braz de Oliviera, editors. *Fernando Pessoa no seu tempo*. Lisbon, Secretaria de Estado da Cultura, 1988.

Lourenço, Frederico. "O não vivido na obra poética de Sophia." *Sophia de Mello Breyner Andresen: Actas do colóquio internacional*, edited by Maria Andresen de Sousa Tavares, Centro Nacional de Cultura, Porto, Porto Editora, pp. 147–51.

Lukács, Georg. "On the Nature and Form of the Essay." *Soul and Form*, by Lukács, translated by Anna Bostock, MIT P, 1974, pp. 1–18.

Macé, Marielle. "Listes de genres: Sur la place de l'essai dans l'imaginaire théorique." *La lecture littéraire*, no. 8, 2005, pp. 129–43.

MacFarland, Thomas. "Field, Constellation, and Aesthetic Object." *New Literary History* vol. 13, no. 3, 1982, pp. 421–47.

Maffie, James. *Aztec Philosophy: Understanding a World in Motion*. U of Colorado P, 2014.

Man, Paul de. *Aesthetic Ideology*. U of Minnesota P, 1996.

Mansfield, Nick. *Masochism: The Art of Power*. Bloomsbury Publishing, 1997.

Marinetti, F. T. "Futurist Manifesto." *The Futurist Moment: Avant-Garde, Avant Guerre, and the Language of Rupture*, by Marjorie Perloff, U of Chicago P, 1997.

Martinho, Fernando J. B. "Pessoa, an Uncomfortable Icon of Portuguese Contemporary Culture." *Portugal: Strategic Options in a European Context*, edited by Fátima Monteiro et al., Lexington Books, 2003, pp. 17–24.

Martinho, José. *Pessoa e a psicanálise*. Almedina, 2001.

Martins, Fernando Cabral. "O *Livro do desassossego* e a escrita heteronímica." *O* Livro do desassossego: *Perspectivas*, edited by Patrícia Soares Martins et al., Esfera do Caos, 2014, pp. 43–48. Central de Poesia 2.

———. "Passo muito depressa no país de Caeiro." *Os poemas sobre Pessoa*, edited by Maria Andresen de Sousa Tavares, Caminho, 2012, pp. 11–20.

Matos Frias, Joana. *Cinefilia e cinefobia no Modernismo português: Vias e desvios*. Afrontamento, 2015.

Maunsell, Jerome Boyd. "The Hauntings of Fernando Pessoa." *Modernism/Modernity*, vol. 19, no. 1, 2012, pp. 115–37.

McGann, Jerome. *A Critique of Modern Textual Criticism*. U of Chicago P, 1983.

McNeill, Patrícia Silva. "Mediating Transnational Reception in Portuguese Modernism: Fernando Pessoa and the English Magazines." *Fernando Pessoa as English Reader and Writer*, special issue of *Portuguese Literary and Cultural Studies*, edited by Patricio Ferari and Jerónimo Pizarro, Tagus Press, 2015.

———. *Yeats and Pessoa: Parallel Poetic Studies*. Legenda, 2010.

Medeiros, Paulo de. "Fernando Pessoa, Singularity, and World Literature." *A Companion to World Literature*, Ken Seigneurie, general editor, vol. 5b, Wiley-Blackwell, 2020, pp. 3291–302.

———. *Pessoa's Geometry of the Abyss: Modernity and the* Book of Disquiet. Legenda, 2013.

———. *O silêncio das sereias: Ensaio sobre o* Livro do desassossego. Tinta-da-china, 2015.

———. "Tal como Lisboa: Representação, Wenders e o espectro de alteridade." *Literatura comparada: Os novos paradigmas*, edited by Margarida L. Losa et al., Associação Portuguesa de Literatura Comparada, 1996, pp. 671–78.

———. "Transnational Pessoa." *Transnational Portuguese Studies*, edited by Hilary Owen and Claire Williams, Liverpool UP, 2020, pp. 299–316.

Mendes, Victor. J., editor. "Pessoa's Alberto Caeiro." Special issue of *Portuguese Literary and Cultural Studies*, vol. 3, 1999.

Mercier, Pascal [Peter Bieri]. *Nachtzug nach Lissabon*. Carl Hanser Verlag, 2004.

———. *Night Train to Lisbon*. Translated by Barbara Harsav, Atlantic, 2009.

Os Mistérios de Lisboa / What the Tourist Should See. Directed by José Fonseca e Costa, JFC Filmes, 2008.

Montaigne, Michel de. *The Complete Works: Essays, Travel Journal, Letters*. Translated by Donald M. Frame, Everyman's Library, 2003.

Monteiro, Adolfo Casais, and José Blanco, editors. *A poesia de Fernando Pessoa*. 2nd ed., Imprensa Nacional–Casa da Moeda, 1985.

Monteiro, George. "Fernando (Antonio Nogueira) Pessoa." *Portuguese Writers*, edited by Monica Rector and Fred M. Clark, Gale, 2004, pp. 5–6. Vol. 287 of *Dictionary of Literary Biography*.

————. *Fernando Pessoa and Nineteenth-Century Anglo-American Literature.* UP of Kentucky, 2000.

————. "First International Symposium on Fernando Pessoa: Seven Unpublished Texts by Jorge de Sena." *Pessoa Plural: A Journal of Fernando Pessoa Studies,* no. 3, 2013, pp. 113–40, https://doi.org/10.7301/Z0W957P0.

————, editor. *The Man Who Never Was: Essays on Fernando Pessoa.* Gávea-Brown Publications, 1982.

————. *The Presence of Pessoa: English, American, and Southern African Literary Responses.* UP of Kentucky, 1998.

Monteiro, Rui. "Razões que nos separam." *Textos teóricos do neo-realismo português,* Comunicação / Seara Nova, 1981, pp. 53–54.

Musil, Robert. *Der Mann ohne Eigenschaften.* Vol. 1, Rowohlt, 2002.

————. *The Man without Qualities.* Translated by Sophie Wilkins and Burton Pike, Picador, 2011.

Namorado, Joaquim. *Aviso à navegação.* Novo Cancioneiro, 1941.

Neumann, Gerhard. "Umkehrung und Ablenkung: Franz Kafka's 'gleitendes Paradox.'" *Deutsche Vierteljahrsschrift für Literaturwissenschaft und Geistesgeschichte,* vol. 42, 1968, pp. 702–44.

Nietzsche, Friedrich. *The Birth of Tragedy.* Translated by Douglas Smith, Oxford UP, 2000.

————. *Jenseits von Gut und Böse: Vorspiel einer Philosophie der Zukunft.* Edited by Giorgio Colli and Mazzino Montinari, De Gruyter, 2012. Vol. 5 of *Kritische Studienausgabe.*

Night Train to Lisbon. Directed by Bille August, Studio Hamburg Fimproduktion / C-Films AG / Cinemate / Bulldog Films / Lusomundo, 2013.

Nogueira, Manuela. *Fernando Pessoa: Imagens de uma vida.* Assírio e Alvim, 2005.

Nolan, Meghan P. "Learning to Circumvent the Limitations of the Written-Self: The Rhetorical Benefits of Poetic Fragmentation and Internet 'Catfishing.'" *Persona Studies,* vol. 1, no. 1, 2015, pp. 53–64, ojs.deakin.edu.au/index.php/ps/article/view/431.

Norden, Bryan Van. *Taking Back Philosophy: A Multicultural Manifesto.* Columbia UP, 2017.

Nye, Robert A. *Masculinity and Male Codes of Honor in Modern France.* Oxford UP, 1933.

Ornellas, Sandro. "Desassossegos da democracia: Notas a partir de Fernando Pessoa e Giorgio Agamben." *Em Tese,* vol. 23, no. 1, Jan.-Apr. 2017, pp. 11–29.

Orpheu: Revista trimestral de literatura. No. 1, Jan.-Mar. 1915.

Patrício, Rita, and Jerónimo Pizarro. Preface. *Obras de Jean Seul de Méluret,* by Fernando Pessoa, edited by Patrício and Pizarro, Imprensa Nacional–Casa da Moeda, 2006, pp. 13–19.

Paz, Octavio. "El desconocido de sí mismo." *Cuadrivio,* by Paz, Joaquín Mortiz, 1965, pp. 131–63.

————. "Fernando Pessoa: El desconocido de sí mismo." *Revista de la Universidad de México,* vol. 16, no. 3, Nov. 1961, pp. 4–7, www.revistadelauniversidad.mx/

articles/c50fd97d-d7ce-4573-86f2-6ae0943caea1/fernando-pessoa-el
-desconocido-de-si-mismo.

———. "Poesía de soledad y poesía de comunión." 1943. *Obras completas*, vol. 13,
Fondo de Cultura Económica, 1999, pp. 234–45.

Pedro, Luís. *Acrónios*. Oficinas gráficas UP, 1932.

Perrone-Moisés, Leyla. *Aquém do eu, alem do outro*. Martins Fontes, 1982.

———. *Pessoa, le sujet éclaté*. Pétra, 2014.

Persona. 1977–85. Facsimile ed., Tinta-da-china, 2019. Box set.

Pessoa, Fernando. *Always Astonished: Selected Prose*. Edited by Edwin Honig, City
Lights Books, 1988.

———. "Antonio Botto e o ideal esthetico em Portugal." *Contemporanea*, no. 3,
July 1922, pp. 121–26.

———. *Argumentos para filmes*. Edited by Patricio Ferrari and Claudia J. Fischer,
Ática, 2011.

———. *The Book of Disquiet*. Translated by Margaret Jull Costa, Serpent's Tail, 1991.

———. *The Book of Disquiet*. Translated by Alfred Mac Adam, Pantheon Books,
1991.

———. *The Book of Disquiet*. Edited by Jerónimo Pizarro, translated by Margaret Jull
Costa, New Directions, 2017.

———. *The Book of Disquiet*. Edited by Jerónimo Pizarro, translated by Margaret Jull
Costa, Serpent's Tail, 2017.

———. *The Book of Disquiet*. Edited and translated by Richard Zenith, Penguin
Books, 2002.

———. *The Book of Disquiet: A Selection*. Translated by Iain Watson, Quartet Books,
1991.

———. *The Book of Disquietude*. Edited and translated by Richard Zenith, Carcanet,
1991.

———. *Cartas entre Fernando Pessoa e os directores da* presença. Edited by Enrico
Martins, Imprensa Nacional–Casa da Moeda, 1998.

———. *A Centenary Pessoa*. Edited by Eugénio Lisboa and L. C. Taylor. Carcanet,
1995.

———. *The Collected Poems of Álvaro de Campos, 1928–1935*. Translated by Chris
Daniels, vol. 2, Shearsman Books, 2009.

———. *The Complete Works of Alberto Caeiro*. Edited by Jerónimo Pizarro and
Patricio Ferrari, translated by Margaret Jull Costa and Ferrari, New Directions, 2020.

———. *Contra Salazar*. Edited by Antonio Apolinário Lourenço, Angelus Novus, 2008.

———. *Correspondência 1905–22*. Edited by Manuela Parreira da Silva, Assírio e
Alvim, 1998.

———. *Correspondência 1923–35*. Edited by Manuela Parreira da Silva, Assírio e
Alvim, 1999.

———. *Crítica: Ensaios, artigos, entrevistas*. Edited by Fernando Cabral Martins,
Assírio e Alvim, 2000.

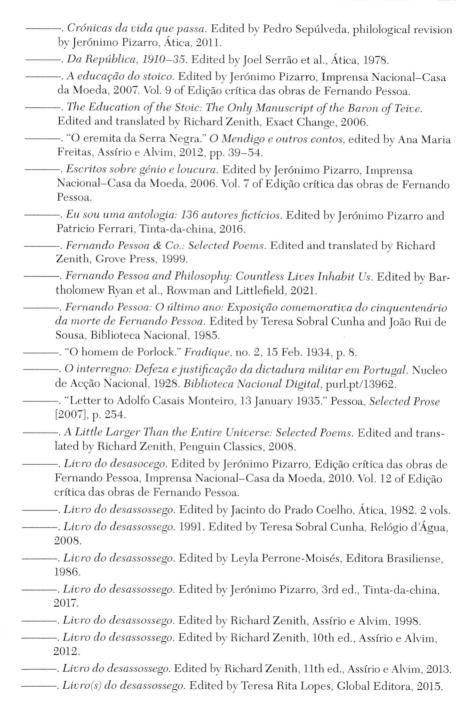

———. *Crónicas da vida que passa*. Edited by Pedro Sepúlveda, philological revision by Jerónimo Pizarro, Ática, 2011.

———. *Da República, 1910–35*. Edited by Joel Serrão et al., Ática, 1978.

———. *A educação do stoico*. Edited by Jerónimo Pizarro, Imprensa Nacional–Casa da Moeda, 2007. Vol. 9 of Edição crítica das obras de Fernando Pessoa.

———. *The Education of the Stoic: The Only Manuscript of the Baron of Teive*. Edited and translated by Richard Zenith, Exact Change, 2006.

———. "O eremita da Serra Negra." *O Mendigo e outros contos*, edited by Ana Maria Freitas, Assírio e Alvim, 2012, pp. 39–54.

———. *Escritos sobre génio e loucura*. Edited by Jerónimo Pizarro, Imprensa Nacional–Casa da Moeda, 2006. Vol. 7 of Edição crítica das obras de Fernando Pessoa.

———. *Eu sou uma antologia: 136 autores fictícios*. Edited by Jerónimo Pizarro and Patricio Ferrari, Tinta-da-china, 2016.

———. *Fernando Pessoa & Co.: Selected Poems*. Edited and translated by Richard Zenith, Grove Press, 1999.

———. *Fernando Pessoa and Philosophy: Countless Lives Inhabit Us*. Edited by Bartholomew Ryan et al., Rowman and Littlefield, 2021.

———. *Fernando Pessoa: O último ano: Exposição comemorativa do cinquentenário da morte de Fernando Pessoa*. Edited by Teresa Sobral Cunha and João Rui de Sousa, Biblioteca Nacional, 1985.

———. "O homem de Porlock." *Fradique*, no. 2, 15 Feb. 1934, p. 8.

———. *O interregno: Defeza e justificação da dictadura militar em Portugal*. Nucleo de Acção Nacional, 1928. *Biblioteca Nacional Digital*, purl.pt/13962.

———. "Letter to Adolfo Casais Monteiro, 13 January 1935." Pessoa, *Selected Prose* [2007], p. 254.

———. *A Little Larger Than the Entire Universe: Selected Poems*. Edited and translated by Richard Zenith, Penguin Classics, 2008.

———. *Livro do desasocego*. Edited by Jerónimo Pizarro, Edição crítica das obras de Fernando Pessoa, Imprensa Nacional–Casa da Moeda, 2010. Vol. 12 of Edição crítica das obras de Fernando Pessoa.

———. *Livro do desassossego*. Edited by Jacinto do Prado Coelho, Ática, 1982. 2 vols.

———. *Livro do desassossego*. 1991. Edited by Teresa Sobral Cunha, Relógio d'Água, 2008.

———. *Livro do desassossego*. Edited by Leyla Perrone-Moisés, Editora Brasiliense, 1986.

———. *Livro do desassossego*. Edited by Jerónimo Pizarro, 3rd ed., Tinta-da-china, 2017.

———. *Livro do desassossego*. Edited by Richard Zenith, Assírio e Alvim, 1998.

———. *Livro do desassossego*. Edited by Richard Zenith, 10th ed., Assírio e Alvim, 2012.

———. *Livro do desassossego*. Edited by Richard Zenith, 11th ed., Assírio e Alvim, 2013.

———. *Livro(s) do desassossego*. Edited by Teresa Rita Lopes, Global Editora, 2015.

———. *Mensagem.* Ática, 1963.

———. "Notas para a recordação do meu mestre Caeiro." Pessoa, *Obra completa de Álvaro de Campos* [2014], pp. 451–88.

———. "A nova poesia portuguesa sociologicamente considerada." *A águia,* 2nd series, no. 4, Apr. 1912, pp. 101–07.

———. "A nova poesia portuguesa sociologicamente considerada." *Textos de crítica e de intervenção,* by Pessoa, Ática, 1980, pp. 13–23.

———. *Novas poesias inéditas.* Edited by Maria do Rosário Marques Sabino and Adelaide Maria Monteiro Sereno, Ática, 1973.

———. *Obra completa de Alberto Caeiro.* Edited by Jerónimo Pizarro and Patricio Ferrari, Tinta-da-china, 2016.

———. *Obra completa de Álvaro de Campos.* Edited by Jerónimo Pizarro and Antonio Cardiello, Tinta-da-china, 2014.

———. *Obra completa de Álvaro de Campos.* Edited by Jerónimo Pizarro and Antonio Cardiello, paperback ed., Tinta-da-china, 2019.

———. *Obra completa de Ricardo Reis.* Edited by Jerónimo Pizarro and Jorge Uribe, Tinta-da-china, 2016.

———. *Obra poética.* Edited by Maria Aliete Galhoz, Nova Aguilar, 1960.

———. *Obras de António Mora.* Edited by Luís Filipe Teixeira Bragança, Imprensa Nacional–Casa da Moeda, 2002. Vol. 6 of Edição crítica das obras de Fernando Pessoa.

———. *Obras em prosa.* Edited by Cleonice Berardinelli, Nova Aguillar, 1986.

———. *Páginas íntimas e de auto-interpretação.* Edited by George Rudolf Lind and Jacinto do Prado Coelho, Ática, 1966.

———. *Pessoa inédito.* Edited by Teresa Rita Lopes, Livros Horizonte, 1993.

———. *Philosophical Essays.* Edited and translated by Nuno Ribeiro, Contra Mundum Press, 2012.

———. *Poemas completos de Alberto Caeiro.* Edited by Teresa Sobral Cunha, Presença, 1994.

———. *Poemas de Alberto Caeiro.* Edited by Ivo Castro, Imprensa Nacional–Casa da Moeda, 2015. Vol. 4 of Edição crítica das obras de Fernando Pessoa.

———. *Poemas de Álvaro de Campos.* Edited by Cleonice Berardinelli, Imprensa Nacional–Casa da Moeda, 1990. Vol. 2 of Edição crítica das obras de Fernando Pessoa.

———. *Poemas de Fernando Pessoa, 1921–30.* Edited by Ivo Castro, Imprensa Nacional–Casa da Moeda, 2001. Vol. 3 of *Poemas de Fernando Pessoa.*

———. *Poemas dramáticos.* Ática, 1952.

———. *Poemas ingleses.* Edited and translated by Jorge de Sena, Ática. 1974.

———. *Poems of Fernando Pessoa.* Edited by Edwig Honig and Susan Brown, City Lights Books, 1986.

———. *Poesia: Antologia mínima.* Edited by Jerónimo Pizarro, Tinta-da-china, 2018.

———. *Poesia inglesa.* Edited and translated by Luísa Freire, preface by Teresa Rita Lopes, Livros Horizonte, 1995.

———. *Poetry: Minimal Anthology.* Translated by John Pedro Schwartz and Robert N. Schwartz, edited by Jerónimo Pizarro, 3rd ed., Emergence Education, 2025.

———. "Prefácio." *Acrónios,* by Luís Pedro, UP Oficinas Gráficas, 1932, pp. 5–8.

———. *Prosa: Antologia mínima.* Edited by Jerónimo Pizarro, Tinta-da-china, 2020.

———. *Prose: Minimal Anthology.* Translated by John Pedro Schwartz and Robert N. Schwartz, edited by Jerónimo Pizarro, 2nd ed., Tinta-da-china, 2025.

———. *O regresso dos deuses e outros escritos de António Mora.* Edited by Manuela Parreira da Silva, Assírio e Alvim, 2013.

———. *Santo António, São João, São Pedro.* Edited by Alfredo Margarido, A Regra do Jogo, 1986.

———. *Selected Poems.* Translated by David Butler, Dedalus Press, 2004.

———. *Selected Poems by Fernando Pessoa.* Edited by Edwin Honig, Swallow Press, 1971.

———. *The Selected Prose of Fernando Pessoa.* Translated by Richard Zenith, Grove Press, 2001.

———. *The Selected Prose of Fernando Pessoa.* Translated by Richard Zenith, reprint ed., Grove Press, 2007.

———. *Sensacionismo e outros ismos.* Edited by Jerónimo Pizarro, Imprensa Nacional–Casa da Moeda, 2009. Vol 10 of Edição crítica das obras de Fernando Pessoa.

———. *Sobre o fascismo, a ditadura militar e Salazar.* Edited by José Barreto, Tinta-da-china, 2015.

———. *Sobre Portugal: Introdução ao problema nacional.* Edited by Joel Serrão et al., Ática, 1978.

———. *Ultimatum e páginas de sociologia política.* Edited by Joel Serrão et al., Ática, 1980.

———. "A Very Original Dinner." *Fernando Pessoa as English Reader and Writer,* special issue of *Portuguese Literary and Cultural Studies,* edited by Jerónimo Pizarro and Patricio Ferrari, no. 28, 2015, pp. 252–73, https://doi.org/10.62791/g02qhk28.

Pierazzo, Elena. *Digital Scholarly Editing: Theories, Models and Methods.* Ashgate, 2015.

———. "A Rationale of Digital Documentary Editions." *Literary and Linguistic Computing,* vol. 26, no. 4, 2011, pp. 463–77.

Pires, Daniel, editor. *Pacheko, Almada e "Contemporânea."* Centro Nacional de Cultura, Bertrand Editora, 1993.

Pittella, Carlos, and Jerónimo Pizarro. *Como Fernando Pessoa pode mudar a sua vida.* Tinta-da-china, 2017.

Pizarro, Jerónimo. "A ansiedade da unidade: Uma teoria da edição." *LEA: Lingue e letterature d'Oriente e d'Occidente,* vol. 5, 2016, pp. 284–311, oajournals.fupress.net/index.php/bsfm-lea/article/view/7716/7714.

———. "Apresentação." Pessoa, *Livro do desasocego,* vol. 1, pp. 7–10.

———. "Editor's Note." *The Book of Disquiet* [New Directions], pp. xvii–xix.

———. *Fernando Pessoa: A Critical Introduction.* Sussex Academic Press, 2020.

———. *La mediación editorial: Sobre la vida póstuma de lo escrito.* Iberoamericana/ Vervuert, 2012.

———. "Os muitos desassossegos." *Revista do centro de estudos portugueses*, vol. 36, no. 55, pp. 11–27, https://doi.org/10.17851/2359-0076.36.55.11-27.

Pizarro, Jerónimo, and Steffen Dix. Introduction. Pizarro and Dix, *Pessoa*, pp. 6–12. *JSTOR*, www.jstor.org/stable/41105303.

———, editors. *Pessoa: The Future of the "Arcas."* Special issue of *Portuguese Studies*, vol. 24, no. 2, 2008.

Pizarro, Jerónimo, and Patricio Ferrari. "Uma biblioteca em expansão: Sobrecapas de livros de Fernando Pessoa / A Growing Library: Dust Jackets from Fernando Pessoa's Book Collection." *Pessoa: Revista de ideias*, no. 3, 2011, pp. 58–96.

Pizarro, Jerónimo, and Teresa Filipe. "Livros, objectos, manuscritos e fotografias: Doação e venda." *Pessoa Plural: A Journal of Fernando Pessoa Studies*, no. 17, spring 2020, https://doi.org/10.26300/0wqk-qf64.

Pizarro, Jerónimo, and Paulo de Medeiros, editors. *Fernando Pessoa and Translation.* Special issue of *The Translator*, vol. 26, no. 4, 2020.

Pizarro, Jerónimo, et al., editors. *Pessoa and Cinema.* Special issue of *Pessoa Plural: A Journal of Fernando Pessoa Studies.* No. 25, June 2024.

Portela, Manuel. "La simulación de los procesos literarios en el *Archivo LdoD.*" *Ilusión y materialidad: Perspectivas sobre el archivo*, edited by Jerónimo Pizarro and Diana P. Guzmán, Ediciones Uniandes, 2018, pp. 353–65.

Portela, Manuel, and António Rito Silva. "A Model for a Virtual *LdoD.*" *Digital Scholarship in the Humanities*, vol. 3, no. 3, Sept. 2015, pp. 354–70, https://doi.org/10.1093/llc/fqu004.

"Portrait of Fernando Pessoa." *WikiArt: Visual Art Encyclopedia*, wikiart.org/en/jose -de-almada-negreiros/portrait-of-fernando-pessoa-1954. Accessed 31 May 2021.

Pound, Ezra. *The Cantos of Ezra Pound.* New Directions, 1996.

———. *Make It New.* Faber and Faber, 1934.

Proust, Marcel. *In Search of Lost Time.* Edited by Christopher Prendergast, translated by Lydia Davis et al., Allen Lane, 2002. 6 vols.

Questão Ibérica. Liga Naval, 1915.

Ramalho-Santos, Irene. "America in Poetry." *America Where? Transatlantic Views of the United States in the Twenty-First Century*, edited by Isabel Caldeira et al., Peter Lang, 2012, pp. 245–81.

———. "A arte da ruminação: Os heterónimos pessoanos revisitados." *Largo mundo alumiado: Estudos em homenagem a Vítor Aguiar e Silva*, edited by Carlos Mendes de Sousa and Rita Patrício, vol. 2, Centro de Estudos Humanísticos, U do Minho, 2004, pp. 829–43.

———. "The Art of Rumination: Pessoa's Heteronyms Revisited." *Journal of Romance Studies*, vol. 3, no. 3, 2003, pp. 9–21.

———. *Atlantic Poets: Fernando Pessoa's Turn in Anglo-American Modernism.* Dartmouth College / UP of New England, 2003.

———. "Being Blind, Being Nothing, Being a Poet: Emily Dickinson 'Reads' Fernando Pessoa." Inside the Mask: The English Poetry of Fernando Pessoa. Symposium on Fernando Pessoa, April 2015, Brown University.

———. Fernando Pessoa and the Lyric: Disquietude, Rumination, Interruption, Inspiration, Constellation. Rowman and Littlefield, 2022.

———. Fernando Pessoa e outros fingidores. Tinta-da-china, 2021.

———. "Narcissus in the Desert. A New Cartography for the American Lyric." Fluid Cartographies: New Modernities, special issue of Journal of Romance Studies, edited by Isabel Capeloa Gil and João Ferreira Duarte, vol. 11, no. 1, 2011, pp. 21–36.

———. "The Tail of the Lizard: Pessoan Disquietude and the Subject of Modernity." Dix and Pizarro, pp. 264–76.

Rimbaud, Arthur. Complete Works, Selected Letters. Edited by Seth Whidden, translated by Wallace Fowlie, U of Chicago P, 1966.

Rito Silva, António, and Manuel Portela. "TEI4LdoD: Textual Encoding and Social Editing in Web 2.0 Environments." Journal of the Text Encoding Initiative, no. 8, 2015, https://doi.org/10.4000/jtei.1171.

Robinson, Peter. "Towards a Theory of Digital Editions." Variants, no. 10, 2013, pp. 105–31.

Rollin, Bernard E. "Nature, Convention, and Genre Theory." Poetics, no. 10, 1981, pp. 127–43.

Romero, Raúl, and René P. Garay. "Epifanía y poema en prosa (El Livro do desassossego de Fernando Pessoa / Bernardo Soares)." Forma breve, no. 2, 2004, pp. 71–80.

Ryan, Bartholomew. Fernando Pessoa. Reaktion Press, 2024.

———. "Into the Nothing with Kierkegaard and Pessoa." Kierkegaard and the Challenges of Infinitude, edited by J. M. Justo et al., Centro de Filosofia da Universidade de Lisboa, 2013, pp. 115–27.

———. "Notebooks, Non-Books and Quasi-Books." Pessoa Plural: A Journal of Fernando Pessoa Studies, no. 7, spring 2015, pp. 318–22, https://doi.org/10.7301/Z0ST7NBG.

Ryan, Bartholomew, et al., editors. Fernando Pessoa and Philosophy: Countless Lives Inhabit Us. Rowman and Littlefield, 2021.

Ryan, Bartholomew, et al., editors. Nietzsche e Pessoa. Tinta-da-china, 2016.

Sá-Carneiro, Mário. Em ouro e alma. Edited by Ricardo Vasconcelos and Jerónimo Pizarro, Tinta-da-china, 2015.

———. Poesia completa. Edited by Ricardo Vasconcelos, Tinta-da-china, 2017.

Sacher-Masoch, Leopold. Venus in Furs. Penguin Books, 2000.

Sadlier, Darlene J. An Introduction to Fernando Pessoa: Modernism and the Paradoxes of Authorship. UP of Florida, 1998.

Sadlier, Darlene J., and Heitor Martins, editors. Fernando Pessoa. Special issue of Indiana Journal of Hispanic Literatures. No. 9, fall 1996.

Sáez Delgado, Antonio. "El eterno desasosiego del Livro do Desassossego o la tentación del texto-Frankenstein." Abriu, no. 5, 2016, pp. 9–12.

Sampaio, Maria de Lurdes. "Ezra Pound and Fernando Pessoa with T. S. Eliot In-Between." Dix and Pizarro, pp. 277–93.

Santos, Boaventura de Sousa. "Between Prospero and Caliban: Colonialism, Postcolonialism, and Inter-Identity." *Portuguese Cultural Studies*, special issue of *Luso-Brazilian Review*, edited by Paulo de Medeiros and Hilary Owen, vol. 39, no. 2, winter 2002, pp. 9–43.

———. *O Estado e a Sociedade em Portugal, 1974–1988*. Edições Afrontamento, 1992.

Santos, Mariana Pinto. "Almada Negreiros and Sonia Delaunay: Simultaneous Contrasts and Futurism." *O Círculo Delaunay / The Delaunay Circle*, edited by Ana Vasconcelos, Fundação Calouste Gulbenkian / Centro de Arte Moderna, 2015, pp. 253–60.

Sapega, Ellen W. "Portugal." Lewis, pp. 137–50.

———. "Saramago's 'Genius': Camões, Adamastor, and Ricardo Reis." *In Dialogue with José Saramago: Essays in Comparative Literature*, edited by Adriana Alves de Paula Martins and Mark Sabine, Manchester Spanish and Portuguese Studies, 2006, pp. 25–35.

Saper, Craig. "Posthumography: The Boundaries of Literature and the Digital Trace." *Rhizomes: Cultural Studies in Emerging Knowledge*, no. 20, summer 2010, www.rhizomes.net/issue20/saper/index.html.

Saramago, José. *O ano da morte de Ricardo Reis*. Caminho, 1984.

———. *The Year of the Death of Ricardo Reis*. Translated by Giovanni Pontiero, Harcourt, 1991.

Sartre, Jean Paul. *The Transcendence of the Ego: A Sketch for a Phenomenological Description*. Translated by Andrew Brown, Routledge, 2004.

Schaeffer, Jean-Marie. "Du texte au genre: Notes sur la problématique générique." *Théorie des genres*, edited by Gérard Genette and Tzvetan Todorov, Seuil, 1986, pp. 179–205.

———. *Qu'est-ce qu'un genre littéraire?* Seuil, 1989.

Schlegel, Friedrich. *Kritische Friedrich-Schlegel-Ausgabe*. Erste Abteilung: Kritische Neuausgabe, vol. 2, Schöningh Verlag / Thomas-Verlag, 1967.

———. *Philosophical Fragments*. Translated by Peter Firchow, U of Minnesota P, 1991.

Schwartz, John Pedro. "Rendering the Formless: Language and Style in *Fausto*." *Pessoa Plural: A Journal of Fernando Pessoa Studies*, no. 14, 2018, pp. 59–83, https://doi.org/10.26300/at6s-bd10.

Schwitzgebel, Eric. "Diversity in Philosophy Departments: Introduction." *American Philosophical Association*, 11 June 2020, blog.apaonline.org/2020/06/11/diversity-in-philosophy-departments-introduction.

Seabra, José Augusto. "Fernando Pessoa e a 'Nova Renascenca' da Europa." *Diário de Notícias*, 12 June 1988, pp. 7–8.

Sebeok, Thomas A., editor. *Myth: A Symposium*. Indiana UP, 1958.

Sedgwick, Eve Kosofsky. *Between Men: English Literature and Male Homosocial Desire*. Columbia UP, 2016.

———. *Epistemology of the Closet*. U of California P, 1990.

Sena, Jorge de. "O heterónimo Fernando Pessoa e os poemas ingleses que publicou." *Poemas ingleses*, Ática, 1974, pp. 13–87.

———. "Introdução ao *Livro do desassossego*." *Fernando Pessoa & Ca. heterónima: Estudos coligidos, 1940–1978*, edited by Mécia de Sena, vol. 2, Edições 70, 1982, pp. 178–242.

———. Preface. *Poesia I*, Edições 70, 1961.

Sepúlveda, Pedro. "Listas do *Desassossego*." *MATLIT: Materialidades da Literatura*, vol. 1, no. 1, 2013, pp. 35–55, https://doi.org/10.14195/2182-8830_1-1_2.

"7 dias." *Expresso*, 18 June 1988, p. 4.

Severino, Alexandrino. *Fernando Pessoa na Africa do Sul: A formação inglesa de Fernando Pessoa*. Lisbon, 1983.

Shaughnessy, Robert. Introduction. *The Cambridge Companion to Shakespeare and Popular Culture*, edited by Shaughnessy, Cambridge UP, 2007, pp. 1–5.

Sidney, Philip. *The Defense of Poesy: Otherwise Known as an Apology for Poetry*. 1595. Edited by Albert S. Cook, Boston, 1890. *Internet Archive*, archive.org/details/defenseofpoesyot00sidn/page/n7/mode/2up.

Silva, Manuela Parreira da. "Raul Leal, o filósofo 'futurista' de *Orpheu*." *Estranhar Pessoa*, no. 2, Oct. 2015, pp. 110–19.

Silva, Nelson da, Jr. *Fernando Pessoa e Freud: Diálogos inquietantes*. Blucher, 2019.

Silva, Patrícia [*published as* Patrícia Silva McNeill]. "Mediating Translational Reception in Portuguese Modernism: Fernando Pessoa and the English Magazines." *Fernando Pessoa as English Reader and Writer*, special issue of *Portuguese Literary and Cultural Studies*, edited by Patricio Ferrari and Jeronimo Pizarro, vol. 28, 2015, pp. 82–108.

———. "The *Orpheu* Generation and the Avant-Garde: Intersecting Literature and the Visual Arts." *Pessoa Plural: A Journal of Fernando Pessoa Studies*, no. 11, spring 2017, pp. 87–113, https://doi .org/10.7301/Z0X0657X.

———. [*published as* Patrícia Silva McNeill]. *Yeats and Pessoa: Parallel Poetic Studies*. Legenda, 2010.

Silva, Sofia de Sousa. *Fernando Pessoa: Para descobrir, conhecer e amar*. Bazar do Tempo, 2016.

———. *Reparar brechas: A relação entre as artes poéticas de Sophia de Mello Breyner Andresen e Adília Lopes e a tradição moderna*. 2007. Pontifícia U Católica do Rio de Janeiro, PhD dissertation.

———. "A vida verdadeira e a errada: Pessoa lido por Sophia." *A mão mais inundada: Ensaios sobre poesia portuguesa moderna e contemporânea*. Oficina Raquel, 2018, pp. 198–210.

Silvestre, Osvaldo Manuel. "O que nos ensinam os novos meios sobre o livro no *Livro do desassossego*." *MATLIT: Revista do programa de doutoramento em materialidades da literatura*, vol. 2, no. 1, 2014, pp. 79–98.

Simões, João Gaspar. *Cartas de Fernando Pessoa a João Gaspar Simões*. Imprensa Nacional–Casa da Moeda, 1982.

———. *Vida e obra de Fernando Pessoa: História duma geração*. Livraria Bertrand, 1950. 2 vols.

Sousa, João Rui de. "Fernando Pessoa e o Estado Novo." *Jornal de Letras*, 14 June 1988.

Sousa, Ronald W. *On Remembering the Hyper-Nation: Saramago's "Historical" Trilogy.* Purdue UP, 2014.

Sousa, Rui. "Os bastidores brasileiros de *Orpheu*: Páginas da revista *Fon-Fon!*, 1912–14." *Pessoa Plural: A Journal of Fernando Pessoa Studies*, no. 7, 2015, pp. 160–81, https://doi.org/10.7301/Z0N58JW0.

———. "Michel de Montaigne em Fernando Pessoa? Uma hipótese de leitura a partir das menções a Francisco Sanches." *Pessoa Plural: A Journal of Fernando Pessoa Studies*, no. 18, 2020, pp. 27–104, https://doi.org/10.26300/wapr-t128.

Steiner, George. "A Man of Many Parts." *The Guardian*, 3 June 2001, www.theguardian.com/books/2001/jun/03/poetry.features1.

Stevens, Wallace. *The Necessary Angel: Essays on Reality and the Imagination.* Vintage Books, 1951.

Stierle, Karlheinz. "Identité du discours et transgression lyrique." *Poétique*, no. 32, Nov. 1977, pp. 422–41.

Strawson, Galen. *The Subject of Experience.* Oxford UP, 2007.

Tabucchi, Antonio. "Bernardo Soares, uomo inquieto e insonne." *Il libro dell'inquietudine*, by Fernando Pessoa, translated by Tabucchi, edited by Maria José de Lancastre, Feltrinelli, 2004, pp. 7–14.

Terlinden, Anne. *Fernando Pessoa: The Bilingual Portuguese Poet.* PU Saint-Louis Bruxelles, 1990.

Terrell, Carroll F. *A Companion to the Cantos of Ezra Pound.* U of California P, 1993.

Thomsen, Mads Rosendahl. *Mapping World Literature: International Canonization and Transnational Literatures.* Continuum, 2008.

Todorov, Tzvetan. "The Notion of Literature." *New Literary History*, vol. 5, no. 1, 1973, pp. 5–16.

Valberg, Jerome J. *Dream, Death, and the Self.* Princeton UP, 2007.

Valdemar, António. "Mensagem na opinião de Soares e de Cunhal." *Tempo Livre*, July-Aug. 2019.

Valéry, Paul. "La crise de l'esprit." *Œuvres*, edited by Jean Hytier, vol. 1., Gallimard, 1957, pp. 988–91.

Verde, Cesário. "O sentimento de um occidental." *Obra completa*, edited by Joel Serrão, Livros Horizonte, 1999, pp. 141–56.

Vieira, Yara Frateschi. *Sob o ramo da bétula: Fernando Pessoa e o erotismo vitoriano.* Editora da Unicamp, 1989.

Vilela, Joana Strichini, and Pedro Fernandes. *LX 80 Lisboa entra numa nova era.* Dom Quixote, 2016.

Visser, Rehan P. "Fernando Pessoa's Art of Living: Ironic Multiples, Multiple Ironies." *The Philosophical Forum*, vol. 50, no. 4, 2019, pp. 435–545, https://doi.org/10.1111/phil.12236.

Wallerstein, Immanuel. *World-Systems Analysis: An Introduction.* Duke UP, 2004.

Warwick Research Collective. *Combined and Uneven Development: Towards a New Theory of World-Literature.* Liverpool UP, 2015.

"We, Orpheu." *Camões: Instituto da Cooperação e da Lingua*, 2024, cvc.instituto
-camoes.pt/area-conhecer-exposicoes-virtuais/nos-os-de-orpheu-eng.html#
.YXRAIylQ1QM.

Werner, Marta L. "Dickinson's Late Hand." *Radical Scatters: Emily Dickinson's Late
Fragments and Related Texts, 1870–1886*, 2010, radicalscatters.unl.edu/latehand
.html.

———. "Document Constellations." *Radical Scatters: Emily Dickinson's Late Fragments and Related Texts, 1870–1886*, 2010, radicalscatters.unl.edu/ind006.html.

———. "'Most Arrows': Autonomy and Intertextuality in Emily Dickinson's Late Fragments." *Radical Scatters: Emily Dickinson's Late Fragments and Related Texts,
1870–1886*, 2010, radicalscatters.unl.edu/mostarrows.html.

———. "'A Woe of Ecstasy': On the Electronic Editing of Emily Dickinson's Late
Fragments." *Radical Scatters: Emily Dickinson's Late Fragments and Related
Texts, 1870–1886*, 2010, radicalscatters.unl.edu/woeofecstacy.html.

Widdowson, Peter. *Literature*. Routledge, 1999.

Williams, Bernard. *Descartes: The Project of Pure Inquiry*. Penguin Books, 1987.

Williams, Raymond. *Marxism and Literature*. Oxford UP, 1977.

Wittgenstein, Ludwig. *Philosophical Investigations*. Translated by G. E. M. Ans-
combe, Blackwell Publishers, 1986.

Woolf, Virginia. *Mrs Dalloway*. Oxford World's Classics, 2000.

Yeats, W. B. "Ego Dominus Tuus." *The Variorum Edition of the Poems of W. B. Yeats*,
edited by Peter Allt and Russell K. Alspach, MacMillan, 1957, pp. 367–71.

Zahavi, Dan. *Self and Other: Exploring Subjectivity, Empathy, and Blame*. Oxford
UP, 2015.

Zahavi, Dan, and Uriah Kriegel. "For-Me-Ness: What It Is and What It Is Not." *Philosophy of Mind and Phenomenology: Conceptual and Empirical Approaches*,
edited by Daniel O. Dahlstrom et al., Routledge, 2015, pp. 36–53.

Zenith, Richard. "Fernando Pessoa's Gay Heteronym?" *Lusosex*, edited by Susan
Quinlan and Fernando Arenas, U of Minneapolis P, 2002, pp. 35–56.

———. *Fotobiografias de Século XX: Fernando Pessoa*. Edited by Joaquim Vieira,
Temas e Debates, 2008.

———. Introduction. Pessoa, *Fernando Pessoa & Co.*, edited by Zenith, pp. 1–36.

———. "*Livro do desassossego*: O romance possível (var.: impossível)." *Congresso
Internacional Fernando Pessoa 2013*, Casa Fernando Pessoa, 2017, pp. 352–66,
www.casafernandopessoa.pt/application/files/7915/1698/4246/CFP_ACTAS_
2013.pdf.

———. *Pessoa: A Biography*. Liveright, 2021.

———. *Pessoa: An Experimental Life*. Allen Lane, 2021.

Zhuangzi. *Zhuangzi: The Essential Writings*. Translated by Brook Ziporyn, Hackett,
2009.

Zweig, Stefan. *Die Welt von Gestern*. Anaconda, 2013.